THE WALTER LYNWOOD FLEMING
LECTURES IN SOUTHERN HISTORY
LOUISIANA STATE UNIVERSITY

The
Wary Fugitives
Four Poets and the South

LOUIS D. RUBIN, JR.

LOUISIANA STATE UNIVERSITY PRESS
Baton Rouge & London

Design: Dwight Agner
Type face: VIP Baskerville
Composition: LSU Press
Printing and binding: Kingsport Press, Inc.

LIBRARY OF CONGRESS CATALOGING IN PUBLICATION DATA

Rubin, Louis Decimus, Jr., 1923–
   The wary fugitives.
   (The Walter Lynwood Fleming lectures in southern history)
   Bibliography: p.
   1. American literature—Southern States—History and criticism.
   2. American literature—20th century—History and criticism.
   3. Poets, American—Tennessee—Nashville.   4. Southern States
in literature.   5. The Fugitive.   I. Title.   II. Series.
   PS261.R677   811'.5'209   77–25479
   ISBN 0–8071–0360–8
   ISBN 0–8071–0454–x pbk.

Winner of the
JULES F. LANDRY AWARD
for 1978

To
ALLEN TATE *and* ROBERT PENN WARREN
And to the memory of
DONALD DAVIDSON *and* JOHN CROWE RANSOM

Contents

Preface

In this book I have concerned myself with four writers: John Crowe Ransom, Allen Tate, Donald Davidson, and Robert Penn Warren. All were members of a group of young poets at Vanderbilt University in the early 1920s, who became known as the Nashville Fugitives and published a little poetry magazine called *The Fugitive*. Later in the decade these poets became interested in the condition of southern and American society and joined with eight other persons, most of them also affiliated with Vanderbilt University, in publishing the symposium known as *I'll Take My Stand*. They became known as Agrarians, and especially during the early 1930s their agrarianism, in various forms, was an active element in the regionalist-proletarian literary controversies of the Depression decade. By the end of the decade, however, the Agrarian enterprise had pretty much come to an end, and in their subsequent writings little more was said about it.

With the possible exception of Donald Davidson, it is not as Agrarians that these men have made their permanent places on the American literary scene. Rather, poetry, fiction, and literary criticism have been the forms in which they have chiefly worked. Much has been written about them as poets, novelists, and critics. Yet their Agrarian writings have not been forgotten. *I'll Take My Stand* has been the subject of several books and numerous articles, and is still in print today, almost a half-century after it first appeared.

What was the relationship between their work as poets, novelists, and critics, and as Agrarian social critics? Or, in a larger context, what is the relationship between modern southern literature and southern life? These are the questions that fascinate me. For in the work of these four writers, we confront a problem that in one way or another concerns most students of literature: the links between imaginative literature and the time and place from which it springs. Since the Nashville writers not only illustrate the relationship in their imaginative work, but at one point in their careers were explicitly concerned to explore the problem, they provide an especially interesting exemplification of what is involved.

I have attempted, therefore, to examine the beginnings of their careers as poets, their involvement in the Fugitive group, their growing interest in their society and in the South, and the symposium they organized and published in 1930. I have then sought to trace, though in considerably less detail than for their earlier work, their subsequent literary careers in terms of the ties with Agrarianism. Thus there are sections on Ransom, Tate, and Davidson before *I'll Take My Stand*, a treatment of the symposium itself, and a section on their later writings.

With Warren, however, the problem was different. Almost all of his writing before 1930 was apprentice work; unlike the others his career dates almost entirely from the 1930s onward. I have therefore discussed his work last of all, in a separate section, and have concentrated almost exclusively on the writing he was doing between 1930 and 1955 or so, or until roughly a quarter-century following his Agrarian involvement. To continue beyond then in any detail, I thought, would take the inquiry too far beyond the concerns of my study.

This book, though published in the author's 54th year, was begun 25 years earlier. For it was while I was, briefly, a graduate student in history at the Johns Hopkins University in 1951 that I wrote a paper for C. Vann Woodward, in which I sought to develop the relationship between the poems of several of the Nashville Fugitives and the Agrarian enterprise known as *I'll Take My Stand: The South and the Agrarian Tradition*. The paper never got beyond first draft form, but it was the starting point for much that I subsequently wrote. Much of what it contained went into an essay on Allen Tate that I published several years afterward, and in one way or another I have kept returning to the subject. My concern with it can only be termed a compulsion, I suppose. In any event, several years ago, during the course of writing a still-uncompleted critical history of southern literature from 1865 to the present, I decided, since I was teaching a graduate seminar on the Fugitives and Agrarians, to jump ahead of where I was then working in the history (the 1880s) and do the chapter on the Fugitives. The next thing I knew I was writing not a chapter but a book. At about the same time I received an invitation to deliver the Walter Lynwood Fleming Lectures in southern history at Louisiana State University for 1975, and I chose for my topic *I'll Take My Stand*. This book, then, represents the results of an intensive effort to get down, for once and for all, my thoughts on a problem that has long fascinated me. I realize that it is a little late to be turning in the final draft of the paper I began in 1951, but I hope that Professor Woodward will accept it even so.

I have many acknowledgments to record. In addition to Vann Woodward, who got me started on this, and whose example and friendship have meant so much to me ever since, I should like specifically to thank my colleagues C. Hugh Holman and William Harmon for reading almost every page of this manuscript several times and making innumerable useful suggestions, and Professor John C. Loos and other members of the Department of History at Louisiana State University at Baton Rouge, for their hospitality on the occasion of the Fleming Lectures. Finally, my gratitude goes to George Core, Lewis P. Simpson, Walter Sullivan, and Thomas Daniel Young.

Louis D. Rubin, Jr.

Acknowledgments

For permission to quote from poems of Donald Davidson, the author is grateful to Mrs. Donald Davidson, Mary Davidson Bell, and to the University of Minnesota Press, publishers of *Poems, 1922–1961*, by Donald Davidson. Copyright © 1924, 1927, 1934, 1935, 1938, 1952, 1966 by Donald Davidson. University of Minnesota Press, Minneapolis.

For permission to quote from poems of John Crowe Ransom, the author is grateful to Mrs. John Crowe Ransom, Helen Ransom Forman, and to Alfred A. Knopf, Inc., publishers of *Selected Poems*, Third Edition, Revised and Enlarged, by John Crowe Ransom. Copyright 1924, 1927, 1934, 1939, 1945, © 1962, 1963, 1969 by Alfred A. Knopf, Inc. Copyright renewed 1952, 1955 by John Crowe Ransom.

For permission to quote from poems of Robert Penn Warren, the author is grateful to Robert Penn Warren and to Random House, Inc., publishers of *Selected Poems 1923–1975*, by Robert Penn Warren. Copyright © 1976 by Robert Penn Warren.

The poems of Allen Tate are excerpted with the permission of Farrar, Straus, & Giroux, Inc., from *Collected Poems 1919–1976* by Allen Tate. Copyright © 1952, 1953, 1970, 1977 by Allen Tate. Copyright 1931, 1932, 1937, 1948 by Charles Scribner's Sons. Renewal copyright © 1959, 1960, 1965 by Allen Tate.

The author is grateful to the editors of the *Southern Review* and the *Sewanee Review* for permission to reprint portions of several chapters of this book which in somewhat different form appeared first in those journals.

1 John Crowe Ransom: The Wary Fugitive

Nashville and Vanderbilt

Although the people of Nashville, Tennessee, liked to refer to their city as "the Athens of the South," because of its several universities and colleges, and although it had a replica of the Parthenon in a public park, as a sign of its cultural accession, the capital city of Tennessee did not in the early 1920s possess much in the way of a literary tradition. As American cities go it was old, its founding dating back into the late eighteenth century, and it had endured its share of history. Andrew Jackson had lived nearby, at the Hermitage. In 1864 a bloody battle had been fought just outside the city limits. Shortly after the Civil War, the Fisk Jubilee Singers had gone forth from the new Negro university founded there to make southern black spirituals famous on several continents. But except for the fact that Mary Noailles Murfree had lived in Nashville in the early 1860s, and the sportswriter-poet Grantland Rice ("when the one great Scorer comes to mark against your name/he writes—not that you won or lost—but how you played the game") was a prominent graduate of Vanderbilt University, there was no particular reason to assume that the city would soon become a citadel, as it were, of twentieth-century American poetry and theory, and more or less the intellectual capital of the southern literary Renascence.

It was in March, 1922, that a group of young men who had grown accustomed to meeting together and criticizing one another's poetry agreed to publish a magazine of verse, which they decided to call *The Fugitive*. Only one of the group, John Crowe Ransom, an English teacher at Vanderbilt, had published much poetry. Ransom had written a book, *Poems About God*, which had come out in 1919 while he was serving as an artillery lieutenant in the American Expeditionary Force in France. Another of the group, a former navy boxer and now mystic seer named Sidney Hirsch, had written plays that had enjoyed limited production. Walter Clyde Curry, also a Vanderbilt English professor, had published sonnets in the *American Poetry Magazine* and was working on a book about Chaucer and the medieval sciences. The others, except for appearances in college magazines and newspapers, were all unpublished writers. When the first issue of *The Fugitive* appeared in April, 1922, the contributions were printed under pen names. Not until the third issue appeared the following October was it revealed that "Roger Prim" was Ransom, "L. Oafer" was Hirsch, "Marpha" was Walter Clyde Curry, "Henry Feathertop" was Allen Tate, "Robin Gallivant" was Donald Davidson, "Philora" was James M. Frank, "Jonathan David" was Stanley Johnson, "Dendric" was Merrill Moore, and "Drimlonigher" and "King Badger" were Alec Brock Stevenson.

In years to come, the founding of *The Fugitive* would be seen as the event that signified the formal invocation of the modern resurgence of letters in the South. Ransom, Tate, and Davidson would become noted poets and critics. Merrill Moore would command something of a national reputation for the prodigiousness with which he turned out sonnets. Robert Penn Warren, who was to join the group a year later, would achieve fame as a poet, novelist, and critic. Cleanth Brooks, who, though never a Fugitive, was a student at Vanderbilt during the 1920s and was closely associated with the group, would become a distinguished critic of literature, a leader in the New Criticism that became the dominant mode of poetry criticism of the mid-twentieth century. With Warren, Brooks would produce a textbook, *Understanding Poetry*, that was to revolutionize the teaching of poetry in colleges and universities. Andrew Nelson Lytle, also associated with the group during the late twenties, would become a well-known novelist; he would join Ransom, Tate, Davidson, and Warren in a volume, *I'll Take My Stand: The South and the Agrarian Tradition*, that when published in 1930 would set off the Nashville Agrarian movement and constitute a controversial and important chapter in the history of southern social thought.

"It was a momentous decision for American literature," Willard Thorp wrote, "when in the fall of 1921 a group of Nashville friends who called themselves Fugitives turned from their discussions of literature and philosophy to the writing of poetry. From their sessions evolved one of the most influential movements in our literary history, suggesting in its pervasiveness the energy radiated by Boston's Transcendental Club of 1836 which included in its informal membership such movers and shakers as Emerson, Margaret Fuller and Orestes Brownson." [1]

The comparison of the Nashville Fugitive and Agrarian poets with the New England Transcendentalists of a century earlier is not inappropriate. It is true, of course, that the Nashville aesthetic, as well as the Nashville politics that developed during the following years, in many respects actively opposed what Ralph Waldo Emerson and the Transcendentalists stood for; and the Agrarians seldom passed up an opportunity to criticize the New Englanders. They did not care for the poetry of ideas, or the transcendental unity of apperception, or for social reformers; and they had little use for Plato, the Pure Idea, the perfectibility of man, abolitionism, or the Higher Law in general. In one of John Ransom's late and most savage poems, "To the Scholars of Harvard," the New England sages are informed that

> Plato, before Plotinus gentled him,
> Spoke the soul's part, and though its vice is known
> We're in his shadow still, and it appears
> Your founders most of all the nations held
> By his scandal-mongering, and established him.[2]

Emerson in particular—the man Herman Melville described as "this Plato who talks thro' his nose"[3]—earned less than good marks from the Nashville poet-critics. Tate called him "the Lucifer of Concord" and "the light-bearer who could see nothing but light, and was fearfully blind"; after Emerson's role has had its effect "New England literature tastes like a sip of cambric tea,"[4] Tate said. For Donald Davidson, Emerson helped cause the Civil War: "His voice was not the voice of America, but of New England, and his plan of salvation was to result not in peaceful unification but in bloody disunion."[5] For Robert Penn Warren he was "a man who lived in words, big words, and not in facts."[6]

All the same, there are some interesting similarities between the rise of the Transcendentalists of the 1830s and 1840s and the Fugitives and Agrarians of the 1920s and 1930s. The American Transcendentalists, as Perry Miller has emphasized, had originated out of the old Calvinist stock; but they had become Unitarians before they embraced Transcendentalism. "In Unitarianism," says Miller, "one half of the Calvinist tradition—that which inculcated caution and sobriety—definitely cast off all allegiance to the other. The idea of decorum, of law and self-control, was institutionalized." The blandness of Unitarianism was admirably suited to the expanding commercial and industrial enterprise of the prospering Boston of the period, for "merchants could most successfully conduct their business if they were not required to lie in the dust and desire to be full of the divine agent within." [7]

But though the old Calvinistic ordering would no longer serve the intellectual needs of the day, "there had been power in it, a power conspicuously absent from the pale negations of Unitarianism." [8] The young theologians and poets who became Transcendentalists were not to be satisfied with a rational, decorous, merchant God. They missed the fervor, the religious spirit, the sense of awe and mystery, of the traditional faith—what Emerson described as the "high tragic school" of the old Calvinists. They felt the loss of the moral ordering of a community that could think of itself, in Jonathan Edwards' words, as "one holy society, one city, one family, one body" whose membership, however distant, "should act as one, in those things that concern the common interest of the whole body, and in those duties and exercises wherein they have to do with their common Lord and head, as seeking of him the common prosperity." [9] Doctrinally, theologically the young Bostonians could not turn back to the old Calvinistic religion; but neither could they be content with what they considered the secular, materialistic faith of commercial Boston. The outcome was transcendentalism, with its celebration of "the presence of God in the soul and in nature, the pure metaphysical essence of the New England tradition." [10]

Now the young men who became the Nashville Fugitives and Agrarians were not the products of New England Congregationalism; most of them were Methodists; several were the sons of Methodist ministers. Ransom, Davidson, and Brooks had grown up in southern communities in which the Protestant churches, both Methodist and Baptist, were still a viable and vigorous force, with a role that was far more than liturgical in scope. As Edwin A. Alderman wrote in 1908, "The fancied home of the cavalier is the home of the nearest approach to puritanism and to the most vital protestant evangelicalism in the world today." [11] Nowadays it is difficult to realize the extent to which small-town community life in the late nineteenth- and early twentieth-century South was structured around religious institutions. "The Church," wrote Howard W. Odum, "was the field for community activities, for certain social relationships, for marriage ceremonies and the training of ministers." [12] In the up-country South, away from the old Tidewater heritage of Anglicanism, the leading denominations were Methodist and Baptist. In particular the Methodist Church South, with its strong hierarchical and pastoral organization, was a formidable community force. In the Old South the Episcopal and Presbyterian churches had represented much of the region's political and financial leadership, but after Reconstruction, as the manufacturing and commercial interests of the New South assumed greater importance, the strength of the Baptists and Methodists in southern communities grew. "A Methodist or a Baptist," wrote Holland Thompson in 1919, "can have none of the former feeling of martyrdom now, when in numbers and wealth his denomination is so powerful." [13] The Methodist church, with its large and increasingly affluent congregations, its active publishing house, its chain of *Christian Advocate* newspapers published throughout the region, its network of denominational colleges and universities, was, especially in the up-country, a notably vital factor in community and state life.

Methodism in the Old South, and in the years after the Civil War, had been a vigorously evangelical faith, strongly Calvinistic, even Puritanical, in its tenets, and very much given to revivalism, camp meetings, and mass conversions. Its chief concern had been personal salvation, not theology. At the same time, however, an element in the church had always strongly supported higher education and social reform; and as the nineteenth century entered into its final decades, such issues came increasingly to the fore. The Methodist clergy was often a highly educated clergy, and emphasis within the church on higher education intensified as church membership grew in financial and social importance and increasingly assumed community leadership. Thus when, in 1873, Bishop Holland Nimmons McTyeire secured from Cornelius Vanderbilt half a million dollars, with the promise of more, to set up a Methodist university in Nashville, there was strong support for it within the General Conference. There was also considerable opposition, however, typified by the declaration by Bishop George F. Pierce that self-made men were better than educated men and that theological training could only mar a preacher: "Give me the evangelist and the revivalist rather than the erudite brother who goes into the pulpit to interpret modern science instead of preaching repentance and faith, or going so deep into geology as to show that Adam was not the first man and that the Deluge was a little local affair." [14]

Notwithstanding, Vanderbilt University was set up, with an endowment far exceeding any enjoyed by other southern schools; and from the start its founders were intent upon creating a first-rate university, comparable to the best institutions of higher education anywhere and with a faculty of outstanding scholars, not all of whom would have to be Methodists. It was in the early 1900s, while young John Crowe Ransom was an undergraduate student there, that the matter of church control came to a head, and the General Conference launched an all-out attempt to gain command over the university's board of trust so as to make sure that orthodox believers were placed in charge of the curriculum. Under Chancellor James C. Kirkland, the university resisted, with powerful allies among the bishops. Eventually the case went before the Supreme Court of Tennessee, which in 1914 decided that the university's board of trust, and not the Methodist college of bishops, was the ultimate controlling body, whereupon the General Conference passed a resolution dissociating itself from Vanderbilt University.

The victory of the Vanderbilt board of trust over the bishops' attempts to keep the university subservient to and within the theological boundaries of the church may be seen as symbolic of the twentieth-century South's break from the constraints of the church-centered community. There would be no more heresy trials such as marked the school's early history, when a faculty member might be discharged for teaching evolution. A Vanderbilt education would now be secular.

What the young gentlemen of the upper South received at Vanderbilt, and at other southern universities as well, was in effect an abrupt and dazzling introduction to some of the chief intellectual currents and impulses of the twentieth-century Western world. Vanderbilt's faculty came to be distinguished beyond those of most southern colleges and universities. Many of the leading professors had been trained in Europe. The faculty brought to Nashville the ideas, attitudes, interests, and sympathies of the intellectual community that lay beyond the Ohio and Potomac rivers, even beyond the Atlantic Ocean. The young southerners, coming to college from orthodox Protestant homes in the towns and villages of the upper South, encountered new ways of looking at church and state, man, God, and the Democratic party.

Furthermore, Nashville itself had developed far beyond the small community of fewer than twenty thousand inhabitants that it had been at the time of the Civil War. By the 1890s its population was close to one hundred thousand. It was very much a New South city, with extensive manufactures. A notable convention center, the city boasted hotels, particularly the famous Maxwell House, famed for their luxury and splendor. There was an active theater and opera season. Donald Davidson has described the entertainment he and his young Vanderbilt friends might enjoy in the first two decades of the twentieth century:

There were informal musical evenings when one found in some friendly house a little orchestra of flute, violins, and piano. There were visits to the Deutscher Verein, then flourishing, that brought together faculty members and students of both Vanderbilt University and Peabody College. Or there might be a private musical session in William Elliott's home with Bill soloing in bass while I ventured a fumbling accompaniment at the piano. Or it might be a holiday expedition up the Cumberland River on Horace Beall's little steamboat, for a literary al fresco affair among the oak trees. . . . Or there were nights at the Vendome Theatre—to see *The Merry Widow,* or something from Victor Herbert, or Kennedy's *The Servant in the House,* or Forbes Robertson in *Hamlet,* or even Geraldine Farrar in *Madame Butterfly*—and afterwards the long walk back to the Vanderbilt campus where Halley's Comet was blazing across the sky above Kissam Hall. It was not exactly Bohemian; nor was it anything like a Parisian salon; but it was not academic, either.[15]

The future Fugitives and Agrarians were in point of fact members of by far the best-educated generation of young southerners since the Civil War. Grinding poverty had all but crushed higher education in the southern states in the decades after the war. The curriculum of a university such as Vanderbilt—like that of the University of North Carolina and the University of Virginia—could now be compared favorably with the better northern and midwestern universities. The cultural shock of the war and the Reconstruction had finally receded.

In the decades leading up to the Civil War there had grown up an intellectual barrier caused by the need to defend and safeguard slavery; as Thomas Nelson Page wrote, "All interference from the outside was repelled as officious and inimical, and all intervention was instantly met with hostility and indignation. [The antebellum South] believed itself the home of liberality when it was, in fact, necessarily intolerant;—of enlightenment, of progress, when it had been so far distanced that it knew not that the world had passed by."[16] During the decades following the war, the barrier had generally remained in place; now it was being lowered, so that the young southerners going off to college in the century's first two decades no longer operated under such intellectual constraints as had hindered their immediate forebears. Like the long-ago Virginians of Jefferson and Madison's day, they could now begin to confront the dominant intellectual trends and influences of their time with receptive minds and eager interest. (What they would eventually decide about some of them is another matter.)

If we look at the early career of John Crowe Ransom, we can see this process almost perfectly exemplified. Ransom was born in Pulaski, Tennessee, in 1888. His father, John James Ransom, was a Methodist minister, as had been his father before him. Dr. Ransom had served as a missionary in Latin America. He was known as a scholar and linguist, and he had translated the Bible into Portuguese. Young Ransom attended preparatory school in Nashville, then enrolled at Vanderbilt in 1903 at the age of fifteen. After a two-year interruption during which he taught school in Mississippi and Tennessee, he was graduated in 1909. A year later he received one of the first Rhodes scholarships and went to England to study at Christ Church College, Oxford. Ransom and his minister father were close intellectual companions. During Ransom's stay at Oxford and afterward, he wrote long letters home describing his studies to his father, discussing philosophical ideas, and setting forth his thoughts on the nature of poetry.

Ransom's philosophy teacher at Vanderbilt had been Collins Denny, later a bishop of the Methodist church. A Virginian, Denny had been educated at the University of Virginia, and he held his own old philosophy teacher there in high esteem. As a result of Denny's veneration of Noah K. Davis, Ransom's college reading in philosophy was restricted to that gentleman. When his tutor at Oxford learned that Ransom had read only Davis—for deductive logic, inductive logic, ethics, and psychology—he was understandably dismayed.[17] But in the light of what was happening in the South, this narrow approach to philosophy is significant. Noah K. Davis was religiously orthodox; in addition to his philosophical treatises he had written a popular work, *The Story of the Nazarene*, which was widely known. His pupil Denny, as teacher of philosophy, held a position that was of considerable importance in this church-affiliated university. It is not surprising that he quarreled repeatedly with Chancellor Kirkland over Kirkland's desire to liberalize Vanderbilt's curriculum. Denny was, Edwin Mims wrote, "a composite of logician, dogmatist, Puritan, and despot."[18] When, in 1910, Denny was elevated into the Methodist episcopacy, he quickly became one of the most aggressive of the bishops attempting to impose theological control over the university. But to take Denny's place on the faculty, Kirkland appointed Herbert Charles Sanborn, Ph.D. *magna cum laude* at the University of Munich, a brilliant linguist and active scholar who greatly admired the German philosophers and psychologists and who contributed frequently to learned journals. It was obvious that future Vanderbilt students would receive a very different kind of intellectual training in logic, ethics, and psychology than Ransom had received—and not from Sanborn alone, but, indirectly, from Ransom as well when he returned to the university as teacher in 1914.

Ransom spent three years in Oxford, during which time he found his interests moving steadily from philosophy and the classics to English literature. If he had at this time made any conscious break with his Methodist upbringing, there is no sign of it. Thomas Daniel Young notes that while at Oxford Ransom published an article on his experiences in the *Methodist Review*, and its reception was such that the editor asked him to write another on Wesleyan education in England.[19] Although he profited from his experience there, and in particular from his friendship with another young American writer, Christopher Morley, he seems never to have been fully at ease in the English educational environment. He warned his family that it was extremely unlikely that he would take a "first" in his exam, for "success on Oxford examinations is very much a question of style and of the psychology of the examiner, and it is almost barred to an undergraduate with American ways of thinking."[20] In later years he wrote a poem, "Philomela," in which he expressed his feeling of a sense of unreality about the literary and intellectual concerns of Oxford. Addressing himself to the literary nightingale, he notes her appearance in Rome, Germany, France, England; "never was she baptised," however. "Not to these shores she came!" he continues:

> How could her delicate dirge run democratic,
> Delivered in a cloudless boundless public place
> To an inordinate race?

He "pernoctated with the Oxford students once," he declares, and, "sick of my dissonance," climbed the hill of Bagley Wood to listen to the nightingale: "Her classics registered a little flat!/I rose, and venomously spat." We Americans are "a bantering breed, sophistical and swarthy," he laments ironically; "Unto more beautiful, persistently more young/Thy fabulous provinces belong."[21] Whatever his respect for the cultural tradition of England and the Continent, he will not, that is to say, settle for an art or a philosophy that is too abstracted from the actualities of everyday American experience.

Ransom returned to the United States in 1913 and for a year taught Latin at the Hotchkiss School, in Lakeville, Connecticut. He also made several visits to New York City, and he seriously considered pursuing a career in journalism. He wrote to his father that he thought that as a writer he would be happiest in a metropolitan center like New York, and when the senior Ransom wrote back to urge the dramatic possibilities of rural life, his son replied that "country conditions operate to produce in country people the qualities of stability, conformity, mental and spiritual inertia, callousness, monotony." The country community is "very well fortified against the intrusion of ideas from without." He felt that morality and art were adversely affected by an isolated rural environment. In coupling the two, he said, "I am not guilty of a mental lapse because I think the two fields are closely related."[22]

When he came back to Vanderbilt to teach English in 1914 he soon found himself teaching Shakespeare to a young Tennessean named Donald Grady Davidson. Born in 1893 in Campbellsville, Tennessee, Davidson had arrived at Vanderbilt as a freshman in 1909, had left school to teach for several years, and was now finishing up his degree. Davidson's people, like Ransom's, were Methodists; his father was a schoolteacher. Davidson too had a sound classical education. He did not take to philosophical studies like Ransom did, but at Vanderbilt he began reading the modern European dramatists, the French novelists, Dostoyevsky, and other writers. One of Davidson's friends was Stanley Johnson, a Nashville native who later wrote an academic novel, *Professor*, which satirized certain members of the Vanderbilt English department of the early 1920s. It was Johnson who introduced Davidson to "a group of Southernized Jews and art-minded Gentiles"[23] in Nashville, one of whom was Sidney Mttron Hirsch.

Hirsch was of considerable importance to the education of the young Fugitive poets. Born in Nashville in 1885, he grew up in a Jewish merchant family. Becoming bored with school, he ran off and joined the navy. A large, powerful man, he won the heavyweight championship of the Pacific Fleet before leaving the navy for a tour of the Far East. He had become interested in Buddhism and Taoism, and he amassed a notable if confusing knowledge of Oriental philosophies, Rosicrucianism, numerology, etymology, astrology, Hebraic lore. He went to Paris, worked as a model for Rodin, became friends with Gertrude Stein and the Irish poet AE (George Russell), and began the study of an assortment of esoteric and neglected languages. He then moved on to New York where, as model and friend of the sculptress Gertrude Vanderbilt Whitney, he continued his study of the occult, wrote one-act plays, and became close friends with Edwin Arlington Robinson. Eventually he came home to Nashville. When in 1913 the Nashville Art Association and the Board of Trade decided to promote a May Festival, Hirsch came forth with a pageant, "The Fire Regained," which was produced with a cast of six hundred, complete with chariot races, three hundred sheep, and one thousand pigeons.

Davidson, Johnson, and another young Tennessean, William Yandell Elliott, the future political theorist, soon began meeting with Sidney Hirsch and his brother Nat for evenings of conversation. Hirsch's sophistication, his friendship with noted writers and artists, his esoteric and mystical discourse fascinated the young men. Soon Davidson invited Ransom to join the group. Ransom's empiricism and his calm, incisive logic provided a fine counterbalance to Hirsch. Walter Clyde Curry, a young South Carolinian who had also joined the Vanderbilt English faculty, began taking part, as did a Vanderbilt undergraduate, Alec Brock Stevenson, Canadian-born son of a professor of Semitic languages at Vanderbilt.

Here was the nucleus of the Fugitives. All during the years 1914–1917 this group of young men met and argued. It was a rich convergence of ideas and attitudes—Hirsch's mysticism, Ransom's hardheaded, speculative empiricism, Stanley Johnson's thorny pragmatism, the young Elliott's ebullient abstractions, Davidson's romantic fervor, Curry's medieval and philological lore. In a letter Elliott wrote to Stevenson when the latter was off in Canada in the summer of 1915, we get an unforgettable picture of the way they talked and argued; Elliott refers to the sessions as "*The* Happiness."[24] One gets a sense of how it must have been as John Ransom, Donald Davidson, and their up-country southern colleagues and friends happily discoursed and theorized on Bergson, Cartesian and Kantian dualism, science, British empiricism, the exploding universe, and Platonic forms. Knowledge, new ideas were open for them to consider. One cannot quite imagine Ransom's and Davidson's fathers, attending college in the South of the 1870s and 1880s, participating so uninhibitedly in similar metaphysical conversations. But the South—in places like Nashville, at least—was not so orthodox now.

Apparently those early pre-Fugitive sessions were chiefly philosophical rather than literary, though one imagines that literature must certainly have been of considerable importance to the group from the start. But a change came. The controversy over *vers libre* was raging in poetic circles at the time, and arguments about it began to arise among the young Tennesseans. One day in the fall of 1916 Ransom led Davidson to a shady spot on the Vanderbilt campus, drew a sheet of paper from his pocket, and announced that he had written a poem—his first. It was entitled "Sunset," and it was in free verse. He read it to Davidson, who was most impressed.[25] Ransom promptly wrote three more, sent them to the *Independent* where they were accepted for publication, and, in effect, the Fugitive poetry movement was under way.

Poems About God

In 1917 John Ransom again showed Davidson some poems. By then both were in the army, for the United States had entered the war and the two young men were at Fort Oglethorpe, Georgia, in training for reserve commissions. The new poems were to become part of a collection which Ransom had left with his friend Christo-

pher Morley during his overseas service. Morley gave
them to Henry Holt and Company. Robert Frost was at
this time reading manuscripts for Holt, and he gave Ransom's verse a positive endorsement. On Frost's recom-
mendation, then, *Poems About God* appeared in April,
1919.

The book was aptly titled. In his preface Ransom announced that, having noticed that his first several poems
all made considerable use of the term God, he decided it
was "the most poetic of all terms possible," and had therefore set out "to treat rather systematically a number of
the occasions on which this term was in use with common
American men." [26] Ransom did not choose to reprint any
of the *Poems About God* in the collections of his selected
poetry until the final *Selected Poems* of 1969. And only two
appeared then. These early poems are, indeed, apprentice
work; they exhibit little of the characteristic manner of
Ransom's mature poetry. There is seldom visible in them
that continuing contrast of a formal, stylized literary language with the pungency of colloquial speech that marks
his best work; nor do they draw importantly upon the
mordant wit and ironic undercutting of the later poetry.
But they do exhibit Ransom's fascination with domestic
imagery, and there is often the undercurrent of violence.
They are written very much in revolt against poetic diction, and they aim at a simplicity of language and reference that sometimes verges upon triteness. One is not
surprised that Robert Frost admired them, for there is
more than a little of Frost's manner in evidence, as in the
conversational tone that is, nonetheless, intensified by the
rhythm and rhyme, as in these lines from "Grace," which
is about the death of a hired man:

> The corn was well above my knees,
> The weeds were more than ankle high,
> And dangerous customers were these,
> We went to work in the heat again,
> I hoped we'd get a bit of breeze

And thought the hired man was used
To God's most blazing cruelties.[27]

In later years Ransom criticized the conventionality of
Frost's technique, suggesting that it was a little less than
entirely audacious. But the Ransom who wrote *Poems
About God* clearly found Frost's way with language extremely attractive, as in these lines from "Geometry":

My window looks upon a wood
That stands as tangled as it stood
When God was centuries too young
To care how right he worked, or wrong,
His patterns in obedient trees . . .

. . . .
Poor little elms beneath the oak!
They thrash their arms around and poke
At tyrant throats, and try to stand
Straight up, like owners of the land;
For they expect the vainest things,
And even the boniest have their flings.[28]

What is most impressive about the poems in this first
collection, however, when viewed in the light of Ransom's
origins and his later development, is their God-searching.
They indicate how unwilling Ransom was, despite his
philosophical bent and his voyaging far from the orthodox Protestantism of his Methodist background, to give
up the traditional religious attitude. The poems are almost all explorations of the human condition in a world
that has moved away from theological certainty. And that
world is generally found to be unavoidable but unsatisfactory. Thus in "Morning,"

Three hours each day we souls,
Who might be angels but are fastened down
With bodies, most infuriating freight,
Sit fattening these frames and skeletons
With filthy food, which they must cast away
Before they feed again.[29]

The biological, material explanation is not to be Plato-
nized away. The flesh is there, and cannot be balked. But

the acceptance is begrudging. Thus in viewing a beautiful woman in "The Cloak Model," a stranger remarks:

> "I wish the moralists would thresh
> (Indeed the thing is very droll)
> God's oldest joke, forever fresh:
> The fact that in the finest flesh
> There isn't any soul."[30]

The early poems do indeed constitute, as the preface suggests, an exploration of the kinds of occasions in which the presence of God is supposed to be observable. But the investigation is an ironic one, for what usually emerges from the poems is the poet's inability to square that presence with his own realistic and logical diagnosis of the situation. Sometimes the point is made good-humoredly, even a trifle fatuously, as in "Noonday Grace," in which father, mother, and son sit down to table, and father offers the blessing, praying that God "Turn not away from us thy face/Till we come to our final resting place." Son thinks

> I love my father's piety,
> I know he's grateful as can be,
> A man that's nearly seventy
> And past his taste for cookery.

But *he* is not past his taste; he prays with total fervency for the food:

> Thank you, good Lord, for dinner-time!
> Gladly I come from the sweat and grime
> To play in your Christian pantomime.

He proceeds to give separate but equal thanks for napkin, platter, centerpiece, milk, yams, country ham, vegetables, corn on the cob, tomatoes, potatoes, beans, cucumbers, corn bread, and so on. On Sunday, he remarks, the preacher had noted the objections to a personal god:

> . . . isn't his sweep of mighty wings
> Meant more for businesses of kings
> Than pulling small men's pretty strings?

He, however, is quite sure that the God he prefers is the one who "helps my mother cook,/And slips to the dining-room door to look." And when it turns out that there is also blackberry pie for dessert, why then, "As long as I keep topside the sod,/I'll love you always, mother and God."[31] The demonstration is meant whimsically, of course; what Ransom is gently undercutting is the convenience of God as the orthodox conceive of Him—as if it were His particular business to keep the Ransom family well nourished. For the young man, God is to be thanked for the excellence of his cuisine; for his father, God is requested to be sure to keep on the job until he dies. The poet is suggesting that whatever God is, he is perhaps not at the beck and call of the Ransom family at mealtime, and that grace before meals—addressed to a personal God—is "a Christian pantomime" of pious sentimentalizing before getting down to the pleasures of the taste buds.

In another "Grace" poem the problem is presented with less lightheartedness. The speaker is concerned with the ugliness and pain of death:

> Who is it beams the merriest
> At killing a man, the laughing one?
> You are the one I nominate,
> God of the rivers of Babylon.

He describes how the hired man and he would work together in the fields, singing hymns, and tells how on one hot day the hired man, who was pious and believed in salvation, suddenly fell from his horse into the furrow:

> . . . it was a foolish kind of sprawl,
> And I found a hulk of heaving meat
> That wouldn't answer me at all.

All about them the day is beautiful—"a fresh breeze made the young corn dance/To a bright green, glorious carnival." He drags the man over into the shade, angry over the thought "of the prayers the fool has prayed/To his God." Then the dying man vomits:

> And God, who had just received full thanks
> For all his kindly daily bread,
> Now called it back again—perhaps
> To see that his birds of the air were fed.

He has seen God provide merciful deaths, he says, but the hired man "in his vomit laid him down,/Denied the decency of blood." The spectacle makes the speaker himself sick, and he too vomits:

> A little lower than the angels he made us
> (Hear his excellent rhetoric),
> A credit we were to him, one of us dead,
> The other half of us lying sick.

Again he views the beautiful Sunday scene about them.

> The young corn smelled its sweetest too,
> And made him goodly frankincense,
> The thrushes offered music up,
> Choired in the wood beyond the fence.

> And while his praises filled the earth
> A solitary crow sailed by,
> And while the whole creation sang
> He cawed—not knowing how to sigh.[32]

Whatever the death signifies, it is horrible and physical—not to be enclosed within the bounds of a comfortable theology that sees God's benevolent hand intervening in every action. This is not merely a poem that points out the difference between sentimental piety and the inexplicability of God's universe. What is being examined is the plausibility of belief itself. For it is obvious that the speaker, like Job, is not prepared to yield his own logic to the mystery. And there is no voice out of the whirlwind that can reconcile him to the orthodox faith; there is only the solitary crow, mocking the Sunday peace, with no logical answer or explanation forthcoming and no basis for believing in spite of logic.

Over the whole performance, however, one has a sense of not merely regret but resentment. That is, the poet explores the disappearance of the Methodist God. He points out, sometimes savagely, sometimes comically, the logical absurdity of the old orthodoxy. But even as he takes aim at the orthodoxy, he seems to be most irked not at those who insist upon holding to it, but at the orthodoxy itself for being logically absurd. He doesn't *want* it to be untenable; and when he depicts its untenableness he is not very happy about it, or about the necessity, as he sees it, of doing so.

For this particular young Tennessee poet, liberation from the intellectual boundaries of the old southern community past, with its theological orthodoxy, albeit necessary, will be begrudging. He will be a modern because he must be, not because he delights in it. He is very much in the position of the young Ralph Waldo Emerson, who accepts the logic of the Unitarianism of Boston, but nonetheless remembers fondly the old Calvinism's emotional fervor, its ordering of the heart and the affections, and wishes he hadn't had to give it up.

Poems About God is a hungry book. What the poet has found thus far, in place of the orthodox Methodist past, appears pretty bland and unappetizing. He consumes it, but with a wry face. He is on the lookout for something better, more pleasing to the palate. It *ought* to exist, somewhere. He will keep an eye out for it.

The Gathering of the Fugitives

When the young Tennesseans reassembled in Nashville after the war, the twice-monthly discussions were resumed. Sidney Hirsch had moved in with his sister and brother-in-law, Mr. and Mrs. James Frank. After a year of teaching in Kentucky, Davidson joined the Vanderbilt English department, where William Yandell Elliott was also teaching. William Frierson, a Vanderbilt senior, became part of the group. By now the talk was centered on poetry and literature rather than philosophy. Ransom and Curry were trading sonnets, and Davidson too was

writing poetry in earnest. Then in November of 1921
Davidson did something that was to be of great importance to the group's make-up. He invited a brilliant young
Vanderbilt student, John Orley Allen Tate, to visit the
next meeting.

Allen Tate was twenty-one years old when he joined
the Fugitives. Tate's father had been less than a financial
success, and the family had moved about considerably
during his youth. He had been irregularly educated at
schools in Louisville and Ashland, Kentucky; Cincinnati,
Ohio; Evansville, Indiana; and at Georgetown University
Preparatory School in the District of Columbia. In classical studies he was far advanced, in mathematics and
science considerably less so.

What Tate brought to the group was an uncompromis-
ing respect for intellectuality, together with an open re-
ceptivity to modernism in language and attitude. He had
already read widely in the French poets and in modern
verse forms; during the Fugitive years he was the one
who kept the group thoroughly in touch with what was
most challenging and vigorous in the literary developments of the early 1920s. Tate did not share Ransom's
skeptical attitude toward what T. S. Eliot, Ezra Pound,
and the Expatriate school represented. There is not in
Tate's work—whether in the early Fugitive days or the
later, more mature poetry of the late 1920s and 1930s—
the evidence of a divided allegiance that one encounters
in Ransom's verse, with the rigor of the new techniques
warring against a traditional sensibility. He was not so
deeply and instinctively drawn toward the older southern
community attitudes; his background was more cosmopolitan and less committed. Acceptance of the failure of
orthodox theology to permit definition of his own identity within it was not for Tate either begrudging or difficult. Though he had a strong feeling for the southern
past, and of his own family's social role within it (along
with a detestation of its erosion), his later commitment

to his origins was more conscious and intellectual than instinctive and reflexive. Whereas in Ransom's writings there is always discernible a certain unease amid the heady currents of modern thought and attitude and a sense of his using modernism as a strategy for coping with what he cannot avoid, Tate is thoroughly at ease in modernism, however much he deplores its values; and as his attitudes begin to coalesce, he is able to work from within it toward a much more radical reformation of those attributes and values he wishes to change.

Tate has depicted himself during those early Nashville days in terms that are less than kind. "My conceit must have been intolerable," he wrote later; and, "you have before you the figure of a twenty-two-year-old prig as disagreeable as you could possibly conjure up, until you see in him several varieties of snobbishness, when he becomes even more disagreeable."[33] To say the least, it is highly unlikely that so unpleasant a youth could have won and held the admiration and affection of his older confreres. The truth is, it seems to me, that it was just those qualities that Tate exaggerates for self-denigration that must have constituted much of his value for Ransom and the other Tennesseans. For Tate *was*, outwardly at least, self-assured; he had learned as a young man to adopt an attitude, a manner of presenting himself; and if he was a bit overly insistent upon it sometimes, he was not afraid to flaunt his intellectual colors boldly and without embarrassment. Even his earliest published poems, in the first issue of *The Fugitive*, show an unhesitating willingness to put forward an intellectual stance and then adhere to it. "To Intellectual Detachment," for example, describes one given to ruthless analysis of others:

> He hung each disparate anguish on the spits
> Parboiled and roasted in his own withering soul.
> God give him peace! He gave none other peace

This he declares of one whose dissecting intelligence

worked on endlessly, "smooth like cold steel, yet feeling without pain" until at last his talent for such vivisection, used always without comparison and as means to an end, destroyed him as well: "It turned on him—he's dead. Shall we detest him?"[34]

Though the poem—surely a respectable accomplishment for a twenty-one-year-old poet—lacks the rich display of language in Tate's later poetry and presents a rather too facile irony at the close, it clearly possesses what was otherwise missing in Fugitive verse, even Ransom's: an achieved, formal position, from which the poem is spoken. Without being used to represent the poet's own groping for the proper attitude, the poem is thus a dramatized argument, reasoned in its premises, exploring the possibilities of the situation. Upon reading it one doesn't feel that the poet is using his poem to illustrate his own personal grappling with the problem; the grappling itself *is* the poem, as displayed by the poet who has already worked out the implications and is now concentrating on presenting them. Nor does the poem seem to apologize for itself; the reader does not feel that the poet is somewhat ashamed and embarrassed at saying what he wants to say in the form of a poem. There is an intellectual boldness to it, a self-assurance that, because it invites no scrutiny of motives, offers no apologies for its own right to exist. And the same is true, with respect to language choice, of such lines as these from Tate's other poem in the first issue of *The Fugitive*, "Sinbad":

> . . . If I could wipe the must
> From the mildewed jam of devilry, and the rust
> Off my lip, the taste of the red preserves
> Of love would be as horrid as one deserves
> Who lusted with wormwood and with sickening myrrh . . .[35]

In retrospect this sort of thing seems to be precisely what the Fugitives, particularly Ransom, most needed to see demonstrated at that stage of their careers. Despite the excellence of some of the lyrics in *Poems About God*, there is an awkwardness, a hesitant, groping quality that comes not merely because Ransom is still fumbling toward a style, but also because he seems to believe that as poet he is obliged not to show any signs of an excessive commitment to a position. Yet Ransom's real talent and cast of mind lay in just such commitment. His dry, rigorous logic, his willingness to search out the implications of an idea or a situation and report them fully, were not best employed in embodying the laborious process of exploration, but in elaborating, with great finesse and subtlety, the outcome. To examine a problem, investigate its implications with keenness of intellect and precision of discrimination, and then set forth his findings was what Ransom had to offer. His gift for extravagance of language and imagery, his ability to dramatize the ultimate implications of a situation, his gleeful, even savage relish for noting and dwelling upon the incongruities and traps of human contradiction and upon logical dead ends—these qualities were impeded by too much linguistic caution and a too-inhibiting self-consciousness. The willingness of his younger colleague to strike a stance in a poem and order everything in accordance with it, to use his formidable, if still immature, resources of rhetoric, vocabulary, and intellect wholeheartedly and without fear of appearing either indiscreet or ridiculous—this must have emboldened Ransom a great deal. What Ransom needed as a poet was the courage of his literary convictions; and he appears to have found encouragement in the example of the young Allen Tate, who did not hesitate to deploy everything at his command and to launch himself fully into the attack. This, I think, was Tate's most useful contribution to the Fugitives.

Tate's influence is evident if we compare the poem Ransom wrote for the first issue of *The Fugitive*, "Ego," with a poem written only a few months later but couched in his mature style, "Philomela," cited earlier. "Ego" is about the poet's decision to cast his lot with the muse and to follow the lead of his fellow Fugitives. He notes the criticism that has been made of him by others (presumably concerning *Poems About God*) to the effect that "a little learning addleth this man's wit" so that "He crieth on our dogmas Counterfeit" and does not respect "duly our tall steeple" but prefers his books. He would prefer, he says, to have been "born dull, born blind," if thereby he "might not estrange my gentle kind,/Nor brag, nor run a solitary race." But being neither dull nor blind, he cannot avoid the estrangement. He addresses his books and also his fellow poets:

> Sages and friends, too often have you seen us
> Deep in the midnight conclave as we used;
> For my part, reverently were you perused;
> No rank or primacy being hatched between us;
>
> For my part, much beholden to you all,
> Giving a little and receiving more . . .

He is made the way he is, and cannot help it; there is "My Demon, always clamoring Up, Begone,/Pursue your gods faster than most of creatures," and he can do no other. So rather than

> Comporting downwards to the general breed;
> I have run further, matching your heat and speed,
> And tracked the Wary Fugitive with you . . .

Having thus made his commitment, acted to alienate himself from his people, he is satisfied with the look of the balance sheet;

> And if an alien, miserably at feud
> With those my generation, I have reason
> To think to salve the fester of my treason:
> A seven of friends exceeds much multitude.

The difficulty, however, is that the poem itself has *not* made its commitment fully. The attitude expressed toward "the general breed" of friends and family is not decisive. That is, he will not "take the vomit where they do," but will seek the company of his fellow bards. His pupils are "young simple snails." To avoid bringing hurt upon his family he should have been "born dull, born blind." Since he is neither, what he thinks and says is certain to offend so pedestrian and unimaginative a group as they. Yet, if we accept his estimate of their worth, there would seem little reason why he should worry much about offending them. However, he also insists that they are "mine own sweet kin" and his "gentle kind"; he is "an alien, miserably at feud" with them, which he seems to think is not very admirable behavior. The claim that "a seven of friends exceeds much multitude" is a bit unconvincing from one who accuses himself of "miserably" feuding with his family and asks that friends come and "acquit me of that stain of pride."[36]

Instead of the emphatically defiant attitude expressed in the next-to-last stanza and in the last line, where the claims of friends and family who would have him desist are treated with the irony that such conviction and such defiance dictate, the rest of the poem wavers in attitude. At times the speaker seems quite satisfied with his choice; at other times he feels extremely guilty for having made it. This is reflected in the images, which are sometimes gentle, sometimes harsh. A poem that might have been written *about* such an ambivalence and fluctuation of attitudes, Ransom's poem instead depicts the ambivalence and the fluctuation *in* the stance of the poem—even though the poem is, in intent at least, "about" the poet's entire satisfaction with the choice he has made. The opinion of the reader is likely to be that the poet is by no means sure of his choice and is reaching about for rhetoric to reinforce it.

When we compare "Ego" with the first published version of "Philomela," which appeared barely one year later, we witness an extraordinary change. This poem, describing his search for a viable poetic stance in the literature of English poetry, as exemplified in the nightingale he hears at Oxford, and his realization that something less precious and rarefied will have to serve his own American muse, also portrays a movement toward a literary commitment. But this time there is no ambivalence on the part of the poet. Although he pretends ironically to feel regret and remorse at his failure to appreciate the nightingale's voice—"I have despaired if we may make us worthy"—there is no question at any point in the poem about what he ultimately thinks of the matter. Though the nightingale has spoken to Ovid, the Teutons, and been "gallicized," he is sure that "Never was she baptised" —the very idea of the nightingale being thus processed for admission to the Protestant heaven is so absurd that we cannot take the nightingale very seriously. "How could her delicate dirge run democratic?" he asks; clearly she is all too precious and bloodless for his taste. From the beginning, it is obvious that he finds "the classic numbers of the nightingale" too removed from the everyday, too divorced from life, to mean very much for him. And when he refers to himself and his fellow Americans as "an inordinate race," dissonant, come from a "barbarous" province and a "bantering breed sophistical and earthy," he is being ironically self-deprecatory, for he doesn't really believe a word of it. The statement that the "fabulous provinces" of the nightingale belong to "more beautiful, persistently more young" nations is another way of saying that as far as the poet is concerned, the famed English poets are lacking in vitality and given to childish attitudinizing about nightingales and Beauty.[37]

The difference between "Ego" and "Philomela" is that the earlier work is a forum for the poet's arguing the pros and cons of his decision to commit himself to his art, whereas the later poem is an instrument of the poet's strategy. Ransom carefully shapes the language, the argument, and the development of "Philomela" to achieve the purpose he wishes. He recites the details of his affair with the traditional English poetic muse, recounting how he decided to renounce the lady; and he puts his language and his wit to work in demonstrating, from the very outset, why that had to be. Ransom's inventiveness, his sense of humor and of the absurd, his playful irony are thus freed to serve his poetic purposes. Because he has already determined that he can't take the nightingale and what it represents seriously, he concentrates on showing why, and throughout pays only a sham homage to the symbol he has rejected, with a beautifully ironic and mockingly humble deference. Unlike "Ego," "Philomela" does indeed have the courage of its commitment, and because it has, it need not insist upon its own earnestness, but can grandly seem to make concessions in order to come down all the more effectively on the chosen side of the argument. From now on, Ransom as poet was the crafty strategist, not the Hamlet-like soul searcher; and he proceeded to produce, all during the 1920s, one poem after another that exhibited his wit and his savage sense of irony.

Terror and Decorum

Chills and Fever, published in 1924, established Ransom as an important American poet. Many of these poems had appeared first in *The Fugitive* and were revised for the book. Two of his most anthologized pieces, "Captain Carpenter" and "Bells for John Whiteside's Daughter," are included. *Grace After Meat*, an English selection of his work, was published in 1924 with an introduction by Robert Graves. In 1927 came *Two Gentlemen in Bonds*, with such poems as "Janet Waking" and "The Equilibrists." For all intents and purposes the major part of Ransom's work as poet was now done; only five poems, "Address to the Scholars of New England," "Painted Head," "Of Margaret," "Prelude to an Evening," and "Old Man Pondered," were added to later collections.

It has often been pointed out how very domestic is Ransom's muse. So many of the situations in his poems are drawn from everyday, middle-class life, and the same is true of many of the most effective images. He concludes "Winter Remembered," a love poem, for example, with:

> Dear love, these fingers that have known your touch,
> And tied our separate forces first together,
> Were ten poor idiot fingers not worth much,
> Ten frozen parsnips hanging in the weather.[38]

The use of parsnips is typical; and so is the command of colloquial idiom when needed: "not worth much"—"hanging in the weather." It has been remarked that what Ransom could do to perfection was set off intensified literary language and the colloquial idiom against each other. Thus in "Captain Carpenter" the much-mauled captain calls out an ironic challenge:

> "To any adversary it is fame
> If he risk to be wounded by my tongue
> Or burnt in two beneath my red heart's flame
> Such are the perils he is cast among.
>
> "But if he can he has a pretty choice
> From an anatomy with little to lose
> Whether he cut out my tongue and take my voice
> Or whether it be my round red heart he choose."[39]

It is the vernacular matter-of-factness of the second line of that latter stanza which makes the speech work; slipped in among a vocabulary and syntax deliberately and flagrantly archaic, it mocks the literary diction and keeps the poem where it must remain: in the realm of sinister playfulness. The same is true of the description of the pet chicken in "Janet Waking," done to death by "a transmogrifying bee":

> It scarcely bled
> But how exceedingly
> And purply did the knot
> Swell with the venom and communicate
> Its rigor! Now the poor comb stood up straight
> But Chucky did not.[40]

Mixed in with the playfulness and the domestic imagery, masked by the wit and the extravagance of language, however, is a considerable supply of violence. Like the young woman of "Vaunting Oak" who had been "instructed of much mortality,"[41] Ransom often dealt with the terrible swiftness and finality of death and the difficulty of its inevitability for humans. Thus in "Miriam Tazewell" an old maid goes forth in her garden after a storm

> To see in the strong sun her lawn deflowered
> Her tulip, iris, peony strung and pelted,
> Pots of geraniums spilled and the stalks naked.

The notable willingness of lewd nature to continue as if nothing important had occurred grieves her: "To Miriam Tazewell the whole world was villain/To prosper when the fragile babes were fallen."[42] The young woman of "Vaunting Oak" would choose the great oak tree as "Our love's symbol" because of its sturdiness and its "long winterings": "Established, you see him there! forever." But her lover knocks on the trunk and shows her the hollow sound of its inner rottenness. The oak, he warns, "before our joy shall have lapsed, even, will be gone." The poem ends with "the tears of a girl remembering her dread."[43] In "Blue Girls" the young ladies of the college are told to

> Tie the white fillets then about your hair
> And think no more of what will come to pass
> Than bluebirds that go walking on the grass
> And chattering on the air.

They are instructed to practice their beauty "before it fail." For the speaker knows "a lady with a terrible tongue, /Blear eyes fallen from blue,/All her perfections tarnished . . ." who not long since "was lovelier than any of you."[44] (It is almost as if he were lamenting the condition of the muse of poetry in the Waste Land time.) One of the most savage of the poems is a sonnet, "Piazza Piece." The first stanza is spoken by "a gentleman in a dustcoat" who addresses a young girl. He warns her to make note of "the roses on your trellis dying/And hear the spectral singing of the moon"—contemplate, that is, the inevitability of age and death. "I must have my lovely lady soon," he tells her. The "lady young in beauty" would prefer not to: she awaits her truelove.

> But what grey man among the vines is this
> Whose words are dry and faint as in a dream?
> Back from my trellis, Sir, before I scream![45]

Not only is the spectacle of death and the maiden sufficiently sinister, but Ransom has infused the transaction with a great deal of suppressed erotic tension: time, one might almost say, as the grim raper.

In other poems the violence is more direct. "Necrological," the first of Ransom's poems to be composed in the mature style of the early 1920s, presents a friar who journeys forth from his monastery to the scene of a battle and contemplates the bare bodies of the slain: "Not all were white; some gory and fabulous/Whom the sword had pierced and then the grey wolf eaten." A dead warrior's mistress lies at his feet clutching his knees. A horse which "had spilled there his little brain" is noted, along with its rider: "the little groin of the knight was spilled by a stone." And so on. The friar can only sit contemplatively, and liken "unto those dead/Whom the kites of heaven solicited with sweet cries."[46] In "Judith of Bethulia," after the lady does in the foe's leader,

> We smote them hiding in our vineyards, barns, annexes,
> And now their white bones clutter the holes of foxes,
> And the chieftain's head, with grinning sockets, and
>   varnished—
> Is it hung on the sky with a hideous epitaphy?
> No, the woman keeps the trophy.[47]

More often in Ransom's poetry, however, the violence and terror are not stated so baldly, but are ironically gentled by the employment of metaphor and diction that are peculiarly bloodless and archaic, so that the effect is made the more sinister in its very covertness. We have seen how in "Piazza Piece" he portrays death as a gentleman in a dustcoat, and how the maiden is made to reply in mannered outrage, "Back from my trellis, Sir, before I scream!" In "Captain Carpenter" the various sallyings-forth of the good captain in pursuit of fame, honor, and duty are each rewarded with physical maiming, but always described in the diction and rhythm of the medieval ballad. A "pretty lady" takes a sword "with all her main/ And twined him of his nose forevermore." A stranger rogue uses a club to "crack his two legs at the shinny part / And let him roll and stick like any tub." The wife of Satan, the she-wolf who "should have made off like a hind," is likewise hostile: "the bitch bit off his arms at the elbows." The captain "parted with his ears" to a black devil, and another "plucked out his sweet blue eyes." Finally "the neatest knave that ever was seen" performs one of the least violently described murders in all of literature: "With gentle apology and touch refined/He pierced him and produced the Captain's heart."[48] The whole wittily archaic, almost sing-song performance, with its ballad stanzas and its extravagant, mock-heroic diction, is a triumph of poetic ambivalence; there is so much violence and gore, even while the language and the form appear to deny them; the linguistic tomfoolery and the grim events serve to undercut each other. When I read "Captain Carpenter" I think of the depiction of the Battle of Hastings in the Bayeux tapestry: the death wounds, the outpouring of blood, the lethal striking home of the Norman arrows are illustrated in the woven medium with such singular absence of realism that they seem peculiarly bloodless, and yet the actual deeds portrayed are terrible. The effect, inherent in the textile, is one of horror made the more sinister by its ambivalence. Just so, in the Ransom poems the language and the technique work both to deny and to reveal the violence, so that one is never quite sure how to take it.

Ransom's poetry, and the philosophy that underlies it, are built upon a dualism. The poetry illustrates and embodies the conflicting claims of the ideal and the real, the spirit and the flesh, and the mature poetry of the Fugitive period seems to constitute a continuing exploration of the human problem involved in that dualistic hypothesis. The poems are based on divisions, usually that of heart versus head. What worried Ransom was the intellectual effort to falsify the perilous balance that he considered life to involve, by a too-strenuous assertion of the ideal, in the form of one variety or another of Platonic abstraction.

It is interesting, however, to see the shift of emphasis in the location of the source of such falsification, as Ransom's poetry develops. In the early *Poems About God* the target is often the old, traditional Protestantism of his upbringing, with what he considered its too-easy anthropomorphism and assurance of fulfillment on the other side of the grave. We have seen how in "Noonday Grace" the speaker refuses to give the thanks to God alone for the bountiful meal; he notes the naivete in the conception of a divinity that "like mother . . . finds it his greatest joy/ To have big dinners for his boy," and he insists ironically that "as long as I keep topside the sod,/ I'll love you always, mother and God."[49] In "Grace" the horribly physical death of the hired man savages the easy notion of a Blessed Redeemer. In the years of *The Fugitive*, however, this particular form of idealistic evasion no longer troubles Ransom; his explorations of the dualistic problem tend to be conducted along other lines, notably the impoverishment of life either through too-rigid social constraint or through unrestrained egotism. His poems of the middle 1920s focus upon the social, domestic scene, and what he insists is the compromised human situation —life caught and defined between the polarities of body and soul, manners and human solitude. Perhaps the finest statement of the paradox comes in "The Equilibrists,"

which was first entitled "History of Two Simple Lovers."
The man is tempted by the physical beauty of his beloved:
"Full of her long white arms and milky skin/He had a
thousand times remembered sin," the poem begins, and

> Body: it was a white field ready for love,
> On her body's field, with the gaunt tower above,
> The lilies grew, beseeching him to take,
> If he would pluck and wear them, bruise and break.

But the affair cannot be consummated, for she says that
giving in to their lust is wrong; and though he knows that
if he disregards her plea, she will readily respond to his
advances, he cannot bring himself to tempt her: "O such
a little thing is Honor, they feel!/But the grey word is between them cold as steel." What ensues is a "torture of
equilibrium":

> They burned with fierce love always to come near,
> But honor beat them back and kept them clear.

The poet, dismayed, asks what is desired. "Would you as-
cend to Heaven and bodiless dwell?/Or take your bodies
honorless to hell?" He points out the ultimate contradiction in their predicament. To yield to the ideal, to obey
the tenets of morality, is to deny the passion of life itself:

> In Heaven you have heard no marriage is,
> No white flesh tinder to your lecheries,
> Your male and female tissue sweetly shaped
> Sublimed away, and furious blood escaped.

On the other hand, to give in to human desire, to heed
only the requirements of passion, is to abandon oneself to
a carnal appetite that can never be assuaged or mastered:

> Great lovers lie in Hell, the stubborn ones
> Infatuate of the flesh upon the bones;
> Stuprate, they rend each other when they kiss,
> The pieces kiss again, no end to this.

This is the human predicament—the dualistic universe
of flesh and spirit, feeling and thought, whereby neither

the mind nor the body may be entirely reconciled—which finds its conclusion only with death. Thus the "Epitaph" with which the poem concludes:

> *Equilibrists lie here: stranger, tread light;*
> *Close, but untouching in each other's sight;*
> *Mouldered the lips and ashy the tall skull.*
> *Let them lie perilous and beautiful.*[50]

Here lies the root of Ransom's fascination with death: the close, the conclusion, the only known solution to existence. In poem after poem Ransom confronts this final realization, whether in pathos or with wry humor. As he remarks of the dead matron in "Here Lies a Lady,"

> But was she not lucky? In flowers and lace and mourning,
> In love and great honor we bade God rest her soul
> After six little spaces of chill, and six of burning.[51]

But though this perilous reconciliation-in-irreconcilement would remain at the center of Ransom's poetry throughout his career, in the poems of the late 1920s and the several written later there is a new emphasis that comes to the fore. We can see it emerging as early as "Armageddon," a poem which won the prize of the Poetry Society of South Carolina for 1923.* This poem depicts the meeting of Christ and Satan at the battle that is to signify the end of the world. The two adversaries, together with their hosts, appear on the plain, ready for combat. Instead of commencing the fight, however, they take to fraternizing, and in one way or another most of the mod-

---

* It is a commentary on the difference between the Nashville Fugitives and the poets who made up the Poetry Society of South Carolina during the years of its notable blossoming in the early 1920s that after Ransom's poem was selected by the judges to receive the prize, the officers of the Charleston group, in particular John Bennett and DuBose Heyward, became alarmed at the possible adverse reaction by the Charleston citizenry that constituted the bulk of the membership if so "atheistic" a poem were to be publicly honored and printed in the society's *Yearbook.* Ultimately the poem was published, not in the *Yearbook* but in a separate little brochure to be distributed "to such members of the society as express a desire to have it."[52] Needless to say, no such civic considerations troubled the Fugitives in their selection of poems for their magazine.

ern modifications and sweetenings of the old traditional gospel are reenacted by Christ during the new-found harmony. All is good will: "the Wolf said Brother to the Lamb,/The True Heir keeping with the poor Imposter." It is only after an old patriarch,

> A goodly liege of old malignant blood,
> Who could not fathom the new brotherhood
> Between the children of the light and dark

makes known his dislike of the proceedings, that Christ is recalled to his mission. Whereupon he "sheds unmannerly his devil's pelf,/Takes ashes from the hearth and smears himself," and rouses his followers, who "with scourge . . . mortify their carnal selves," and "whet the ax-heads on the helves/And seek the Prince Beelzebub and minions." As the battle is readied, Christ and his followers sing "of death and glory and no complaisance," while the Antichrist and his armies "Make songs of innocence and no bloodshed." As the battle grows imminent,

> The immortal Adversary shook his head:
> If now they fought too long, then he would famish;
> And if much blood was shed, why, he was squeamish:
> "These Armageddons weary me much," he said.[53]

Clearly this poem of 1923 presages the later Ransom of *God Without Thunder* and the making of the Agrarian symposium, *I'll Take My Stand*. For it is a poem about religious orthodoxy, and instead of occupying himself with the logical inadequacy of the old Methodist theology that he had rejected, Ransom is now satirizing the modern-day Social Gospel and the forces of rationalism and urbanity in the church, suggesting religious belief has been so watered down that it no longer distinguishes between good and evil. The ironic note at the end—Antichrist has seen his Armageddons come and go and is still in business as usual—does not cancel out the clear evidence that the poet is expressing a strong preference for the attitude toward Christianity that he had known as a youth, with its active, personal, unambiguous moral ordering. The duality is still very much present—Antichrist is by no means the entire villain of the piece—but Ransom focuses his sarcasm on the idealistic theorizing of modern, post-Darwinian theology, with its optimism, its preference for liturgical form rather than evangelical fervor, its alliance with wealth and ease, its interpretation of the Scriptures as a literary document rather than as divine revelation, and its relativistic refusal to confront evil. Whatever the deficiencies of the older theology when interpreted in the light of modern science and reason, it had provided the conviction of right and wrong and furnished Commandments by which men could define themselves.

What we have, in short, is an extremely sophisticated, witty, urbane poem written in advocacy of a return to That Old Time Religion, which, the poet suggests, with respect to its moral ordering at any rate, would be good enough for him. We shall see what the ultimate implications of such an attitude will prove to be, insofar as Ransom's social views are concerned, when we take up the Agrarian adventure. Meanwhile, we turn to another poem, "Antique Harvesters," first published in 1925, to see another and different manifestation of the same kind of impatience with modernity.

"Antique Harvesters" is not the first poem of Ransom's in which the South becomes explicitly a theme. In 1924 he published "Old Mansion," which describes a sophisticated modern as he observes an old house, "a Southern manor." Evidences of the mansion's former glory are still very much visible. A graveyard is "not distant, possibly not external/To the property"; it is a place of the past, and though "Stability was the character of its rectangle," now "Decay was the tone of old brick and shingle." It will not be there long, he thinks, "And one had best hurry to enter it if one can." So he goes up to the door and knocks. But he is refused entry. He is quite certain that the old

mansion will soon crumble to dust, but it reminds him of
his own evanescence:

> How loving from my dying weed the feather curled
> On the languid air; and I went with courage shaken
> To dip, alas, into some unseemlier world.[54]

In this particular poem, obviously, the Old South is indeed dead, and the modern man can find no ingress to it.
The tone, however, is one of regret, and the change from
that antique way of life to the "unseemlier world" he now
inhabits, if inescapable, is not without its disadvantages.

A year later, however, and "Antique Harvesters" approaches the same problem with a considerably changed
strategy. The locale is specifically identified: "Of the Mississippi the bank sinister,/and of the Ohio the bank sinister." It is harvest time in the South, and the prospects are
not bounteous; rather, the scene is one of decline, and
those who assemble are old: "dry, grey, spare,/And mild
as yellow air." Someone hears the croak of a raven's funeral wing; the thought is of death. This is hardly pleasing to the young men, who "would be joying in the song/
Of passionate birds." But the old are not to be despised:
"Trust not but the old endure, and shall be older/Than
the scornful beholder." The harvesters begin the harvest:
"One spot has special yield? 'On this spot stood/Heroes
and drenched it with their only blood.'" The talk is of
the past, of tradition and causes cherished and lost, as
is proper for old men. Then they pause, for a hunting
party comes along:

> Here come the hunters, keepers of a rite;
> The horn, the hounds, the lank mares coursing by
> Straddled with archetypes of chivalry;
> And the fox, lovely ritualist, in flight
> Offering his unearthly ghost to quarry,
> And the fields, themselves to harry.

It is a very southern hunt portrayal; the hunters are of

the rural South, and they straddle their bony nags, not the chivalry itself but rustic archetypes of chivalry—onetime Confederate cavalrymen perhaps, fallen on threadbare days but pursuing their ritual as of old. It is indeed a rite, a communal observance designed to commemorate and reaffirm through repetition. So is the harvesting ritual; "Resume, harvesters," the speaker declares. What they harvest is "a treasure of full bronze/Which you will garner for the Lady." Time and mortality will soon take over: "Pluck fast, dreamers; prove as you amble slowly/Not less than men, not wholly." Thus the harvest takes on a religious significance, and the ritual is tribute to the Lady.

Now the young men—the young poets?—are to be instructed: "Bare the arms, dainty youths, bend the knees/Under bronze burdens," for it is only through all the seasons and stages of life that "you will have known/Your famous Lady's image." The young men must, that is, live and die in Dixie. There follows a precautionary admonition. If persons come and suggest that their careers will fare better in other areas, they must not give ear: "Angry as wasp-music be your cry then," and they are told what to retort:

> Forsake the Proud Lady, of the heart of fire,
> The look of snow, to the praise of a dwindled choir,
> Sons of degenerate specters that were men? . . . .

No indeed, the young must not leave the homeland to the care of the old alone; it is theirs, and they must continue to honor the tradition: "The sons of the fathers shall keep her, worthy of/What these have done in love." They must do so, for the South they serve is still very much alive, and has in no way ceased to be worthy of their fealty: "True, it is said of our Lady, she ageth./But see, if you peep shrewdly, she hath not stooped . . . ." It is true that the old men who have toiled for so long in her service have declined, but "Take no thought of her servitors that have drooped,/For we are nothing . . . ." And if the South is thought to be diminished or other than it once was, if change and mortality are what are to be considered, then these are but the common lot everywhere: "Why, the ribs of the earth subsist frail as a breath/If but God wearieth."[55] Where in "Old Mansion" there was no entry for the young modern, and death, the graveyard, was "possibly not external" to the property, now the South and its tradition are alive and available, and no more given over to dying than anywhere else. The need to "dip, alas, into some unseemlier world" is not only an imperative no longer, but the very suggestion is to be rejected with anger.

Beyond that, there is a crucial fusion of imagery in "Antique Harvesters." Instead of being portrayed as a crumbling "old mansion," the South is now seen in terms of the land. The tilling of the land is made into the garnering of treasure for our Lady—in other words, into a religious act. Identification with the South therefore constitutes identification with the religious attitude; the harvesting becomes a way of serving both the South and the Lord. It is as if the modern poet has discovered a strategy whereby it becomes possible to recapture the fervor, faith, and moral ordering of the old-time religious outlook, through a renewed concern with the South and its tradition. And there is one more, very important element added: the transaction is depicted as a ritual, complete with myth. For Ransom this is highly significant, for where ritual and myth are present, he held, then art is possible. "Manners, rites, and arts are so close to each other," he wrote in the late 1930s, "that often their occasions must be confused, and it does not matter much if they are. . . . Many works of art embody ritual, and art is often apparently content to be the handmaiden to religion. . . . We know also that works of art have been dedicated to the ceremonious life of society, communicating chivalry, or some much easier code; art serving manners."[56]

We have here, it seems to me, set forth explicitly in "Antique Harvesters," a strategy whereby through fealty to the southern land the old, forsaken communal ordering of religion is to be made possible, and this in turn will provide the ceremony of poetry. Just as the young Ralph Waldo Emerson had discovered in Transcendentalism a way to regain the emotional fervor and moral ordering of the old Calvinism which was so wanting in the bland Boston Unitarianism of his day, so now Ransom was discovering a path back to his own religious and social heritage. In the poem "Antique Harvesters" we have the prescription for *I'll Take My Stand*, in which a group of southern men of letters announced that the South, which had gone whoring after the strange gods of industrialism and modernism, must return to its old community heritage, forsake the modern, urban doctrine of progress, and loyally defend a traditional agricultural, rural way of life, in order to make possible the harmonious, mannered society in which the fine arts and the arts of living alike flourish. Ransom had traveled a long way from the young man who had once informed his father that rural life stultifies morality and is baneful for art and religion. He had come back to his origins.

Poetry and Miraculism

It is John Ransom's poems that chiefly distinguish the quality of verse in *The Fugitive*. When, in his early thirties, the decision was made to publish a magazine, he was prepared to move into his mature style, and the larger part of his most distinguished verse was first published in its pages. The other important poets to come out of the group were younger than he, and in their instances we read the successive issues of *The Fugitive* today to study the beginnings of their achievement. To be sure, Donald Davidson published some of the best of his early poetry in later issues of the magazine; but it was in the years following the demise of *The Fugitive* in 1925 that Allen Tate produced almost all the poetry he chose to include in his several volumes of later years. As for Robert Penn Warren, when he was made a member of the group in the spring of 1924, he was only a precocious eighteen-year-old college junior.

Upon the suggestion of Sidney Hirsch, the group decided, in March, 1922, to publish a poetry magazine. The preface of the first issue announced that inasmuch as "a literary phase known rather euphemistically as southern literature has expired, like any other stream whose source is stopped up," *The Fugitive* was thereby enabled to be born. Its editors wished its readers to know that "THE FUGITIVE flees from nothing faster than from the high-caste Brahmins of the Old South."[57] It was to be edited by the group as a whole, with each member having a vote on poems to be included. Not until the fourth issue, December, 1922, were the magazine's pages opened to outside contributors. Thereafter the contributors included Robert Graves, Witter Bynner, William Alexander Percy, Hart Crane, Louis Untermeyer, L. A. G. Strong, John Gould Fletcher, Joseph Auslander, Olive Tilford Dargan, and George Dillon, though poems by the Fugitives always made up the bulk of the magazine's contents. One outside contributor, Laura Riding Gottshalk, the New York-born wife of a professor of history at the University of Louisville, was later made a member of the Fugitive group, though she did not attend regular meetings. Members not represented in the first two issues, such as William Yandell Elliott and William Frierson, contributed later on. As new members were taken into the Fugitives, their work was published. These included not only Warren but Jesse and Ridley Wills. Another Nashville resident, Alfred Starr, was made a member, but published no poems. A Vanderbilt undergraduate, Andrew Nelson Lytle, though never formally a member of the Fugitive group, published one poem in the magazine.

Although the regular meetings continued throughout the magazine's tenure, it is a mistake to imagine that these occasions represented the sole or even the primary forum for the principal member poets. When one reads the excellent account of the magazine's history by Louise Cowan, one sees that fairly early on the Fugitives began separating into two factions, even though the group identity was always insisted upon and there was never a time when lines were rigidly drawn.[58] On the one hand there were Ransom, Tate, and Davidson, all three of whom were already professional men of letters, or were on their way to that status. However much they differed among themselves—Ransom and Tate especially went through a period of considerable distancing, while Davidson was never quite the modernist in his verse—these three represented something of a modernist faction, interested in language, intellectually committed, and very much open to influence from the main poetic currents of the day. As might be expected, they spent a considerable amount of time in one another's company, and the regular meetings of the full group came to constitute more or less formal gatherings, separate and apart from their own close association. The other faction, centering on Hirsch, Stanley Johnson, Alec Stevenson, James Marshall Frank, and William Yandell Elliott, tended to oppose modernism, obscurantism (as they termed it), overintellectuality, and too-sordid reference, and held out for the poetry of high style and elevated subject matter. Not especially committed to either group were Walter Clyde Curry, Merrill Moore, the Wills brothers, and latecomers such as Warren.

As *The Fugitive* developed, it soon ceased to be a friendly diversion for Ransom, Tate, and Davidson, who were deadly serious about poetry and professionally ambitious for their work, and rapidly moved into the front lines of the literary campaigns of the 1920s. Writing and publishing verse was not an avocation for them; it represented an increasingly important professional activity. The magazine's growing fame—it was widely praised and reviewed, and attracted the admiring attention of such major contemporary literary figures as T. S. Eliot—was not only a tribute to the good taste of the group but an index of the increasing importance of the work of the leading Fugitives. It was only natural that the members of the group who were fully committed to poetry, and whose own work was constantly developing and changing as they extended their interests, should come increasingly to the fore. They began, too, to become interested in criticism and theory, and to publish their thoughts as editorials and articles.

It was Ransom whose personality and commitment provided the strongest and most pervasive influence in the Fugitive meetings. Not only was he the oldest member of the group and the sole poet who in the early 1920s had something of a national reputation as a poet and essayist, but as a member of the Vanderbilt English faculty he had taught most of the others. Because of his kindness and his genuine modesty, he was able to deal with the younger men as friend rather than as master. It might be noted at this point that at no time was the group or the magazine ever formally affiliated with Vanderbilt University. When the group proposed publishing a magazine, the chairman of the Vanderbilt English Department, Edwin Mims, at first tried to discourage them from doing so, though afterwards he went out of his way to praise the magazine and the poets as exemplary of the awakening in southern intellectual and cultural life. Mims's chief contribution to the group (and it was of much importance) was that he made a place on his faculty for Ransom and Davidson, and that—in notable contrast to most academic literary scholars of the time—he accepted creative work and was willing to consider it as important as literary scholarship in assessing the professional activity of his staff. But it was not until the year 1956, long after the group had broken up and its members had dispersed, at the time of the

Fugitives' reunion, that Vanderbilt University ever formally recognized and honored the poets who had won worldwide distinction for it.

Ransom's influence on the younger Fugitives was decisive. Genial, good-humored, he was also a rigorous logician, and he thrived on debate. In such discussion and argumentation he refined and honed the ideas that eventually became his critical essays. This habit was ingrained early in his life; when he and his father would discuss ideas at the dinner table, as apparently they often did, the dialogue often grew so emphatic that Ransom's mother would warn them to lower their voices lest the neighbors think they were quarreling. The Fugitive sessions meant a great deal to Ransom, as did those other occasions in his life when he would debate and discuss ideas with friends. With former pupils and fellow poets such as Allen Tate he carried on an extensive correspondence, devoted almost entirely to poetics.

Ransom never lost his small-town, middle-class attitudes and interests. This is apparent not only in his poetry, which, as we have seen, centered usually on domestic situations, but in his life. He was an enthusiastic athlete and card player; he loved to play tennis and golf, and was a passionate sports fan. Ransom thrived on good company and good talk, and did not seek out the company of scholars and writers in preference to that of other kinds of citizens.

For all his gregariousness and heartiness, there was a private quality to him, which one notices almost from the beginning, a recess of personality that never came out, and yet was very much a part of him. He liked to win, whether in discussion or in sports or in his career. When he received only a high "second" on his Oxford examinations, he cabled to his parents that "It is the first time I have ever failed at a critical moment and it will be a good lesson for me. I consider it a moral defeat rather than intellectual; bad enough but still one that can be remedied."[59] He was extremely ambitious, though he kept it well under control and usually out of sight. In the early 1920s, when *The Fugitive* was being published, there were times when book reviewers and critics would refer to the group as John Crowe Ransom's pupils, and to Ransom as their leader and the editor of *The Fugitive*. The better part of valor, given the situation and the sensitivities involved, would have been for Ransom to make it clear on such occasions that he was neither editor of the magazine nor "leader" of the group, and his persistent failure to do so resulted in some tension and ill feelings, particularly when he continued to resist the move on the part of some of the members to name an annual editor in order to provide the administrative authority that was necessary to the magazine's continued operation. Insisting that the magazine had always functioned without an editor, he objected to having his own name appear in a subordinate position in the magazine. His professional fortunes were too deeply involved, he said.[60] The point is that upon such occasions and at such junctures, none of the other Fugitives, no matter how friendly they were with Ransom, could ever discuss personal matters and motives frankly with him; there was always a kind of reserve about him which made him hold back his private thoughts.

Along with this went a quality of mind that was a continuing source of some puzzlement even to those who knew him best. He seemed to formulate his opinions and his ideas as the result of a rigorous reasoning process, and to use such a process to discipline and subjugate his emotions, so that he held not merely views but systematized intellectual positions, from which he could move by logic to cover his entire experience, and he could order that experience with a consistency that was very important to him. We can see this trait at work early in his career, in the letters he wrote to his father about his decision to stay in the Northeast, in which, having declared that he believed rural life unproductive of moral development for its inhabitants, he proceeded to set forth formally in some detail his definition of morality in order that, he explained, he would not be misunderstood. We notice it again in the preface he wrote to *Poems About God*, in which he explains his decision to compose the poems included in that book: having written several poems in which the term *God* was used, he said, he came to the conclusion that "this was the most poetic of all terms possible," and then "simply likened myself to a diligent apprentice and went to work to treat rather systematically a number of the occasions on which this term was in use with common American men."[61]

One rather doubts that the poems got themselves written in quite that way, though this is not to say that it was not entirely possible that Ransom thought that was what he was doing. In any event, it seems undeniable that his philosophical stance was no merely catch-as-catch-can affair, but a highly sophisticated and logically developed position which, depending upon the form it took, might be extended into poetry, politics, society, philosophy, theology, and whatever, and still reflect a consistent attitude. The dualistic base upon which Ransom built his hypotheses and out of which he created his poetry is predicated upon the rival claims of the intellect and the feelings, the reason and the emotions, the idea and the fact. His definition of poetry is of a logical structure and a seeming textural "irrelevance" of language, which work against and upon each other to produce the unique artifact which is the poem, and which thereby, in the transaction between the idea and the physical image, produce a kind of suspended "miraculous" knowledge of the nature of reality, which is there not for use but for contemplation. What might seem odd—or perhaps not so odd—is that his bias is against Platonic poetry, the poetry of ideas, which he sees as falsifying the rich, contingent materiality of the world through forcing the unique items of experience into a straitjacket of abstraction. Writing on "The

Future of Poetry" in *The Fugitive* for February, 1924, he declares that "no art and no religion is possible until we make allowances, until we manage to keep quiet the *enfant terrible* of logic that plays havoc with the other faculties."[62] This approach, which so influenced the aesthetic of his pupils (Tate, "Tension in Poetry"; Warren, "Pure and Impure Poetry"; and Brooks, "The Language of Paradox"), involves a kind of Armageddon of its own: the contending forces of structure and texture, head and heart, meet and grapple with each other, and out of the combat comes a communique from the battlefield, which is the poem, and which also announces the peace settlement. It is usually Ransom's habit to portray the forces of the head, which he is apt to term Platonizing, scientific, structural, abstract, predatory, as the aggressor in such a battle. In a brilliant essay of the 1930s, "Poetry: A Note on Ontology," he presents the matter this way: "The aesthetic moment appears as a curious moment of suspension; between the Platonism in us, which is militant, always sciencing and devouring, and a starved inhibited aspiration towards innocence which, if it could only be free, would like to respect and know the object as it might of its own accord reveal itself."[63]

Without attempting any kind of psychological inquiry, one is nonetheless impelled to point out that the author of that brilliant definition was a reasoner of the first magnitude, a rigorous conceptual thinker who moved toward his conclusions with inexorable logic. With Ransom it is never the flash of intuition, the sudden deduction that produces results, but the relentless dialectical development. Louise Cowan's description of his critical thought is apt: "what must be seen as underlying all Ransom's critical thought is the formation, by abstraction, of some general notion of how things ought to be and then, later, the discovery, in an encounter with the actual world, that things are not after all quite so simple."[64] It was Ransom's tough-minded empiricism, his inductive powers, that impressed his students. Davidson recalled that "always he was, as he politely declared at many a Fugitive meeting, 'literal-minded'—a term he used just before rending to bits with calm, analytical pincers some too airy fancy that one of us had bounced into in a mere fit of rhyme."[65] Tate remembers that in his literature classes Ransom "was teaching, whatever course he taught, the dialectic, the motions of one of the most distinguished minds in the United States. He never gave us 'conclusions' that we could hand back to him in papers and examinations. He was thinking aloud, and it was the subtle, unpredictably precise emotions of his intelligence that created the drama of his classes."[66]

All of which might seem a long way removed from the Methodist theology of his origins. But was it? In his later years, reviewing his pupil Cleanth Brooks and John Edward Hardy's edition of the 1645 edition of Milton's poems, he made an interesting observation. Discussing Brooks's critical method of pouncing upon a paradox or an irony in a poem and then his proceeding "to wrestle as much of the poem as possible under it as the 'dominating' figure," he remarks that Brooks's "dominating" figure is likely to have philosophical or religious implications, and pronounces the method to be "homiletic." He goes on to say that both he and Brooks, as the children of Methodist ministers, "equally had theology in our blood," and were accustomed to hearing sermons "where the preacher unpacked the whole burden of his theology from a single figurative phrase of Scripture taken out of context." Then he likened Brooks's theologism to that of Duns Scotus, "who preached as all critics know the individuality or *haecceitas* of the well-regarded object." Brooks, he says, "does not want the poem to have a formal shape, but simply to unfold its own metaphorical energy."[67] Now whatever might be the case with Brooks, it seems obvious that John Crowe Ransom was no stranger to homiletic technique in his argumentation. The dialectic method he used was not open-ended in its possibilities; he started out from strongly held moral, social, and ethical premises, and what he always moved toward, with masterful skill and subtlety of discrimination, was the extension and re-affirmation of those premises in terms of the chosen context of the argument. Much of Ransom's philosophy and his aesthetics, as Professor Daniel Young's excellent biography reveals, was present, though in rather rudimentary form, from the beginning of his career. We find him, for example, reporting to his family from Oxford that he intended to "write an attempt at the analysis of morality and later a higher affair on the restatement and the relative importance, under the theory, of the conventional virtues." [68] The conclusion, be it noted, has already been reached; the writer's task is to work on the analysis that will produce it. We have his statement, which Louise Cowan records, that "he has never departed from the religion learned from his father at the turn of the century." [69] And we have him setting forth for his father, while he was teaching at the Hotchkiss School in 1913, a theory of poetry that contains the essence of the position he was to develop with subtlety and detail over the next thirty years: "Words have a double nature: they stand for things and are associated inseparably with thought; they also have definite second values, like the notes on the piano . . . . Poetry is invented when men see this double nature." [70]

Ransom's poetics aims to recapture the claim to knowledge of the world from the scientists and the abstract philosophers by claiming for poetry a more complete, more comprehensive reality, based not merely upon its logical structure but upon the recalcitrant and unique particularities of its texture. The poem, through the imaginative and creative clash of these opposing tendencies, provides "the world's body"—the "body and solid substance of the world" in which we live, the "fulness of poetry, which is counterpart to the world's fulness." [71] It is no accident that the product of this process is "miraculous" —an entity that cannot be apprehended through its idea structure or its physical texture of imagery alone. Ransom points to metaphysical poetry, which for him is the ultimate kind of poetry, as one whereby, through the use of a metaphor extended until it becomes a conceit, the idea structure and the verbal and imagic texture produce a miraculism or supernaturalism. "Specifically, the miraculism arises," he declares, "when the poet discovers by analogy an identity between objects which is partial, though it should be considerable, and proceeds to an identification which is complete." [72] Then, significantly, he goes on to declare that

From the strict point of view of literary criticism it must be insisted that the miraculism which produces the humblest conceit is the same miraculism which supplies to religions their substantive content. (This is said to assert the dignity not of the conceits but of the religions.) It is the poet and nobody else who gives to the God a nature, a form, faculties, and a history; to the God, most comprehensive of all terms, which, if there were no poetic impulse to actualize or "find" Him, would remain the driest and deadest among Platonic ideas, with all intension sacrificed to infinite extension. The myths are conceits, born of metaphors. Religions are periodically produced by poets and destroyed by naturalists. [73]

We have already seen how, writing to his father to justify his wish to remain in the Northeast and live in a city rather than return to rural Tennessee, Ransom put his case on moral grounds, declaring that rural life was unproductive of morality. He apologized for seeming to be using the word "artist" and "moralist" interchangeably, and said, it may be recalled, that he is "not guilty of a mental lapse because I think the two fields are closely related." [74] The identification of the artist and the moralist, of poetry and religion, was never to be dropped. We have noted, too, that in a piece on "The Future of Poetry" in *The Fugitive* he declared that neither art nor religion is possible until the logical, rationalizing consciousness is suppressed.[75] It should be no surprise, therefore, to find him proclaiming in the uniqueness of the poem the affirmation of the "world's body," the miraculism that actualizes the knowledge of God, and the creation of poetry as a religious act. What he has done, within the much broader and more sophisticated context of his literary and philosophical studies, is to reaffirm the rightness of the religious faith in which he was reared. He has, in effect, reasoned his reliance upon religious belief through poetic theory, in order to "quiet the *enfant terrible*" of a destructive logic. Being a young man not of the orthodox Methodism of the late nineteenth-century South, but a twentieth-century southerner educated at Vanderbilt and Oxford and unable to accept the kind of literal, revealed Protestant theology he chides in his *Poems About God*, he had to employ the logic of ontology and aesthetics to arrive at a justification for the religious impulse through poetry, and vice versa.

A Reaffirmation

It is precisely this logical process that constitutes the book that Ransom published in 1930, *God Without Thunder*, subtitled "an unorthodox defense of orthodoxy," and dedicated to his father. This remarkable though too seldom remarked book begins with the author's apology to "S.M.H."—Sidney Mttron Hirsch—for using the unorthodox tools of rigorous analysis to deal with a true and orthodox view of religion. He has, he says, drawn upon "the cold and not very fastidious terms of an Occidental logic" to define the myths, the sacred objects and supernaturalism of the faith. He does so, he says, because modern society has lost the most and the best of its myths, and as a result is "stricken with an unheard-of poverty of mind and unhappiness of life." He therefore sets out to explain to the world, in particular to the American portion of it, "as if in simple untechnical monosyllables, the function of the myths in human civilization," and also "why one myth may be better than another." [76]

God Without Thunder is a complex, relentlessly reasoned book principally concerned with demonstrating the inadequacy of scientific knowledge as an explanation of reality, the unconscious or hidden dependence of science upon extrascientific assumptions, the necessity of such assumptions—whether called myths or "universals" or "ghosts" or gods—for a true knowledge of nature and reality, and the error of Occidental Christianity in its worship of Christ as Logos—the Law, the Word, the idea—rather than its old belief in the supremacy of the Old Testament God of mystery and awe. Christ, he declares, was *"the Demigod who knew he was the Demigod and refused to set up as a God."* [77] But the Western church, with its doctrine that the Holy Ghost—the "presence" or spirit—descends from the Son as well as from the Father, glorified the rational principle by enshrining the Logos. He criticizes modern theology for being so intimidated by the claims of science and rationality that it sanctifies these as God and removes from religion the sense of man's limitation and dependence upon God, so that man becomes a god to himself. Only through the myth become Myth, the belief in a reality that is larger and greater than the demonstrable reality of science and of human reason, can men regain the condition of wonder and dependence, the belief in a supernatural God they can fear and love, and whose commandments will represent for them the deepest wisdom. Ransom's prescription, therefore, is a concerted and conscious return to orthodoxy: *"With whatever religious institution a modern man may be connected, let him try to turn it back towards orthodoxy,"* he declares in conclusion, italicizing his words for emphasis: *"Let him insist on a virile and concrete God, and accept no principle as a substitute. Let him restore to God the thunder. Let him resist the usurpation of the Godhead by the soft modern version of the Christ,* and try to keep the Christ for what he professed to be: the Demi-god who came to do honor to the God." [78]

God Without Thunder is a polemic, argued with patient and remorseless logic. It is not without importance that it started out, in the middle 1920s, as a book on aesthetics, entitled "The Third Moment," which Ransom withdrew from consideration for publication after submitting it to Henry Holt and Company.[79] He had become convinced that the health of the arts was ultimately dependent upon the religious attitude, and that it was necessary to defend that first and foremost. Meanwhile his interest in the South had been renewing itself during the middle and late years of the 1920s, and he and Allen Tate had been exchanging letters in which they pondered ways of defending the ways and the beliefs of their region. As we shall see, the Scopes evolution trial in Dayton, Tennessee, during the summer of 1925 had helped to cause both of them to reexamine their attitudes; the spectacle of the massed battalions of scientists, lawyers, journalists, and liberal theologians bombarding with ridicule and smug scientific logic the pitiful troops of rural Tennessee fundamentalism had made them look around for ways to defend southern religious attitudes. When Edwin Mims asked Ransom to join other southern intellectuals in a disavowal of the defenders of the antievolution statute, Ransom declined emphatically.[80]

Thus *God Without Thunder*, as it unfolded in Ransom's mind, ultimately developed into a vigorous attack on the assumptions of science, and a reaffirmation of the need for supernaturalism. He had also become convinced that much of the discontent of modern society was the result of its apotheosis of science in its applied form, industrialism. The modern American city he now saw in terms far different from those he had once advanced to his father in defense of his youthful desire to remain in the urban Northeast; it was now artificial, mechanical, "the most impressive transformation of natural environment that has yet appeared on this planet."[81] The metropolis, the home and source of applied science and the glorification of reason, "tickles its inhabitants so pleasantly with the sense of their ruthless domination of nature"[82] and thus shields them from reality. At the same time, industrialism is ruthless and brutal, degrading the dignity and enjoyment of labor, predatory in its nature, geared entirely toward producing more and more material goods as impersonally and as rapidly as possible, for which new markets must be endlessly created. Under such conditions, neither genuine religious faith nor aesthetic enjoyment is possible, for these are dependent upon a view of reality as ultimately mysterious, suprarational, a view that is not scientific and predatory but ritualistic and contemplative.

If the city was the science-deified society incarnate, and if its industrialism was antireligious and antiaesthetic, then where was the community to be found that did not worship science? Where was the place in which the religious and aesthetic sensibility might properly find its home? The answer, for Ransom, was apparent, and it became increasingly obvious during the late 1920s: the community of his origins, the South. But the region was changing; it was coming, particularly in cities like Nashville, to look and behave more and more like the urban Northeast. To the extent, therefore, that the South was putting aside its traditional values and moving to embrace the industrial *ethos* of the urban Northeast, it was destroying many of its most admirable and satisfying characteristics. The task, therefore, was to recall the region to its senses, and imbue its lagging citizenry with a determination to resist such self-betrayal. The result was his involvement in *I'll Take My Stand*.

It is this process, which we find more or less adumbrated in *God Without Thunder*, that the historian Frank Owsley doubtless had in mind when he suggested that Ransom had reasoned rather than felt himself into Agrarianism.[83] This is quite true, provided we understand what is meant. It is not that Ransom's decision to defend the South with renewed fervor is merely the result of a dialectical process whereby his search for a defense of poetry led him toward the defense of the religious attitude, which in turn necessitated the dethronement of science and therefore the urban community that applied science had created. That is undoubtedly the way he reasoned the thing out; but what we must not forget is that, as we have seen, Ransom started out from some deeply ingrained premises. We recall how he intended, when young, to write a philosophical book defending the conventional virtues—*i.e.*, those of the community in which he had grown up. The attachment to the South, which Ransom clearly associated with the kind of agricultural, Protestant community in which his Methodist father had lived and worked, was always there. Even when he was declaring with strenuous logic his desire to dwell in the urban Northeast because it was there that art and morality were stimulated, he made it clear that he was not "scornful of Tennessee," for he did not "know any land more delightful for climate or landscape or people or cooking."[84]

At no point did Ransom ever give up his strong personal preference for the southern community ways he knew as a child. In *Poems About God*, his poem "The School" was already ridiculing the bright young Hellenist who had thought himself too gifted and precious for his home and the homefolks:

> Equipped with Grecian thoughts, how could I live
> Among my father's folk? My father's house
> Was narrow and his fields were nauseous.
> I kicked his clods for being common dirt.
> Worthy a world which never could be Greek;
> Cursed the paternity that planted me
> One green leaf in a wilderness of autumn;
> And wept, as fitting such a fruitful spirit
> Sealed in a yellow tomb.

Providentially, a pair of blue eyes and a coin combine to reconcile him to his origins; the sentimental and intellectual objections swiftly vanish, once love and livelihood are forthcoming: "And what are dead Greek empires to me then?/Dishonored, by Apollo, and forgot."[85] His poems of the *Fugitive* years are filled with the southern domestic imagery that is Ransom's metier, and it is drawn, like the subject matter of the early poetry, from the life around him. Clearly it is in the particularities of southern experience that he found the stuff of his poems, and, as important, their *meaning*. One of his most significant poems is "Conrad in Twilight," published originally in *The Fugitive* for February–March, 1922, in which (I quote the revised version in the *Selected Poems*, 1963) an elderly man is seated in his garden in the autumn of the year. Someone—his wife, perhaps—urges him to come into the house, and he is reminded of his neuralgia and other ills that will not be gentled by such exposure to the element. "Conrad! you've forgotten asthma," she adds. Inside the house it will be comfortable and he will be safe from the elements:

> The log on Conrad's hearth is blazing
> Slippers and pipe and tea are served,
> Butter and toast are meant for pleasing!

But he stays on in the moldy garden nonetheless, and poet describes why, and what it means:

> Autumn days in our section
> Are the most used-up thing on earth
> (Or in the waters under the earth)
> Having no more color or predilection
> Than cornstalks too wet for the fire,
> A ribbon rotting on the byre,
> A man's face as weathered as straw
> By the summer's flare and winter's flaw.[86]

He will not go into the house because he is aging, like the season, and because the garden is where he belongs for a while, for he too is "used-up," and he can see in the declining garden a kind of reality, and the significance of his place in it, that the house with its thick brick walls and blazing fireplace contrive to hide from him. (Nothing could be further distanced than this man in his garden is from Ransom's description of the city, previously quoted as "the most impressive transformation of natural environment that has yet appeared on this planet.") He is, insofar as he is a physical man, much like the abandoned cornstalks, the ribbon left from some outdoor occasion during the good weather; that at least is one aspect of the meaning of his life, which may not be left out of reckoning. He will go back into the house after a while; he is not merely a thing of nature, and he knows it very well; but for now he wishes to sit outside in the dying garden and think about the end of season, and in his own way symbolically take part in mortality. He is engaged, we might say, in aesthetic contemplation, the impulse, as he phrases it in *God Without Thunder*, "to contemplate for its own sake the object as a concrete object, or as an inexhaustible complex of attributes." [87]

For our purposes, what is important is that in this poem, written in 1922, Ransom has chosen the southern rural scene as the imagery for what he wants to say about life, time, and mortality. He finds in the imagery the emblems that pronounce the meaning, and he uses the colloquial idiom of the region to express it: "the most used-up thing on earth"—"as weathered as straw." The idea, therefore, that Ransom's discovery of the virtues of the agrarian South is the outcome of a lengthy and open-ended logical process is misleading. The evidence of a poem such as "Conrad in Twilight" shows that what he thought and felt about religion, man in nature, abstraction, science, and aesthetics* was already implicit in the way he looked at the southern scene, well before he began the rational,

---

* When in the 1930s Ransom again revised this poem, he retitled it "Master's in the Garden Again" and dedicated it to the memory of the poet Thomas Hardy.

dialectical exploration that resulted in *God Without Thunder* and Agrarianism. To date his defense of the South from the reaction to the Scopes trial is likewise to oversimplify. The views that he set out to champion and to defend in the late 1920s are already manifest in "Conrad in Twilight," "Armageddon," and "Antique Harvesters," all written before Clarence Darrow, H. L. Mencken, and William Jennings Bryan gathered in Dayton, Tennessee. To use a later term that Ransom adapted from Hegel, the "Concrete Universal," the concrete image was already there, and what he was engaged in doing in his dialectic was adducing the universality.

He is not considered an "autobiographical" poet, and his poetics would appear to leave little room for first-person lyric self-justification. All the same, it might be noted how often his poetry describes just such a cycle of early identification, then alienation, then ultimate reaffirmation as we have recognized in his career. One would hardly call a poem such as "Armageddon" a personal poem, since assuredly Ransom did not think of himself as Jesus Christ, but the return to orthodoxy in the poem, after a time when "the rubric and the holy paternoster/ Were jangled strangely with the dithyramb," comes fairly close to describing Ransom's own intellectual progression.[88] Even more to the point is a delightful poem, "Amphibious Crocodile," published in the last issue of *The Fugitive* in 1925, which Ransom perversely declined to include among his *Selected Poems* until he revised it for the third edition of 1969 and reprinted it under the title of "Crocodile." The thing is pure vintage Ransom. The basic action resembles that of "Philomela," but with more low comedy. Robert Crocodile of the state of Florida arises from the water, cleanses his toes, acquires clothes, raincoat, overshoes, umbrella, becomes the social dandy.

> At length in grey spats he must cross the ocean.
> So this is Paris? Lafayette, we are here.

> Bring us sweet wines and none of your French beer.
> And he weeps on Notre Dame with proper emotion.

He visits the scene of the late war to observe the trenches, "all green slime and water." It is all Robert can do to keep from plunging in, such is his nostalgia. But he recovers his presence, journeys to England, and is presented to King George: "Who is the gentleman whose teeth are so large?/That is Mr. Crocodile the renowned aesthete."

Once in Britain he tries English country sports, but does not ride well. When he rises to speak at the Union (as Ransom once did), he feels awkward and unlovely; "I wonder, says he, if I am the sort of creature/To live by projects, travel, affaires de coeur?" He meditates marriage, but decides against it. He considers High Church, "sips of the Eucharist," then turns to Freud, and sets up as psychoanalyst. He becomes the philosopher:

> Great is his learning. He learns to discuss
> Pure being, both the Who's Who and What's What,
> Affirms that A is A, refutes that B is not.
> This is a clean life, without mud and muss.

The intellectual effort is difficult, however, and Robert Crocodile soon wearies of the necessity

> To whittle the tree of being to a point
> While the deep-sea urge cries Largo, and every joint
> Tingles with gross desire of lying at length . . .

And such is his basic love and need for his primal element that one fine day, the news appears in the fashionable literary reviews that the renowned Robert Crocodile has departed. He has disappeared; his friends cannot find him, his lady loves write in vain, he is gone from sight, gone home:

> Crocodile hangs his pretty clothes on a limb
> And lies with his fathers, and with his mothers too,
> And his brothers and sisters as it seems right to do;
> The family religion is good enough for him.

We view him finally, at peace with the elements and with himself:

> Full length he lies and goes as water goes,
> He weeps for joy and welters in the flood,
> Floating he lies extended many a rood,
> And quite invisible but for the end of his nose.[89]

The poem has been proclaimed a satire on the American tourist, and perhaps it is, but I daresay that it is rather the other way around, and cosmopolitan intellectual and social life of the 1920s is what is being satirized. Ransom is not only on Robert Crocodile's side; he *is*, playfully, Robert Crocodile, and after a lengthy journey among the literati and the philosophers he has determined that "the family religion is good enough for him," at home in unsophisticated places with his kinfolk. "Amphibious Crocodile" is good fun, but the intellectual journey therein chronicled is one that Ransom himself made, and in the year 1925 he had pretty much come back home.

Let him not deceive us, however; behind the playfulness and whimsy there was passion and steel. It was no sporting junket that he made, but one in which he was grappling with the most profound problems of life, career, and belief. He had a compulsion to make logical sense of himself and his experience. He was powerfully drawn toward logic and reason, and he was also mightily attached to everyday middle-class institutions and the old religious community.

Unless we understand that Ransom's penchant for logical argumentation, his relentless dialectic, was in part at least a way of organizing and systematizing an intense emotional life, a method of discipline for his strenuous imagination, we will miss an essential truth about this very passionate man and poet. For Ransom, as those of his fellow Fugitives who have written about him all attest, was by no means the friendly, avuncular man of reason that his genial manner and his courtly demeanor seemed to indicate; far from it. He did indeed have a formidable, analytical mind; he took ideas very seriously, and his thinking was methodical and rigorous. He was, as Thomas Daniel Young writes, always willing to debate almost any issue at any time;[90] it was his way of thinking. But there was more to the man than the thought; the same mind that worked out the poetics and the theory wrote the poems. He insisted on poetry as a way of knowing the world, superior in its fullness of apprehension to the partial truths of science and philosophy, and there can be no doubt that he believed this because he perceived it thus in himself. Out of this amiable and unpretentious but ultimately very private and strong-willed man came some of the best poetry of the twentieth century, and also some provocative and creative thinking about poetry and society, and these were the product of passion disciplined by logic and made formally felicitous by strategy. Ransom was no sweet reasoner; that was only his tactical method. He held strong convictions, felt emotions powerfully; and when he took his stand, he meant it.

2 Allen Tate:
The Poetry of Modernism

Early Years

On the occasion of Allen Tate's sixtieth birthday, John
Ransom wrote of Tate's arrival at Vanderbilt in 1918 and of
his impact on the Fugitive poets as the commencement
of a mission. Tate, he said, was possessed of a knowledge
of literary matters "which were not the property of our
region at that time," and could write "in the consciousness of a body of literature which was unknown to his fellow students, and to my faculty associates and myself, unless it was by the purest hearsay."[1] Tate knew the writing
of the twentieth century, both in English and in French.
He was quoting Remy de Gourmont on the "dissociation
of ideas"; he introduced Ransom to Eliot's critical essays
and poems. He brought literary modernism to Nashville.

Ransom and his fellow Tennesseans were not without
awareness of contemporary poetry, of course; we have
seen that Ransom was well acquainted with Frost's work,
for example. But what Tate carried to them was tidings of
a literature that was "modern" not merely in attitude but

in language and form as well. He was, as Louise Cowan says, of the newer generation—a generation just young enough to have missed World War I but old enough to sense the disillusion in its wake.[2] When he joined the Fugitive meetings at the age of 21, he introduced a sophistication, and a kind of intellectual boldness, that not even Ransom had hitherto encountered. He had, Ransom said later, an attitude toward literature that was already professional, and no hesitation whatever in conducting himself accordingly. What he was writing puzzled Ransom, but also fascinated him: "I figured that perhaps he had really discovered a way to the top which might be worth knowing," he wrote. "It would consist in assuming topographically the terrain where the top writers seem to inhabit, and plunging with all one's might into the current of ideas and language within which they moved so splendidly."[3]

It has not been sufficiently remarked, I think, that Tate's relationship to the Fugitives differed from that of all the other members in one important respect. He was, in that Tennessee community, something of an outsider, even though his older brothers had attended Vanderbilt and he had gone to grammar school in the city for parts of two winters earlier in his life. He came from Kentucky and other places, and his antecedents and loyalties were Virginian. He had not the experience of, and instinctive identification with, the kind of small-town Methodist- and Baptist-dominated community of the upper South that Ransom and the several of the others knew. Not only was his own father not a Methodist clergyman like Ransom's; John Orley Tate was an Episcopalian long since turned Free Thinker, while his wife was Presbyterian—and in the southern social hierarchy the Episcopalians and Presbyterians constituted the social elite. Thus the sophistication Allen Tate brought to Vanderbilt was not merely intellectual but social as well. Interestingly, Ransom describes his impact on the group in the terms sug-

gested above. "As champion of the new literature—
though ever so fastidious in his elections—among people
who did not know anything about it," he writes, "and
were as likely as not to resist it when they were made to
know, Allen had *a mission in Tennessee which he was ten
years discharging, during his intermittent residence with us.*"[4]
(The italics are mine.) Obviously Tate not only swiftly
made a place for himself, but as an enthusiastic newcomer,
it was apparently his influence that helped the others to
recognize their own intentions and to move ahead on
their business with a new assurance.

But if the advent of Tate meant so much to the Fugitives, it was as true the other way around. For it was at
Vanderbilt that Allen Tate found himself and his vocation. While a student there he was able to recognize and
bring together his talents and his interests, and discover
the focus that henceforth would make possible the direction and emphasis of his adult career. Doubtless something of the sort would have occurred wherever he might
have gone to college; it was in part a matter of growing
into maturity. But more is involved that that; Vanderbilt
was just the right place for Tate, the one place in which
he could most advantageously realize his potentialities
and derive the maximum profit from what was available
to him both in the classroom and, of even more importance, outside it.

Tate was born November 19, 1899, in Winchester,
Kentucky. His family lineage is of considerable interest in
understanding his later career. From his mother's side—
she was named Eleanor Parke Custis Varnell—he came
originally from a Roman Catholic family, that arrived in
colonial Maryland during the late seventeenth century.
At the outbreak of the Civil War his maternal grandfather, a lapsed Catholic, owned 200,000 acres of western
timberland in five states and kept 81 slaves. Tate's mother
was born in Fairfax County, Virginia, at Chestnut Grove,
which was destroyed by invading yankees during the war.

She spent her girlhood in Washington, D.C., St. Louis, and, for a time, in Mt. Vernon, Illinois, with the family of her uncle, John Stewart Bogan. Her mother, Susan Armistead Bogan, was a great-granddaughter of Colonel Fielding Lewis, of Kenmore, Fredericksburg, Virginia, the Revolutionary War patriot whose second wife was George Washington's sister. On Tate's father's side, the lineage was as long, but not as patrician. The Tates were Scotch-Irish and came to America in the mid-eighteenth century, while the Allens were descended from Robert Allen, who arrived at Port Tobacco, Maryland, in 1690, where he was for six years the indentured servant of a cabinetmaker (at one time Allen Tate enjoyed making furniture). The Allens migrated westward to Kentucky, and transferred their allegiance from the Methodist to the Episcopal Church. The Tates migrated down through Virginia into the Carolinas, and later to Tennessee. Tate's grandfather, James Tate, originally of Fishing Creek Plantation, Chester County, South Carolina, came to Kentucky about 1840, as a schoolmaster, bearing with him a Bible and a Latin grammar. When Tate's father, John Orley Tate, fell in love with Eleanor Varnell, her father insisted that he supervise the family lumber business in Mount Vernon, Illinois.[5]

Tate's origins, particularly on his mother's side, were thus of the antebellum Virginia gentry, and this fact was forcefully borne in on him during his childhood. Doubtless it was of consolation to his mother, for her marriage was not a notably successful one. Young Allen spent his summers with his mother in Washington, in Fairfax County, Virginia, or at the various Virginia and Maryland springs which during the early 1900s still retained much of their social popularity as a mecca for the upper stratum of Virginia society. His father was not successful as a businessman, and the family moved about from place to place. Tate attended schools irregularly, acquiring a considerable education in the classics and in music, but with wide gaps in mathematics and the sciences that he had to make up upon entering Vanderbilt in 1918. Finances, meanwhile, went from bad to worse, and there was also something of a scandal involving his father, so that after Tate was about eight his mother spent a considerable amount of time away from her husband, taking her three sons with her. The middle son, Benjamin, became a successful businessman in Cincinnati and after 1920 was the family's principal support.[6]

The point of all this is that we have in Tate's background certain elements that are largely absent in that of the other leading Fugitives, and we may be sure that he was aware of them. On his mother's side he was descended from the planter aristocracy of northern Virginia, and there was the knowledge, on his mother's part and therefore forcefully handed down to him, that had it not been for the Civil War, the status of gentleman landowner might have been his. His roots went back almost to the beginnings of the English colonies (it might be noted that Tate's youngest son, born in 1969, had a great-great-grandfather born before the adoption of the United States Constitution), and there was a tradition of status and leadership in the early years of the nation. Tate has written that until he was thirty he had always thought he had been born in Virginia, not Kentucky; his father disabused him of this notion. His mother, he said, always bent reality to her wishes.[7] At the same time, it must be said that Eleanor Parke Custis Varnell had, from a Virginia standpoint, so far as such things go, married a trifle "beneath her," in that the Allens and the Tates, though they had done well in Kentucky, were of a yeoman rather than a patrician strain (in which respect they were much like the families of Tate's fellow Fugitives). Furthermore, there had been a sharp decline in the family fortunes, and, as one supposes, a corresponding emphasis upon maintaining the appearances that go with status. Such things were, from all accounts, not without importance in the society at the Virginia springs and in northern Virginia, where young Tate spent his summers.

That this had its impact on him is obvious from the fiction he published in the 1930s, much of which is almost entirely given over to the ramifications of such matters, proclaimed and then dissected with a wry and ironic intelligence. In his biography of Stonewall Jackson (1928), which is his first book, we several times come upon this kind of remark: "Tom Jackson was almost painfully aware of his social predicament and of the decline of his branch of the Jackson family." Again, "Doubtless much of his desire for personal distinction rose in the discrepancy between his inherited family pride and the poverty that had humbled his branch of the Jackson family."[8] And, mockingly, "If Major Jackson should happen to live in the year 1900, he will see a whole people, some of them deprived of their birthright, but all of them sorely afflicted with the delusion of ancient grandeur."[9]

Tate has told us frankly about his childhood. Very early he became a voracious reader; his mother, herself a confirmed reader of novels who often read a book a day, surely encouraged him to read, but at the same time she would seem to have disparaged his intellectual leanings. He quotes her as once saying, "Son, put that book down and go out and play with Henry. You are straining your mind and you know your mind isn't very strong."[10] As a small child he had a large, bulging forehead, which the family interpreted as "water on the brain";[11] in a very late poem, "The Swimmers," there is an allusion to "Tate, with the water on his brain."[12] He felt the need, he says, to prove his intellectual distinction and refute the family verdict. At the same time, the constant moving about—"we might as well have been living, and I been born, in a tavern at a cross-roads,"[13]—contributed to a family situation of uncertainty and instability, and his mother's social attitudes served to intensify his loneliness, for she approved of very few others as eligible playmates for her son.

At the various schools he attended there was another difficulty, for he was, he says, "always the 'new boy,'" who had to "win my masculine standing at every new school by fist-fighting the bully. I don't think I ever won; for if my mind was weak, my physique was weaker; and I usually came off with a torn shirt or a bloody nose."[14] Tate passes over this with few words, but one can well imagine what he must have endured. He pictures a childhood characterized by much loneliness, a pervasive sense of being different from his peers and all too vulnerable to their physical bullying; a strong mother who instilled in him a sense of family status that contrasted painfully with present insecurity; a father who had disgraced himself and with whom he had little or no rapport; and a general sense of decline and fall, of personal and familial failure, and much unhappiness. This may seem rather strong, but it is pretty much what Tate's own description suggests.

He entered Vanderbilt in the fall of 1918, having first been tutored in mathematics in order to pass the entrance examination. It was not long before his intellectual prowess attracted the attention of his teachers. Walter Clyde Curry lent him books and encouraged him to write poetry. In John Crowe Ransom's class he found his lifelong mentor; as we have seen, the older poet was astonished at the young man's maturity. "It was my rule," Ransom wrote later, "to follow old pedagogical custom and prescribe elementary exercises to the freshmen, but he would have none of that. He wrote essays about the literary imagination, with corollary excursions into linguistics and metaphysics; they were slightly bewildering to me in more ways than one."[15] He met Donald Davidson, Alec Brock Stevenson, took part in and eventually became president of the Calumet Club, a literary society composed of faculty and students. He joined Phi Delta Theta fraternity, and published a poem in the campus humor

magazine. Then in the fall of 1921 he was taken by Davidson to a meeting of the Fugitives. There he encountered
Sydney Mttron Hirsch; "it was plain that I had been invited to hear him talk," he says.[16] Tate fitted immediately
into the group; it was not long before he was trading
poems with his elders, and his active presence would seem
to have helped to confirm the group's shift in emphasis
from philosophy to poetry. He found Hirsch's mysticism
and his vision of the poet as occult seer hard to take, but
the formidable logic and the calm reason with which Ransom went at the analysis of poetry impressed him mightily. The warmth and enthusiasm of Davidson developed
into a strong friendship.

At Vanderbilt, Tate found himself. His brilliant intellect and his bookishness were no longer social liabilities,
but distinct assets. The sophistication and the formal pol-
ish that a rather withdrawn and insecure young man had
erected as a defense to keep the world at a distance became, in the social environment of a university campus
and among young men and women who were striving to
seem and be worldly-wise adults, qualities that elicited
admiration and attention. No recluse now, he thrived on
the campus scene, both in its literary and its social aspects.
The university professors whose classes he attended were
prepared, in a way that he had seldom previously encountered, to recognize his remarkable intellectual merit.
And among his new literary friends, too, he found little
disposition to measure one's worth and status economically. If one's family had clung to ancestral distinction as a
way of countering the evidence of a gentility worn thin, if
one felt the private humiliation of knowing that such
claims were not quite so valid as one made them out to
be, the occasion for that sort of thing had notably diminished. If anything it was the other way around, for a Virginia ancestry was a source of honor at Vanderbilt and in
Nashville, accepted more or less at face value, with none
of the qualifications that might have been evidenced in

the social milieu of Kentucky and Virginia. The Fugitives were, after all, from middle-class Tennessee stock, of Methodist rather than Episcopalian or Presbyterian backgrounds, or else from Southern Jewish families. But more than that, they did not *think* along genealogical lines. What they valued was what he really valued most; literature, ideas, the life of the mind. All this he came to realize in Nashville, and for the rest of his life he lived by it.

What he got at Vanderbilt, as part of his education, was a confirmed sense of the dignity in the profession of letters and of the potentiality of poetry as a legitimate mode of dealing with human experience. Ransom says of Tate that "his personality is as whole and undivided, and it is as steady, as it is vivid," and suggests that in whatever time he might have been born, he would have found his role.[17] The Fugitive association provided Tate in the early 1920s with the realization, which was both liberating and determining, that he was a *writer*, and in so doing, it offered the method whereby his intensely creative imagination could achieve the focus and the discipline that would allow it to find constructive expression. More than that, it helped determine the direction of his art.

There seems, in retrospect, little doubt that Tate would have become a writer, no matter where he had been sent to college. But Vanderbilt was decisive for the form that his work would take; it put him in touch with Ransom and Davidson and a little later with Warren and with what was most authentic and creative in the southern aesthetic life of his day. As we have seen with Ransom, from the time of *Poems About God* onward that poet was engaged in coming to grips with a redefinition of the southern community experience, as he knew it in his own life, with its deep roots in religious and social attitudes, as that experience moved into confrontation with the ideas, values, and attitudes of the twentieth century intellectual and social milieu. Out of this confrontation, he was writing poems that dramatized the meaning of its human dimensions, and his wrestling with the problem was bringing to bear the powers of a formidable logician. Davidson, as we shall see, was also dealing with the problem, but in a different way and on a different level: he was intent upon finding the form for a passionate emotional response to his times. Tate was, by dint of his family background and his experience, potentially more receptive to the literary forms and attitudes of modernism, which he would soon come to use with great authority. What the example of his friends gave him was the sense of the inevitability of grappling with the problems of one's personal identity in society, and also of its *mattering*. Not only the example of Ransom and Davidson, but the very nature of the Fugitive group itself—a group of highly intelligent, sensitive men, whom he could respect and think of as his peers, engaged in a communal enterprise involving the use of the mind and the writing of poetry—served as a counterweight to any inclination toward a romantic withdrawal from the disorder of the world.

One thinks of the Virginia novelist James Branch Cabell, whose background and family situation were in so many ways similar to Tate's, but who was of an antecedent generation. Cabell's response to the disorder and confusion of his times was to move into an ironic detachment, a saucy, witty spoofing of the seriousness of his situation. He used his considerable intellectual powers and his sense of the incongruity and futility of his own social responses to write a series of brilliant, archly mannered comedies in which the problems of his times and the fact of his personal confusion are fastidiously mocked. A comment Tate made about Cabell and Ellen Glasgow in a letter to Davidson in 1929 comes to mind: "Those two novelists are fine examples of running with the hare and hunting with the hounds. Miss Glasgow has everything that I have learned to detest in the transformation of the Virginia character—the feeble and offensive assumption of past superiority along with casting a vote for Hoover:

she exhibits the 'aristocratic' manners of the South and shows how ridiculous they are; she is an incredible old snob who would not receive in her house a 'man of the people' (as she would put it) and yet she wrote a novel proving the sterling worth of a man born in a circus tent, the whole atmosphere of the novel being that of sniffing and calculating condescension. The people like Miss Glasgow and Cabell convince outsiders that all Southerners are snobs and pretenders." [18]

One need not agree with Tate's estimate of the two Richmonders (and, indeed, in the 1930s his attitude toward Miss Glasgow would change) to recognize what is involved in respect to his own family background. He was criticizing the direction that his own life and art could have taken. Tate might well have gone that way: toward a personal escape into detached satire—in which instance he would have been prevented, or at any rate hindered, from drawing upon the great theme of the literature of his own era: the spiritual and moral dislocation of Western society in the face of the decline of the older religious and social ordering. The potentialities were there, and as we shall see, can be discerned in his earliest poetry. But the example of the Fugitives helped to keep him from moving into the personal evasion of withdrawal and satire, through helping him to realize the stake he still had in the community, for all its disorder in his time, and the potentialities for a meaningful exploration of the nature of the spiritual malaise of his generation. A writer such as Cabell could not do this, and did not need to do it, for the years of Cabell's artistic maturity were the 1910s and 1920s, when the American condition seemed, in the words of the famous Viennese proverb, a situation that was hopeless but not serious, and in which a Cabell or a Mencken could find the creative image for much of his best work. But by the time that Tate came into his artistic maturity, that response would not serve—thus the decline of Cabell's and Mencken's reputations after 1930.

What was needed was not the ability to transcend, but to confront: and it was in that context that Tate's finest work would be done. This is what Nashville helped make possible for Allen Tate.

Eliot and Ransom as Models

Tate was a senior at Vanderbilt when he became a member of the Fugitives. He did not, however, graduate at the end of that school year of 1922. In April he was forced to withdraw from Vanderbilt because of a threat of tuberculosis and was sent by his doctor to Valle Crucis, in the North Carolina mountains. There he continued to write poems and send them on for discussion at the Fugitive meetings, and he corresponded steadily with Donald Davidson. In September of 1922 he was allowed to leave the mountains, and after a brief stop in Nashville went on to Ashland, Kentucky, where he worked, with less than notable success, for his brother Ben in the coal business. By the following February he was able to return to Vanderbilt, where he finished up his work that spring and summer.

The ten-month period spent away from college was important for him. He was made to confront his future prospects. The excitement and the heady optimism attendant upon his success at Vanderbilt were abruptly suspended; removed from the academic and literary milieu, off by himself in the mountains, and with the possibility, for awhile at least, that his disease might prove fatal, he engaged in a stocktaking. He concluded—and a subsequent episode with his brother's colliery enterprise only confirmed it—that his future lay with literature. At the same time, it does not appear that he contemplated the kind of academic career that Ransom and Davidson were pursuing. Unlike them, he wanted to enter the arena as a full-time writer, to attempt to make his living through his writing, and this meant New York City. The encouragement he had already found with his poetry was intensified by the reception his poems got from the New Orleans literary magazine *The Double-Dealer*, and by the friendships he was making with literary figures such as the young poet Hart Crane and the critic Gorham Munson. Crane read his poems in the *Double-Dealer*, wrote to say he admired them, and that clearly Tate had been reading Eliot. Tate had not been, he says, but he got hold of Eliot's poems at once, and was overwhelmed.[19] Crane also sent him some back numbers of *The Little Review*, and Tate absorbed these. He went on to immerse himself in the moderns, and was soon convinced not only that his destiny lay with them, but that fame and fortune might speedily be his in the literary field.

The poetry that he was turning out during the period, though distinguished by its verbal audacity and moments of genuine poetic excitement, was at a far remove from what he would be writing in the late 1920s and the early 1930s. He had not yet found either his voice or his theme. These would come only after he had begun mastering the techniques of Eliot and others that he was finding so exciting. As was true of many another promising young poet, his taste and his critical judgment were well in advance of his ability to put what he knew into practice in his own writing.

The stance that young Tate tended to take in his early poetry was, not unpredictably, that of the world-weary, jaded sophisticate. He has seen all, experienced much, suffered much, and is wistfully cynical: the doomed romantic become old before his time. Not all of his early work is of the *fin de siecle* mode, but a great deal of it is. Thus "Sinbad," quoted earlier, in the first issue of *The Fugitive*: the adventurer has "sailed too long over that monstered ocean/Ever to grapple with the sinews of an emotion/Like this slave-girl's." If he could but be young and innocent again, it would be different, but he has seen too much. It is true that "her thin mouth to save/My soul

I can't forget, nor her slack eyes," but "The oasis of age is sand and lies." and "She's just a fancy." It is Browning out of Dowson and William Alexander Percy—except for one metaphor that, put into action, takes over.

> If I could wipe the must
> From the mildewed jars of devilry, and the rust
> Off my lip,

it begins, but then instead of the expected extension of the thought by means of other figures of speech, he proceeds to extend the specific figure to see just how far it can go:

> the taste of the red preserves
> Of love would be as honied as one deserves
> Who lusted with wormwood and with sickening myrrh. . . .[20]

A few years later he would no doubt have omitted "of love" and let "red preserves" carry the meaning, thus strengthening his image by effecting a sexual and hunting pun as well, and he would have found a more arresting adjective than "sickening," in order to force the sense of the myrrh's being cloyed into an image that could be intellectually shocking as well as sensual. But Radcliffe Squires is quite correct when he insists that at this point in the poem the performance is closer to Elizabethan soliloquy than to Victorian monologue.[21] Indeed the language is much more violent and stunning than the occasion warrants, or than the overall meaning of the poem can absorb, and so what follows is anticlimax. Nor has Tate yet learned his later strategy of coupling intellectually violent adjectives with neutral nouns—but there is no doubt that here is a young poet who is not going to let the language of a poem play second fiddle to the ideas.

Tate did not reprint "Sinbad" in any of his volumes, nor has most of his early *Fugitive* work been reprinted. The earliest of his poems that he included in his later collections is the "Horatian Epode to the Duchess of Malfi," which first appeared in *The Fugitive* for October 1922.

This poem, which John Crowe Ransom praised in an editorial prefacing that issue of the magazine as an example of modernist work "so perfected that we [nonmodernists] would not wish it to be otherwise,"[22] is a commentary on a very Ransomic theme: the swift passing of beauty. Again, operating very much in Ransom's bailiwick, the poet considers the matter of whether the body's death is also the spirit's. But what Tate does with the subject, and how he goes about it, are handled very much in his own style, not Ransom's. The poem addresses itself to the Duchess of Webster in the play, who died young. She is told that "The stage is about to be swept of corpses" (bodies in the earliest version). She has "no more chance" of meaningful survival beyond the grave than an "infusorian/Lodged in a hollow molar of an eohippus"—a minute protozoan in a primitive fossilized horse. She must not "prattle" of "remergence with the *ontos on*"—there must be no nonsense spoken about the immortality of the spirit.[23] This sardonic discounting of all but the naturalistic attitude toward death serves in fact to raise just this issue, and in the remainder of the poem it is explored.

At the outset of this poem, clearly, Tate develops the idiom in which he would henceforth do most of his work: a highly intellectual frame of reference, in which through vocabulary and allusion he depicts the ultimate futility of intellection, suggested through forcing an emotional context upon the intellectual object. At this stage of the game there is a certain amount of shocking the bourgeoisie in his stance; the learning is a bit self-conscious. One has little doubt of the dismay that it must have created among most of the Fugitives when read aloud. All the same, it is precisely through the strategy of cramming the maximum emotional violence into his intellectual abstractions that Tate would be able to make his commentary on the dissociation and fragmentation of the modern sensibility, which would become his primary theme.

He follows Eliot's lead, but much more than for Eliot his emphasis is on the painful experience of the spiritual disorder, rather than on the philosophical and theological significance of it.

The "difficulty" that would henceforth characterize much of Tate's poetry, its refusal to yield to easy paraphrase or immediate logical coherence of imagery, constitutes his way of rendering the urgency of that experience. Unlike Ransom's, his own use of literary reference and erudite vocabulary is not for playful extravagance, the phrasing of something reasonably simple in fanciful literary language to make ironic deprecation and qualification even while stating it. "Sweet ladies, long may ye bloom, and toughly I hope ye may thole," Ransom declares;[24] he uses the archaic *thole* rather than *endure* and the adverb *toughly* to mean *vigorously* rather than *strongly* or *roughly*, and addressing the sweet housewives as he is doing, he achieves a fine fancifulness to belie the actual tidings, which are of the brevity of mortal life. Tate plays no such gallant games, not even in the commencement of the "Horatian Epode," where he is being somewhat mockingly histrionic in mode of address. He speaks of infusorian, eohippus, the *ontos on*, later on of Probability, Katharsis and so on, not as erudite circumlocutions of more ordinary words, but because these are the level on which he wishes to conduct his statement, so as both to jar the reader's complacency and to present his case in ultimate rather than in everyday terms. He uses his intellections and his abstractions violently; he wants to drive home the emotional implications of consciousness.

Having set the stage for his inquiry, he proposes an analogy to the Duchess' plight:

> As (the form requires the myth)
> A Greek girl stood once in the prytaneum
> Of Carneades, hearing mouthings of Probability,
> Then mindful of love dashed her brain on a megalith.[25]

"The form requires the myth"—an echo of Pound's "the age demanded an image/of its own accellerated grimace," no doubt, as Squires points out,[26] but also the ironic assertion to the inhibiting self-consciousness; *i.e.*, to write a Horatian epode, one must properly introduce a mythological comparison, and also, in order to feel the pathos of the Duchess of Malfi's wasted beauty, one must grant a significance of more than animal extinction to her dying. Thus we are told of a girl who, upon hearing the philosopher Carneades discourse on the impossibility of any exact knowledge of truth, leaped to her death in despair of ever knowing love. You also, the poet then tells the Duchess, go to your own death as welcome respite from life, "And I am filled with a pity of beholding skulls./ There was no pride like yours."

Still, when he thinks of "the void coming after," the impossibility of knowing whether anything lies beyond the body's dying, which "the 'strict gesture'" of her death has in no way changed, the "straight line of pessimism" is split "into two infinities":

> It is moot whether there be divinities
> As I finish this play by Webster:
> The street-cars are still running however
> And the katharsis fades in the warm water of a yawn.[27]

Webster's naturalistic bias has called into question the existence of all truths that transcend the animalistic, but the question has not been settled. On the other hand, life goes on, whatever the attempts to explain its meaning may turn up, and after the reader thinks for a while about the tragedy he has read, the torpidity of the everyday routine of sensation reasserts itself.

The poem is, beyond doubt, Eliotesque, as most commentators agree (or perhaps Poundlike). Eliot's "Whispers of Immortality," which begins "Webster was much possessed by death," and discourses on the beholding of skulls, is involved, as is "Mr. Eliot's Sunday Morning Service," with its Greek phrase and with Sweeney shifting

"from ham to ham/Stirring the waters in his bath.[28]*
There is, however, a difference in overall tone, and the
difference would only be further developed in Tate's
later poetry. Even in Eliot's most desperate verse, including *The Waste Land*, there is always a kind of wry, urbane
distancing of the violence and the desperation; *The Waste
Land* is a demonstration, in five parts, of the wretched
condition of the world, but the poet always holds back,
retaining his poise even while depicting the chaos (this is
part of the tactics). The *persona* speaking the lines remains on his dignity, aloof from the reader—which is a
way of making his point. In Tate's poem, despite the distancing assertion of the close, to the effect that he has finished reading a play and is retiring into the routine of the
everyday, no such separation is involved. The *persona* is
himself personally involved; the rage is his own; the strategy of the poem is not that of a diagnosis of the situation,
but an enactment of it within the consciousness of the
speaker. Many years later Tate would write that "as I
look back upon my own verse, written over more than
twenty-five years, I see plainly that its main theme is man
suffering from unbelief; and I cannot for a moment suppose that this man is some other than myself."[30] This
is doubtless true; what is certain is that the strategy of
his poetry involves the creation of a *persona* engaged in
doing just that. This is the stance that Tate assumes in
most of his poetry, and the argument is conducted within
his own sensibility. As a poet Tate never holds back;
he plunges into the melee, and when there is confusion
within the poem, it is because he is working out the meaning from within. His work is almost never elegiac—not

* Surely the "warm water" referred to in Tate's poem is of this sort, and
not "the salivation which accompanies yawning," as Mr. Squires would have
it![29] The poet says he is yawning, not spitting. The "warm water" I take to be
the creature comfort, the indolent immersion in the here and now. If Mr.
Squires's reading is adopted, then what with the "hollow molar" of the first
stanza, it is almost as if one were reading the "Duchess of Malfi" while re-
clined in a dentist's chair.

even the "Ode to the Confederate Dead"—because his way of telling a poem is not reflective, but participatory. However much the writing of the poem may be, as he often insisted, an act of calculation, the strategy he uses for speaking the lines is that of an active, ardent, engaged consciousness. What goes on is fought out within the sensibility of a created *persona*.

Tate's headlong immersion in Eliot and what Eliot's poetry and poetics stood for was the occasion for temporary hostilities with Ransom during the period just after his graduation from Vanderbilt in 1923. There was a dispute over *The Waste Land*, which in retrospect seems clearly to have been a dispute over the direction that Tate was taking in his career. He had returned to Vanderbilt in February, 1923, to finish up his college work, and had roomed with a remarkable young sophomore from Guthrie, Kentucky, Robert Penn Warren, and Ridley Wills, a cousin to Jesse and a Fugitive himself. When *The Waste Land* appeared, Tate and Warren were very much taken with it. Warren illustrated the poem with four murals on the walls of their dormitory room. Tate remembered, years afterward, the rats creeping softly through the vegetation, and the typist putting a record on the Gramophone. One night Tate and Wills, who had decided that the tone of the older Fugitives was all too grave, retired to the local beanery and by dawn produced a book, *The Golden Mean*—the title was a sarcastic reference to one of Professor Edwin Mims's catch-phrases—in which among other things there was a parody of *The Waste Land* by Tate, ending with the words *Shanty Shanty Shanty*.[31]

By the end of the summer of 1923 Tate had finished making up his credits and was graduated summa cum laude, with the diploma dated 1922 so that he might graduate with his class.

During that summer Ransom, who was away teaching in Colorado, published an article in the *Literary Review* of the *New York Evening Post* (July 14, 1923), entitled "Waste

Lands." It had to do with modernism in poetry, and its result was to enrage Tate. Ransom began with a formal definition of poetry as being based on maturity. The poet, he declared, "is not to put an extravagant value on the freshness of his youthful passions, but to make sure that the work of art wants for its material the passion mellowed and toned and understood long after the event: 'recollected in tranquillity,' to use the best of all the literary dogmas." For literature requires the enrichment of the data of the world by the imagination, and this involves not the hot, impulsive passion of youth but the patient contemplation of the mature artist, who waits for the magic to happen in his imagination. Eliot's new poem, Ransom declared, is the "apotheosis of modernity," composed in extreme disconnection: "I do not know just how many parts the poem is supposed to have, but to me there are something like fifty parts which offer no bridges the one to the other and which are quite distinct in time, place, action, persons, tone, and nearly all the unities to which art is accustomed." The attempt would seem to be that of accomplishing a chaotic wilderness, in which both poet and reader are to be bewildered. "The fragments," he declared, "could not be joined on any principle and remain what they are. And that is because they are at different stages of fertilization; they are not the children of a single act of birth." The material was incapable of synthesis, and the difficulty is peculiarly an American one, for "our native poets are after novelty; they believe, as Mr. Eliot does in one of his prose chapters, that each age must have its own form." Compared with Eliot's earlier work, which was generally whole and mature, the new poem "takes a number of years out of this author's history, restores him intellectually to his minority." Clearly it will not become a permanent part of the language of poetry.[32]

Tate obviously viewed Ransom's article not merely as an attack on *The Waste Land*, but as a calculated affront to his own advocacy of that poem. He therefore rushed into print with a reply, published in *The Literary Review* for August 4, in which he declared that Ransom's article "violates so thoroughly the principle of free inquiry" and is so poor an example of so-called philosophical criticism that readers should consider the flaws in the method thereby illustrated. He proclaimed Ransom's ignorance of contemporary theories of artistic inspiration, denounced his conclusions about the workings of consciousness, and said that Ransom's objections to the supposed chaos of *The Waste Land* were the result of an inability to discover the poem's structure because of his inability to perceive Eliot's irony. Eliot's alleged failure to duplicate the achievements of his earlier work was in reality the result of his free intelligence, which "cannot harbor a closed system." Tradition hardly means sameness, he said. In any event, Ransom's method of attack "is not likely to give T. S. Eliot much concern. And my excuse for this extended objection is that Mr. Ransom is not alone. He is a *genre*."[33]

Ransom responded to the onslaught of his younger colleague with a personal comment. Tate, he told the readers of *The Literary Review*, was not an enemy, but a former pupil, and had sent him a copy of the letter "with certain waggish additions for my private benefit." His younger friend had "for two years suffered the damning experience of being a pupil in my classes, and I take it his letter is but a proper token of his final emancipation, composed upon the occasion of his accession to the ripe age of twenty-three."[34] This in turn angered Tate, who considered Ransom's letter an attack *ad hominem*, whereas his had not been, he felt, and it was some time before the rift between them was healed.

There was, of course, truth to what Ransom said: Tate's attack was indeed something of an assertion of his independence of his teacher. But however much the younger poet's assault may have been less than good manners—"How he ever forgave me I do not know," Tate wrote many years later, "and I do not want to know,"[35]—there was more to it than merely the need to assert his freedom. For Ransom's strictures upon *The Waste Land* (which, it must be said, time has hardly ratified) went beyond a critical judgment of the poem's shortcomings; he was savaging not merely Eliot but a poetic mode of which his young student and colleague was an enthusiastic adherent, and Ransom knew that very well. I think that Tate sensed that both the substance and the manner of Ransom's attack were possibly inspired not only by Eliot's poem but by the ubiquitous presence, right there in the Fugitive group, of a brilliant and brash young man who was conducting himself—and going about the business of writing poems—with less than entire respect and reverence for established reputation and age.

A little of that feeling is discernible, I think, even in Ransom's laudation upon Tate's sixtieth birthday, quoted earlier, in his way of speaking of Tate in the Fugitive days, in which he recalled his envy of Tate's disconcerting habit of "assuming topographically the terrain where the top writers seem to inhabit, and plunging with all one's might into the current of ideas and language within which they moved so splendidly."[36] Transfer that back to the early 1920s, when Tate was indeed a brash newcomer and Ransom a still-young but already published poet striving mightily to develop his own reputation, and we get a sense of what must have been involved. Ransom had couched his attack on *The Waste Land* in terms of the chaotic sensibility and brashness of passionate youth as against the superior reflectiveness of maturity, and he singled out in Eliot's poem precisely the qualities that various of the older Fugitives were constantly censuring in Tate's work: the apparent disunity, the difficulty of language and reference, the seeming lack of control and the formlessness. Whether Ransom realized that in lambasting *The Waste Land* he was administering a rebuke to Tate is moot. All the same, we may note that he cited *The Waste*

Land in 1923 as "the apotheosis of modernity," and that
in 1959 he referred to Tate as having a mission in Nashville as "champion of the new literature . . . among people who did not know anything about it, and were as
likely as not to resist it when they were made to know."[37]

In effect, then, Ransom was telling Tate, as Tate saw it,
that he was too young to be able to know what he was doing with poetry, and this at a time when Tate was enthusi-
astically going about the business of being a modernist
and was beginning to establish a reputation for his poetry. The result was that Tate impetuously lashed back at
the rebuke. He could take such criticism from the tradi-
tionalists among the Fugitives such as Hirsch, Elliott,
Frank, Johnson, Stevenson, and so forth, for he knew
they were not really professionally committed to the
muse. But when John Ransom emerged from behind his
customary stance as man of reason and delivered a critical broadside along the same lines, that was something
else again, for he respected Ransom's opinions on poetry
in a way that he did not respect most of the others.

In retrospect, of course, it seems clear that what Ransom was really doing was arguing with himself, with Eliot
and Tate playing the role of scapegoat, the externalized
and properly denounced manifestations of certain tendencies which were very much a part of Ransom's own
inner identity. *The Waste Land* was Ransom's *bête noire*,
and by attacking it he sought to banish to an outer Thrace
his own inner recognition of the threat of moral disorder
and social and spiritual chaos, which if not kept in check
might imperil the equilibrium that he was able to maintain through the application of his rigorous logical powers. His art, and his philosophy, consisted of keeping the
terror and decorum in creative tension through an insistence upon his own poetic synthesis: it was his definition
of poetry, and his way of writing it. Eliot (and Tate)
seemed to him to be giving up the attempt, yielding to
the terror and making their poetry out of the capitula-

tion, and what disturbed him was that they were apparently succeeding. While Ransom was searching for the image of the good society by which he could give external, objective social form to his dualistic philosophical convictions about religion and art, here were Eliot and Tate, *as poets* (Eliot as theorist was another matter), willingly immersing themselves in the destructive element itself.

As for Tate, what dismayed him about Ransom's attack was the refusal of his older colleague to recognize that Eliot (and himself) were not for a minute abandoning unity and form, but instead were working from within the irrationality and chaos to give these form and meaning. *The Waste Land* was not a surrender to passion, an abandonment of all attempt at order, but an ordered, structured representation of the spiritual and social chaos of the day, searching out and delineating the human failure involved in it. It was fully as much the product of "emotion recollected in tranquillity" as was Ransom's poetry, or Wordsworth's. That Ransom could not and would not see this in Eliot's work exasperated Tate; for he knew that it was there and that it was part of Ransom's poetry as well as of Eliot's and his own. He recognized, indeed, that Ransom and Eliot were as poets and thinkers far more similar than different. When a few years later he met Eliot, he said as much to Davidson: "Ransom and Eliot are more alike than any other two people alive; I have always suspected this, now I am convinced. It is very hard for me to distinguish the influences they have had on me; they merge. It is quite proper, and quite amusing, that John from the beginning seems to have had an instinctive dislike of Eliot. The poetry of both is highly original; it is very much alike."[38]

Modernism

Tate stayed on in Nashville through 1923, taught school in Lumberport, West Virginia, in the spring of 1924, then made his long-meditated descent upon New York. There he met various of the literati, pondered whether he should attempt to live there permanently, and returned south to spend the summer of 1924 in Guthrie, Kentucky, with his friend Robert Penn Warren. It was in Guthrie that he met the future novelist Caroline Gordon, and in November they were married in New York City, where Tate had returned a month earlier to find work. In New York, Tate worked at free lancing for newspapers and magazines, began a biography of Stonewall Jackson, and soon was writing some of his best poems. He and his wife saw much of Malcolm Cowley, Edmund Wilson, Mark Van Doren, Hart Crane, and others. For a while Tate had a job helping to edit a pulp-paper love story magazine, *Telling Tales*. After several years city life began to pall, and the Tates rented an old farmhouse in New York State, where they hoped to find the quiet that would permit steady writing. But they took in Hart Crane, who was then without a job, and after a time the inevitable quarrel occurred, and there was considerable tension. The Tates stayed on through the summer of 1926, then moved back to the Village, where Tate got a part-time job as janitor of the building in which they lived, and continued with his writing. In 1928 he received a Guggenheim fellowship, and they sailed for England, moving on to Paris after that.

Tate's first volume of verse, *Mr. Pope and Other Poems*, appeared in 1928. The title poem, originally published in *The Nation* for September 2, 1925, exemplifies the swift advance of his art in the course of only a couple of years. The poem is rather more of a set piece than much of Tate's work; its subject is limited and the technique essentially descriptive. But in its economy and precision it represents a considerable gain in craftsmanship over the ardent but somewhat diffuse work of the early 1920s. The poem is in four stanzas of four lines each, and it opens with a description of the poet in London. When Pope went about the city, all that he observed was proper and Augustan: "Strict was the glint of pearl and gold sedans." He was an object of curiosity because of his fame and because of his physical deformity: "Ladies leaned out more of fear than pity/For Pope's tight back was rather a goat's than man's." But now he is dead, and in the disintegration of the dust of his body, we see the swift diminution of the importance that Pope could command as a man:

> The urn gets hollow, cobwebs brittle as stones
> Weave to the funeral shell a frivolous rust.
>
> And he who dribbled couplets like a snake
> Coiled to a lithe precision in the sun
> Is missing. The jar is empty: you may break
> It only to find that Mr. Pope is gone.

After his death, in other words, the human being who created the poetry is no longer within reach. The poems remain: the crisp severity of the couplets is what we have. In this respect there is the sense that the poems are the apt memorial to the man, for just as the living poet's physical grotesqueness inspired fear, so the poems he made, with their savage, mannered satire, are described in terms of a coiled snake in the bright sunlight. The couplets contain the man's personality as the world saw it, and now that the poet is gone, for better or worse that is the only personality that survives. In life he was respected, whether in fear or admiration, and was distanced; he was *Mr.* Pope, whom one knew or else knew about, liked and respected perhaps but did not take liberties with. Now Mr. Pope, who kept his private counsel, is removed.

It is the final stanza of the poem, in particular the last sentence, that has caused the most critical discussion:

What requisitions of a verity
Prompted the wit and rage between his teeth
One cannot say. Around a crooked tree
A moral climbs whose name should be a wreath.[39]

Various commentators have sought to interpret just what Tate is saying in the final sentence. Radcliffe Squires, in his excellent book on Tate, views the poem as dealing with the way that readers of poetry seek to biographize, to possess the man (the moral) rather than the aesthetic experience of the poem (the wreath): "The nature of Pope's poetry cannot be found in the discoverable man, yet the world would have it so." Squires sees the poem as a precocious announcement of what would later be called the New Criticism.[40] M. E. Bradford says that Tate "does not deny that the motives behind a man's creations are rooted in 'personality' (hence the organic figure, the tree; and its peculiarity, crookedness). But he insists that, if the artist is to be loyal to his craft, it is the handiwork that should interest us, the thing made and not the subliminal causes of its fashioning. Therefore, upon a crooked tree (the Pope *with us*: the work, not the urn) gathers a moral (*i.e.* aesthetic) that deserves a poem."[41] For Ferman Bishop, Tate, through the figure of the tree, is identifying organic nature with the moral essence of Pope, thus expressing the hope that as a poet, he too can achieve the immortality of time in nature.[42] John L. Stewart, who does not approve of Tate's willingness to publish "difficult" lines and sees it as an attention-getting device, says that the last stanza is Tate on the subject of Tate: "the mysterious artist, maimed, feared, enjoying his last triumph over the ordinary citizen by withdrawing and refusing to let others into his secret meaning."[43] And so on.

Are the lines really so obscure as that? And if Squires and Bradford are right, isn't Tate doing what they say he has written a poem about the importance of not doing; using the poem to make a personal moral observation rather than produce an aesthetic statement? I think it is rather a different matter. Tate wasn't preaching a sermon. He begins the last stanza by remarking that no one can know what the personal needs to express truth were that caused the poet to dribble the witty and savage couplets—we shall never know *why* he wrote poems. Then he declares that "Around a crooked tree"—that is, a thing beautiful and growing, though formed in duress and strain: the hunchback who wrote "The Dunciad"—"a moral climbs"—surely a vine—which is the poetry he left, and that brings about the reputation and estimation that the Poetry of Ideas he produced has achieved. This is not only what we now see when we look for the poet, but because it exists it will forever cloak the grotesque shape and adorn the personality of the long-since-hidden man who wrote the poems. This Pope, "whose name"— that is, Pope: His Poetry, the fused entities which are undistinguishable, so that when we speak of Pope we mean the poetry which contains the personality expressed in them—"should be a wreath"—deserves our honor and our tribute.

Such a paraphrase may gloss the line, but it cannot communicate the compacted wit and riddle—the "lithe precision" of the poem, for it is the interplay of the images with the intensified intellectual statement, with each modifying and almost interchanging with the other, that gives the poem its forcefulness. The cohesion of the thought and the metaphor is "strict" indeed: felicitous but meticulous and constrained, both mannered and amicable, which is what Tate is saying about Alexander Pope's poetry. "Mr. Pope" is probably Allen Tate's most finished poem; there are others that have more to say and in both content and range are more important than it, but in this, the first poem of his maturity, there is a formal expertness that he would never surpass.

"Mr. Pope" is also interesting, it seems to me, in what it shows of Tate himself. The stance that is ascribed to Pope is rather like the stance that Tate himself elected to adopt.

He had been instructed by his Virginia mother to look to his manners and to hold to his dignity and station, of course, and one rather imagines that a studied aloofness had early provided a way of dealing with a world that was not always gentle in its behavior. Once he reached college age, such a bearing had been a positive advantage. When he went North, however, like many Southerners before and after him he became highly conscious of the way that his habitual manners and his automatic attitudes and social assumptions set him off from the company in which he now found himself, and superficially at least, helped give him an identity.

It is from the time that Tate went to New York that his interest in southern history begins to play an important role in his thinking and writing. In *The Fugitive* for October, 1922, he had published a poem, "The Battle of Murfreesboro," which depicted an old Confederate veteran walking about the town dreaming of long-dead beauty, and ended with a note on the futility of his search now that "no bottle yields its cork/And skyscrapers tower in New York." [44] But with his move to New York, and his predictable experience of provincial unease in the metropolis, the awareness of his southern origins and attitudes became much more important to him. In Nashville he could confidently identify himself with modernism and cosmopolitan sophistication, for the value of the southern identity went unquestioned and unremarked; but in New York it was another matter.

However much he was fascinated with the literary life and its opportunities, there were qualities about such life in New York that he found both tawdry and disturbing, and which compared less than favorably with the southern community. He was surprised at what seemed the cliqueishness, the addiction to certain fashionable ideas, the too-close alliance of literature and marketplace. Like many a provincial before him, he was put off by the impersonality of the city, the lack of an accessible social context beyond the small, narrow associations with his fellow writers. There was a sense of isolation, of being part of a little intellectual and literary circle that was cut off from the rest of the city and the world. In the South, money was important, as were material possessions; but in the metropolis it was as if the entire fabric of the society were made up out of economics and had no cohesion or concern beyond or larger than it. In a society in which the cash nexus seemed to be the only reality, could there be any social stability beyond the marketplace, any permanence beyond the fluctuation of financial status?

Tate's reaction to this was both emotional and intellectual, personal and social. Thus the portrait of Mr. Pope in London, a man who, living in a city in an earlier day, commanded the respect and the fear of the wealthy in their pearl and gold sedans by virtue of the savage integrity and slashing wit of his pen, and who, however they may have considered him strange, was not to be trifled with. The key word, it seems to me, is *strict*. In the "Horatian Epode," he had referred to the "'strict gesture'" of the duchess' death, placing the words in quotation marks. There the adjective was used to connote the resolute integrity of the duchess' final behavior, as against the compromise and calculation of those about her. In "Mr. Pope" it suggests the civility the poet enforced upon his society, and also the rigid pride with which he knew to conduct himself in such a society, while keeping his own council.

Andrew Lytle has an interesting description of Tate in New York. Younger than Tate, he was given an introduction to him through their mutual friend and former teacher Ransom, and he called upon him:

At any rate the day I presented myself at the basement entrance of 27 Bank Street I was met with a severe and courteous formality—it was as if the eyes reflected but did not see what was before them. Later I came to recognize this as a mask to keep the world at a distance, because of the artist's necessity to be saved interruptions while at work; or merely to save himself boredom, which he cannot hide. I learned the necessity for withdrawal in his house, as I learned that the artist's discipline is almost its only reward. Once a caller asked for Katherine Anne Porter at this same address and was received with grave decorum and told, with a bow, "The ladies of the house are at the riot in Union Square." The bow, as well as the words, was a conscious emphasis upon the irony of his situation, the common situation of the artist living in New York, belonging to no cliques, and demanding that the profession of letters be accepted as a profession.[45]

The artist, and also the southerner. The eighteenth-century city which Mr. Pope inhabited was not the Old South, but there was, especially in retrospect, a great deal of the eighteenth century about the Old South, particularly in its Virginia manifestations.

In an article also published in 1925, Tate remarks that antebellum "Southern culture consisted, in essence, in a reflowering of eighteenth-century English manners and in the backwash, sterilized, of liberal thought from that century," along with certain other ingredients, and of the Old South's literary tastes that all literate persons "knew something of Pope, or should have—that whatever is is right, if it is what you approved of."[46] Some years later Tate noted, in explaining why his Virginia-born mother used to refer to the fact that her grandfather had "known Mr. Poe," that "she was of the era when all eminent men, living or recently dead, were 'Mr.'"[47] Just so, it is *Mr.* Pope in this poem of 1925, and it seems clear to me that Tate was constructing not only a commentary on the relationship between art and biography, but a kind of social ideal, which is that of the artist as he might best present himself to society, and also the proper stance for the man of integrity, whether he be the man of letters or the aristocrat, in a world of artistic and social confusion. It is as if, in this poem, he comes upon a way of viewing his times, and his place within them, that is both a strategy and an attitude, and which can function both on the level of personal and of social and artistic consciousness.

Following "Mr. Pope," one encounters the same image of mannered, proud reserve in various other works. For example, in "Fragment of a Meditation" he describes Poe as "exemplar of dignity, a gentleman/Who raised the black flag of the lower mind;/Hated in life by all; in death praised."[48] The "Elegy: Jefferson Davis: 1808–1889," speaks of the Confederate president as "He who wore out the perfect mask/Orestes fled in night and day."[49] In the "Ode to the Confederate Dead" the dead soldiers are made to "praise the arrogant circumstance" of their slain comrades, while the modern Southerners are shown as dressed "In the ribboned coats of grim felicity."[50] And in Tate's novel, *The Fathers* (1938), when the Buchan home (modeled on the Bogan family place, Pleasant Hill, where Tate's mother grew up) is about to be burned by the Yankees, the Buchan overseer describes what happened as follows:

"When the officer says I'll give you half an hour, the major looked at him. You know how the major is," he said in a pure voice. His eyes shone. "The major looked at him. He held himself up and, Mr. Posey, you know how he is when he don't like folks. Polite. That's what he was. He was polite to that Yankee. He come down to the bottom step and said, 'There is *nothing* that you can give to me, sir,' and walked back into the house."[51]

The freezingly polite disdain with which Major Buchan treats the yankee officer, followed by his suicide by hanging inside the mansion that symbolized his estate and which in its destruction by fire would exemplify the death of the Old South, is the lonely response of a man of order and principle to overwhelming chaos and disaster. The response of the man of letters to the same is an equally strict disdain, and the confrontation of the implications of the situation within the work of literature. For Tate's seizing upon the figure of the eighteenth-century artist and gentleman to provide the image for his literary and social critique is—and this is important to realize—not a retreat from the modern world into a nostalgic antiquarianism and ancestor-worship. However much Tate's imagination was stirred by the aesthetic possibilities of the antebellum, aristocratic South, it was never really a recoverable objective for him. Rather, it afforded him a point of view, and an instrument of strategy in his transactions with the life, values, and attitudes of his own day. Poetically, socially, politically, philosophically, Tate was a modernist, nor was that modernism ever begrudging, as in Ransom's instance. It was simply a fact, which he accepted without cavil.

This is by no means to say that Tate thereby accepted the disorder, depersonalization, and vulgarization that he and many others saw as characterizing an urban, secular society based on economic determinism and industrial capitalism. Modern consciousness, he insisted, was fragmented into what he later referred to as "the illiberal specializations that the nineteenth century has proliferated into the modern world: specializations in which means are divorced from ends, action from sensibility, matter from mind, society from the individual, religion from moral agency, love from lust, poetry from thought, communion from experience, and mankind in the community from men in the crowd." [52] The point is that Tate recognized the actuality of his existence as a creature of such a world and the necessity of his participation in it. Modernism is the way that he views his experience; he cannot pretend otherwise. When Ransom refers to "we moderns," he is pretending, for strategic reasons, to adopt a way of perceiving reality that is perhaps only partially his own. Tate does not customarily say "we," but simply "modern man," in which category he unhesitatingly includes himself. (Davidson, as we shall see, would not even make the concession.) What Tate would like is to change it; and if that was ever to happen, he saw his own role in the doing, as poet and man of letters, as one of attempting to arrest the dehumanization of language, and to write his poetry as a way of identifying the dehumanization.

It is important, in this respect, to consider what he later wrote of his friend Hart Crane: "Crane was never *alienated*. He did not reject, he simply could not achieve, in his own life, the full human condition: he did not for the moment suppose that there was a substitute for it."[53] For Tate, Crane was the exemplar of the modern American poet. His failure with *The Bridge*, he declared in an earlier essay on the poet, was that of "the romantic modern poet of the age of science (who) attempts to impose his will upon experience and to possess the world." Crane's "defect lay in his inability to face out the moral criticism implied in the failure" to do what he wished to do.[54] The modernism of a poet like Crane, therefore, did not involve a willing yielding to the *results* of modernism; rather, Crane raged against these. Crane's tragedy arose in his attempt to overcome the limitations of modernism without understanding how much of his response to modern experience was based, unconsciously, on the acceptance of many of the premises of the condition he detested. In other words, acceptance of the fact of modernism does not necessarily involve approval of it; but the only way to overcome it involves an understanding of the contradictions within it and within oneself as a modern. Unless this is done, the attempt to transcend its limitations will be doomed.

The eighteenth-century and Old South reference, then, represented the discovery on Tate's part of a way of ordering his response to the modernism within himself and all around him. It was, to repeat, a strategy, not an end in itself. The failure to understand the difference—and many of Tate's polemical opponents did not, or professed not to—is a failure to understand not merely Agrarianism, which Tate and his Nashville friends would soon espouse, but the creative dynamics of his literary imagination. One cannot account for poems such as "Mr. Pope" or "Ode to the Confederate Dead" or "Mediterranean" if one sees the moral impulse underlying them as only an erudite nostalgia, or *I'll Take My Stand* as a back-to-the-plantation movement. The *language* of Tate's work is never antiquarian or nostalgic, and neither is the moral attitude; it is the historical stance that seems to come from the past, and that is something else again.

The Dead Confederates

Tate's first published book was *Stonewall Jackson: The Good Soldier* (1928). Beyond the fact that from time to time it contains certain striking observations about the Old South, I can find little in it that justifies its being taken with much more seriousness than, say, one ought to take Henry James's biography of William Wetmore Story. I do not think it was one of Tate's important works. It was an exercise, done to earn bread and to shock the Brahmins—a game played for the fun of it. *Jefferson Davis: His Rise and Fall* (1929) is a trifle better, primarily because it is much better written and because, being the account of a politician rather than a soldier, it affords the author considerably more opportunity for dealing programmatically with southern society. But neither of these two works should be considered as much more than incidental to Tate's literary career. He was not an historian; he lacked the chief requirement of historian or biographer, which is the desire to discover what happened in the past through its study, and from that to attempt to understand what it might have meant. Tate had already decided what Jackson's and Davis's lives were supposed to mean before he began the books, and mainly he worked at fitting the biographical material into his thesis. Indeed, both narratives, and in particular *Davis*, are polemical works: Tate is arguing for his modern interpretation of southern history, not trying to uncover that history. And as always with works so thoroughly polemical in design, he oversimplifies, he slights what would refute his thesis, and he manages to rob the subject of what, had he truly set out to write history, he could certainly have contributed: the sense of its immense complexity. Even though *The Fathers* is fiction, it is far more profound history than the two biographies. We should look on both biographies, I think, as exercises in trying to do with little commitment what in "Ode to the Confederate Dead" he concentrates on showing the extreme difficulty of anyone's doing. Their thinness is, I think, in its own way a tribute to the accuracy of the insight of the poem.

Tate began the Confederate Ode in 1925–1926. It was first published in 1927 and thereafter revised several times before its ultimate version in his *Selected Poems* in 1937. In 1938 he wrote an extended commentary on the poem, "Narcissus as Narcissus," which is one of the better examples of a poet's explanation of the process whereby he wrote one of his poems—though Tate has said on a later occasion that "I don't think I really did it that way. Maybe a little of it was true, but it was partly rationalizing."[55] The poem quickly became Tate's best-known and most often anthologized work.

The first draft of "Ode to the Confederate Dead" was written while the Tates were living, on a meager income indeed, on the farm near Patterson, New York. It was a crucial time in his career. He had been away from the South for several years. He had made something of a name for himself in New York intellectual and literary circles, though almost entirely of a "highbrow" sort: that is to say, his reputation was mostly among the better literary critics and the readers of the little magazines and the journals of advanced opinion such as the *New Republic* and *The Nation*. The eagerness with which he had gone northward in expectation of a prominent literary career had by now been significantly qualified; he was up against the commercial and popular orientation of the publishing industry. As we have seen, a decade before, the youth-ful John Crowe Ransom had been excited at the intellec-tual and literary prospects that he thought would be his in the Northeast. Ransom, however, went back to Ten-nessee and did not attempt to try them out. Tate had now gone through the same process, and he *had* man-aged a living out of it. What he found, as we have seen, was not only that the financial prospects for a full-time poet and critic in the literary marketplace were less than overwhelming, but that the state of the literary cosmos as made manifest in the metropolis was not without its rele-vance to the state of American society as a whole. The modernism he had so zestfully espoused during his stu-dent days in Nashville had ramifications that he had not anticipated. The fragmentation and cultural disorder to which the poetry he most admired constituted a response was emblematic of a society that encompassed grave con-tradictions within itself. There *was* a Waste Land, in short, and its boundaries included his own country as well as the England in which T. S. Eliot was living.

If this was so, then where, in the scheme of things, was Allen Tate? As a poet, what was his role? In "Mr. Pope" we have seen how the problem presented itself. What he did now was to begin examining his particular tradition, and its meaning, or lack of it, for himself. All his life he had heard about the Confederacy and his identity as a southerner and descendant of early Virginians. What did these mean? It had been easy, when he was younger, sim-ply to dismiss such things as antiquarianism, romantic posturing, aristocratic pretense, and to identify himself with the sophistication and urbane condescension of modernism. But now he had seen something of what that sophistication involved, and the values, or lack of them, on which it was based. The advanced thought of the me-tropolis indeed condescended to the provincial places where he had grown up and gone to school; but on just what grounds? Was the presumption of superiority justi-

fied? And if *he* was not of the metropolis, and the values
and attitudes it cherished were inimical to his own in so
many respects, then of what place *was* he? He had left
those provinces so eagerly and so confidently; he had
thought that while they might be all right for his academic friends, secure as they were with their wives and
families, they were not nearly exciting or stimulating
enough for himself. Now he was not so sure.

It was not that he wished to go back, even if he could.
For better or for worse, there he was, in the urban Northeast, writing for a living. But what elements were there
about the kind of life, the attitudes toward the community, about the places he had once known, which were
so obviously missing in the society he now lived in, and
which—as he increasingly realized—were all the more
lacking for the fact of their absence not even being realized? How might they be recreated, if indeed they could
ever be? And he was forced, too, to realize that if such
elements were still present in the South, it was not because of but in spite of the attitudes toward their desir-
ability that most enlightened southerners now held, on
the conscious level at any rate. Nashville *wanted* to be like
New York, or thought it did; Murfreesboro wanted to be
like Nashville, and so on. As for the Virginia that his
mother had so revered, it didn't know what it wanted to
be, and didn't think about it (or about anything else) very
much anyway; when it did, it liked to imagine itself as still
being the kind of aristocratic traditional society that his
mother had talked about so often, with the smug references to "Mr. Jefferson" and "Mr. Madison" and so forth,
but this seemed increasingly little more than a snobbish
mannerism, an enfeebled, romantic posturing belied by
its everyday commercial ethos and having little that was
creative and vigorous about it. And as for Kentucky—
what it thought it wanted was to be like Virginia, and
mostly it couldn't manage even that. So just where, as a
Kentuckian of Virginian antecedents who had gone to col-

lege in Tennessee and was now living in a rented farmhouse near the urban substation of New York City known
as Patterson, did that leave him? Was he, like the persona
of the poem by Poe that he had read so often in his boyhood, out of space, out of time? Hardly that. But if not,
where *in* time and place did he belong?

In October of 1925 Tate published an article in *The
Nation*, entitled "Last Days of the Charming Lady," in
which he surveyed the lack of a vigorous literary tradition
in the South. The region's antebellum literary culture, he
said, had been the unventuresome, eighteenth-century,
energyless charm of an aristocracy of social privilege
founded in a rigid social order. Now that the order was
disintegrating, its literature could offer only the sentimental escape from ideas of a James Branch Cabell, while
the new generation embraced the boosterism and commercial bounderism of the rest of America. The surviving southern aristocracy has "no tradition of ideas, no
consciousness of moral and spiritual values, as an inheritance; it has simply lost a prerogative based on property."
There had been, in the northern Virginia and Charleston areas of the Old South, societies distinguished for
graces of living, if not for literary achievement, but these
were going fast. Thus the present-day southern author
was without a foundation in regional self-inquiry, and if
he was to make out of his own openness to experience
and readiness to explore new forms a literature that would
speak to his southern circumstance, he would have to do
it from without: by making use of the cosmopolitan culture of Western Europe. "It is pretty certain," he concluded, "that the Southern variety of American writer
must first see himself, if at all, through other eyes. For he
of all Americans is privy to the emotions founded in the
state of knowing himself to be a foreigner at home."[56]

The diagnosis, of course, not only fitted Tate's case
(and would fit Faulkner's and Wolfe's and that of the
other southern writers, all of whom would draw deeply

upon the techniques and attitudes of advanced twentieth-century literary thought), but it stated, topically and matter-of-factly, the central anguish that "Ode to the Confederate Dead" would explore: the final sentence is almost a *precis* of the situation in the poem. In 1965 he told an interviewer that "One morning, the first line popped into my head: 'Row after row with strict impunity.' I said, well, where do you go from there? I had no grand design. Of course it was about a cemetery, it was an elegy, in fact the poem was called *elegy* instead of *ode* at first. And then I wrote the second line and moved on step by step."[57] Notice that when Tate thought about a cemetery, he at once associated it with the South. Furthermore, he joins the key adjective *strict* with *impunity*—the impunity, the freedom from further humiliation and punishment, is because of death, and it is 'strict'—ordered, proper, unassailable. If we remember Tate's use of the same adjective in "Mr. Pope," in which he also described the glint of the pearl and gold sedan cars in Pope's London as "strict," we have the interesting congruence of the image of the tombstones of the dead Confederate soldiers with the self-esteem and respect which Alexander Pope was able to enforce upon his fellow citizens. In other words, what he sees in the dead soldiers is something of that same pride and "arrogant circumstance" that the poet who "dribbled couplets like a snake/ Coiled to a lithe precision in the sun" could command, and who after his death deserved a wreath for the moral ferocity of his art. But these dead southern soldiers left no poems: only tombstones:

> Row after row with strict impunity
> The headstones yield their names to the element,
> The wind whirrs without recollection . . .* (17)

The narrator, who we soon come to realize is standing by

* The discussion that follows is based on the final, 1936 version of the poem, as it appears in *The Swimmers and Other Poems* (New York: Charles Scribner's Sons, 1970), pp. 17–20. Page numbers are given parenthetically.

the gate of the military cemetery watching the leaves pile up in the troughs between the graves, is musing upon the way in which the proud integrity of the soldiers, however inviolable in death, is forgotten in time. No more than the leaves being blown about the graves are the dead men immune to such oblivion. The leaves, "of nature the casual sacrament/To the seasonal eternity of death," (17) are, in the long measurement of eternity, equally as permanent as the soldiers; the watcher at the gate mockingly imagines them as possessed of similar ultimate self-importance, so that like the soldiers they might see themselves with Calvinistic self-assurance as "driven by the fierce scrutiny/Of heaven to their election in the vast breath"* where they "sough the rumors of mortality." (17)

So begins Tate's poem. If the watcher at the Confederate cemetery gate is a modern southerner, who sees the inroads of nature on the tombstones of the once-proud soldiers of the Lost Cause, and ironically meditates upon the seeming likeness of the soldiers to the leaves insofar as the natural world is concerned (the wind which "whirrs without recollection"), then what he confronts is the absence of any lasting meaning to the tradition other than what human memory might afford. But if so, the leaves piling up alongside the graves suggest the neglect of the graves by the living, too. Autumn or not, it is not a well-tended cemetery. In other words, the modern southerner, whom we may assume is the poet, ponders his historical tradition and its erosion, and this is the situation with which the poem will concern itself.

---

* John L. Stewart, in his attempt at debunking Tate's poetry in *The Burden of Time*, uses the first version of the ode, and of the lines "Then, in uncertainty of their election,/Of their business in the vast breath," declares, "What a deal of words to say that the leaves were blown about helter-skelter!" failing entirely to get the theological point.[58] Mr. Stewart's political bias, which underlies most of the judgments of *The Burden of Time*, no doubt prevented him from recognizing the Calvinistic image; it may be that he imagined that the word *election* refers to what customarily takes place on the first Tuesday after the first Monday in ambitious November.

Tate called the poem an "ode," he wrote later, in part out of a sense of irony: neither the classical Pindaric ode nor the seventeenth-century imitation of it would have permitted a purely subjective meditation, a lone man standing by a gate, rather than a public celebration.[59] The poem, for that matter, is not about the dead Confederate soldiers at all; it is about the modern man's sense of being distanced from them. When Tate sent the draft of the poem to Donald Davidson, his fellow Fugitive objected that "the Confederate dead become a peg on which you hang an argument." He admired the craft, but "its beauty is a cold beauty," he said. "And where, O Allen Tate, are the dead? You have buried them completely out of sight —with them yourself and me. God help us, I must say."[60] But that is precisely the point of Tate's poem (and as we shall see, what Tate could do here was precisely what Davidson as artist could neither understand nor approve.) Tate was interested not in patriotic homage, but in what was ultimately perhaps a more important form of tribute: an attempt to understand why one of his fragmented time and place was no longer able to celebrate what the Confederate soldiers had been in their time. His attitude toward that, as Radcliffe Squires notes, was one of despair.[61] Davidson could not envision the backward look as being a problem; Tate knew better.

Therefore "autumn is desolation" in the cemetery for the man at the gate, who tries to muster the proper memorial rhetoric for the occasion, but cannot sustain it. Thus

> where these memories grow
> From the inexhaustible bodies that are not
> Dead, but feed the grass row after rich row . . . (17)

Instead of what should follow the commemorative phrase "that are not/Dead," he can only envision the bodies manuring the soil—that, and not the customary assertion of how the spirit of the dead warriors lives on, is all the immortality he can manage. He thinks of how the seasons—

"Ambitious November with the humors of the year"—
have worn away at the stone monuments, until the look
of inhuman, impenetrable inquiry upon the face of a
stone angel,

> The brute curiosity of an angel's stare
> Turns you, like them, to stone,
> Transforms the heaving air . . . (17)

The man at the gate is overwhelmed by the terrible distance between himself—as a man presumably linked
with the dead soldiers as a matter of familial and social
heritage—and the graves before him, and at the incom-
prehensibility of the relationship as it appears to him. He
feels suffocation, submersion, as if the oppressive air
were turned to water that enveloped him:

> Till plunged to a heavier world below
> You shift your sea-space blindly
> Heaving, turning like the blind crab. (17)

It is as if he were trapped, with no direction or purpose.
Then he recovers himself, focuses on the physical scene
before him: "Dazed by the wind, only the wind/The leaves
flying, plunge" (17). That refrain is what he sees, and so
what he can be sure he knows: what is literally and physically in his eyesight.

Now he thinks of the dead soldiers as they were in
their hour of battle, when they knew the immediate actuality of war,

> Those midnight restitutions of the blood
> You know—the immitigable pines, the smoky frieze
> Of the sky, the sudden call . . . (18)

The soldiers in their time did not question what reality
was; it was all about and within them, and filled with life-
and-death meaning. There was for them no Problem of
Knowledge; like the Greek philosophers—"the rage . . .
of muted Zeno and Parmenides" (18)—they did not con-
fuse subjective sensible appearance with ultimate reality.

They went into battle assuming that in thus fighting they could accomplish certain real objectives, and the attainment of such objectives—those of their society—was more important to them than the risk they would run of losing their lives:

> You who have waited for the angry resolution
> Of those desires that should be yours tomorrow,
> You know the unimportant shrift of death
> And praise the vision
> And praise the arrogant circumstance
> Of those who fall . . . (18)

At this point in the poem the speaker comes closest to realizing for himself, as Tate says, the active faith of the dead, and the metre is thus at its most cadenced.[62] Note the image of "arrogant circumstance" that comes to mind at this moment. Again, this time as if it were the dead soldiers who were praising the valor of their comrades, the implication is that the dead were able to enforce and to know respect for themselves: the pride that comes of being able to believe fully in one's conduct and circumstance and to act accordingly. The man at the cemetery gate admires that capacity, and he envies it. But he cannot sustain his belief, and at that point the rhetoric breaks down: "Rank upon rank, hurried beyond decision—/ Here by the sagging gate, stopped by the wall . . ." (18) is followed again by the refrain, "Seeing, seeing only the leaves/Flying, plunge and expire." (18) The dead, whatever their arrogant circumstance, have ended up here in the leaf-strewn, neglected cemetery. Both the dead and the man at the gate are "stopped by the wall." The wall separates the observer from the cemetery as the barrier which imprisons the modern in his own sensibility prevents him from believing in what the dead soldiers stood for and died for, even from understanding how in their time they could have felt the certainty that they did.

The wall, however, is also the barrier that stands between men, whether moderns or those of an earlier time, and ultimate knowledge; for the dead soldiers were mowed down in battle, "hurried beyond decision," and for all their certainty about what they were doing, at the moment when they fell, so far as the man at the gate can tell, they were really no closer to discovering reality than he is in his own far less confident circumstance. With this gloomy thought—the conjecture that the dead soldiers might well have been just as futile in their conduct as he is, and had only thought they were otherwise; the "cir-cum*stance*" is that of a "fall"—he is again undone by the helplessness of the situation, so that he can focus only upon the literal scene of the leaves falling.

Ironically now, he becomes the military historian, the professional antiquarian: "Turn your eyes to the immod-erate past,/Turn to the inscrutable infantry rising/De-mons out of the earth—" (18). If you look at the dead in terms of the heroic rhetoric of the Memorial Day ora-tions, he suggests, you will find nothing in which you can ultimately believe: "they will not last." He recites the slo-gans and the names of the battles.

> Stonewall, Stonewall, and the sunken fields of hemp,
> Shiloh, Antietam, Malvern Hill, Bull Run.
> Lost in that orient of the thick-and-fast
> You will curse the setting sun. (18)

The four Civil War battles were all ended without victory for one side or the other when dusk made impossible further combat operations, while if Stonewall Jackson had lived to lead his corps in the Battle of Gettysburg the opportunity of the second day's fighting in the wheat fields might not have been lost—at least so I interpret the specific referents. The historian, caught up in the ac-counts of the war, will like the Confederates lament the lost military opportunities; but must then like the poet lament the dying of the light, the end of a day in which men could believe and act decisively. So the historical vision fails, too, and again we get the refrain, "Cursing only the leaves crying/Like an old man in a storm" (18)— cursing nothing except dumb nature. This is followed by an instant in which receding memory almost produces a real sensation: "You hear the shout . . ." One may come close to believing he can hear the cry of actual battle, but then

> the crazy hemlocks point
> With troubled fingers to the silence which
> Smothers you, a mummy, in time. (18)

Nature itself seems to participate in the delusion; the tall trees appear deranged (one is reminded of certain paintings by Van Gogh), and in their disturbance, to be indicating something important which is not visible, but should be. Yet all the man at the gate can see is the trees. He feels the emptiness, an all-pervading silence which mocks the momentarily imagined noise, and like the heaving air earlier in the poem, is suffocating in its total enclosing. The modern man at the gate is a mummy, lifeless and entombed, separated from the heroic circumstance by the envelopment of time:

> The hound bitch
> Toothless and dying, in a musty cellar
> Hears the wind only. (19)

It has been only a naturalistic, animal response; in Tate's explanation, "the failure of the vision throws the man back upon himself, but upon himself he cannot bring to bear the force of sustained imagination. He sees himself in random images . . . of something lower than he ought to be: the human image is only that of preserved death (the mummy); but if he is alive he is an old hunter, dying." [63]

At this point the poem changes. Until then it has been the private meditation of the modern man at the gate, and it has concentrated upon his several attempts, each doomed to failure, to identify his own sensibility and his own occasion with that of the dead soldiers. The poem

has focused upon the ultimate impossibility of his doing
so. With this realization, the man at the gate now turns, as
it were, to address his fellow moderns, in something of a
Confederate Memorial Day address—but of a very different sort than the customary celebration of defeated
southern valor. What, he proposes, shall be our attitude
toward the dead soldiers? Now that they are dead and
their material bodies compacted with the elements, and
what they were is unavailable to us—"the salt of their
blood/Stiffens the saltier oblivion of the sea . . ."—what
shall we moderns make of them:

> What shall we who count our days and bow
> Our heads with a commemorial woe
> In the ribboned coats of grim felicity,
> What shall we say of the bones, unclean,
> Whose verdurous anonymity will grow?
> The ragged arms, the ragged heads and eyes
> Lost in these acres of the insane green? (19)

The woe is "commemorial" both in that the speaker figu-
ratively addresses his fellow moderns of the southern
persuasion who, with him, go through the motions of
mourning the dead heroes, and also because the plight
in which he sees himself is the plight of all his fellows,
whether they know it or not: cut off from the past, and
from the capacity to act communally and heroically. They
are "civilized," wearing "ribboned coats," but what effects
of well-being they can manage are "grim": a desperate,
tenacious contriving of urbanity and stoic resolution in
the face of emptiness. In their very propriety they are
separated from the dead soldiers, who are part of the dirt,
the "verdurous anonymity" of the earth. The grim prim-
ness, the civilized circumstance, is temporary and momentary; soon the moderns too will be compacted with
nature and lose their contrived self-importance. They
face the same oblivion that the dead soldiers have found,
but without the purposefulness and belief which the soldiers felt in their time.

But the interrogation breaks down. The rhetorical questions have no answer in any kind of communal response.

> The grey lean spiders come, they come and go;
> In a tangle of willows without light
> The singular screech-owl's tight
> Invisible lyric seeds the mind
> With the furious murmur of their chivalry. (19)

The vision of the thicket of darkness, the weavings of the grey spiders (as if they were the slain Confederates), is of an impenetrable wall, this time of nature, broken only by the piercing sound of the owl's cry, with its suggestion of the lost echoing of valor. Out in the underbrush and forest beyond the cemetery, in the growing darkness, the memory of the heroic possibility would now seem to have been distilled into nature, as if it were something wild that was no longer available to the desperately felicitous moderns. Or is it that the modern man at the gate suspects that his own notions of the lost time of chivalry are no more than the imagined personification of something animal and natural? It works both ways. Whichever the explanation, there is anguish and loneliness. (And there is, after all, really no memorial throng at the cemetery gate; the speaker only imagines that, too.) He can merely return to the scene before him: the refrain, "only the leaves flying, plunge and expire."

But this time he holds to that image and develops it:

> We shall say only the leaves whispering
> In the improbable mist of nightfall
> That flies on multiple wing . . . (19)

The leaves are now personified: they whisper, and the coming darkness, with the night birds, becomes mysterious, unspecific. Past and present merge in mist; heroic illusion and natural fact become a single incomprehensible obscurity:

Night is the beginning and the end
And in between the ends of distraction
Waits mute speculation, the patient curse
That stones the eyes . . . (19)

For the man at the gate, the attempt to understand appears useless, because the goal is impossible. Sealed off
from the past, from any hope of his being capable of
fathoming how the dead soldiers could have acted meaningfully and believed in their actions, the modern observer has only the ingrained habit of speculation, which
will not let him rest. Locked within himself, he can contemplate only himself—"or like the jaguar leaps/For his
own image in a jungle pool, his victim." (19) He is the
trapped animal of naturalism, whose self-consciousness
and capacity for wanting to discover meaning beyond nature only condemn him to frustration and self-hatred.
"This figure of the jaguar," Tate wrote, "is the only explicit rendering of the Narcissus motif in the poem, but
instead of a youth gazing into a pool, a predatory beast
stares at a jungle stream and leaps to devour himself." [64]

With this despairing conclusion, "Ode to the Confederate Dead" might logically have ended—the realization
of the total inability of the man at the gate to make anything of his heritage. He had sought to invoke for himself the reality of the Confederate past, had been unable
to find in it any meaning that was transferrable to him,
and so had ended with a picture of himself as no more
than a biological creature, imprisoned within his own
sensibility, doomed to return into the nothingness from
which he had come. The society in which he had been
born and grown up had been importantly formed by that
past, but it had been repudiated, and since the repudiation had been in favor of a life without meaning or belief,
there could be no place for himself outside his own society, either. He would indeed have been, as he said of the
southern writer in "Last Days of the Charming Lady," an

American "whose emotions were founded upon knowing himself to be a foreigner at home."[65] That is what the poem has developed.

But the poem does not end there. There are two more stanzas to come, and they are definitive for both this poem and to what Tate would be thinking and writing in the next decade. Instead of the poem's culminating with the figure of the predatory animal leaping to narcissistic self-destruction, the man at the gate asks another question: "What shall we say who have knowledge/Carried to the heart?" (19)

Tate later explained the figure as follows: "This is Pascal's war between heart and head, between *finesse* and *geometrie*."[66] But if the man at the gate and his fellow moderns—those who are concerned with the erosion of the capacity for belief (by no means all of them, to be sure)—have "knowledge carried to the heart," which is to say, possess a sensibility which does not willingly split apart thought and feeling, but would unify them, then the jaguar about to pounce upon his reflection in the water and thus destroy himself will not quite do for the last word on the modern predicament. Rather, it appears that despite the solipsism and failure to be able to act intelligently upon one's deeply felt convictions, the aptitude for the kind of wholehearted response to life exemplified by the dead Confederate soldiers has not died out. What is missing is not the capacity but the social circumstance. That is to say, the conditions of contemporary society, the public assumptions, the tenor of everyday twentieth-century economic and social life, serve to prevent the rendering of the True Account. This is the implication—though not the overt conclusion—of the figure concerning those who "have knowledge/Carried to the heart."

There follows a statement that would seem to belie any likelihood whatever of doing anything about it.

> Shall we take the act
> To the grave? Shall we, more hopeful, set up the grave
> In the house? The ravenous grave? (19)

The image came, Tate says, from a friend's account of a dream in which he awoke to find himself in a room, surrounded by the coffins of his ancestors.[67] Shall those who are like the man at the gate remain silent and live out their lives with the private knowledge that the condition of the present time is not as it should be? Or shall they, in a romantic affirmation of despair, make a virtue out of hopelessness and consciously celebrate decay and death? This was the way of the *fin de siecle*, the "Gone with the Wind" school. Southern poetry of the early twentieth century was full of the note, and in some of his early work in *The Fugitive*, Tate had essayed it: the langorous assertion, by a world-weary surviving memorialist, of the death of the gods.

Without any warrant for it other than Tate's ancestral Virginia ties and his notable passion for Edgar Allen Poe —and neither of these as such are in the poem—I find myself wanting to read a pun into the poem here: to read the last three words quoted above as "The Raven-ous Grave." I do not mean by this that the poet is making any such pun, but that what Tate means by setting up "the ravenous grave" in the house is the sort of thing that takes place in Poe's often-quoted poem: the reveling in a kind of decadent, thrilled morbidity. Shall we, he asks in effect, write funeral poems, in which death is made into life, as the only positive response to a world of death-in-life? (In 1949 Tate wrote that "everything in Poe is dead: the houses, the rooms, the furniture, to say nothing of nature and of human beings," and, "He could feel little but the pressure of his predicament, and his perceptual powers remained undeveloped.")[68] This is one alternative to the situation as set forth in "Ode to the Confederate Dead." Shall we elect it? he asks. It is not quite a rhetorical question, though almost so. He will not seriously consider making that choice, but neither is it to be dismissed as absurd.

Instead Tate closes his poem by leaving the question open:

> Leave now
> The shut gate and the decomposing wall:
> The gentle serpent, green in the mulberry bush,
> Riots with his tongue through the hush—
> Sentinel of the grave who counts us all! (20)

Tate's explication here is that "the closing image, that of the serpent, is the ancient symbol of time, and I tried to give it the credibility of the commonplace by placing it in a mulberry bush—with the faint hope that the silkworm would somehow be explicit. But time is also death. If that is so, then space, or the Becoming, is life; and I believe there is not a single spatial symbol in the poem."[69] Radcliffe Squires makes an interesting observation about this: "If Tate had thought longer about his symbol he might have remembered that when Aeneas prays at his father's grave, a serpent wriggles up from the earth. That serpent was the spirit of his lineage, the spirit of the past, present, and future of the house."[70] Precisely; no conscious allusion to the *Aeneid* (a work that Tate often makes use of in other poems, as in "Aeneas at Washington") is necessary to make the point that the "Ode to the Confederate Dead" does not conclude in blank despair, either historical or moral. "Leave now" the gate and wall that keep us from the spirit of the dead soldiers, he says, and one possible conclusion is that one is to give up the attempt to make any sense of them or of one's relationship to them. But if the man at the gate is leaving the Confederate cemetery, he is going back into the city of his time; and what he takes with him, finally, is life: for the serpent, whatever he represents, is indubitably alive and green, which is a very different thing from the splayed leaves piled up in the graveyard. If time is the solution to the riddle, it is an affirmation of continuing life, with its own problems.

The poem, in short, ends with the emblem of life in time and in nature. The gentle serpent is *sentinel* of the grave. Alive, "rioting with his tongue through the hush," he guards the cemetery and the memory of the dead Confederates from attack. This particular serpent may not be coiled to a lithe precision in the sun; and neither is "Ode to the Confederate Dead" dribbled forth in heroic couplets. All the same, it is not beyond the boundaries of legitimate comment on the poem to suggest what Mr. Squires proposed: that if the man at the gate is a poet, and if (as in a sense, all such poems are) this one is about the writing of poetry, then insofar as the future exploration of his own identity in history and society was concerned, the modern poet at the Confederate cemetery gate still had a great deal to write about.

It is not that I am insisting upon a "happy ending" to the anguish in the "Ode to the Confederate Dead." It is not an optimistic poem. But neither is it a surrender to the Waste Land. What it does is to dramatize the difficulty of the present, in terms of Tate's own historical and social concerns. And closing as it does with the image of the gentle serpent, the moving, continuing, exploring symbol of life in time, it asserts a continuity of experience that joins past and future as part of the ongoing human problems of meaning and belief. This is what one takes, finally, from the poem.

Participant in a Waste Land

Tate wrote several others of his best poems during the period 1925–1927, while he was living in New York and environs and attempting to earn a threadbare living for himself and family by journalism. There is no question that the time was one of much self-scrutiny; having arrived at his full powers as a poet, he was engaged in attempting to define what he was doing and why, and he wrote poems to help find out. Poems such as "Causerie," "Retroduction to American History," and "The Subway" are explorations of his response to the metropolitan experience. "Causerie," for example, takes off from a description in the *New York Times* of a party on the stage of the Earl Carroll Theatre, at which a chorus girl, Joyce Hawley, is reported to have bathed in the nude in a bathtub filled with wine.[71] Tate uses the occasion to depict in the form of a reverie of a man who cannot fall asleep, the erosion of the heroic possibility in modern life. The early Elizabethan adventurers who discovered and explored the American continent were those who could rest only when they had

> scanned the earth,
> Alert on the utmost foothill of the mountains;
> They were the men who climbed the topmost screen
> Of the world, if sleep but lay behind it,
> Sworn to the portage of our confirmed sensations,
> Seeking our image in the farthest hills.

He and his generation, however, realize the futility of such restless searching, and "know our end/A packet of worm-seed, a garden of spent tissues." The speaker is unable to get to sleep not because he has himself, like Macbeth perhaps, murdered sleep; he can assign no great amount of conscious deviltry to himself, nor has he made a fetish of easy rectitude. The trouble is that "this innermost disturbance is a babble . . ."—and one that leads to nowhere worth going except to the grave. The lines that sleeplessness leaves on the face are like the wrinkles of aging. Death at least means something, Matthew Arnold's definition of religion for instance:

> "morality touched with emotion,"
> The syllable and full measure of affirmation.

Let life be left to the pursuit of various delusions.

"Where is your house, in which room stands your bed?"
he asks himself. He is somewhere in the city. If there was
a place where he had belonged ancestrally, it is nothing
any more: a ruin in the wilderness: "Blood history is the
murmur of grasshoppers." He has a daughter now; what
of that? The family geneology that produced her seems
meaningless: "Let her not read history lest knowledge /
Of her fathers instruct her to be a petty bawd."

What is missing is any kind of true religious belief, with
its assumption of an ultimate reality beyond the aging
human body—"resurrection is our weakest clause of religion." He names certain of his friends who confront that
problem:

> John Ransom, boasting hardy
> entelechies yet botched in the head, lacking grace;
> Warren thirsty in Kentucky, his hair in the rain, asleep;
> None so unbaptized as Edmund Wilson the unwearied . . . .

They, like himself, wait in vain for revelation of meaning.
To the modern world, God is dead:

> In Christ we have lived, on the flood of Christ borne up,
> Who now is a precipitate flood of silence,
> We a drenched wreck off an imponderable shore . . .

Unlike the early English explorers, no new continent of
adventure and discovery waits for him and his kind: "A
jagged cloud is our memory of shore / Whenever we figure
hills beyond ultimate ranges." What once was thought of
as God's heaven is now a bank of cumulus cloud, past
which is empty space. Yet there remains the persisting
desire for meaning, for knowing; from what impulse
does it come, if all is matter and machine? As a poet the
very language he uses seems to rise, cliché-ridden and
pseudoliterary, out of some ancestral insistence upon
value and meaning, to await his personal modification
and use in his time:

> It rises in the throat, it climbs the tongue,
> It perches there for secret tutelage
> And gets it, of inscrutable instruction—

The poem moves to the speaker's comment on the substitution, in his own time, of abstract psychological and sociological interpretation for personal judgment of good and evil. The absence of public outrage over such a flagrant obscenity as the Joyce Hawley winebath (for which Earl Carroll was subsequently arrested) is the exemplification, one imagines, of "an age of abstract experience" in which

> fornication
> Is self-expression, adjunct to Christian euphoria,
> And whores become delinquents; delinquents, patients;
> Patients, wards of society. Whores, by that rule,
> Are precious.

The final stanza is a kind of exasperated, ironic dismissal of the age, consciously fustian and rhetorical, in the conventional *o tempora, o mores* style, whereby the sleepless reverie is converted into impotent bluster—for the speaker is himself of the age he condemns and can come up with nothing better than irritated expostulation:*

> Was it for this that Lucius
> Became the ass of Thessaly? For this did Kyd
> Unlock the lion of passion on the stage?
> To litter a race of politic pimps? To glut
> The Capitol with the progeny of thieves—
> Where now the antique courtesy of your myths
> Goes in to sleep under a still shadow?

* John Stewart misses the point: "The rage between Tate's teeth suddenly collapses into peevishness," he declares, forgetting that the poem is the dramatic monologue of an insomniac who, though he may denounce the degradation of a godless time, has nothing more definitive than "peevishness" to offer as rebuke, and can do that only in the imitative style of the Elizabethan melodrama.[72] Stewart's reading of Tate's poems, as I have already suggested, is informed by an odd kind of resolute impatience, which works against his considerable ability to explicate Tate's work. Again and again he will, after making some very shrewd comments on a difficult poem, follow it by an apparently programmatic refusal to grant any merit either to the work or the technique that has so obviously engaged his attention.

Poems such as "Causerie" and "Retroduction to American History" are Tate's depiction of the Waste Land. But we miss their import if we see them as declamatory pieces written by a disapproving observer. Tate is writing, as almost always, about *himself*; he is describing a society of which he is a part, and whose tendencies he, however regretfully, shares. He is not, as I fear some of those who have written in reverent admiration of the Nashville Fugitives have assumed, the austere moralist of the old school who observes the sins of modernism with disdain from the lofty vantage point of a superior social and religious heritage. If he were only that, he would have had little that was worthwhile to say about his time and place. Tate is a *participant*, not a spectator. Because he is also the inheritor of a set of social and moral attitudes uncongenial to the modern world, he can bring to bear, through self-scrutiny, critical judgment upon the errors and inadequacies of modernism as he perceives them within himself. But he could not understand the society he censures if he did not recognize within his own sensibility the tendencies he deplores. What he is doing in his poetry is composing, out of the modern circumstance, a portrait of the moral disorder and spiritual hunger that he sees both around him and within him. The great power of his best poetry comes out of that self-scrutiny. No one without a tremendous sympathy for the attitudes of twentieth-century American society, as well as a growing conviction of their inadequacies, could have composed such lines as these from the sonnet entitled "The Subway":[73]

> Harshly articulate, musical steel shell
> Of angry worship, hurled religiously
> Upon your business of humility
> Into the iron forestries of hell

What Tate wishes to show about the subway is its self-destructive, Satanic ugliness, its debasement of dignity and beauty for the sake of efficiency. But he realizes that the attitudes that created it include those of misdirected love, warped aesthetic craving, mistaken pride; it is hurtling toward hell not merely mechanistically but *religiously*, and in so doing it has its own beauty and grandeur.

It would have been easy to describe the artifact of the subway as godless bedlam personified; but Tate sees its symbolic virtues and its fatal attraction, too, because he can feel them within himself. M. E. Bradford makes it all too simple: "Its matter is infernal, and the hell it explores nothing but manmade and contemporary—the fruitage of wars in the cortex, the self-destructive impetus of rationalism." "The speaker, however," says Bradford, "is aware of the satanism in the rush of his fellows in 'their business of humility' down 'into the iron forestries of hell.'"[74] True, but also and equally of the speaker's *own* tendencies along that line; otherwise he could not have described the subway as vividly as he did, for he would have missed its fatal beauty as the "dark accurate plunger" and its function as the "harshly articulate, musical steel shell/Of angry worship" of power and ambition. As poet Tate almost never takes the stance of the disapproving, smug, superior traditionalist deploring the mistakes and misdeeds of the godless moderns who were not fortunate enough to have been born in the southern part of heaven. The poems of the period 1925–1927, exploring the urban circumstance, are *confessional*; if we ignore this, we not only cheapen them, but fail to grasp the unique sense of their pathos.

Home Thoughts From Abroad

In September of 1928, Tate sailed for England with his family. He had received a Guggenheim Fellowship, and planned a year abroad completing his biography of Jefferson Davis and writing a long poem (it was never finished). In London he met Eliot and Herbert Read, and visited Oxford where his fellow Fugitive Robert Penn

Warren was studying. Eliot he found impressive and (at first) somewhat distant. We have seen how in his courteousness and self-possession he reminded Tate of Ransom. "I should say that his character, far from being weak, is almost overdeveloped," he wrote Davidson. "It is both amusing and impressive to observe the attitude of the English towards him. It is almost worship, and it contains no reservation. . . . There is something very American about Eliot's whole procedure, and I like it. He came here unknown and without influence. In fifteen years he has become the undisputed literary dictator of London. What I like is that he doesn't seem to feel the role."[75] But Tate did not really care for England. In late November of 1928 the Tates proceeded to Paris. There he met various of the American literary expatriates, among them Ernest Hemingway, whose fiction he had previously reviewed. He and Hemingway got along very well together. With him he visited Gertrude Stein; "She is really a delightful woman and mad as the March Hare," he wrote to Mark Van Doren.[76] In Paris he also encountered two previous acquaintances who would remain his close friends, Ford Madox Ford (Hueffer) and the American poet John Peale Bishop. It was Bishop who introduced him to F. Scott Fitzgerald. When Ford departed for America in late January, 1929, he turned over his apartment rent-free to the Tates for the next six months.

The year that Tate spent in England and on the continent was important in his development. It represented, as for many American writers, the journey back to the fountain and source of literature, the locus of cultural value. For Tate it must have meant, in anticipation, the ultimate end of provincialism, the arrival upon the scene of the mainstream of the literary tradition in which he worked. It had been the French Symbolists who had opened the door to poetic craftsmanship for him. Eliot, the American writer he most admired, had found his spiritual home in England, where he had become not only the Great Cham of British letters, but a pillar of the Anglican Church as well.

In 1926 Tate had reviewed Eliot's *Poems: 1909–1925* for the *New Republic*, and had recognized in Eliot the same "cultural disinheritance" under which he labored, and had seen Eliot as moving toward a poetry so centered upon ideas that its ultimate development would be criticism, a critical philosophy of the present state of European literature. Eliot's poetry had drawn its impetus from "the desperate atmosphere of isolation" within a period of great disorder. What Eliot had done, however, instead of continuing to explore the disorder within himself as personal attitude, Tate wrote, was to erect a critical position for dealing with it. As the position became more coherent, the experience of the disorder, instead of serving as the impetus for poetry, was being made into precondition for thinking it out: "The intellectual conception is now so complete that he suddenly finds there is no symbolism, no expressive correspondence, no poetry, for it. An emotional poetry uncensored by reason would be intolerable to his neoclassical predilections."[77]

This was apt criticism of the Eliot of the late 1920s; it was also excellent cautionary criticism for Tate. For when he wrote the review he was busily engaged in making poetry out of the experience of spiritual disorder; in analyzing Eliot he was in effect examining the requirements of his own imagination, and warning himself against taking an easy way out of what for him remained a very creative dilemma. That was all well and good —for 1926. But several more years of continued immersion in the destructive element was a great deal of destructive element indeed, and not only were there limits to just how much of it a man could take, but poetry could hardly keep arriving indefinitely out of a condition of such withering cultural and moral isolation.

When Tate went to Europe he was looking for a new ambiance, an accessible and usable moral and aesthetic vantage point from which he could view and understand his situation. Eliot had moved into the Anglican Church and had found in it a way to deal with the secular disorder. Furthermore, sequences of what would become *Ash Wednesday* were appearing in print, so that apparently Eliot had managed to remain a poet in the doing. And Tate in the meantime had come to think a bit differently about the importance of conceptual thought for a poet. As he wrote in a review of *Ash Wednesday* published in *Hound and Horn* in 1931, "If a young mind is incapable of moral philosophy, a mind without moral philosophy is incapable of understanding poetry. For poetry, of all the arts, demands a serenity of view and a settled temper of the mind, and most of all the power to detach one's own needs from the experience set forth in the poem."[78] This was good Eliotesque doctrine; whether it was in 1931 or whenever, precisely the appropriate formulation for Tate's own instance is another matter. But Tate was tremendously influenced by Eliot's example during the 1920s. It was not that he was imitative—for the poetry he produced was not really Eliotesque in any important way —so much as that in Eliot he found a kindred imagination facing up to the same problems of language, meaning, and belief that he was facing, and it was only to be expected that the particular solutions Eliot advanced for such problems would receive Tate's respectful attention.

It is notable that he saw Eliot's literary conquest of London as an American enterprise. Tate never really accepted Eliot as an English poet; he recognized in him something of the same sly breed of practical cat as Ransom. Many years later when Tate collaborated with Lord David Cecil on an anthology of modern British and American poetry, Eliot was allotted to Cecil's care, but even so Tate devoted a goodly portion of his remarks on American poetry to this supposedly British bard, declaring for that occasion that Eliot was neither British nor American, but both.[79] I think that Tate always viewed Eliot's English allegiance and his Anglicanism as a strategy for coping with an American sense of disorder; I do not mean by this that he saw it as casuistic or hypocritical, but rather as a conscious act of the willed intellect, done to further certain strongly felt emotional convictions. (This was probably why Eliot reminded him so much of his fellow Fugitive Ransom.) And I think he was strongly tempted by Eliot's example, even to the extent of considering Catholicism himself. In February of 1929, from Paris, he wrote to Davidson, after commiserating with his friend about the conditions that worked against literary creativity in both their lives, that "I am more and more heading towards Catholicism. We have reached a condition of the spirit where no further compromise is possible. That is the lesson taught us by the Victorians who failed to unite naturalism and the religious spirit; we've got to do away with one or the other; and I can never capitulate to naturalism." And, "There is no dualism without religion, and there is no religion without a Church; nor can there be a Church without dogma. Protestantism is virtually naturalism; when morality lacks the authority of dogma, it becomes private and irresponsible, and from this it is only a step to naturalism."[80]

Davidson wrote back urging him against it: "Surely you must not, like Eliot, give up the ghost in favor of a combination of classic-Anglo-Catholic-Conservative, principally because that combination (good as it may be) isn't good enough for you, however much its elements may attract you, or even serve your poetical purposes now and then."[81] Tate did not make the move—partly, I think, because he realized that for him at this time it would be *only* a strategy, an intellectual act. He could not view religious belief apart from a social context; if a society's economic and political underpinnings were ultimately religious, the converse was equally true: that the conviction of a living faith was deeply manifested in a social fabric. And the English situation, however much it suited Eliot, was not for Tate; if he was anything, he was an American from the South, and emphatically he was *something*.

It is interesting that it was to Davidson that he had expressed his drift, as he saw it, toward Catholicism, for Donald Davidson, as we shall see, was at this time the exemplar for him of so much that he admired and valued about the South. In his review of Eliot's *Poems 1909–1925* Tate had described the work as "a return of the Anglo-French colonial idea to its home."[82] Elsewhere Tate had expressed the view that New England had more or less dehistorized itself; its provenance had been ideas, and ideas were, one assumes, not subject to the immobility of a social texture grounded in history. In any event, Tate's own southern heritage was presumably not open to removal abroad.

The fierce, if thwarted, loyalty that we have seen expressed in "Ode to the Confederate Dead" was emblematic of Tate's strong attachment to a social context, whose unraveling he found deeply painful. Eliot, living as an English citizen and an Anglican communicant, remained even so an American Puritan; in his move he was affirming his own social and intellectual tradition. But for Tate to make a similar attempt would not produce the same result. His southern American ties involved what Eliot's largely did not: a visible, tangible historical and social allegiance, still embodied, however inadequately, in a specific place. In "Last Days of the Charming Lady" he had declared that the southern writer could draw upon European culture and sensibility in a way that the New Englander could not, *because* his own heritage did not involve the "interdependency of a religion and a society." There was not, that is, a southern *religion*. "It is pretty certain," he had said, "that the Southern variety of American writer must first see himself, if at all, through other eyes"[83]—by which he meant the perspective of Europe. Well, now he had done so, not only intellectually but geographically.

If we want to understand something of what was involved in this, we might look at two poems that Tate wrote while in Europe in 1928–1929. On the surface, they may seem very different and even contradictory in their content. One of the poems is "The Cross," published first in the *Saturday Review of Literature* in January of 1930. Tate remarked years later that it was the only "explicitly Christian" poem he had ever written, and also that at the time he had no idea of becoming a Catholic.[84] The evidence of the letter to Davidson, however, contradicts the latter recollection. "The Cross" is one of Tate's most difficult and beautiful poems. It has been ably explicated by R. K. Meiners, Radcliffe Squires, and Robert Dupree, whose insights I shall draw on while subverting them to my own purposes here.[85] The poem begins with a statement of partial belief:

> There is a place that some men know,
> I cannot see the whole of it
> Nor how I came there.[86]

The "place" is "The Cross"—that is, the speaker is powerfully drawn to Christian faith, but cannot accept all its implications; nor does he feel entirely secure in his reasons for being there. Then comes a depiction of the impact of the Resurrection:

> Long ago
> Flame burst out of a secret pit
> Crushing the world with such a light
> The day-sky fell to moonless black,
> The kingly sun to hateful night
> For those, once seeing, turning back

The blinding clarity of the light of Christ's word made the natural world and pagan belief meaningless and dark to all who had seen it. I take it that the lines that follow are based on the paradox that life is existence in time, which is mortality, while if death is the redemption, and love of God is the setting aside of the pleasures of the senses and the material world, then to believe in God and the resurrection is to have to disbelieve in life—in the very condition of mortality out of which the love of God is formed:

> For love so hates mortality
> Which is the providence of life
> She will not let it blessèd be
> But curses it with mortal strife,
> Until beside the blinding rood
> Within that world-destroying pit
> —Like young wolves that have tasted blood,
> Of death, men taste no more of it.

Thus those who have found their way to belief and so to relinquishment of all stake in the concerns and exigencies of the world have become so hungry for God that they lose all appetite for mortality—for the providence of life. (I take the 'it' of the last line above to refer to mortality, just as the previous use of that pronoun does.) But though they have reached that position alongside the cross—the relinquishment of the world and the belief in resurrection, they are nonetheless still men and cannot know existence beyond the grave:

> So blind, in so severe a place
> (All life before in the black grave)
> The last alternatives they face
> Of life, without the life to save,
> Being from all salvation weaned—
> A stag charged both at heel and head:

Their last alternatives are whether to live or to die, but since they disbelieve in the values of mortal existence, they have no stake in choosing life rather than death, since for them the providence of life—Being—is a condition in which there can be no possible salvation. Thus they are like the stag attacked at both heel and head: if they elect to live they choose mortality, which is death, while if they choose death they are choosing just that: non-life. ("The grave's a fine and private place/But none, I think, do there embrace.") Once having come to the belief which affords that realization, they can no longer credit the world they must inhabit, and yet mortal life *is* the world. To live with belief, therefore, is to inhabit a world in which one cannot believe, and also, to view that world as hell on earth: "Who would come back is turned a fiend/Instructed by the fiery dead."

Tate was not composing a topical poem, of course, but he was certainly writing about his own situation in the late 1920s. And when he says that in approaching the cross—in moving toward a Christian belief that some men can know—he cannot see it whole or understand how he came there, he is expressing from the start his own dilemma. Some men may know the place, but his own understanding of it is only partial, because he cannot fully accept the world-destroying implications of Christian belief. Yet if one does not believe, there is no meaning to the world other than animal mortality. He cannot accept a view of life as only physical and biological; at the same time he cannot disabuse himself of the reality and the necessity of living in the world. Belief in the cross—in the doctrine of the Catholic Church—is the only alternative to an unacceptable naturalistic interpretation of existence, yet he cannot accept its corollary of the world as nothingness: he cannot "see the whole of it."

Catholicism thus, for him at this time, remains an urgent idea, a world-destroying abstraction that cannot fully describe his own experience, however much it appeals to him. He sets his imagery in terms of a place, of a burning pit, with the light of the rood within it so blinding that all else is as night. The flame is world-devouring; it consumes the things of the world. Now if we look back at the poem he wrote in 1925–1927, "Ode to the Confederate Dead," we may recall another such pit:

> What shall we say who have knowledge
> Carried to the heart? Shall we take the act
> To the grave? Shall we, more hopeful, set up the grave
> In the house? The ravenous grave?[87]

In that poem the grave—of decay and death, or at most the celebration of dying as the alternative to death-in-life —is posed as seemingly the only place left for those who can not tolerate the failure of religious belief that is the condition of modern man. But the speaker cannot accept that solution. The grave is *ravenous*—it consumes life. In "The Cross" the pit is likewise life-consuming, ravenous; in both poems the logical alternative to the pit is the state of hopelessness, "mute speculation, the patient curse/ That stones the eyes,"[88] or "Being from all salvation weaned."

But as we have seen, "Ode to the Confederate Dead" did not close on that note, but rather with the image of the "gentle serpent, green in the mulberry bush," who "riots with his tongue through the hush—" and who is "sentinel of the grave who counts us all."[89] If the image of the serpent is of the continuing exploration of life in time and nature, guardian of the grave, but not dead like the splayed leaves being blown about the cemetery, then the *mode* of experience of the "Ode to the Confederate Dead" is, however desperate, an alternative to the ravenous, world-destroying pit. And that mode of experience is the continuing search for meaning in the present through contemplation of man in time and history. The difficulties of such a search, the peril of hopelessness that it involves, are obvious; but as an alternative to the "black grave," it does at least exist. Here we recall Donald Davidson's remarks to Tate, quoted earlier, when informed of his friend's thought of becoming a Catholic: "Surely you must not, like Eliot, *give up the ghost* in favor of a combination of classic-Anglo-Catholic-Conservative" (italics mine). Davidson had indeed hit upon the problem as it was presenting itself to Tate, right down to the very metaphor itself. For Tate at this time in his career to follow the poet he so admired into Catholicism seemed finally, a life-abdicating step, an escape, which he could not take.

It is against the background of the concerns presented in "The Cross" that another important poem that Tate wrote during his first European sojourn should be read. "Message From Abroad," the several parts of which were first published separately, is dedicated to Andrew Lytle, bears a date, "Paris, November 1929," and is prefaced by a quotation: "Their faces are bony and sharp but very red, although their ancestors nearly two hundred years have dwelt by the miasmal banks of tidewaters where malarial fever makes men gaunt and dosing with quinine shakes them as with a palsy.—Traveller to America (1799)."[90] It is a poem about the relationship of men to history—specifically, that of an American to his own unfabled past, written from self-imposed exile in Europe. "What years of the other times, what centuries/Broken, divided up and claimed?" the speaker asks. Where is his own bit of history that is needed "to keep us/Fearless, not worried as the hare scurrying/Without memory . . ." He looks around him at the well-chronicled and appropriately humanized European scene:

> Provence,
> The Renascence, the age of Pericles, each
> A broad, rich-carpeted stair to pride
> With manhood now the cost—they're easy to follow
> For the ways taken are all notorious,
> Lettered, sculptured, and rhymed

But for Americans no such appropriately mapped and garnished history is available, for they are

> lost,
> Not by poetry and statues timed,
> Shattered by sunlight and the impartial sleet.

Viewing his own history, across the ocean, he sees "only/The bent eaves and the windows cracked,/The thin grass picked by the wind,/Heaved by the mole . . ."—these, and the American pioneer,

> the man red-faced and tall seen, leaning
> In the day of his strength
> Not as a pine, but the stiff form
> Against the west pillar,
> Hearing the ox-cart in the street—
> His shadow gliding, a long nigger
> Gliding at his feet.

This is the history he had inherited, and it is a very different and less glamorous version than the European model. The red-faced man—American, pioneer, Virginia planter and slaveholder—went west for gain. The shadow, "a long nigger gliding at his feet," suggests both the economic motive of his pioneering and also the curse of human slavery bequeathed to his heirs. From abroad, in the centers of civilization and culture, the American can only look back to this for his historical legacy.

The second part of the poem describes the journey away from that heritage, back to Europe. "Wanderers to the east, wanderers west," it begins. A wanderer is not so much a purposeful explorer as a drifter, looking for a place but not with anything specific in mind. In depicting both his own eastward and the earlier westward migration in that way, Tate is suggesting that all Americans are exiles, and that their heritage is based upon rootlessness. On the trip back "the ship mounted/The depths of night—/How absolute the sea!" The ocean is the absolute darkness and blankness of eternity, the condition which leads men to look for places. Beneath the ocean are drowned men—who did not make it to the New World— but the voyage over the ocean also decisively isolates the voyager from his time and place:

> The red-faced man, ceased wandering,
> Never came to the boulevards
> Nor covertly spat in the sawdust

Sunk in his collar
Shuffling the cards

The speaker can find, in Paris, no emotional link with his American past. The American pioneer set down his roots over the ocean, and his image bears no relationship to the European scene, in which he would be an awkward, uncomfortable, crude visitor, out of place amid the monuments and the art galleries and the salons. (In a way, this is Tate's highly unplayful version of Ransom's "Amphibious Crocodile.") Because the exile is separated from his heritage, all avenues seem equally open to him to travel, since none leads homeward:

The man with the red face, the stiff back,
I cannot see in the rainfall
, Down Saint-Michel by the quays,
At the corner the wind speaking
Destiny, the four ways.

The final section of the poem is in the form of an address to the bony, red-faced men of America who are his forebears, and concerns the distance between them and the speaker:

I cannot see you
The incorruptibles,
Yours was a secret fate,
The stiff-back liars, the dupes:
The universal blue
Of heaven rots,
Your anger is out of date—

Presumably the Americans are incorruptible because they have not been touched by the boulevards, salons, and art galleries—by the sophisticated hopelessness of modern urban society. There was an innocence about them in their ambition, their plotting and scheming for land westward. As M. E. Bradford says, they are like the dead Confederate soldiers of the Confederate Ode;[91] they believed in "the angry resolution/Of those desires that should be yours tomorrow," and their circumstance was

accordingly arrogant in its presumption of the importance of the individual will. Their recovery is what the
speaker of "Message From Abroad" meditates: "What
did you say mornings? Evenings, what?" For better or for
worse, his own identity in time, if it is to be found, lies in

> The bent eaves
> On the cracked house,
> The ghost of a hound. . . .

He must return home, if his own history is to have any
significance, for

> That man red-faced and tall
> Will cast no shadow
> From the province of the drowned.

The point is, as I see it, that *he* does not belong abroad.
The "drowned" are not the Europeans; nor does one assume that they are such American expatriates as Henry
James or T. S. Eliot;* they are those such as himself who,
by reason of their particular heritage, cannot live and
create apart from their native society.

The relationship of this poem to "The Cross" is autobiographical. That is, both were written by the same man,
a southern American poet in Europe. In one is recorded
the tremendous attraction to Catholicism, and its reluctant rejection in that it fails to enable him to define his
own life; in its meaning it is "world-destroying," and he
cannot accept that view of the world. The second poem
chronicles the poet's inability, in Europe, to discover his
own history and heritage; in Europe the bony, red-faced
American will cast no shadow for him. The Cross—God's
love—"hates mortality/Which is the providence of life";
and since mortality is life in time, true religious belief can

---

* In his essay on Emily Dickinson, written at about this time, Tate says of
James that he "found himself in the post-Emersonic world, and he could not,
without violating the detachment proper to an artist, undo Emerson's work;
he had that kind of intelligence which refuses to break its head against history. There was left to him only the value, the historic role, of rejection."
James's way was not his way, but for James it was "a victory" in that he thereby
refused "to engage the full force of the enemy." So much for "aestheticism." [92]

permit no historical identity, for it is timeless. This the speaker is unable to accept; he will go home and try to explore, in history, what he is in his mortality. In Bradford's words, "even with only 'bent eaves' behind him to go on, the speaker must face up to what he is and begin to define himself there. History cannot be avoided."[93]

Tate was ready. He completed his biography of Jefferson Davis on July 14, 1929, then spent the remainder of that summer in Brittany. In July he learned by telegram that his mother had died in Monteagle, Tennessee. In September the Tates returned to Paris, and on January 1, 1930, sailed for New York. For two years he had been in correspondence with Donald Davidson and John Crowe Ransom about the need for a symposium that would set forth their views on the South. Now *I'll Take My Stand* was under way.

3 Donald Davidson:
The Poet as Southerner

A Man of Loyalties

Allen Tate was still in France in late 1929 when Donald
Davidson wrote to urge his return to the United States as
soon as possible. The symposium on southern problems
that the two of them and John Crowe Ransom had been
exchanging ideas about by letter was still only a scheme.
"I do not think it can really develop until you get back to
the States," Davidson told his friend,

for I cannot swing it by myself, busy and distracted as I am
now, and I sadly need advice, comfort, and the aid of a strong
right arm. There is nobody around here who has either sufficient zeal or wisdom to pitch into the business wholeheartedly.
Ransom, you know, never was a man to push anything. He will
give moral support, he will write, he will be a strong man in
conference, but he does not energize. Andrew Lytle is terrific-
ally interested, but he has to get his Forrest biography out of
the way before all else. I simply cannot fit the project into my
routine until things loosen up a bit, but I am ready to do all that
I can do under the circumstances. I lead an incredible life,

hardly ever relaxing from the round of hard driving work. In a month or two, however, I may be better organized.[1]

Tate returned that winter, and *I'll Take My Stand* got under way. But it was Davidson who made it work. Tate could, and did, provide generative ideas, and was able to find a publisher for the venture, but Donald Davidson was the organizer and the energizer, as all the others readily admitted. He was indispensable to the Agrarian program, just as in the early years of the decade he had been vital to the publication of *The Fugitive*. "Busy and distracted" as he was—and continued to be throughout his life—Davidson always found time to get such work done. If Ransom gave the Fugitives their direction and purpose, and Tate gave them their professional nerve, it was Davidson who provided the cohesion, loyalty, and warmth of temperament that made their joint enterprises fruitful. There is no way that his value to the group can be overstated; if his ultimate place in the literary firmament has come to be less important than that of Tate, Ransom, and Robert Penn Warren, his role in twentieth-century southern literary history is solidly established. For without him, there could hardly have been either a continuing poetry group in Nashville in the 1920s or an Agrarian movement in the 1930s.

Davidson's family was of pioneer Tennessee stock.[2] His great-grandfather came to America from Scotland in the late eighteenth century and was located in Tennessee before 1805. Donald Davidson's father, William Bluford Davidson, earned a bachelor's degree at Holbrook Normal School in Ohio, studied further at schools in Winchester, Tennessee, and Troy, Alabama, and became a school teacher. In 1892 he married Elma Wells, and their first child, Donald Grady, was born on August 18, 1893, at Campbellsville, Tennessee, where the elder Davidson was principal of the school. Donald Davidson grew up in Pulaski, Lynnville, and other Tennessee communities. His father was cultivated in the classical languages and literatures, and his mother was an accomplished musician. A number of his great-uncles were Confederate veterans, and his mother's mother, Rebecca Mar Patton Wells, who lived with the family, told him many tales about the federal occupation of Middle Tennessee during the War.

Davidson attended school at Lynnville Academy and at Branham and Hughes School, one of the South's better-known preparatory schools. In 1909 his father moved to Bell Buckle, Tennessee, to be principal of the high school there. The famous Sawney Webb School for Boys was also located in that community, and the elder Webb made it possible for the young Davidson to use a loan, which had been established for Webb School graduates, to enter Vanderbilt University in 1909. After a year in college, he ran out of money and spent the next four years as a school teacher in Cedar Hill and Mooresville, Tennessee, until he had saved enough to reenter college. Even so, when he returned to Vanderbilt in 1914, he had to support himself by teaching English and German at Wallace University School in Nashville.

At Vanderbilt, Davidson took courses under Walter Clyde Curry and John Crowe Ransom, with whom he soon became friends, and with Edwin Mims. He found Mims's stirring readings of the American poets especially exciting. Curry introduced him to the modern European dramatists. His education continued out of the classroom as well. His fellow students Ben and Varnell Tate, whose younger brother he would later come to know very well indeed, loaned him the works of DeMaupassant. Another English teacher, Lawrence G. Painter, had encouraged him to read Dostoyevsky. Alec Brock Stevenson, whose father was professor of religion, made him acquainted with Joseph Conrad. It was through Stevenson and two other young men, William Yandell Elliott and Stanley Johnson, that he met Sidney Mttron Hirsch, and soon there began the philosophical and literary discussions at the Hirsch family apartment, to which Ransom began coming as well, that after the First World War resulted in *The Fugitive*.

Davidson was doing very little writing at the time; music was an almost equally strong interest for him, and he considered applying for studies in musicology at Harvard University. When the United States entered the war Davidson, like Ransom, was admitted to Officers' Training School. He was commissioned second lieutenant in August, 1917, and in July of the next year embarked for France with the 324th Infantry Regiment of the 81st (Wildcat) Division. Before he sailed, however, he was married to Theresa Sherrer, a girl from Ohio he had met two years earlier. The 81st Division was moved up into position for the attack on the Hindenberg Line, and on November 9 went into action in the Manhuelle Woods, losing over two hundred men and undergoing heavy artillery shelling. Following the armistice on November 11, the division undertook a three-week march to Chatillion-sur-Seine, where it awaited eventual shipment home. It was not until the late spring of 1919 that the division embarked for the United States, arriving in Charleston, South Carolina, in mid-June.[3]

Throughout the time he was in the army, Davidson carried with him a packet of his friend Ransom's poems. In France he attempted some verse of his own, and wrote to his wife to send him a copy of Amy Lowell's *Tendencies in Modern American Poetry*. As soon as he was demobilized he stopped off at Nashville, where he found that there was no vacancy for him in the Vanderbilt English department that year, and then hurried to rejoin his wife and infant daughter at Oberlin, Ohio. He sought work in advertising, journalism, and teaching in the Cleveland area without success, until finally he received an appointment to teach English at Kentucky Wesleyan College. The next year Edwin Mims arranged an instructorship at Vanderbilt, where he could also work on his master's degree. He found a summer job as a reporter for the Nashville *Tennessean*, was happily reunited with Ransom and his other friends, and the meetings of the discussion group, now held at Hirsch's brother-in-law James M. Frank's home, were soon in full force.

When the Fugitives decided in early 1922 to undertake publication of a poetry magazine, Davidson was enthralled. Tate's skepticism was not for him. "I could hardly believe, at first, that my *friends* really would go through with this bold undertaking," he remembered later. "I thought it bold, indeed—but not folly. When all agreed that we should, we *must* publish a magazine, it was for me one of my moments of highest, undiluted joy—one of the few such moments of peculiar elation and, I could almost say, of triumph."⁴ Such a reaction, I believe, was characteristic of the man. Publication of a poetry magazine by the group involved the translation into action of shared ideas and ideals. He was never the man of detached, ironic contemplation that his friends Ransom and Tate were; he did not tend to see ideas apart from their practical and immediate embodiment and consequences, any more than he could view poetry as separate from its social content. Throughout his life he was always involved in "doing things"—projects such as the editing of the Nashville *Tennessean* book page, the writing, editing, and periodic revision of numerous textbooks, and, in the 1950s, political activities involved in resistance to the civil rights edicts. Although he was an intensely private man, he cherished his friendships, and delighted in group projects. Philosophy, aesthetics were not his metier; back before World War I, listening to his friends Hirsch, Ransom, Elliott, and Johnson disputing the concepts of philosophy at the Hirsch apartment, he had felt himself "destined to be but a shy guest at the feast of the world's great culture," he remembered, "if the banquet were to consist of the categories of Kant and the heresies of Hegel."⁵ Yet perhaps more than anyone else, he relished the sessions, for he gloried in being with his good friends.

In particular, his friendship with Tate was extremely close all during the 1920s. Tate's conceptual mind impressed him mightily, and his emotional involvement in what he believed in was inspiriting. Tate had the habit of consciously adopting a strategy and then ordering all his outer defenses accordingly, which appealed strongly to Davidson's penchant for action—whereupon he entered into the operation without any of Tate's ironic reservations. For Davidson it was not a matter of strategy; it was total commitment. This in turn gratified Tate, who admired his friend's loyalty and enthusiasm.

The relationship between the two, so important to the forming of *I'll Take My Stand*, is exemplified in the letters they were exchanging during 1928 and 1929, when Tate was in Paris. Davidson and Ransom had long been in agreement that they should "do something" about the southern situation, and from time to time had discussed editing a book, or something along that line, without, however, coming to any conclusion. Ransom was busy with his book on aesthetics, and was not the man to organize such things. Davidson, for his part, needed something to stir him into action. Meanwhile Tate was wrestling with his growing sense of rootlessness and the futility of the literary situation of the day. It was during the period, as we have seen, that Tate was strongly contemplating religious conversion, but could not equate the spiritual compromises of such a step with the actualities and needs of his own life. One has the feeling that the choice presented to him, as Tate saw it then, was an either/or affair: either the attempt to become a Catholic, with all that this would mean, or the attempt to involve himself in the social situation of his times as a southerner, in active willed strategy directed at the reformation of southern culture. Being a poet in the metropolis, without any additional allegiance, was no longer enough. Whether or not the alternative was as clear as that (and such a neat formulation omits the spiritual travail involved), the outcome in effect was that Tate decided it was appropriate to "do something" about the South, whereupon he sent Davidson and Warren a lengthy plan of action, involving all manner of immediate and long-range objectives, along with a proposed table of contents, with possible contributors, for the book defending the South.[6]

Davidson's reaction was only to be expected. He had written to his friend a few paragraphs about a proposed book, and by return mail he had gotten back a detailed battle plan. He was delighted. "To you goes the credit for defining sharply and ambitiously the loose aspirations that have been rattling around in our heads," he told Tate. "It's a tremendous stimulus just to have your letter with its grand outline of activities, and though I've been a long time in answering, I want you to know that your letter shook me up from top to toe and filled me with a new fire."[7] Each man had thus supplied a need for the other: Davidson had given Tate, not only by his remarks about a southern book but, even more important at that juncture, simply by being himself and having the concerns he had, the hint for an assertion of identity and definition that Tate was ready to act upon, and in return Tate had thereupon offered a strategy, imaginative yet practical, specific yet open-ended, for whole-souled intellectual combat.

It is not too much to say that the discovery of Agrarianism made possible Tate's return to Tennessee. His years at Vanderbilt, as a member of the Fugitives, had been the finest and most enjoyable of his life, but eventually he had, as a poet, outgrown the association and had found it necessary to pursue his literary career in the Northeast. I doubt that, strictly as a literary man, Tate could for some years have gone back to live in the South. But Agrarianism was something that would involve him intellectually and programmatically with his friends again, and he could believe in its importance. In turn, Tate's coming

back and his presence on the Tennessee scene made it
easier for Davidson to put his loyalties and convictions
into application, in action.

Yet unlike Davidson, Tate never really believed in the
practical effectiveness of Agrarianism as a force in everyday southern life. It remained a cultural strategy for him.
"We are not in the least divided," he felt it necessary to
write Davidson just before he left for the United States,
"but we exhibit two sorts of minds. You and Andrew
[Lytle] seem to constitute one sort—the belief in the
eventual success, in the practical sense, of the movement.
The other mind is that of Ransom and Warren and myself. I gather that Ransom agrees with me that the issue
on the plane of action is uncertain. At least I am wholly
skeptical on that point; but the skepticism is one of hop-
ing to be convinced, not by standing aside to watch the
spectacle, but by exerting myself. In other words, I believe that there is enough value to satisfy me in the affirmation, in all its consequences, including action, of value.
If other goods proceed from that, all the better."[8] As we
shall see, Tate was mistaken in his estimate of what Ransom's attitude would be once the book was published, or
so I think, but in assessing the difference between Davidson's approach and his own, he was quite accurate.

The Outland Piper

In the early 1920s, however, all this was far in the future
when the two friends were involved with the other Fugitives in bringing out their poetry magazine. At this time
Davidson was not really very much interested in the condition of the South, or overtly concerned with its problems. The first issue of *The Fugitive*, it will be remembered, contained a statement of purpose in which the
poets insisted upon their emancipation from the then-
moribund tradition of southern letters. Louise Cowan is
quite right when she notes that "it was only through break-

ing with 'Southern literature,' as it was then piously conceived, that they could find the way to what they realized years later was the genuine Southern tradition."[9] Identification with the southern literary milieu meant, in the early 1920s, acceptance of the genteel pastelry of southern local color writing, with its regional pieties and eulogistic Confederate sentimentality. To write poems about the real world in which they were living, it was necessary that they get freed of all such inhibiting allegiances. Indeed, when in 1923 Harriet Monroe, editor of *Poetry*, published a review of DuBose Heyward's and Hervey Allen's *Carolina Chansons* in which she urged Southern poets to "accept the challenge of a region so specialized in beauty, so rich in racial tang and prejudice, so jewel-weighted with a heroic past," Tate and Davidson were indignant.[10] Davidson prefaced the next issue of *The Fugitive*, for July, 1923, with the remark that "it is difficult to applaud the limitations she proposes for Southern poets." Serious southern writers, he said, "will guffaw at the fiction that the Southern writer of today must embalm and serve up as an ancient dish."[11]

The poems that Davidson was composing in the early 1920s had mostly to do with demon pipers, tigers, dragons, and the like; they were musical, romantic, and the language was more like that of the early Yeats than of T. S. Eliot or even of the Yeats of post-1910. The pen name he chose for the work that appeared in the first two numbers of *The Fugitive*, "Robin Gallivant," suited perfectly the approach to the poems. The opening lines of "A Demon Brother," which appeared in the first issue, are vastly different in tone from his late work and, curiously and unconsciously, accurate in their implications for what he would later become:

> *Old man, what are you looking for?*
> *Why do you tremble so, at the window peering in?*
> *—A Brother of mine! That's what I'm looking for!*
> *Someone I sought and lost of noble kin.*

Whereupon the account begins. "I heard strange songs when I was young,/piping to songs of an outland tongue." The speaker tells how he followed the piper, for "something in that outland tongue/Drew me away,—for I was young!" He followed "that alien piper—so like me" to the deserted end of an unknown street. The piper warns him to "'follow me no more,'" for

> "Though I be of thy father bred,
>   And though I speak from thine own brood,
>   Yet I am but of demon blood;
>   And follow not my piping sweet
>   To find the walking world a cheat . . ."

The speaker has heard the admonition, but cannot heed it, and he has followed ever since, wondering that the demon brother's piping "Left me to know a world's deceit" and to seek an unknown kin. Then the poem closes with the voice of the interrogator again and the reply of the now-old man:

> *Old Man, is it songs you are looking for?*
> *Music lost in the leaf that the year has shed?*
> *—A Brother of mine! That's what I'm looking for!*
> *The sight of a kinsman's face before I am dead.*[12]

In the revised version of this poem, retitled "An Outland Piper" and made into the title poem of Davidson's first book, the query and the answer which frame the lyric are omitted, and the rest of the poem considerably revised. (In his last collection, *Poems 1922–1961*, Davidson apparently went back to the original title.) But the original version, however inferior poetically, pronounces the theme of Davidson's career as poet. For as poet and as Agrarian, he would indeed be looking for "someone I sought and lost of noble kin"—the image of the southern forebear of days gone by, the "Tall Man," whether as pioneer Tennessean or Confederate hero, who could stand up for what he believed and not give in to "the world's deceit" as practiced in the twentieth century. As poet and Agrarian,

Davidson looked back at a time when, as he saw it, the materialistic, characterless tempo of modern industrial existence had not yet destroyed the good society. He did indeed seek "the sight of a kinsman's face before I am dead"—which is to say, a community to which he could willingly belong and in which he could truly believe.

Tate's impact on Davidson's work at this time was extremely important, and was largely responsible for a change in Davidson's work that became visible in 1923 and 1924. Divorcing his muse from the early, wistful romanticism, Davidson became for a time much more direct and modernistic and the vocabulary of his work much more colloquial. But if he gave in—temporarily— to the call of modernism, he put up quite a resistance. Thus in *The Fugitive* for October, 1923, he published a poem entitled "Old Harp," in which he set up a contrast between the past and present by depicting a harp that had been used in olden days to sing of

> old, old things
> In tongues men have forgot,
> Of sleeping, barrowed kings
> That wait new Camelot . . .

The harp had accompanied Viking songs, sung by warriors filled with the excitement of discovery, who had viewed "blue cliffs slowly rifting/That guard enchanted bays." Now the harp reposes in a museum; the man who once played it is dead:

> Here is no singing tongue.
> Only the mute cool rust
> Fingers thee, loosely strung.
> And men read, as read they must
> What once was sung.[13]

Though the poem is about music, and by implication a critique of the musicless nature of modern free verse, we see that Davidson is already employing the heroic past as rebuke to the confused present. No political or social

context is given; the issue is aesthetic; but obviously those
Vikings anticipate in spirit and attitude the "long-haired
hunters watching the Tennessee hills/In the land of the
big rivers for something." [14] An interesting difference,
however, is the somewhat reluctant concession, in the
next-to-last line, to the effect that the modern men *must*
read "what once was sung." This early lament for the lost
past, then, involves the realization, if stated only as an
afterthought, that the moderns have no choice but to live
by and in the circumstances of a changed time.

This is also what Davidson contended when, in the final issue of *The Fugitive*, for December, 1925, he published a review of R. C. Trevelyan's *Thatmyris, or Is There
A Future for Poetry?* Davidson deals with the author's
theory that modern poetry has developed from naïve
primitive song, and in so doing is operating under a disadvantage. Trevelyan, he says, "refers to the loss which
we have suffered in that poetry is no longer chanted or
sung, as if the movement of the race from unsophistica-
tion were something to be ashamed of. One who thinks
twice will reflect that primitive poetry was sung because it
could not be read, not necessarily because singing was
more artistic or advantageous." "Why be apologetic at
all?" he continues. As art has evolved, the arts have become specialized, and if poetry is less the "popular and
social art" it was, it has made gains as well. "In short,
though American and English soldiers in France had no
native epic to chant as they went into battle, no songs of
Roland and Beowulfs, it would be hard to say that the
state of poetry on that account is one of degradation." He
closes the optimistic statement that the nature of poetry is
change and flexibility: "The strangest thing in contemporary poetry is that innovation and conservatism exist
side by side. It will probably always be so!" [15]

For Donald Davidson that attitude was odd doctrine—
and soon to be discarded. It was, however, more or less
what Tate had insisted in his defense of "The Waste

Land" against Ransom's strictures. I find it difficult to account for otherwise than by the influence of Tate on Davidson's sensibilities at this time. If we examine certain Davidson poems of the late issues of *The Fugitive* we can also see the same attraction at work. In "Hit or Miss," the last poem he published in the magazine, we encounter a stanza such as this one:

> Or if from the puffed white mouth of a toad
> I heard a syllabled exhortation
> Or actually saw disintegration
> Bubbling the hardest stone on the road.[16]

The choice of the adjectives, the imagic violence in the personification of disintegration as "bubbling" the stone, seem much closer to Tate's poetics than to Davidson's customary emphasis on musicality. In another poem, "The Wolf," in *The Fugitive* for August–September, 1923, he portrays a Sweeney-like rural storekeeper as a beast of prey:

> Drooling, like one who should be crunching bones,
>   He mouths the figured column of his kill.
> A sneaking blast rattles the locked door.
>   The cat looks on, oracular and still.[17]

Here the language is not so complex, but the imprint of modernism is present even so: the image in the second line has a radical quality that does violence to customary poetic expectations. Only Tate, of all the Fugitives, would have used images that on the literal level clash so drastically. There is also more than a little hint of Eliot here in the savage, dissecting objectivity of the description.

   Tate maintained, in the 1940s, when he looked back at *The Fugitive* period, that during this time Davidson "began to write poems that I think are still among his best."[18] It is easy to say why Tate felt this way: not only because the poems of his friend were coming much closer to his own preferences for poetic language and attitude, but because Davidson's best poems of this period have an objectivity about them, a self-sufficiency that does not depend on the preconceived sympathy of reader for poet and subject matter that is true of even Davidson's best later work. Davidson isn't invoking an attitude, but rendering an experience. The best of his poems of this period—"The Swinging Bridge," "Prelude in a Garden" (in which the influence of Ransom is most strong), "Swan and Exile," "Cross Section of a Landscape," "Not Long Green"—are, in this sense, the most formally accomplished work that Davidson was ever to do. His later work would be more rich, perhaps, and certainly more characteristic of his sensibility, but these short poems of the mid-1920s are not only more bold as poems, but they give a tantalizing glimpse of the kind of poet Davidson might have become had he continued along such lines of development.

There is room to consider only one such: "Not Long Green," which appeared in *The Fugitive* for June, 1925, and was subsequently reprinted, slightly revised, as "Apple and Mole." (I cite the revised version.)[19] The poem describes the incursion of a mole into a meadow where an apple tree tops a hill:

> For a high heavy time on the long green bough
> Hangs the apple of a summer that is shaken
> From its flat hot road to its apple-topped hill
> With the scraping of a mole that would awaken.

Though the summer seems long and endless, the mole is working away,

> Snuffling under grass and lusty clover
> With a sure blunt snout and capable paws
> Up the long green slope past the beeches and the haws
> For the summer must be shaken and over.

The apple hangs, ripe and heavy, but meanwhile the mole "is butting out a path, he is shoveling a furrow,/Till the tree will be aquiver feeling mole at the root," until at length the "root will be sapless and the twig will be dry . . . ." The summer is done, the seemingly endless reason of greenness is over,

> The apple is too old, it has worms at the core,
> And the long green summer will be green no more.
> The apple will fall and not awaken.

Over and beyond its primary and beautiful depiction of seasonal growth and death "Apple and Mole" is a powerful indictment, the rape of nature by a predatory inhabitant. Louise Cowan declares "long green" to be a pun, emphasized by its fourfold repetition in the poem;[20] whether or not this is so, the poem does suggest, the more so upon rereading, the intrusion of the commercial spirit into the rural garden; the mole "with a sure blunt snout and capable paws" would be materialistic avarice, the industrial ethos. The apple which will "fall and not awaken" is the fruit of the garden, and, one would assume, of the region. The blind mole, powerful, efficient, timeless, manages to bring down the tree which "is tall . . . . green"— and tallness is Davidson's favorite word for the old heroes.

Cowan remarks that the poem is that in which "Davidson's true poetic voice emerges, undistorted by attitudes foreign to his own talent"[21]—by which she means, I take it, that Davidson ceases to follow Tate's example insofar as the use of intensified, intellectual imagery and reference is involved, and that he no longer involves himself in any sort of self-conscious irony. But there is still an important respect in which Davidson continues, in this poem, to adhere to Tate's or Ransom's poetics. The poem is a contained unit; it is not a vehicle of expression for an attitude, but an artifact. No matter how intensely the man feels about what he is writing, as poet he has no emotion. He does not use the poem as forum for enunciating his views; rather, he uses the views as material for the poem. The power of the poem—and it is a very powerful lyric—comes in the vividness of Davidson's depiction of the mole, and in the use of mole, apple, tree, and meadow to show the self-destructive rhythm of the natural world. Davidson is intent on capturing this, and he builds up the sense of remorseless, accelerating fatality through skillful use of rhythm—anapest, dactyls, insertion of an entire extra line in the second stanza. The process culminates with the moment when the mole reaches the roots: "Till the tree will be aquiver feeling mole at the root"—a most adroit union of rhythm, meaning, and sound.

This is Davidson at his very best. His friend of later years, Robert Frost, would have been appreciative of what he did there. It is pastorale, southern style: and what makes it so effective is the way that the poem describes and by inference makes its point without explicit judgment. The thing is not done doctrinally, and nothing is forced either in the imagery or the conclusion to be drawn from it. We feel no sense of being manipulated; the conclusion is inescapable, and all the more powerful because of its seeming objectivity. When we end, we sense that there is more to it than a mole and an apple, so we read back over the lines, and the allegory becomes more pointed. There is no contrived interpretation; the deck is not stacked. It begins and ends as a poem about nature, and the poet accepts what he sees without moving in himself to take sides. This is what Davidson was capable of at this stage in his career. But instead of this kind of development going farther into deeper and richer exploration, it changes, and he abandons disinterested artistic observation, as it were, to enter the struggle. The immediate result is "The Tall Men." As we shall see, there is a gain involved, in the new range and scope that are thereby afforded. But there is also a loss.

Break-up of the Fugitives

It is because of the change that comes in Davidson's poems shortly after this lyric, I think, that Tate's departure from the Nashville scene for New York was a deprivation for Davidson most of all. Despite the continued correspondence between the two, Davidson lost the example, the encouragement, and the inspiriting force of the Fugitive who had most to teach him. Ransom's personality, his way of doing things, were too aloof and formal; for all their years of association, he and Davidson were never really intimate personal friends, so much as fellow workers. With Tate, the ties were much more intimate, and their gradual diminution, over the years, was a source of great sadness to Davidson.

The truth was that as Tate went to New York and entered the wider literary scene, and as his sophistication both in literary and general cultural matters grew apace, imperceptibly but steadily Davidson was left behind. We get hints of this all through their correspondence of the late 1920s, when Tate was writing from London and Paris, as in his cautionary remark in late 1929, cited earlier, when he pointed out that his own view of the value of *I'll Take My Stand* and the Agrarian enterprise was of a different sort than Davidson's; unlike Davidson he could not believe in any real practical outcome for the enterprise. Again, in December of 1929, we find Tate objecting to an article in which Davidson had attacked Hemingway's writing as "scientific ministration." Tate urged Davidson to take another look at Hemingway: "There is nothing scientific about Hemingway." Then he went on to make a point that he felt was crucial. "We must not get so lost in our vision of what novelists should do to the Southern scene that we reject the version of 'reality' given us by writers who are not Southern. In short, to do that is to commit provincialism at its least attractive level. . . . I don't think we can afford to give the opposition the slight-

est chance to say that we aren't as disinterested as to literature as any critics can possibly be. Shouldn't we keep the
two things distinct? Otherwise logic brings us back to
Thomas Nelson Page." [22]

Davidson admitted, in his reply, that there was justice
in what Tate had said. "I've felt for quite a while that I
was in danger of losing balance and becoming merely a
cantankerous localist, and your admonishment warms
my conscience to its task." [23] But for all his good intentions and his desire to please his friend, Davidson simply
could not permanently maintain the kind of distinction
that Tate as a literary man was insisting upon; his involvement in the idea of Agrarianism was so complete in
its manifestations that it came to dominate everything he
did and thought.

We can see the way this could work if we examine the
remarkable review of Theodore Dreiser's *An American
Tragedy* that Davidson wrote in his column "The Spyglass"
for the Nashville *Tennessean*'s book page on January 31,
1926. Davidson was bowled over by Dreiser's novel. "It is
a complete presentation, methodical, unsparing, and yet
somehow tender and pitying, of a being who could perhaps exist in this time in no land but America, yet who is
so fully and poignantly imagined that he partakes of universality," he declared. He found *An American Tragedy*
"an overwhelming book; a book convincing, terrible, and
true; a book that tears you away from whatever you are
doing and incorporates you into itself, a massive and pitiful document of human verity; a book from which may
be gained, as from George Eliot's *Romola*, an overpower-
ing sense of the reality of evil. . . . What is there, I ask
myself, that this man Dreiser does not know about human
beings?" And Davidson sees the universality of Dreiser's
vision, to its relevance for "all of us poor puzzled creatures, born willy-nilly into a world we do not understand
and forced to leave it before we have really had a chance
to understand it, not always perhaps like Clyde Griffiths,

with innocent blood on our hand, but certainly, like him, finding it terrifying difficult to adjust ourselves and our fine dreams to all its complex forces."[24]

That was Davidson's first, open, unqualified response. But within two months' time, reviewing T. S. Stribling's *Teeftallow*, he is saying of Stribling's character that "he has not even the dignity of ambition and consuming passion that somewhat dignify that other worm of modern American fiction, Dreiser's Clyde Griffiths."[25] Stribling has written a novel in which life in Tennessee is portrayed unfavorably, and Davidson objects to the negativism of the portrait; since Dreiser also portrayed life in dreary terms, he therefore uses Dreiser to attack the viewpoint. Dreiser's fiction, which had made so powerful an impact upon Davidson, now becomes the victim of a theory about the proper approach to the portrayal of regional life, and is thereafter denounced for what it represents as subject matter, rather than for what it is as art. Thus he concludes his 1935 essay on "Regionalism and Nationalism in American Literature" with the plea that we must not be deluded "into thinking that a novel about a ploughboy is only a regional curiosity, but a novel about a bellboy, a national masterpiece"[26]—a novel that when he first read it had touched him so deeply is now only an example of metropolitan debasement of taste. It is not that Davidson has contradicted himself; rather, he has allowed his Agrarian concerns to override his literary judgment, so that he ends up denigrating the value of what, as a reviewer with no ideological ax to grind, he had earlier found quite universal and powerful.

Davidson's involvement in the southern situation, which upon the commencement of *I'll Take My Stand* would become a lifelong preoccupation, was stimulated by the Scopes trial. Curiously enough, his immediate public responses were surprisingly mild. He wrote a piece for the *Saturday Review of Literature* for May 15, 1926, on "The Artist as Southerner," in which he surveyed the southern literary scene, discoursed on the difficulty the serious contemporary writer finds in using southern materials, insisted that there was much light as well as darkness about the contemporary southern scene, praised Edwin Mims's recently published *The Advancing South* for its depiction of the contrasts in progressivism and reaction existing in the South, and suggested that the southern artist might attempt to make use of the positive aspects of his regional heritage. "Fundamentalism, in one aspect, is blind and belligerent ignorance," he wrote; "in another, it represents a fierce clinging to poetic supernaturalism against the encroachments of cold logic; it stands for moral seriousness. The Southerner should hesitate to scorn these qualities, for, however much they may now be perverted to bigoted and unfruitful uses, they belong to the bone and sinew of his nature as they once belonged to Milton, who was both Puritan and Cavalier." And he closed by urging the southern writer "to remain in his own country and fight the battle out. For it may be his privilege to discover, in himself and in his art, something of the bold and inclusive American character that Whitman celebrated in prophecy."[27] This was hardly written with the ferocity with which Davidson would later champion the cause of the South against the metropolis, though all the themes are there. He was still feeling his way; the important thing, however, was that events in Dayton, Tennessee, and elsewhere had gotten him to thinking seriously about himself as a Southerner, and to examining his relationship to the place of his birth and his residence.

In another essay, "First Fruits of Dayton: The Intellectual Evolution in Dixie," published in *The Forum* for June, 1928, Davidson was still adhering publicly to a moderate line. Noting the ridicule and anathema heaped upon the South during and after the Scopes trial, he insisted that there was nothing monolithic about the South, and that it contained a progressive as well as a reactionary direction. "We may take comfort in the creation—or re-creation of

Duke University, with its endowment of millions," he declared. "We may recall that Chancellor Kirkland's answer to the Dayton episode was to build new laboratories on the Vanderbilt campus. We may rejoice in the press, the *Journal of Social Sciences* [*sic*], the notable activities of the University of North Carolina. . . . Anti-evolution statutes are straw barriers against a great wind."

Davidson conceded that the South was not only making progress, but was going to have progress forced upon it. He urged the South to be careful, deliberate, however, to choose only "that ideal of progress" that "affirms and does not destroy the local individuality and true characteristics of the South." There was never a time, he said, "when the South needed its provincialism more—if by provincialism is meant its heritage of individual character, the whole bundle of ways that make the South Southern."

If the South adopted northern ways blindly, then "what problems are to be visited upon the South, what strikes, agitations, nervous retchings of society, wage slavery, graft, mountebankery, idiocies of merchant princes?" He declared that "to make Charleston over into the precise image of Pittsburgh would be a worse crime than the Dayton crime." And, warming to his task toward the end, he asserted that "Those who advocate progress without any positive regard for the genius of the South may presently find themselves in the unenviable company of the carpet-baggers and scalawags of the first reconstruction. They shall be as persons without a country—barren and importunate exiles—dwelling in a land that loves them not, that they have helped to kill." He wanted the progress of the South "to be organic. . . . And as growth means improvement of what you have, not mere addition or change, the first step toward progress is for the South to turn back upon itself, to rediscover itself, to examine its ideals, to evaluate the past with reference to the present, and the present with reference to the past."[28]

To those familiar with the Davidson of *I'll Take My*

Stand and afterward, this seems mild doctrine. In letters
to Tate he had been expressing himself far more strongly
on the subject. But it might be remembered that to break
publicly, as Davidson and his friends did, with the general progressive meliorism of the period was not a step to
be taken casually. Certainly it was not enlightened self-
interest, at the Vanderbilt of Chancellor Kirkland and
Edwin Mims, to defend the fundamentalist side of the
Dayton controversy even obliquely, as Davidson and
Ransom were doing. Tate, in New York, might speak his
mind as he saw fit; he had no institutional dependence,
and desired none. Davidson was not nearly so much the
free agent.

Tate recognized this clearly when he wrote to Davidson in 1927 about their plans, just getting under way
then, for the enterprise that would ultimately result in *I'll
Take My Stand*: "as I somewhat fiercely told John [Ran-
som], it seems to me that your willingness to oppose the
New South carries with it a willingness to lose your jobs."[29]
Edwin Mims would not be especially pleased with having
his poet-professors come down even philosophically on
the side of what seemed to him just that reactionary impulse in the South that he and the New South liberals
had been struggling against all their lives. And Mims ran
the Vanderbilt English Department as he saw fit; he was
not exactly a meliorist when it came to that. Ransom and
Davidson knew very well that for all their growing renown as poets, they would be no match for Mims if the
battle lines were drawn in university power politics, and
that Kirkland, who though originally a professor of English had never paid any heed to the putative needs of
poets and had not even bothered to subscribe to *The Fugitive* when invited to do so, would stand behind Mims.

Tate had early run afoul of Mims; in the brashness of
youth he had not scrupled as an undergraduate to make
known his contempt for Mims's Victorian approach to
the cultivation of the muse, and Mims had responded,

using his vastly superior arsenal to keep the arrogant young bard in his place. Tate's failure to get the fellowship that would have enabled him to pursue graduate study at Vanderbilt was generally thought by his friends to have been Mims's doing, and later on Tate found out that Mims had even used his influence in efforts to block later opportunities that he had sought elsewhere. And Tate had replied in kind, in the only way he could: he had dealt Mims a backhanded compliment and registered his scorn for his critical limitations in his essay "Last Days of the Charming Lady," in *The Nation*.[30]

Ransom and Davidson, who had roots in Nashville and who were temperamentally unsuited to the kind of uncertain financial existence that Tate had elected when he set out to make his way in the literary marketplace, were understandably reluctant to make the overt break with Mims or with Mims's political and social views concerning the South, which they must have realized was eventually coming. And it must be pointed out, too, that they felt some personal loyalty to Mims; he had, after all, employed them and advanced them in rank, and had, if very much on his own terms, made a place for poets on his faculty at a time when few English departments went in for keeping working poets on the premises.

The breakup of the old Fugitive organization in 1924 and 1925—though the group continued occasionally to convene after the magazine was discontinued in 1925, the allegiance was never the same—had affected Ransom and Davidson with a severity that it had not done for Tate, who by this time was getting established in New York literary circles and did not depend on the magazine for an outlet for his verse or upon the association for his literary identity. Ransom talked increasingly of leaving Nashville, though it would be ten years before he did, and then only after the Agrarian enterprise had all but foundered. Davidson was unhappy with his situation; he edited the Nashville *Tennessean's* book page and taught his classes, and felt that he did not have the time to do his writing. Theresa Davidson, who had a law degree, was earning a respectable salary at the Vanderbilt University Law School, but saw little chance of ever making a place for herself as a practicing attorney in Nashville.

After *The Fugitive* was discontinued, there was considerable discussion about attempting to set up a Nashville poetry society. Ransom and certain others of the Fugitives took the idea very seriously, and meetings of the old Fugitive group were filled with much disputation and wrangling. I have been unable to find out just what this society was to do, but to judge from Davidson's letters to Tate it was apparently to be something more than a mere poetry society, and Ransom seems to have been much involved in the planning. Davidson was quite skeptical; such issues as public participation, the relationship of such a venture to the old Fugitive group and to southern literature and the like were involved. "You can see," he wrote to Tate, "that I have gradually gotten into the role of the Opposition among the Fugitives. Since you left, and since Stanley [Johnson] adopted the role of Ishmael and went to live on the Cumberland, there has been nobody to create a disturbance except me. And when it comes to an oral argument, I make a feeble showing; it's hard for me to make out a case."[31]

The truth is that Davidson in the period 1925–1926 was at a crossroads in his career. As the Fugitive enterprise had developed, he had been drawn more and more toward Tate's position, and closer toward modernism in verse. Tate's departure for New York had served at first to accentuate this tendency; Davidson's poetry, as we have seen, had grown increasingly contemporary in idiom and attitude. He missed Tate's presence very much. He wanted and needed the kind of group commitment, the communal enterprise, that the Fugitive relationship and publication of the magazine had provided, and which was no longer forthcoming. His discontent and sense of drifting came to a head with the dispute over the proposed poetry society. "I am disgusted with myself for getting upset over so small a matter, but it is annoying beyond words," he wrote to Tate.[32] In truth it was no small matter for him, for it symbolized the unanchored nature of his position.

Tate, in New York, recognized what was going on with his friend. When Davidson had first written to him about the way things were going, he had responded with a letter (November 26, 1925) that expressed the issue very clearly.[33] He agreed with Davidson's suspicion of the proposed poetry society, and he felt that the preoccupation of his former Fugitive colleagues with such matters was emblematic of an unstable and highly contrived intellectual and social situation, full of petty tensions and false issues, in which they were so involved that they could no longer see the real world as it actually existed. He told Davidson that "you build up defenses for this artificial world in a desperate attempt to make it a reality, and all the time the real world not only passes you by but you automatically oppose it and contemn it a little." For his part, he said, he was determined "not to be misled into an acceptance of false issues in which life becomes dully insufferable to the participant and a little ridiculous to the observer."

What he was telling Davidson in effect was that if he wished to continue to develop as a contemporary poet he had better think long and hard about getting out of Nashville and away from Vanderbilt. Davidson was "one of the best friends" he had ever had, he told him, but he was convinced that "our roles are being interchanged by necessity, and I am about to be Mentor. You are wiser in the expedient details of life; but I'm damned if you're very farsighted." There was an atmosphere of defeatism in the Fugitive venture, he said; all the group, including himself, had tended to use poetry as a way of warding off the confusion and stress of the everyday world, by adopt-

ing the pose of the sensitive soul. If Ransom and Davidson and their friends thought that by establishing a poetry society that would protect the values of poetry and
art in Nashville, they could reform the commonwealth,
they were sorely mistaken. "I remember John once alluded to those persons who escaped common American life by running off to Washington Square!" he said.
"Well, if John is living common American life why is his
subject-matter a melange of Church, State, Kings, romantic maidens, all heaved up in an intellectual sigh!"

He suggested to Davidson that he might be able to get
him a job teaching at Columbia University. The Columbia English faculty wasn't made up of pedants, he declared; "they actually want men who are capable of something outside the academic routine, and they have many
of that sort. In short, if you are interested I'll talk about it
to certain acquaintances of mine; the first person I'll see
will be Mark Van Doren, who already knows of you very
pleasantly. New York isn't a paradise; but once you left
your classroom, your life would be your own, whether
for dipsomania or haircloth shirts and ashes. For I very
much suspect that you would find character and not code
to be the prevailing criterion."

It was upon receipt of this letter that Davidson unbur-
dened himself about his situation in Nashville. It "*is* really
horrifying," he replied. He described his revulsion at the
local wrangling. He would very much like to have Tate
get him an opportunity to leave Nashville and join the
Columbia faculty, he said—*if* he would not have to make
a great financial sacrifice. "I am restless, and all the more
because I feel that I'm caught in a blind alley," he said.
"And this is true even though I should really prefer to stay
in the South, if only I were financially independent."[34]
Ransom, he said, was planning to take a job in the East,
too.

An odd business, truly. Here, only a few years before
the three men were to take the lead in the proclamation

of the Agrarian manifesto, calling upon the South to turn away from the industrial society and forsake the metropolitan ethos, Allen Tate was promising Donald Davidson that he would help to find him a teaching job in New York City, while John Crowe Ransom was meditating a move to the Northeast. Within a few years Tate himself would be headed back south to Clarksville, Tennessee, and Ransom and Davidson would be hard at work turning Vanderbilt into a veritable citadel of intellectual resistance to eastern values.

What might have happened, one may well wonder, if Davidson had pursued Tate's suggestion and accepted a teaching position in the Northeast? It is difficult to say. Given his considerable gift for the music of poetry, it is possible that if he had continued along the lines of the exploratory modernism that he was developing in 1924 and 1925, his place in the history of American poetry might have been very different, and perhaps more important, than it turned out to be. In moving to the Tennessee material, as he did soon afterward, Davidson largely ceased to use the form of poetry as a vehicle for self-examination and began using it to celebrate a predetermined intellectual and social position, with the result that though his advocacy and evocation of that position was often eloquent and powerful indeed, his language thereafter lacked the element of tension between self and society, public and private identity, tradition and modern circumstance, that made for the creative resolution of poetry such as Tate's and Ransom's. The turn to Agrarianism for Davidson was not merely the discovery of a theme; it was also, and to the ultimate disadvantage of his poetry, the move from dialectic to rhetoric, from—to use Yeats's formulation—the quarrel with oneself to the quarrel with others. From this point onward in his career, Davidson largely ceased to explore the nature of his personal relationship to what he publicly believed in, and began to define himself rhetorically in accordance with such belief.

But the question is not only unanswerable; it is, in retrospect, irrelevant. One cannot really imagine Donald Davidson cutting loose from Vanderbilt and Nashville, for all his unhappiness with the way things were going after *The Fugitive* came to an end. For one thing, the reservation he expressed to Tate in answer to his friend's offer to look for a place for him at Columbia—that he could not afford any reduction in family income—is significant. The hard times that Davidson had known as a youth, the straitened circumstances that forced him to give up college for several years, and upon his return to Vanderbilt continue full-time teaching while he completed his classes, had left their mark on him. All his life he felt financially insecure, and was almost constantly engaged in various projects to supplement his academic income. And to do his work Davidson very much required the social context of a known and assured community identity; to cut himself loose from his accustomed moorings, as Tate had done, and to seek his future as a writer in the vast, impersonal life of the metropolis, was hardly for him. However much, in the year 1925, he may have come to feel isolated and alienated from his friends in Nashville, his life and his work remained bound in with his relationship to his community in a thousand ways that he himself did not perhaps realize. What he really desired was not a complete break with Nashville and the South, but a way whereby he could view that identity as intellectually and emotionally creative and respectable, and thus overcome the self-doubts he was feeling about it.

This was what the idea of Agrarianism, once it was sufficiently articulated, could and did offer him, and we are not surprised that when once the southern project began, Davidson fell thoroughly in with it and championed it with an enthusiasm that was without reservation and entirely whole-souled. Here was a way to *act*; here was a cause in which one could *believe*; and during the years from 1926–1927 onward, Davidson's response grew in conviction and in passion. The more specific the plan of action became, the more programmatical and articulated the group's strategy and tactics, the greater was Davidson's satisfaction. He responded to the letter Tate wrote him from abroad setting forth a detailed program for their venture, with the same unfeigned kind of joy that he had earlier displayed on the occasion when the Fugitives had agreed to publish a poetry magazine. *His* friends were doing this. They were acting together, in concert. He desired nothing better than to have the men he most admired working with him on a cause that all believed in. Modest to a fault, he happily subordinated his own interests to those of the group endeavor, marveled at the virtuosity of his friends, felt himself privileged to be united with them. Not for him the philosophical reservations and ironic qualifications of some of the others, the pragmatic skepticism of the ultimate worth of the great endeavor; it was enough for him to have a goal and be striving with good friends toward its achievement.

The Tall Men

In March of 1926 Davidson sent Tate copies of some new poems, among them "Fire on Belmont Street" and "The Long Street." The first-named eventually became the final poem of *The Tall Men*.[35] With this poem, which won the Southern Prize of the Poetry Society at South Carolina for 1926, Davidson moved authoritatively into the mode that would dominate his poetry for the rest of his career. It is dramatic, it is in blank verse, and its language is the intensified diction of everyday speech, with little of the wordplay and imagic ambivalence of Ransom's and Tate's verse. It deals with the Tennessee scene, posits the heroic past against the mundane present, and is designed

as a rebuke to the moderns for their failure to live up
to the ideals and achievements of their forebears. The
poem begins with a modern day Nashville businessman,
alarmed because there is a fire on the street on which he
lives:

> He was a worthy citizen of the town.
> "Where is the fire?" he babbled as he ran.
> "The fire! The fire!" Spat between pursy breaths
> He dropped his question, stuck his gross right hand
> Against his watch-chain, ran, and stared, and sobbed,
> *Out Belmont Street? My God, that's where I live!* (179)

Distraught because his house may be in danger, he
hurries, bereft of dignity and without thought of anything except his own self-interest, in frantic alarm at the
prospect of disaster. Others seem to join him—"blobs of
heels/Pecking the night with hurry." The speaker joins
in the rush, but though "clamorous/As all the plump
mad mob, shouting like them," his alarm is not for the
burning house, but for the peril from within the city that
threatens to destroy it. The city is in no danger from
without—there is no natural catastrophe imminent; no
dragon has emerged from an old sewer; the ghosts of the
Indians slain by the pioneer ancestors of the citizenry
have not "Come back with devil-medicine to bombard/
Your bungalows." (179) Rather, the fire is the wrath of
heaven at the urban industrial wasteland that the modern citizenry have made:

> Why God has come alive
> To damn you all, or else the smoke and soot
> Have turned back to live coals again for shame
> On this gray city, blinded, soiled, and kicked
> By fat blind fools.

The modern metropolis, grimy and gray from the smoke
of its factories, morally blind in its complacency and materialism, is what is wrong; the fire, the danger come
from what it and its people have become. "The city's
burning up?/Why, good! Then let her burn!" (180)

Yet even though the narrator had joined in the first precipitate flight of the citizenry, he is not really a participant in the public panic. God has come alive to damn *you all*, not *us*. As far as he is concerned, the city might just as well be consumed by flame, so corrupt has it become.

The narrator, unlike the citizenry, sees what is happening in racial perspective. He recalls an incident in ancient Anglo-Saxon history, from the Finnsburg Fragment, in which King Hnaef and his sixty Danish warriors, having gained the palace of the Finns, hold it against the enemy. These warriors, remote ancestors of the Tall Men who settled Tennessee,

> Surrounded were, yet held the door and died
> While the strange light of swords and helmets made
> The place like day.

But what shall their modern descendants do, who would hold the door shut against

> the press
> Of brazen muscles? Who can conquer wheels
> Gigantically coiled with mass of iron
> Against frail human fingers? (180)

The enemy the Tennesseans face now is not a hostile army, but the age of the machine, the pressure of materialistic industrial society which would strip the land of its beauty, create a wasteland of asphalt and concrete and steel, and rob the people of the old heritage of individuality and resourcefulness. The fire that threatens the citizenry is

> invisible fire that feeds
> On your quick brains, your beds, your homes, your steeples,
> Fire in your sons' brains and in your daughters',
> Fire like a dream of Hell in all your world.

What the citizenry must do is to flee from the artificial, materialistic kind of world, go back to the natural world their forefathers inhabited, "Fly from the wrath of fire to the hills / Where water is and the slow peace of time"

(181). They must regain their heritage, reclaim their country and land, look beneath the artificiality of urban society to the enduring earth they inherited and are in imminent danger of losing.

The poet then recalls a "place where beech-trees droop their boughs/Down-slanting, and where the dark cedars grow/With stubborn roots . . ." There, he recalls, his father had once said

> Pointing a low mound out to me: 'My son,
> Stand on this Indian's grave and plainly ask,
> *Indian, what did you die for?* And he'll say,
> *Nothing!* (181)

The Indians whose land it was before the white settlers had dispossessed them have indeed died for nothing, if the land is now "Waxing in steel and stone, nursing the fire/That eats and blackens . . ." The sacrifice made for the land, the blood shed by redmen and by whites, can have no meaning if the soil is to be used only for the rootless, materialistic urban society of the modern city. The poet urges his fellow Tennesseans to remember

> Hnaef and his sixty warriors
> Greedy for battle-joy. Remember the rifles
> Talking men's talk into the Tennessee darkness
> And the long-haired hunters watching the Tennessee hills
> In the land of big rivers for something. (181)

The statement is unequivocal, without ironic qualification of any sort: the modern-day inhabitants of Nashville can restore meaning and purpose to their lives, escape the contemporary wasteland of the city, only if they reclaim their heritage, and move to make themselves worthy of the land their forebears dared their all to settle.

Clearly "Fire on Belmont Street," and the other sequences of the poem of which it became the epilogue, represent a definitive turn in Davidson's art. The poem is at the opposite pole from Davidson's friend Tate's "Ode to the Confederate Dead," written at about the same time.

Tate's poem was told from the point of view of the modern, who is separated from his heritage and examines, from the cemetery gate, the enormous distance between himself and the "arrogant circumstance" of the older time of the dead soldiers. One recalls Davidson's objection to Tate's poem: "And where, O Allen Tate, are the dead?" The point of Tate's poem was just that: the extreme difficulty of recovering them. Davidson's speaker, though a resident of the modern-day city, encounters no such difficulty: not only can he summon up the spirit of the Tall Men who slew the Indians and captured Tennessee, but he can go back to the earliest recorded records of the race and envision himself and his fellow Tennesseans as facing the same challenge as the Danes who fought at Finnsburg. The ancient warriors who were their forebears had held the doors against the Finns; now the modern Tennesseans must hold off the impersonal industrial might of the machine. The peril is within; the way to throw it off is to return to the old virtues, to "the hills/ Where water is and the slow peace of time." Davidson's persona, though he joins in the general clamor, is not really part of it; the worthy "citizen of the town" is depicted most unfavorably, as harried, out of breath, obese, slow afoot—"God has come alive/To damn you all . . ." By contrast, in Tate's poem the modern southerner uses the first person plural—". . . we who count our days and bow/Our heads with a commemorial woe/In the ribboned coats of grim felicity . . ."

To his own satisfaction if not to Tate's, Davidson had resolved the problem of identity. Having written "Fire on Belmont Street" and "The Long Street," he was at work with increasing assurance, as he wrote to Tate, on "a closely related group or scheme of poems which I am gradually building up. These will, in a roughly unified way, present what I intend to be a fairly complex portrait of a person (say myself) definitely located in Tennessee, sensitive to what is going on as well as what has gone on for some hundreds of years." Note the phrase "definitely located in Tennessee": the doubt and the restlessness of the previous year were ended, Davidson was sure now that Tennessee was where he belonged, and so now he undertook to characterize his life and his experience in terms of that identification.

He called his poem "The Long Street"; when published in 1927 it was titled *The Tall Men*.* The opening poem, "Prologue: The Long Street," presents the contemporary scene, the poet in the city, "Pacing the long street where is no summer/But only burning summer—looking for spring/That is not . . ." (116) In the city the seasons are remote, life is purposeless. "Steel answers steel. Dust whirls./Skulls hurry past with the pale flesh yet clinging/And a little hair." This is Davidson's contemporary wasteland, and there are strong echoes of Eliot's. What meaning, he asks, is there in the city of the present, "How shall we meet again . . ." (116)

For answer—and for Davidson there *is* an answer; his wasteland, he is confident, can indeed be reinvigorated—he turns back to the past. "The Tall Men," the first poem, looks back at the pioneers who settled the land. "In twos and threes the tall men/Strode in the valleys. Their palisades were pitched/In the Cumberland hills." They knew their business, and they molded bullets "for words that said: 'Give way, Red Man./You have lived long enough. . . .'" Thus they came across the mountains, settled the land, and began the process that has now "left me here/Flung up from sleep against the breakfast table/Like numb and helpless driftwood." (118)

The modern Tennessean, a prisoner of the city, rides to his job on a trolley car and works in an office where a northern business associate asks him why it is that "you Tennesseans" are so tall. For answer the poet tells of the

* I shall use the version first published in *Lee in the Mountains and Other Poems* (1949), rather than the 1927 text, for my commentary. Page references are to *Poems 1922–1961*, and are given parenthetically.

Indian-fighting past, and of one McCrory who stood sentinel at night guarding against Indian attack. There follows a description of the onslaught and of its repulse.

The poet recalls certain Tall Men who once lived on the land: John Sevier, Andrew Jackson, Davy Crockett, and of how unhappy they would be with what has happened to their land and its people. He thinks mournfully that "I was not there" at the battles they fought, whether against Indians or British. "I have not sung/Old songs or danced old tunes. I have read a book." (124) His lot is the city, with its mass transportation, its creature comforts, its mechanical conveniences. He is separated from his tradition by the years.

But though at this point the poem might seem to be moving close to the situation of Tate's "Confederate Ode," in actuality the similarity is only apparent. Davidson's modern speaker is not really cut off from the past; rather, he is out of place in the present, and infinitely prefers the values of the past, and he seems to blame his present unsatisfactory circumstance not on the fact that *he* is a modern, but on the historical and social circumstances that force him to play so false a *role*. His heart is with the men of the old time; he views the present from their vantage point, and with their values.

Clearly this is a very different affair from Tate's watcher at the cemetery gate, who envies the men of the old time their capacity for belief and action, but cannot view experience in such fashion himself. The truth is that Davidson's poem is basically pastoral in mode—the rebuke of the complex present through depiction of the simpler, more heroic past—while the mode of Tate's is participatory and confessional, written to show and share the anguish of the complex present. One can understand why Tate, in encouraging Davidson to work ahead on his poem, said that he himself "couldn't even begin it; Ransom probably has too much of the same poison in his system as I have to do it." But as one reads on in Tate's letter to his friend about *The Tall Men*, it is clear that Tate had serious reservations about the whole enterprise. He felt that Davidson was attempting a poem in the grand style when Davidson did not really, as a poet, believe in it himself. "I am convinced," he wrote Davidson, "that Milton himself could not write a Paradise Lost now."[36]

As a modern man, Davidson, he felt, could not believe in the unqualified accessibility of the past in the way that he was attempting to present it in his poem. Thus in order to present it as he was doing, Davidson was having to oversimplify, to assert in rhetoric what privately he was not nearly so convinced about; he was having to leave out too much that he knew. "Minds are less important for literature than cultures," Tate wrote him: "our minds are as good as they ever were, but our culture is dissolving. . . . You can't escape it even in Tennessee!" Davidson, he said, was attempting to *create* a theme, and that was impossible: "Themes are or are not available. . . . You can't put your epic of Tennessee into the minds of Tennesseans; the precondition of your writing is that it must (in an equivalent of spiritual intensity) be there." Davidson's poem was *thin*—its texture did not embody life, but only a rhetorical marshaling of evidence: "you are attempting to envisage an experience of the first order with a symbolism of a lower order: you are trying to write a history of your mind, but your mind is not so simple as you think; it cannot be so homogenously accounted for as your schematism would lead one to believe. At the present moment you represent the convergence of forces that will not be adequately represented by reference to a Tennessee history, and the result is thinness; the symbols seem trivial."[37]

Davidson could not accept Tate's critique. Conceding its relevance, he insisted that Tate's reservations "indicate difficulties, perhaps, that can be ironed out." He was *not* writing an epic for Tennesseans, he declared; "Good lord, surely not an epic . . . ." Rather he was, just as Tate said, composing a "history of a mind—my mind, to an extent—and therefore I come within your requirement of subjectivity for modern poetry."[38] But as we shall see, Tate was closer to the mark than Davidson was willing to concede.

Having begun with memories of the pioneer days, Davidson's poem proceeds to recapitulate the historical experience of a Tennessean. In the second section, "The Sod of Battlefields," a modern city dweller goes motoring among the Civil War battlefields about Nashville. There are still veterans of those campaigns alive, old men

> who creep to the sun
> In the winter of a time that heeds them not.
> They are the proof of ancient differences
> Not yet committed to the grave. They warm
> Their bones with names that are not names to them
> But panoplied moments . . . (126)

He recalls tales told to him by his grandmother, about the time when the Yankees came, and of how three local boys were executed as spies. But now those memories grow faint. He uses for refrain the Civil War song: "*And the years creep slowly by, Lorena.*" Nowadays pneumonia, not bullets, threatens Lee's army.

> The Union is saved. Lee has surrendered forever.
> Today, Lorena, it is forbidden to be
> A Southerner. One is American now;
> Propounds the pig's conception of the state—
> The constitution of, by, for the pig—(131)

But life goes on, with movies and Sunday drives, and the moderns do not remember. But he does: "But have I forgotten these/Cool scouts, hidden in a wild-plum thicket,/ Once in an autumn dusk near Ewell's Farm . . ." (131) Has he forgotten the men who fought at Franklin, those who suffered defeat under Hood at Nashville—"The withered army, the slow retreat, the rain/Fallen on huddled shoulders?" The question is rhetorical; his body, that of a Tennessean, is "woven from dead and living . . . Broken but never tamed, risen from the bloody sod/Walking suddenly alive in a new morning." (132) The historical identity for which Tate's watcher at the cemetery gate sought vainly is achieved through the act of memory. But it is achieved at the expense of divorcing his sympathies entirely from the circumstance of those other moderns who like himself motor about the battlefield, and who live in the urban community that he too inhabits.

In the next section, "Geography of the Brain," Davidson describes the modern man, brain disembodied from living flesh, existing and earning his living in the urban metropolis, dependent upon machines and on the products of world trade, until the brain "grows aghast/To hunch in tailored robes of state alone," dismisses the things that surround it,

> summons up
> The map of all its native circumstance,
> And suddenly it is attended, it is alive. (134)

The man thinks of his origins, the past that is part of his identity. We have a description of a farm in rural Tennessee, close to the wilderness, and then a song to the dignity of farm labor, with memories of white and black men at work in the fields. He recalls a time when his father would tell him stories about his grandfather, about country life, with fiddlers and corn-shucking days. There was his great-grandfather, "neat with beard and white moustache," who kept thoroughbred horses, and was himself "a thoroughbred/And kept slaves." But his father prefers to tell him "About Julius Caesar or Captain John Smith or read/Out of Plutarch's Lives," (137) and sing him some of the old songs and ballads. His father recalls the days of the Ku Klux, too. Then the poet remembers the old black woman who worked for them, and who told him a story about a ghost (a variation of Mark Twain's famous "Golden Arm" tale).

This leads the poet to take up the matter of race relations. "Black man, when you and I were young together,/

We knew each other's hearts," he declares. The poet is no longer a child, and you "perhaps unfortunately/Are no longer a child," but they still understand each other "Better maybe than others." An ancient wall lies between them; men say it once might have been crossed. "But now I cannot/Forget that I was master, and you can hardly/Forget that you were slave." The two of them did not build the wall, but "there it painfully is./Let us not bruise our foreheads on the wall." (140) This is Davidson's only direct reference to that aspect of the Tennessee heritage that involves white-black relations. It is moderate enough for the year when it was written, and hardly presages Davidson's own determined public effort to marshal southern opposition to school desegregation a quarter-century later. Still, it represents, as does nothing that Tate, Ransom, or Warren were writing in verse at the time, the direct assertion that the matter of his Tennessee heritage is specifically bound up with the advocacy of the traditional southern racial beliefs. The essential difference between this passage in Davidson's poem and lines such as those in Tate's "Message from Abroad" in which the image of the Virginia planter is seen, "His shadow gliding, a long nigger/Gliding at his feet"[39] is that where Tate depicts race as part of the complex heritage of guilt and achievement that is his birthright as a southerner, Davidson expresses his position programatically: he does not accept it, so much as take his political and social stand on it.

The section continues with a depiction of the elements of romance in the southern tradition, and concludes with the assertion that the history and the rural life of Tennessee are part of his being, existing as elements of his personality today,

> Steady within the modern brain which draws
> Attendants grim or beautiful together,
> Asking of motley splendor out of the past
> A stubborn unity of courage, only
> A wall against confusions of this night. (142)

The fourth long poem of the sequence, "The Faring," is perhaps the most readable of all. It is narrative, describing the call to the colors in 1917, in which the Tennesseans, having fared westward across the ocean in earlier days, now voyage eastward again, back to the place of their Saxon and Norman heritage. There is a magnificent description of the troopship packed with soldiers, sailing from New York. The tall soldiers crowd the railings watching:

> They saw the immense
> Vertical lift of the piled buildings sway and whirl
>   as the ship
> Wheeled in the harbor, nosed and let loose by tugs,
> Saw the wisps of white on packed ferryboats and people,
> Looking with farewell motions. They saw the sun
> Dropping behind New York. (144)

Arrived in England, they are objects of curiosity. Someone notes the divisional insignia:

> "Why, what's that on your sleeve?"
>   "A wildcat, sonny,
> To scratch the Germans' eyes out."
>   (A wildcat snarling
> Emblem of western mountains where tall men strode
> Once with long rifles. The Decherd rifles are clipped
> To a neater weapon. The faces are unchanged.) (145)

They cross over the English Channel to France, and move along roads where the Roman legions marched and Napoleon galloped. Now "The husky guns/Rumbled at twilight from the Western Front," (146) and the Tennesseans are ready for battle.

There follows a marvelously vivid action sequence, portraying the preparations for battle. The Tennesseans are posted to guard against an enemy assault. Again one McCrory, who in the poem earlier had stood sentinel against Indian attack in the wilderness, watches in the night. An artillery barrage explodes, McCrory shouts *"Down, down, you men,"* (149) fires the flare pistol that

gives the alarm to the battery guns, then sees the enemy
coming on, summons the troops up from the dugout,
and the tall men repel the German attack, in much the
same fashion as against the Indians a century earlier. Afterward the armistice ends the fighting, the living soldiers speak one after another of what they have seen and
done, and after them the dead; and at last the tall men
come home, landing in Charleston,

> And June beats hot on spacious trains—we are going
> Home through a landscape strange. We had never known
> It was like this. Trees . . . earth . . . sky. (156)

The poem that follows, "Conversation in a Bedroom,"
is mostly satire; tossing restlessly as he seeks sleep, the
speaker imagines himself tempted by the devil, offered a
Faustian compact, and is shown the beauties of post-war
American life that can be his if he will sell his soul. Davidson satirizes aesthetes, snobs, wealthy dilettantes, cultists,
expatriates, Anglophiliacs, devotees of primitivism, flap-
pers, intellectuals—there is a bitter portrait of T. S. Eliot
as defeatist worshipper of despair, and so on. None of
this is particularly convincing, for it is all done with such
withering contempt that it is difficult to take the modern
scene seriously. Davidson will not concede any virtue to
modern culture; he is not tempted by it in the slightest.
His depiction of the lions of the literary life in the metropolis is far different from the way that such things appeared to him barely two years earlier, when Tate had
offered to find a teaching post for him at Columbia University.

Davidson seems to have attempted to externalize everything that was wrong with the cultural attitude of the
1920s—as if he himself were of another age and time
and had no stake in modern attitudes. When Tate would
have fought it out in the poem, Davidson already knows
what he thinks. Thus the devil's temptation cannot be
made very tempting, and so the poem lacks excitement.

The whole modern wasteland is rejected, as dawn comes and opens the prospects of renewed life.

The next section, "The Breaking Mold," constitutes a look at the speaker's religious past: the northern European pagan origins, the Christianization of the Goths, the Reformation, the defeat of the Scotch Highlanders at Culloden, the flight to America, the evangelical Protestantism of the frontier. Davidson deals with the nature of his belief in God, which he cannot equate with orthodox, revealed Christianity:

> It is
> My soul that will not be contained in the dead
> Plaster that other hands have made. It is cramped
> And like a child within the womb it must
> Be gone from that which gave it life. It rends,
> It cleaves its way, and there is agony. (170)

He is, he says, three men. One is the pagan northerner who wonders where his sword, hound, charger, ashen spear, the throng of men feasting in the smoky hall have gone. What is he doing as Christian believer?

> Who gave me over to Hebrews?
> After a thousand years I have not learned
> The voice of the Hebrew God or the Hebrew way. (171)

The second man is a Methodist: "the hymns of country choirs haunt my tongue." The Ten Commandments, the remembered words of preachers regulate his conduct. "The words of God are written in the Book/Which I will keep beloved though earth may speak/A different language unto those who read her." The third man is one who lives in the world, "content to know what things do/Or can be made to do." No enquirer after absolute causes, he would "rather walk/The observant friend of the world as it looks to be . . ." (171)

To the evangelist who "called to me on the curb" he asks this question: "How can three alien men be reconciled/In one warm mind . . . ?" He would ask

                    a scroll
        Written anew, for where I pass are lions
        Walking chainless and devils that will not flee. (172)

What is noteworthy about this assertion of his divided
spiritual heritage is that it seems to pose no real problem
of identity; the assertion of the tripartite loyalties evokes
no anguish of contradiction, no sense of such elements
warring one upon another with himself as battleground.
There is nothing in this episode remotely resembling
Tate's poem "The Cross," with its depiction of the speaker
as torn between secular life on earth, and a religious belief
that would deny the world as without meaning; nor does
one think of Ransom's "Armageddon," with its ironic,
sardonic depiction of rival theologies. We recall that Davidson wrote to Tate in 1929 that "I seem to be bothered
less by religious matters than by anything else."[40] This
was probably true; however much the attitudes toward
community and order derived from his Methodist origins were central to the way that he looked at the world
and at the relationship of the individual to the community, these took the form of secular rather than religious
concerns. One might well contend that his idea of the
agrarian South and the community of true believers was
essentially a religious impulse, but its manifestation was
secular in reference. In any event, the religious presentation in "The Breaking Mould" lacks urgency. It is not examined, merely presented.

    "Epithalamion," the final section of *The Tall Men* be-
fore the Epilogue, is concerned with love and marriage.
It is addressed to the woman he loves. Whatever the
storms and darkness, the two of them together know that

                    storms will pass,
        And we shall stay in our firm element
        Of human love, our *primum mobile*. (173)

In their life together they shall remember "*morning by
morning, night by night, the love / That, coming once, has come*

to us forever." (174) The poet must consider that he is a Tennessean, but she is an Ohioan, "And in being faithful to you I have been unfaithful/Maybe, this once, to my own." Southern girls were attractive, "But I was a willing traitor when you came." (175) He describes her, in her liveliness, pride, clear-eyed brightness, and quickness. Then he imagines to himself "maybe an older meeting" (176) when an Ohio girl might have given water to some Confederate prisoner en route to a northern prison camp, or even "still an earlier meeting" (176) when some young Goth, on the Frisian coast, bearing an offer of peace, felt love for a Frankish girl whose eyes responded to his own glance. Thus his marriage to an Ohioan is made historically appropriate to the annals of the Tall Men. The section ends with a love poem in rhyme, celebrating the bridal day, with the conclusion,

> Let the long street a solemn music speak
> And larger beauties break
> From this wide world that is our marriage room,
> And April grass and every April bloom,
> And Hymen cry and now your joyance make,
> And drink the skies' sweet influence while ye may.
> Go forth, my love, for still it is our bridal day. (178)

Such is Davidson's "history of a mind—my mind, to an extent." The "Epilogue: Fire on Belmont Street" which ends *The Tall Men*, as we have seen, urges the modern Tennesseans to reassert their true inheritance, break with the false divinities of materialism and hedonism that are modern urban life, and remember the Tall Men looking out boldly and resolutely into the darkness of the wilderness night.

The Southern Identification

When Tate, in his correspondence with Davidson, referred to the new poem as an "epic," he was doubtless prompted to do so by the way in which the poem celebrates the Tennessee experience, depicting the evolution of the tall men historically, racially, and even mythically. Davidson, in insisting that it was not an epic but the history of a mind that resembled his own, was contending that the experience therein recounted was designed to examine what he himself was. The approach, he declared, was subjective. But Tate's contention is correct; in the form that *The Tall Men* is cast, the examination is really of the Tall Men and how they came to be, and the poet is allying himself with them and their history, not inspecting their credentials to speak for him. Neither the beginning nor the ending of the poem is set up in such a way as to make the sequence appear as an investigation by the poet of his own consciousness. Indeed, the epilogue directly addresses itself to the Tennesseans, urging them to turn back to their heritage, with the poet joining in their ranks even while making his exhortation. It is an act of complete identification. There is no self-scrutinizing involved in it; even the particular events of the poet's life that might distinguish him from his fellow Tennesseans, such as his marriage to a northern girl, are justified as representative incidents that might equally have occurred in the recent or remote history of the race. Davidson was not really investigating his beliefs; he was ordering and ritualizing the inheritance of his people, and depicting his own experience as emblematic of that of his fellow Tennesseans. He does not ask the question, Who Am I? Rather he sets out to show that This Is What We Are, assuming the identity of public and private consciousness without a qualm.

The Tall Men is a different kind of poem from almost anything that Davidson had attempted before in verse; the closest comparison to it among works by his fellow Fugitives might well be Ransom's "Antique Harvesters," which also sets forth an identification and urges the South to reclaim its heritage. In both poems the poet, having come upon his identity, proceeds to proclaim its mean-

ing. Ransom, however, stays out of the poem, except perhaps as his always identifiable persona is involved in the
ironies of the language; Davidson dramatizes his participation in the discovery, and his poem constitutes an act
of personal identification and an expression of his fealty.
Tate wrote no poems such as this; he used this approach
only in his biographies of Jackson and Davis. As poet he
was concerned to explore the difficulties of attempting
such identification.

Upon being sent a copy of the complete manuscript of
what ultimately became *The Tall Men* in 1926, Tate was
appalled. "I do not believe it was your intention to write a
poem; you wished to do something else," he told Davidson. He did not think that Davidson had made the material into a poem. His disagreement was not with Davidson's ideas; "I am personally inclined to believe that
Southerners are better men than Yankees, that the fall of
the South made a state for the pig, and that some sort of
love is the keynote of ethics," he wrote. "But if I *dis*believed these doctrines, I should feel as much interest in
them, *as poetry*, as I do believing them." He thought that
"in general, the *form* of the poem is still in your mind."
He strongly urged Davidson to hold off on sending the
poem out: "For God's sake, Don, don't publish the poem
in its present state. The material has great possibilities,
but it is not yet mastered."[41]

Davidson apparently replied at length, defending himself, but his letter does not survive. When Tate reiterated
his belief concerning the failure of *The Tall Men* in a later
letter, Davidson waited a while before replying again,
causing Tate to fear that he had been too severe in his
criticism. However, Davidson assured him that, though
the criticism had indeed bothered him, there was no disruption in their friendship: "My present feeling about it
reduces to this: it would be wrong no doubt for *you* to
write *The Long Street* as it has been written, but it isn't
wrong for *me* to do so."[42]

Meanwhile Tate had sent him the manuscript of several poems, including "Ode to the Confederate Dead," and a few weeks later Davidson gave his views on them. It was in this letter that he asked, "Where, O Allen Tate, are the dead?" He found Tate's poems admirable, he said, but they did not touch him; "I clap my hands just as I might for a difficult series of Liszt cadenzas, performed with great skill, but my enthusiasm has no passion in it." Tate's poetry was "so astringent that it bites and dissolves what it touches." Tate's conviction that the world was in a terrible condition was so pervasive, he declared, that it got into his poetry, and made every poem into an aesthetic discussion. "The Confederate dead become a peg on which you hang an argument whose lines, however sonorous and beautiful in a strict proud way, leave me wondering why you wrote a poem on the subject at all . . . . Your *Elegy* is not for the Confederate dead, but for your own dead emotion, or mine (*you* think)." The poem's "beauty is a cold beauty."[43]

This exchange marks, it seems to me, the end of the close relationship between Davidson and Tate *as fellow modern poets*. They could and did work intimately together as Agrarians, but from this point on, their diverging aims as poets became so obvious that no real literary give-and-take was possible. It is true that a few years later, when Davidson sent Tate the first draft of "Lee in the Mountains," Tate complimented him highly and made valuable suggestions for revision; but it was expert technical advice, given from the outside, as it were, for Tate could not share Davidson's idea of what a poem should be. He helped Davidson refine and develop the tactics of Davidson's kind of poem, but no longer did he make the effort to get Davidson to understand his view as to what constituted the proper strategy for a poem.[44]

What had happened was that Davidson had willed himself into a complete identification, both as a man and *as a poet*, with the Agrarian cause he would spend much of the remainder of his life defending. His commitment to Agrarianism differed crucially from Tate's, in that for Davidson it was an enterprise for redeeming the South and the nation from the social, political, and moral evils of industrialism, urbanism, and materialism, while for Tate it was a conscious strategy for dealing with his social and aesthetic experience. I do not mean by this that Tate did not believe in the virtues of Agrarianism, or that his personal commitment to it was either half-hearted or partial. But for Tate it was never a way of life; it was a way of interpreting life. Thus where Tate could compose Agrarian essays, asserting the value of the Agrarian premises, and could write poems in which such values are portrayed, he could not see those values *as* the substance of his experience, and so write Agrarian poems. In other words, he might write poetry *about* Agrarian topics, but not *as* an Agrarian. They were separate occupations. As an Agrarian he set forth Agrarian doctrine; as a poet he commented upon his experience, of which Agrarianism was an important principle of formulation. Davidson, by contrast, wrote his poetry and prose *as* an Agrarian, and saw the programmatical application of Agrarianism as constituting the core of his experience. The success or failure of Davidson's poem, therefore, was to be judged, from his standpoint, by the eloquence with which it expressed his Agrarian views. The difference was irreconcilable; friends and associates though Davidson and Tate would remain for many years to come, what joined them from now on was not the art of poetry, but the South and the memory of the earlier Fugitive association.

For Davidson's poetry, the identification of his life and art with Agrarianism meant that its reception would come largely to depend upon whether or not the reader could sympathize with and share the political and social attitudes expressed in it. The reader who could bring to the poem something approaching the same loyalties and concerns that Davidson put into it, might find it eloquent and moving. The southern allegiance was, for him, Truth, in the way that a religion contemplates Truth—not the *fact* that *he* felt the allegiance, but the nature of the allegiance itself. He could not and would not make the distinction between art and life that Tate considered essential. When Ransom in later years lost interest in Agrarianism and moved into pure literary criticism, Davidson was baffled at what he felt was the desertion, referring on one occasion to "John Ransom's most recent essay in refined aesthetics, which I hold to be a misuse of his great gifts. . . ."[45] Apparently he felt that the various topical Agrarian economic essays that Ransom wrote during the early 1930s were *not* a misuse of Ransom's gifts.

So far as Davidson was concerned, the onset of the Agrarian allegiance unleashed in him the creative release he had felt was lagging before its advent. Beginning with *The Tall Men* he produced a torrent of verse, as well as a steady stream of critical and historical essays and articles in which he took his stand in no uncertain terms. Many of his poems have moments of great beauty; at least one, "Lee in the Mountains," is a triumph. But almost every one depends upon the reader's ability to identify with the social and political attitude of the poet. What Tate had written him earlier about *The Tall Men*—"if I *dis*believed these doctrines, I should feel as much interest in them, *as poetry*, as I do believing them"—was not part of Davidson's poetics, with the inevitable result that his reputation as a poet fell steadily behind that of the others. In 1940, when Tate referred to his work in a letter as constituting a defense of the South, and being thereby lacking in universality, he was hurt. "You say I conceive myself as the 'spokesman' for a culture and a people!" he replied. "What foolishness! You talk like a New York *Times* reviewer, not like yourself." Yet in the same letter he objected to Delmore Schwartz's review of Tate's poems not because it wasn't good, but because "*conceivably* somebody might have been found to do an essay on Tate who

should be nearer to the corpus and spiritus of your poetry than Schwartz can ever be."[46] He wanted, that is, an
Agrarian reviewer; any other approach to Tate's poetry
had to be misguided, no matter how sympathetic.

Of the work of himself and his friends, Davidson wrote
many years later that

Our total purpose was to seek the image of the South which we
could cherish with high conviction and to give it, wherever we
could, the finality of art in those forms, fictional, poetical, or
dramatic, that have the character of myth and therefore, resting on belief, secure belief in others and, unlike arguments, are
unanswerable, arc in themselves fulfilled and complete. Such
was the total purpose, of which the so-called "Agrarian" movement was but a declaratory preface.[47]

This is about as eloquent a statement of Donald Davidson's life work as could be made, and is characteristic of
the man. But neither Tate nor Ransom nor Robert Penn
Warren would have agreed with the statement that their
own purpose as poets was to seek the image of the South.
Rather, they would have insisted that as poets they were
concerned with seeking the image of God and man in the
world, and that the South, however much they cherished
it, was and could be only a setting, a mode, for anchoring
that image in language.

For this, and other reasons, it was Davidson who was
the heart of Agrarianism, and all the others knew it. When
the disintegration of the Fugitive group began setting in
during the 1920s, he had been unhappy and uncomfortable, missing the sense of fraternity and partnership in
the joint effort. Tate's departure for New York had left
a gap in his world that could not be filled. As Ransom
moved away from poetry toward poetics and philosophy
in the middle 1920s, the ties between him and Davidson
had become weaker. But now, as the Agrarian enterprise
began building momentum, the balance shifted. If Tate
and he had grown apart on poetics, Agrarianism united
them once again. Tate came back to Tennessee. Ransom

moved decisively and actively into the strategy of Agrarianism. New recruits were picked up: not only Andrew Lytle, but John Donald Wade, Frank Owsley, Lyle Lanier. For Davidson there was once more the sense of being part of a dynamic, active enterprise with his friends. Selfless in his efforts and his advocacy, open and unspoiled, loyal and determined, he gloried in their common cause, and he never went back on it. The Agrarian enterprise invigorated and inspired him. Like the narrator of *The Tall Men*, after a night of tossing and turning and self-doubt, he woke to its advocacy, "alive in a new morning."

4 The Agrarian Enterprise: *I'll Take My Stand*

The Agrarian Venture

The "Southern" book that Donald Davidson, Allen Tate, and John Crowe Ransom planned, *I'll Take My Stand: The South and the Agrarian Tradition*, was published by Harper and Brothers on November 30, 1930. The authors were Twelve Southerners, most of them associated with Vanderbilt University. It was no accident that the enterprise was centered upon Vanderbilt, or that it came to fruition just when it did. In one sense, as we have seen, it was a logical, though not an inevitable, result of the Nashville Fugitive poetry group of the early 1920s, but its origins go farther back than that.

The leading figures among the Agrarians—Ransom, Tate, Warren, Davidson, and the future novelist Andrew Nelson Lytle—all came out of the upper South, and grew up in the years when the South was entering the twentieth century. All were from small towns. They had been born into a region that was predominantly rural and agricultural, and they had lived in communities that were more or less settled, ordered, religiously orthodox, with social lines well defined, but without great extremes of wealth and poverty among the white inhabitants. They had been sent to Vanderbilt University for their educations because it was the leading university of the upper South.

These young men had been born into one kind of society, and had grown into another, and they were part of the change. They were, as their fathers and grandfathers had not been, citizens of modern America. Yet they were still very much imbued with the values, attitudes, and habits of mind and emotion of that earlier, premodern South, and they remained strongly affected by its instinctive community loyalties and pieties.

We have seen that at the outset of their literary careers the leading Fugitive poets cared and thought very little about the South or about the nature of their society. They associated self-conscious southernism with the United Daughters of the Confederacy and the Ku Klux Klan, and southern literature with the wan posturings of local color and costume romance. Not until the middle 1920s did any noticeable amount of disenchantment with the contemporary American scene become discernible in their writings. It came, I think, only after the three leading Fugitives (Warren was not yet involved to any great extent) began to achieve a certain amount of literary success and recognition. It was only when the euphoria of the Fugitive publishing endeavor and the excitement of writing poems and becoming part of the literary world began subsiding, that they began to look at the situation around them more critically and ask some questions that as the decade grew older became more and more urgently formulated.

They were poets now, young men of letters. They lived in a society in which books, magazines, the fine arts in general were supposedly prospering as never before, so

far as sales and numbers of books and magazines printed
were concerned. Yet between the best literature and the
mass-produced, mass-marketed entertainment of the period, as symbolized by Hollywood and the mass magazines, an enormous gap had developed, whereby the
standards of taste and judgment in which they believed
bore little or no relationship to the vast pabulum of sentimental trash that flooded the newsstands, bookstores,
theaters, and music halls. In being commercialized, taste
was also being vulgarized. Meanwhile the best literature,
the best art for the most part had little or no remunera-
tive popular audience. It seemed to exist in a little world
of its own, read by its initiates only, separated from all except its devotees by a barrier of language and sophistication that protected it from adulteration at the cost of its
being made inaccessible to all except a tiny segment of
the reading public. In self-defense, literature that attempted to count for anything as literature had turned its
back on the interests and tastes of a general audience.

As for the trappings of political, social, and economic
life in what had now become the Age of Coolidge, they
saw little that they could respect. Politics was banal, petty,
without much in the way of ideals or leadership involved.
The business of the nation, as the president himself confirmed, was business; and commercial zeal seemed to be
all that mattered to anyone. Stock prices soared; real estate developments mushroomed; Rotary and the Booster
clubs were rampant; the more vulgar techniques of mass
advertising were employed without restraint to create
new consumer demand for a vast outpouring of new
products. The moral letdown after the war to end wars
had spawned what seemed to be a commercial civilization
without parallel. From pulpit and political platform alike
the virtues of salesmanship were extolled. The hypoc-
risy of Prohibition had turned big city restaurants into
speakeasies and produced an orgy of crime and gang-

sterism. It was the age of the flapper, the hip-pocket flask.

Malcolm Cowley described American life as it looked to young writers during those times:

Something oppressed them, some force was preventing them from doing their best work. They did not understand its nature, but they tried to exorcise it by giving it names—it was the stupidity of the crowd, it was hurry and haste, it was Mass Production, Babbittry, Our Business Civilization; or perhaps it was the Machine, which had been developed to satisfy men's needs, but which was now controlling those needs and forcing its standardized products upon us by means of omnipresent advertising and omnipresent vulgarity—the Voice of the Machine, the Tyranny of the Mob. The same social mechanism that fed and clothed the body was starving the emotions, was closing every path toward creativeness and self-expression.[1]

Cowley and his friends went to Europe; they became expatriates; they issued little magazines and proclaimed the Waste Land; and they wrote the literature of the Lost Generation, which was if not their best work then very good work indeed. And most of them did not come back home again for good until the stock market crashed, whereupon many of them became Marxists and called for the proletariat to rise and overturn the capitalistic system.

With the southerners it was another matter. They were both of the period and apart from it. The South had come late to the new ways, had participated least in it, and because it was predominantly agricultural had begun to experience what would later be called the Great Depression well before the stock market crash of 1929. The young Fugitives were Modernists, but with a difference. They had brought to their modernism and to the urban culture of the 1920s the memories and the attitudes of a different kind of society, which their parents had known and which was still present all about them in many ways while they were growing up. That society had been small city, small town, rural. It had been, if sometimes narrowly sectarian, religious in its moral and ethical assumptions, and in a threadbare way to be sure, traditional in its pieties and loyalties. Not only that, but there had been a common history, which had involved them all, and which had not been forgotten; it offered them a set of pieties and loyalties, and helped to focus their grievances. In short, they had experienced what it was to belong to a closely knit human community, and to deal and be dealt with by others on the terms of individual personality that a functioning community identity could offer its members. That community had been far from perfect; for some, membership had been on highly disadvantageous terms. Indeed, one entire group of people were in crucial respects barred from many of its advantages and exploited economically for the benefit of the more fortunate members. But even so it had been a community, not merely an economic or political association, and particularly for those who had not been in too disadvantaged a relationship to it, it offered its strong attractions. At least they thought and behaved as if it did.

During the years in which these young men were born and were growing up, the up-country South was beginning to be importantly affected by urbanization. Historians tell us that except for certain localities here and there, the New South proclaimed by Henry W. Grady had brought little change to the southern scene for many years. There was considerable oratory about it, but the sum total of manufacturing and cities remained quite small. It was not until after the turn of the century that the economy of the region began to feel strongly the impact of industrialization. Once it did, however, the progress was rapid enough. The First World War brought some real money into the region for the first time in more than a half century, and the cities flourished. When the war was over the South was ready to enter into the industrial dispensation with unsurpassed enthusiasm, and the manufacturer and the real estate promoter flourished in the 1920s as never before. As a northern newspaper reporter wrote at the end of the decade, "the clamor of

Chambers of Commerce, the seductive propaganda of city and state industrial development boards, the rattling knives and forks and pepful jollities of Rotarians, Kiwanians, Lions, and Exchange clubs are filling the erstwhile languorous wisteria-scented air with such a din these days that every visitor must recognize immediately a land of business progress." A few years earlier a southern commentator, Gerald Johnson, had declared of his region that in hundreds of towns from the Rio Grande to the Potomac "there is no God but Advertising, and Atlanta is his prophet."[2]

The belated but swift coming of industrialization and urbanization made itself felt not only economically, of course, but politically, socially, educationally, and culturally. Edwin Mims of Vanderbilt was quick to proclaim the relationship: "Looms and furnaces," he wrote, "factories and stores, railroads and water power, have led to the prosperity of the few and the well-being of the many, and these have been largely responsible for the symphony orchestra and the Parthenon of Nashville, the grand opera seasons of Atlanta and Chattanooga, the County Court House of Memphis, the Tennessee War Memorial Auditorium, and the increasing architectural beauty of colleges that stretch from Charlottesville to New Orleans." Nor was Mims loath to attribute the literary quickening to the same cause—and to number among its benefits the Fugitives of Nashville. Praising Ransom and Davidson in particular for their originality and lack of sentimentality, he cited them as examples of the fact that "more men and more women are writing fiction, poetry, plays, and literary criticism than at any time in the past quarter of a century, and . . . are displaying a critical intelligence, a sense of literary values, and a reaction against sentimentalism and romance which has not been hitherto regarded as characteristic of Southern writing."[3]

Of course Mims was quite right in making the connection. The leading Fugitives *were* the product of a South that was far more cosmopolitan, critical, realistic, and in touch with the chief ideas, forces, and developments in contemporary letters of the time than had ever before been true of southern writers. But once the first fine excitement of contact with the values and attitudes of modernity had begun to wear off, the several Fugitives who became professional men of letters began to ask questions. Was there a South, from which they were being so vigorously dislodged, that had characteristics not available in the modern urban, industrial society and that was very much worth preserving? Looking at the life of their country in the 1920s, viewing the way in which the South was attempting to emulate the urban, industrialized ways of the Northeast, they were by no means enthusiastic about the prospect. The inheritance that linked them not with the currents of modernism but with the more traditional, rural and small town ways now being threatened with extinction, began to reassert itself.

They had been zealous to escape from the village; now they began, for the first time, to recognize the attractiveness of the kind of community experience and the sense of individual identity that the old ways had afforded, and to realize that these qualities were increasingly absent in the life that was being created by the forces of progress and modernism. Metropolitan life seemed huge, impersonal. A complex industrial society enforced greater and greater specialization upon its members. The tremendous diversification of occupations and interests caused a fragmentation into economic pressure groups and narrowly defined professional coteries. This in turn brought a greater and greater distancing from the everyday concerns of the mass of one's fellow citizens. An overriding importance had come to be placed upon the display of material wealth in a society where rapid accumulation of such wealth now appeared quite possible. The swiftness of change within the expanding city, and the distancing from the familiar ways of the town and countryside, engendered a sense of rootlessness. And so on. Whatever their disagreement with the values of the earlier community, and whatever their feeling of having been constrained by its attitudes, they had at least known who they were, and felt that others knew and cared to know. But as part of industrial, urban society, they were being, as Emerson had complained about the Northeast of his own time, "reckoned in the hundred, or the thousand." The prospect was not appetizing, and the more they thought about it, the less they liked what was happening to themselves and to their native region.

If any single event focused the concern of some of the future Agrarians upon what was happening to the post-World War I South, it was probably the Scopes trial of 1925. When John T. Scopes, a schoolteacher, was arraigned before a court in Dayton, Tennessee, on July 10 of that year, on charges of having violated a newly enacted state law forbidding the teaching of evolution in public school classrooms, the case became a national *cause célèbre*. William Jennings Bryan joined in the prosecution of Scopes, and Clarence Darrow headed up the defense. Noted scientists and other expert witnesses were called to testify on Scopes's behalf. H. L. Mencken, Joseph Wood Krutch, and others came down to cover the trial, and sent back scathing descriptions of the ignorance, illogic, and barbarity of the Tennessee fundamentalists. The thing became a three-ring circus, with Darrow making Bryan appear ridiculous on the witness stand, and Mencken and others regaling the nation with depictions of fundamentalist bumpkins and of the rural South in general. Embarrassed southern progressives such as Edwin Mims and Chancellor Kirkland of Vanderbilt joined in the condemnation of the fundamentalists; Kirkland announced that "the answer to the episode at Dayton is the building of new laboratories on the Vanderbilt campus for the teaching of science."[4]

Ransom, Tate, and Davidson were not primitive fundamentalists, of course, and they did not cherish any great respect for bumpkinry and ignorance. Yet the spectacle of the rural South being held up to ridicule and contempt by Mencken, Darrow, and the other apostles of advanced urban cosmopolitan wisdom for having dared, however naïvely and illogically, to assert a faith in the Bible and in the primacy of religious truth over science, stirred them to anger. Was the matter so one-sided as the national press made it appear? Were the religious "superstition" and "supernaturalism" so vehemently denounced by Mencken and his imitators merely aspects of unlettered rural barbarism, bigotry, and ignorance, as was being proclaimed everywhere, or were they, as expressed at Dayton, grotesquely emblematic of a society that was not yet willing to surrender its religious convictions to the commercial materialism and glib scientism of urban America? In any event, were the moral, ethical, and spiritual characteristics of the kind of society extolled by Darrow and Mencken so very much superior to those of the rural South, that the conflict should be depicted, as was done by *The Nation*, as one of "the State of Tennessee *vs.* Truth"?[5]

What they felt most keenly was the supineness of the South in the face of the onslaught against it. If there were attributes of southern community experience that were still very much alive and that could offer a more humane, satisfying life than seemed possible in the urban, industrial society of the Northeast, then it seemed tragic to allow the case for that life and for the human values it represented to rest with the naïve defense set forth by the fundamentalists of Dayton. Surely there was more to be said for the southern heritage than that.

In expressing disenchantment and dismay over the mechanization and commercialization of American life of the 1920s, of course, they were by no means alone. Such commentators as Lewis Mumford, Walter Lippmann, Krutch, James Truslow Adams, Ralph Borsodi, Stuart

Chase, Robert and Helen Lynd, and numerous others were stridently attacking what Adams called "Our Business Civilization." In England, D. H. Lawrence was registering his disapproval of the industrial dispensation, and T. S. Eliot and others were depicting the society of the city as a wasteland of spiritual and moral decay. Scott Fitzgerald's *The Great Gatsby* savagely depicted the corruption of the American ideal by the lure of easy money; the vulgar and tawdry materialism that polluted Jay Gatsby's dream was emblematic of the time and the place. Many of the criticisms of contemporary society that *I'll Take My Stand* would make were already being expressed by thoughtful observers who were appalled by the ugliness, the materialism, and the cultural and social chaos of the age.

The future Agrarians, however, had a special and unique perspective from which they could view what was happening to modern America. They were southerners. The very tardiness with which the South had entered the modern age afforded them a sharp and still viable contrast with contemporary urban life. Although the cities of the South, with Nashville very much in the vanguard, were eagerly taking up the institutions and the slogans of modernism, the South as a whole was still backward, and by no means yet fully transformed into an industrial society. It seemed to them not so much a problem in recovering, so much as of retaining, attitudes, arrangements, and relationships that made possible a more satisfying kind of human existence than what they saw and read about in the large urban centers of the Northeast. If only the South could be made to see what it was doing to its still-viable community life, and how it was jeopardizing its inmost human and social values, by its uncritical and eager pursuit of more and more industrialization, urbanization, mechanization, then it might have second thoughts about becoming "a 'new South' which will be only an undistinguished replica of the usual industrial community."[6] (xxi)

This was the conclusion they reached in the late years of the 1920s, and that prompted the organization of their symposium. For each of them, however, to reach that conclusion had involved a separate journey growing out of their own individual needs as poets and citizens. Where earlier they had thought about poetry and poetics almost exclusively, they came now to think about society and the South as well. By the late twenties each of the leading Fugitive poets had by various routes arrived at a position wherein they were impelled to undertake a strong critique of the direction which they saw modern American society taking, and each perceived, in the life of the region into which they had been born and had grown up, certain strong correctives to that situation. Looking back upon it, we can see many factors that had brought them to the decision: the condition of poetry, the state of religion, the economy, social relationships, the long heritage of separateness that southern history had bequeathed them, the reentry of the South into the national experience, the continuing experience of being different, the sense of foreboding bred into them by their region's past which made them ill at ease in Zion, and many other things besides.

By early 1927 Davidson was writing to Tate that he was thinking about writing a book on "the Southern tradition —where it is, where it isn't, what and how and so on." Meanwhile Tate and Ransom were exchanging letters on a "Southern symposium of prose." Davidson was delighted with that prospect; "I'll join in and go the limit," he wrote. There was talk of founding a southern magazine, though Tate was skeptical. "If there were a Southern magazine," Davidson wrote Tate in early 1929, "intelligently conducted and aimed specifically, under the doctrine of provincialism, at renewing a certain sort of sectional consciousness and drawing separate groups of Southern thought together, something might be done to save the South from civilization." Davidson and Ransom were now talking about putting together a southern symposium. On the Vanderbilt faculty were others, not poets, who were drawn into the conversations. John Donald Wade, biographer of *Augustus Baldwin Longstreet*, and Frank Owsley, historian of states' rights and the Confederacy, were keenly interested, as was the young Andrew Nelson Lytle. Plans were still vague. Then in August of 1929, Tate wrote to Davidson from France. He had already written to Warren he said, and had proposed "the formation of a society, or an academy of Southern *positive* reactionaries made up at first of people of our own group." This group was to be expanded; the members would draw up a philosophical constitution and look toward acquiring a daily newspaper, a weekly magazine, and a quarterly review. He then proposed a detailed table of contents for a southern symposium, with suggested contributors. This was the impetus needed to get the project moving. Soon Ransom and Davidson were lining up contributors.[7] Early in 1930 Tate returned from France, and through his agency a contract was signed with Harper and Brothers for a symposium on the South. The book was put together during the winter and spring, and delivered to the publishers.

I'll Take My Stand: The South and the Agrarian Tradition, by Twelve Southerners, was dedicated "in love and admiration" to the historian Walter Lynwood Fleming. It consisted of a "Statement of Principles" followed by essays by each of the contributors.

The "Statement of Principles," drafted by Ransom and accepted after revision by the others, began with the assertion that all of the participants "tend to support a Southern way of life as against what may be called the American or prevailing way," and declared that "the best terms in which to represent the distinction are contained in the phrase, Agrarian *versus* Industrial." (ix)

In their prefatory statement the Agrarians expressed their displeasure at the way that the South was beginning

to adopt the American industrial ideal, and their conviction that younger southerners must be persuaded to
come back to the support of the older tradition. Other
American sections, too, they said, faced the same problem, and they hoped that "a national agrarian movement"
might be possible. Defining industrialism as "the decision
of society to invest its economic resources in the applied
sciences," they charged that the result had meant an enslavement of human energies. (xi) Theoretically, science
could render labor easier and assure economic security to
the laborer, but in practice it had brutalized labor and
caused widespread insecurity of employment. Applied
science was based on the labor-saving capacity of the machine; it assumed that labor itself was evil, and that its
material product was good. Labor was practiced solely for
its material rewards, as on an assembly line, not as an act
of one of the happy functions of human life. The evils of
overproduction, unemployment, and inequality in the
distribution of wealth that have followed had been ignored, with the ultimate result likely to be an economic
superorganization such as the Soviet system.

Although industrialism has produced "more time in
which to consume, and many more products to be consumed," its tempo has brutalized and hurried our satisfactions, the Agrarian statement continued. (xiv) The average man is not prepared to enlarge his consuming time
indefinitely; the price has been satiety and aimlessness,
resulting in a loss of vocation. Nor does an industrial society encourage religion, for religion is the submission to a
nature that is fairly inscrutable, while industrialism provides the illusion of mastery and destroys the sense of nature as "something mysterial and contingent." (xiv) The
God of nature becomes merely an amiable superfluity.
As for the fine arts, they depend upon a free and disinterested observation of nature, and so are impossible in
an industrial age. In the same way, the amenities of life
suffer from the brutalization and commercialism since

they depend upon a right relation of man-to-man that industrialism destroys. Education is no remedy; the arts and humanities must grow out of the conditions of life, not be applied from the top.

The tempo of industrial life is increasing, for its very nature involves an ever-increasing production and consumption. Modern advertising and salesmanship thus arise to stimulate consumption in order to keep the machines running. But each day the task grows more difficult. To this false system, with its built-in apprehension of crisis, men are enslaving themselves. "Men are prepared to sacrifice their private dignity and happiness to an abstract social ideal, and without asking whether the social ideal produces the welfare of any individual man whatsoever." This, declared the Agrarians, "is absurd." (xviii)

Having set forth the evils of an industrial society, the Statement of Principles had relatively little to say about what an agrarian society would be like. Technically it would be "one in which agriculture is the leading vocation, whether for wealth, for pleasure, or for prestige—a form of labor that is pursued with intelligence and leisure." Such a society would exist wherever industrialism was not allowed to destroy it. Its theory was that "the culture of the soil is the best and most sensitive of vocations," and should therefore enjoy economic preference and be the principal form of labor. (xix)

The statement closed with some topical questions. How can a small community resist industrial development? How could southern and western agrarians unite? Should agrarians seek to capture the Democratic party or form a new one? What legislation might best further agrarianism and undo some of the ravages of industrialism? The Agrarians did not pretend to have the answers, they said, but were united in the conviction that something could be done if a people wished to throw off the yoke of industrialism. To say that nothing could be done about industrialism was pusillanimous, and for a "community, section, race, or age" to admit it was to doom itself to impotence. (xx)

It will be noted that nowhere in the "Statement of Principles" was any specific Agrarian economic program advanced. It was concerned with delineating the evils of industrialism, and not with what might be done to palliate or remove them. Agrarianism was assumed to be the natural condition of man in society when industrialism was not allowed to violate it, and what the Twelve Southerners were agreed upon was that the violation should be resisted.

Of the twelve individual essays in the volume, John Ransom's "Reconstructed but Unregenerate" came first, more or less as the keynote essay. Ransom began by noting the historical opposition of the South to the American progressive ideal, and asserting an identity between southern conservative attitudes and European culture; "the European principles had better look to the South if they are to be perpetuated in this country." (3) Unlike the American pioneering ideology, European (and southern) life was based upon a truce with nature which made possible leisure, security, and intellectual freedom. The American progressive ideal, by contrast, was committed to winning victories over nature not for a particular end but from force of habit, and without any recollection of what pioneering was for. The twin concepts of progress and service which characterized American life involve unrelenting exploitation of nature and of people. The Old South, which had never conceded that the increase of material prosperity was the duty of man or the measure of culture, had pioneered its way to a sufficiently comfortable estate, then had ceased pioneering and proceeded to enjoy the fruits of a stable establishment. But the Civil War had ruined the establishment; northern industrialism had conquered; and the impoverished South was threatening to move to emulate the progressive North in order to restore its material prosperity. The question now was whether the South would grudgingly allow itself only so much industrialism as was necessary to survive, or whether it would adopt the progressive ethics wholeheartedly and thus remove the last substantial American barrier to endless industrialism. If resistance was to be offered, then it would require rekindling in southerners a knowledge of and pride in their sectional identity, and the mapping of a concerted program of political action by southern leaders, involving cooperation with agrarian elements elsewhere.

Donald Davidson's "A Mirror for Artists" followed Ransom's essay. Davidson analyzed the condition of the fine arts under industrialism. Viewing the arts as commodities rather than as organic manifestations of human needs and aspirations, industrialism separated art from life, and the artist's response has been to move toward alienation from his society. The commercial elevation of mass taste has meant vulgarization; in defense the artist has cultivated his aloofness from society or his opposition to it. The dissociated artist "sings for himself. He develops not only a peculiar set of ideas, more and more personal to himself, but a personal style that in time becomes the 'unique' style demanded of modern poets, highly idiomatic, perhaps obscure." (44) The only hope for the health of the arts lies in the repudiation of the supremacy of industrialism; only in this way can harmony be regained between society and artist. Thus the artist "must step into the ranks and bear the brunt of the battle against the common foe." (51) As for the southern artist, his hope lies in the reassertion of an agrarian southern society in which he can work in harmony with his milieu, as he cannot under the industrial dispensation. His role, therefore, is to enlist in the agrarian cause, "become a person first of all, even though for the time being he may become less of an artist. He must enter the common arena and become a citizen." (60)

Next came Frank Owsley's "The Irrepressible Conflict," an overview of American history that linked the sectional conflict of 1861–1865 with the present Agrarian venture, as responses to the onslaught of northern industrialism.

The Arkansas poet John Gould Fletcher, who had lived in England for many years, followed with an essay entitled "Education, Past and Present," in which American public education was attacked as a standardizing, leveling, industrializing force, and a call was issued to revamp education in the South to make possible an intellectual elite.

The Vanderbilt psychologist Lyle Lanier contributed "A Critique of the Philosophy of Progress," which encapsulated Western intellectual history from medieval times to the present to show that the rise of science and materialism had led to a breakdown of the family and religion, and that the ultimate result of industrialism, if not checked, would be revolutionary convulsions and communism.

Allen Tate's "Remarks on the Southern Religion" declared the Old South to have formed a proper religious attitude, involving a view of history and society that was traditional, contemplative, and humane, but without a foundation in proper religious dogma, which left the postwar section open to the industrial exploitation of nature. If the South would regain its tradition, it must therefore do so by an act of the will. The southerner "must use an instrument, which is political, and so unrealistic and pretentious that he cannot believe it, to reestablish a private self-contained and essentially spiritual life. I say that he must do this; but that remains to be seen." (175)

The essay following Tate's was Herman Clarence Nixon's "Whither Southern Economy?" Nixon, who had recently left Vanderbilt to be professor of political science at Tulane University, examined the South's economy, showed how the farmer had been steadily impoverished by industrialism, and declared that only the reassertion of agrarian economy could save it from economic and spiritual conquest by an acquisitive industrial society.

Andrew Nelson Lytle's "The Hind Tit" provided the appropriate contrast to Nixon's factual, statistically informed analysis. Lytle, playwright, actor, and soon-to-be novelist, had done considerable family farming himself, and he was deeply loyal to up-country rural ways. Lamenting the betrayal of the American ideal by industrialization, he branded industrialism as the temptress that could wreck the self-sufficiency of rural life. Urging the farmer to resist the seductive lures of "progressive," money-making, mechanized farming, he asserted that "a farm is not a place to grow wealthy; it is a place to grow corn." (205) He then painted a picture of old-style farm culture, showing its routines, its relationships, its rituals, and declared that the Agrarian South should dread industrialism "like a pizen snake," (234) insisting that the farmer resolutely refuse to have any traffic with the money economy, since it meant disaster. Once accept the economic advantages of the machine, he said, and spiritual slavery followed. The southern farmer must hold on to his own and not give up; "if we have to spit in the water-bucket to keep it our own, we had better do it." (245)

The next essay, Robert Penn Warren's "The Briar Patch," constituted an attempt to deal with the presence of the black man in the agrarian South. Since I shall discuss this essay later, it will suffice here to say only that it constitutes an attempt to show that the black man's true needs are best served by maintaining his place in a segregated rural South. But that place, to be what it should be, must be equal as well as separate, Warren felt compelled to point out—with consequences that we shall examine later.

John Donald Wade's "The Life and Death of Cousin

Lucius" is not an essay so much as a familiar sketch of a landowner patterned on Wade's uncle. Wade shows us Cousin Lucius when a very small child moving with his family and their slaves from South Carolina to Georgia, growing up, experiencing the war, going to college and becoming a teacher, settling into a life as teacher, farmer, husband, and then banker. The years go by, and Lucius's economic conservatism seems out of place as the New South spirit takes over, but when hard times reassert themselves, he appears not so unwise after all. Finally one morning as he walks out into his fields, he dies. The point of Wade's beautiful sketch, however, is not so much what happens, as that it portrays a man living decently and honestly on the land and in his community, over the course of a lifetime that encompasses change, destruction, and opportunity. Because he is true to himself and to others, his life has been imbued with dignity and love. Here, Wade tells his southern readers, is what it can signify to be a southerner and a gentleman, as those terms have meaning. What, he suggests by implication, can the urban metropolis and its values offer to them that could be finer or even as fine?

The next to last essay, "William Remington: a Study in Individualism," by Henry Blue Klein, a former Vanderbilt student and journalist, describes how a young man of sensibility and intellect decides to live in the South and work to keep his region free of industrial progress; this is the weakest of the essays in the book.

The final sketch, Stark Young's "Not in Memoriam, but in Defense," is of considerably more stature. Young, a native Mississippian, had long since ceased to live in the South; he had taught at Amherst, then become drama critic for the *New Republic*, and was well known as a critic, translator of Chekhov, and a playwright and novelist. The addition of so noted a literary figure as Young to the Agrarian cause represented an accomplishment, particularly in securing proper attention from the national press; there was some apprehension, however, that Young might make the occasion into an excuse for a sentimental excursion. Young's essay began with the proposition that any return to the southern past would be both impossible and undesirable. He concentrated upon the need to reassert the aristocratic values in a commercialized society, and defended provincialism as a better index to the objectives of civilization than the standards of the progressive metropolis could offer. Change was inevitable, he concluded, but in change one could be true to oneself and so remain unchanged.

When *I'll Take My Stand* appeared the South and the nation were in the process of sliding ever more rapidly down into the trough of the Great Depression. The book seemed, therefore, more a response to the immediate issues of the times than had been intended, and the reviews tended to treat it as such. "The truth is," Davidson wrote a few years later, "that *I'll Take My Stand* was by necessity a general study, preliminary to a specific application which we hoped the times would permit us, with others, to work out slowly and critically. The emergencies of 1930 and later years made such deliberate procedure impossible."[8] Within a few years' time the coming of the New Deal so changed the relationship of government and of economic and social planning to the problems and possibilities of southern life that many of the specific hypotheses upon which the essays of *I'll Take My Stand* had been predicated had been significantly altered. What relevance the book had as a document about the immediate topical concerns of southern society, therefore, was in crucial respects outdated. Yet unlike many another book more specifically designed to cope with the southern situation in seemingly more practical and expedient terms, it did not drop out of public view once the immediate occasion of its publication had passed. Almost a half-century later the volume is still read and discussed. It seems obvious, therefore, that it was not the practicality of *I'll Take My Stand* that mattered. Was it, in fact, a book about farming at all? This is the question I now want to take up.

Agrarianism and Farming

If there was one principle upon which the twelve contributors to the symposium could agree, it was that the industrialization and urbanization that were expanding their hold upon the southern states in the 1920s constituted a severe threat to the traditional community life and social ordering of the region. All of them subscribed to the "Statement of Principles" which prefaced the volume, and which asserted their dissatisfaction with "the melancholy fact that the South itself has wavered a little and shown signs of wanting to join up behind the common American industrial ideal. It is against that tendency that this book is written. The younger Southerners, who are being converted frequently to the industrial gospel, must come back to the support of the Southern tradition. They must be persuaded to look very critically at the advantages of becoming a 'new South' which will be only an undistinguished replica of the usual industrial community." (xx–xxi)

The agrarianism that they advocated as the proper course for the South to follow was based upon that conviction—as the statement of principles put it, all of them "tend to support a Southern way of life against what may be called the American or prevailing way; and all as much as agree that the best terms in which to represent the distinction are contained in the phrase, Agrarian *versus* Industrial." (xix) *Agrarian*, however, was defined in general terms, and the course of action to be followed varied from essay to essay. Stark Young, for example, begins his essay with the sensible remark that "if anything is clear, it is that we can never go back" and that "dead days are gone, and if by some chance they should return, we should find them intolerable." (328) He sees in the present South "much of the old life surviving, the old practices that belong with the land, the old beliefs and standards," then notes "the gradual blend of these with later ideas and conditions, the onrush of new powers in money, industry, and communication," and when he writes about his ideal southerner, he assumes that his "family lived in a big house, not without elegance, hospitality, and affection." (333) It is clear that what Young hopes for is the determined retention of the manners, graces, and attributes of an aristocratic social relationship as a way of civilizing the vulgarity and crudeness of nouveau-riche urban America.

This is in a very different key from Andrew Lytle's injunction to his fellow southerners—who are plainly not landed aristocracy but small farmers of the up-country—to "do what we did after the war and the Reconstruction: return to our looms, our handcrafts, our reproducing stock. Throw out the radio and take down the fiddle from the wall. Forsake the movies for the play-parties and the square dances." (234) Lytle was exaggerating his position for effect, but not only was he obviously proposing a response far more specific and more positive than Young had in mind, but he was conceiving of the nature of agrarianism in terms of an entirely different class of the population. What was for Young the need to preserve an attitude toward the world was for Lytle a course of social and economic action.

Similarly, when John Crowe Ransom remarked that the business of the southern agriculturalist "seemed to be rather to envelop both his work and his play with a leisure that permitted the activity of intelligence," (12) he was clearly approaching the pursuit of agriculture with very different assumptions about what was important to it than was Herman Clarence Nixon. The latter might or might not have agreed with Ransom's analysis, but farming for him was a practical, economic activity. There was, he wrote, "a tendency to burden the farmer [which is] observable in the sphere of general taxation, which is becoming constantly heavier on agricultural lands and capital without regard to income. Readjustments are necessary to give the southern farmers and other farmers a square deal in the fields of tariffs and taxation." (195) Are the two Agrarians writing about the same thing? If so, then they conceive of what is involved in it in very different ways. Surely what one sees as central to agrarianism is very different from the concerns of the other.

Allen Tate, in his essay on the southern religion, is concerned with how the southerner may regain a lost tradition. The region was without a proper religious foundation for its society, he contends, because of its theological reliance upon a Calvinistic Protestantism fundamentally at odds with the southerner's concrete, self-sufficient, personal, dramatic (rather than ideological or intellectual) way of life. To regain his tradition, therefore, the southerner cannot fall back upon the tenets of his theology; he must consciously and actively will the tradition back into existence, however pretentious such an intellectual act may be.

Ransom, by contrast, describes an Agrarian South for which any such act of the naked, intellectual will would seem not merely incongruous but almost a betrayal of its nature. A dozen times in his essay Ransom praises the placidity of southern life. He reiterates in laudatory fashion such terms as *line of least resistance, routine, leisure, comfortable, stable, inertia*, and *truce with nature*. What he finds most admirable about the Agrarian South is what it assumes and values instinctively; an aggressive act of the will such as Tate proposes would be a contradiction, philosophically at any rate, of the whole Agrarian rationale.

Such variance in assumptions and ideas is indicative, I think, of more than merely a matter of individual differences in methods of approach. It signifies a fundamental division, apparent almost from the outset of the Agrarian enterprise and manifested throughout *I'll Take My Stand*, of what agrarianism was about and what role and expectations it was to involve.

In the letter which served to formulate the direction that the project would take, Tate had proposed to Davidson "a Southern movement," and this involved setting up a southern academy and drawing up a philosophical constitution which "should set forth, under our leading idea, a complete social, philosophical, literary, economic, and religious system," which together with other steps would *"create an intellectual situation interior to the South."*[9] It is interesting that in none of his correspondence with Davidson, up to the very eve of publication of *I'll Take My Stand*, did Tate deal in the terms *agrarian* and *industrial*. This is an important point; for Tate was not thinking in terms of a socioeconomic program, even one so general as to oppose an agricultural allegiance to one favoring industrialization. Even his call for an economist, I believe, was not for an advocate of agrarian economics, but for one who might write in refutation of the policies of the commercial, profit-oriented economy of the American industrial establishment. What he was after was an overt, articulated southern intellectual consciousness, which would make itself heard in all aspects of public experience.

Where did the specific agrarian-versus-industrial formulation of *I'll Take My Stand* come from? The source is not difficult to find. It is a key feature of Ransom's book *God Without Thunder*, in which Ransom developed at length his theory that the industrial society is opposed to the agrarian, and that in espousing industrialism Western man in general, and man in the United States in particular, had placed himself in a false, predatory relationship to nature. As Ransom saw it, only in a nonindustrial, agrarian community could labor know true dignity, and man enjoy the humane, leisured life in which belief in an all-powerful God who could be feared and loved is possible.

The kind of community that Ransom and the others had grown up in, the small-town and rural South of the 1890s and early 1900s, had been agricultural rather than industrial, and they saw the order and stability of that earlier kind of community as preferable to the dissociation and instability of modern urban society. Thus it was logical that Ransom would view the only feasible and workable response to the economic disorder, religious confusion, and social dislocation of the 1920s as the reassertion and restoration of an agrarian social and economic order.

In Ransom's mind, an agrarian society and a religious, traditional, aesthetic life were one and the same. We can see this clearly in his definition of the farmer in his essay in *I'll Take My Stand*:

He identifies himself with a spot of ground, and this ground carries a good deal of meaning; it defines itself for him as nature. He would till it not too hurriedly and not too mechanically to observe in it the contingency and the infinitude of nature; and so his life acquires its philosophical and even its cosmic consciousness. A man can contemplate and explore, respect and love, an object as substantial as a farm or a native province. But he cannot contemplate nor explore, respect nor love, a mere turnover, such as an assemblage of "national resources," a pile of money, a volume of produce, a market, or a credit system. (19–20)

Now this may well be so, and there is no reason to believe that the other Agrarians seriously disagreed. All the same, it ought to be noted that Ransom's premises about the causal relationship of religion and society were diametrically opposed to those of Allen Tate. Ransom sees the return to an agrarian society as the only way to restore the religious life. Tate, by contrast, declared twice in his essay that it was the other way around: "the social structure depends upon the economic structure," he says, "and economic conviction is the secular image of religion." (168) And again, "economy is the secular image of religious conviction." (175) Tate wrote of the Old South that "The Old Southerners were highly critical of the kinds of work to be done. They planted no corn that they could not enjoy; they grew no cotton that did not directly contribute to the upkeep of a rich private life; and they knew no history for the sake of knowing it, but simply for the sake of contemplating it and seeing in it an image of themselves." (172) Ransom, in the quotation cited above, declares that the farmer's life "*acquires* its philosophical and even its cosmic consciousness" (italics mine) as the result of his identification with the soil, as agriculturalist.

The point may seem narrow, yet I think that it is decisive in its implications. For if one is dissatisfied with the materialism and disorder of twentieth-century American society, and wishes to protest against it and to urge something better, it makes a great deal of difference whether one assumes that the economic mode determines the philosophical and religious, or vice versa. If the former, then the first and crucial need is to change the economic mode; if the latter, then a change in the economic mode can only be brought about by a change in what and how one believes in the way of a theology and a philosophy. To change the economic mode without first changing the moral and religious values, one must have another economic program to propose in its stead; if the proposed program by its very nature goes against certain other strongly felt social and economic needs and values, then one is in trouble.

Donald Davidson, replying to hostile criticism five years after *I'll Take My Stand* had appeared, wrote that the prevailing schools of economic thought all "held that economics determines life and set up an abstract economic existence as the governor of man's efforts. We believed that life determines economics, or ought to do so, and that economics is no more than an instrument around the use of which should gather many more motives than economic ones. . . . The virtue of the Southern agrarian tradition was that it mixed up a great many motives with the economic motive, thus enriching it and reducing it to its proper subordination."[10] But though this might have been the intention of the Nashville Agrarians, it was nevertheless true that by describing their endeavor as one of "Agrarian *versus* Industrial," as Ransom did in the Statement of Principles, the thrust of the book was made into an economics-premised argument. "Mixing up" other motives with the economic drive did not suffice to subordinate it sufficiently. Davidson, noting the mistake in tactics, wrote later that it had "puzzled our critics, who had somehow learned to think of 'agrarian' in the strictly occupational terms used by newspapers and professional economists," whereas "to us it signified a complete order of society based ultimately upon the land."[11] But it was not only that the term *agrarian* was in general usage associated with the cultivation of land, and at least since the days of the Roman Agrarian Laws had always been so associated; more importantly, it seemed to base the argument of the group upon an economic occupation rather than upon a mode of looking at the moral foundations of human experience. A last-minute attempt by Tate and Warren to change the title of the volume to *Tracts Against Communism* was the result, though not a very practical one, of a belated realization of polemical weaknesses of the title that was actually used. Ransom and Davidson opposed the change, both for practical problems of publication deadlines and advance publicity, and because to them the formulation seemed essentially correct. But Tate's warning that the use of the title would leave the group at the mercy of hostile critics who "need only to draw portraits of us plowing or cleaning a spring to make hash of us before we get a hearing"[12] proved only too true, as Davidson later conceded. At the same time, however, there is no reason to suppose that the term Agrarian of itself bothered Tate; his own suggested subtitle, "The Agrarian Tradition," made use of it, too. In any event, merely changing the title at the last minute would not have importantly altered the reception of the book, for the reason that the very presentation of the idea as one of "agrarian *versus* industrial" had caused the book to take the form that it did.

It would be interesting to know just how and when it happened that a book designed to "do something" about the South was made into a specifically focused advocacy of agrarianism. I would guess that the transaction occurred subsequent to Tate's letter to Davidson from Paris on August 10, 1929, in the course of conversations between Ransom, Davidson, and several of the other potential contributors at Vanderbilt, before Tate returned to the scene the following spring. To judge from the account in Virginia Rock's definitive study of the formation of the book, it was not until early 1930 that the specific word *Agrarian* began to be importantly used in their deliberations. I would hypothesize that the Agrarian formulation was advanced by Ransom, taken up by Davidson as providing a concrete schematization of the enterprise, and thereafter applied by the various contributors in different ways.

There can be no doubt that in this respect it was quite convenient. It enabled, for example, H. C. Nixon, whose views on social structure and economic authority were in certain respects at variance with those of several of the others, to join in without too much adjustment, thus giving the group its political economist, for Nixon did feel strongly that the southern farm economy was very much at the mercy of corporate finance and a protection-oriented federal government. It tied in beautifully with the history of southern sectionalism, which historically had been based on an agricultural-industrial opposition and had centered upon the protective tariff, and thus gave Frank Owsley his point of departure. It finessed the problem of the low-country–up-country, Populist-aristocrat schism, since an Agrarian could be anyone who lived on the land, whether dirt farmer or plantation grandee. It allowed full impulse to Andrew Lytle's strong attachment to rural southern folkways, making possible an impassioned plea to the farmer to forsake new-fangled fashion in favor of the old rural customs. For Davidson it provided the kind of organizing principle that could allow him to focus all his notions of regional loyalty, southern patriotism, distaste for cosmopolitan urban values, distrust of ideological formulations and oversimplifications, and fierce identification with the rural Tennessee of his origins. As for Ransom, the term *Agrarian*, with its image of field and harvest, not only offered the kind of concrete metaphor of the good life that had prompted his poem, "Antique Harvesters," but it carried with it certain philosophical and even theological connotations that pleased his need for an intellectual system, in a way that a word such as *agriculturalist* or *ruralist* or *traditionalist* could never do. For not only did Agrarian imply tillers of the soil, but believers in the beauty and dignity of life on the land as well. It had an intellectual respectability that at the same time invoked a practical sense of social and economic identity. An Agrarian, one might say, was a farmer with a philosophy.

The participants who seem most to have found the Agrarian formulation a handicap were Tate and Stark Young and, for different reasons, Warren. In Warren's instance it was obvious to him that the coming of factories and payrolls to the South held out to the black man attractions that could not be summarily dismissed as disabling and dehumanizing. However much he might assume—as Warren did at this juncture—that segregation was an inescapable condition, it was all too clear that to ask the black man to acquiesce willingly in rural poverty and tenant farming, when the coming of industrialism would mean jobs, cash money, and schools, was hardly realistic. Setting out to demonstrate that the black man had a stake in the rural and small-town South, Warren was quite

aware that his customary situation there was less than
idyllic, and that public and private policy were designed
to keep him in that disadvantaged position. Warren had to
come down hard, therefore, on the potential advantages
of the black man's place in the humanized southern community, as opposed to what industrialism might bring in
the way of attenuated race hatred, and had therefore to
insist accordingly that it was up to the white man to in-
sure that the black man was allotted an acceptable place
in such a community. "If the Southern white man feels
that the agrarian life has a certain irreplaceable value in
his society, and if he hopes to maintain its integrity in the
face of industrialism or its dignity in the face of agricultural depression, he must find a place for the negro in his
scheme," he declared. (263) Warren was forced, therefore, implicitly to criticize agricultural polity as actually
practiced in the South: The white man "must remember
that the strawberry or the cotton bale tells no tale in the
open market concerning its origins," (264) he wrote. It
seems obvious that Warren would have been happier if
his argument could have been made without reference to
the tilling of soil; for the way for the black man to achieve
the kind of self-sufficiency and self-respect that Warren
saw as necessary, while remaining in a racially separate
society, clearly led through such untraditional ways as vocational education, greater literacy, improvement of economic conditions, and (though Warren tried his best to
keep from making the overt statement) political fran-
chise. The truth is that the only way Warren could have
logically fitted southern racial segregation into an Agrarian argument was to have produced a standard Thomas
Nelson Page depiction of the black man as a happy, child-
like peasant, and Warren knew better than that.

The result was an essay that satisfied nobody, least of
all Warren. Some of the Agrarians, in particular Davidson and Owsley, were shocked at its heretical premises; as
Davidson wrote to Tate, Warren had not concentrated on

the Agrarian aspect: "It makes only two or three points that bear on our principles at all." There were all too many "implications which I am sure we don't accept—they are 'progressive' implications, with a pretty strong smack of latter-day sociology." He could not understand how Warren could have written it, "at least not the Red Warren I know. The very language, the catchwords, somehow don't fit. I am almost inclined to doubt whether RED ACTUALLY WROTE THIS ESSAY!"[13] It would seem in retrospect that the Agrarians would have been much better advised to have asked someone such as Stark Young to write on the black man in an Agrarian South; had he been willing, Young could have rung the changes on the joys of the old plantation.

Young's discomfort with the Agrarian approach—he later declared that he had never really been an Agrarian—was not with its social realism, or lack of it, but with its economic and social focus. What he meant with his essay was not a defense of a farming economy at all. Although the southern attitudes that he valued were, as he said, originally based upon the economics of the plantation South, they were no longer tied nearly so specifically to a particular economic and social context. They consisted of certain qualities of mind and spirit, certain human and humane values, that were, he said, the product of the South's landed heritage, were aristocratic in their nature, and provided the southerner of good family with a distinction in manners and attitude that he felt contrasted favorably with the ways of general America as a whole and the urban Northeast in particular. These were such things as private and public honor, disdain for mass opinion, courtesy, dignity, self-respect, a scorn of the more crass sort of money worship, a sense of social complexity, a belief in family, a disinclination to enshrine profit-making above cultural worth, individuality, leisure, and a pride in one's own provincial identity. Not only did this set of virtues not especially characterize dirt farmers, whether northern or southern, however much it may have fitted the landed non-metropolitan gentry of any region, but if these *are* the agrarian virtues, then there is something that is more than a little embarrassing about participation in a programmatic Agrarian movement (and it is this, I think, that accounts for Young's discomfort with it). For the Agrarian scheme, as promulgated by Ransom, Davidson, Lytle, and the others, was an ideology, a social program, a joint intellectual stratagem, not instinctive behavior but an act of the will, and Stark Young's ideal gentleman-aristocrat would have felt more than somewhat uncomfortable in the presence of anything so immoderate as that. The very term *agrarianism*, with its connotations of a ruling ideology and doctrinal authority, would surely cause uneasiness. It would involve a kind of violation of repose, an affair of cerebration rather than of habitual attitude and accustomed mode.

Stark Young was simply too sophisticated, I think, to be apt to conceive seriously of the restoration of the dirt farmer to the ideological center of the republic; that sort of thing had gone out with Thomas Jefferson. He could cherish his memories of the old folks at home, and in his fiction could envision the black man as happy peasant; but lacking, as Allen Tate did not, the apprehension of a growing moral and ethical crisis in the society, he could only view the purpose of *I'll Take My Stand* as an assertion of the continuing value of aristocratic standards. "It is impossible to believe," he wrote, "that a Southerner of good class, with a father who was a gentleman of honorable standards, pride, and formal conceptions, could regard many of our present leaders, however heroic they appear in the tabloids and in the unconscious lapses of great editorial writers, with quite the naïvete of some self-made foreman in a shoe factory, of some Bowery child, born out of a magnificent, ancient spiritual tradition, but muddled with the crass American life around him. For this inheritance of ours, together with all we have learned, all there is outside to profit by, the South must find its own use." (358) But how? And precisely to what use? Young didn't say, but certainly the Agrarian program of action did not seem, in any literal sense, either feasible or important to him.

With Tate it was another matter entirely. Like Young, Tate did not envision the Agrarian program as a feasible course of practical social reform, as he pointed out to Davidson (about Ransom's attitude, however, he was wrong; Ransom became much more literally involved in agrarianism as a social program than Tate anticipated). But Tate was by no means willing to separate the kind of aristocratic virtues and attitudes which Young so esteemed from the social and moral situation in which they must function. He may have agreed (I am sure he did) that to the extent that such habits and attitudes characterized southern society, they had been imposed upon it from the top—as Young put it, "our traditional southern characteristics derive from the landed class." (337) But he knew very well that if such characteristics were to have any value beyond that of social snobbery, they had to be more than personal gestures; they had to be grounded in the life and the values of a society, and exist as the expression of not merely economic but moral and religious conviction. They must be elemental to the society's existence as well as ornamental; however creative, nostalgia would not do.

Young was in habit and attitude a conservative; Tate was a radical, a conservative revolutionary who sought fundamental reconstruction. (He liked to call himself a reactionary.) At the same time, however, Tate was not so simple as to think that any kind of attempt at literal restoration of an Agrarian ordering for the South was possible, in the sense of a collective political, social, and economic movement being made into public policy in the South. What he sought, as he wrote to Davidson, was "an intellectual situation interior to the South"—which is to

say, a marshaling of informed southern opinion, the conscious awakening of the region's intelligentsia to the values inherent in southern community life and to the way
in which those values were being menaced by the region's
capitulation to the urban and industrial forces that domi-
nated twentieth-century American life. He wanted the
makers of southern opinion to be made aware of how
much their instinctively held, but largely unexamined,
beliefs in what their society should be and how it should
be constituted were endangered by the largely contradictory implications of their own present political, economic,
and social thinking. The South was swiftly becoming, he
thought, what it largely did not want to be, and it would
continue to do so until and unless informed southern
opinion could be made to see what was happening. At
bottom, he was convinced, the problem was philosophical,
religious; to put the South's economic and social house in
proper order, there would first have to occur a recognition of and conscious allegiance to certain basic, underlying premises about the nature of man and society. He
envisioned the joint effort of himself and his friends as a
movement designed to bring about just such a recognition
and awareness. If they could dramatize the crisis, make
conscious the unconsciously held assumptions, force a re-
examination of attitudes about society and man so that
contradictions might be recognized and self-defeating responses and actions identified as such, then something
might be accomplished. This, he thought, could be the
role of southern intellectuals; by constituting themselves
as an Academy, they could, like the *Encyclopédistes* of pre-
Revolutionary France (to whom Tate likened the group
many years later),[14] have a genuine impact upon regional
opinion. As he wrote somewhat later of Poe and the profession of letters in the South, Poe "meant business," and
"until the desperate men today who mean business can
become an independent class, there will be no profession
of letters anywhere in America."[15]

Given Tate's set of objectives, the specific Agrarian formulation was a formidable handicap. Not only did it imply that regional economics came first, but also that the thinking southerner's hope of regaining his tradition could be possible only by actively favoring a reshaping of twentieth-century southern economic life along specific nineteenth-century lines. If this was not what Ransom, Davidson, and the others *meant*, it was what the connotations of the word *Agrarian* implied.

So if the movement that Tate proposed had any chance of directing southern opinion toward an examination of the true moral and religious beliefs of the southern community and thus forcing a reassessment of the wisdom of much of the South's acceptance of modernism, some crippling limitations were thereby incurred. It was one thing to be opposed to the tawdry slogans of boosterism and what Ransom termed the Gospel of Progress; it was another to tell a farmer to weave his own jeans rather than buy them at a store because it threatened his Agrarian values not to do so. It was one thing to favor Thomas Jefferson's formulation of moral judgment as "'taste'— reliance on custom, breeding, ingrained moral decision," as against John Adams' use of "'a process of moral reasoning,' which forces the individual to think out from abstract principles his rôle at a critical moment of action," to use Tate's formulation. (170) It was another thing to oppose public high school and college educational opportunities for most white and all black southerners, as John Gould Fletcher did, because "what is the good of sending an unspoiled country boy or girl to a city high school and still later to a college, if after some seven years' sophisticated flirting with knowledge he or she has to return and unwillingly take up ploughing and washing dishes again?" (119) The necessity of having to accept Fletcher's views on public education in order to take part in Tate's "intellectual situation interior to the South" would alone have alienated many, if not most, thinking southerners. Yet given the Agrarian formulation, Fletcher's views (which, however, I suspect would in their intransigent hyperbole have pleased Tate) on secondary and higher education were quite proper. Again, this was not what Ransom and most of the others meant by "agrarian *versus* industrial"; but it was what, by using the term *agrarianism*, they were made to seem to mean.

As Tate had predicted, the way that *I'll Take My Stand* was set forth played into the hands of the group's opponents. The *Macon Telegraph*, for example, declared that the Agrarians "desire horses and buggies and music boxes to replace automobiles and radios. They want huge Georgian plantation homes with well filled slave quarters to take the place of suburbs and industrial villages." Writing in *The Nation*, Henry Hazlitt asserted that if the Agrarian attitude toward progress had prevailed in the past, "we should still be in the savage stage—assuming that we had at least accepted such technological advances as flint and the spearhead." W. B. Hesseltine, in the *Chattanooga News*, ridiculed the Agrarians' foolishness in "apotheosizing agrarian culture, and elevating the yeoman farmer to a pedestal"; the history of the South from Jamestown to the Scopes trial, he said, was a horrible example of the spiritual failure of agrarianism. H. L. Mencken declared that the South "can no more revive the simple society of the Jeffersonian era than England can revive that of Queen Anne. The mills and factories are there to stay, and they must be faced."[16]

All these things being so, it seems very obvious to me that given the true objectives of the leading members of the group, the specific Agrarian delineation was a strategic error of considerable magnitude. It was *not* the moral and social virtues of a farm economy that Tate, Ransom Davidson, and Warren were really concerned with, and their arguments were both blunted in formulation and distorted in their impact by being so designated. What Davidson said in 1935 was what they were truly about

"I am sure that at first we did not do much thinking in strictly economic terms. Uppermost in our minds was our feeling of intense disgust with the spiritual disorder of modern life—its destruction of human integrity and its lack of purpose; and, with this, we had a decided sense of impending fatality. We wanted a life which through its own conditions and purposefulness would engender naturally (rather than by artificial stimulation), order, leisure, character, stability, and that would also, in the larger sense, be aesthetically enjoyable."[17]

This was what all of them were after. But as Davidson goes on to say, as their thinking developed they "realized that the good life of the Old South, in its best period, and the life of our own South so far as it was still characteristic, was not to be separated from the agrarian tradition which was and is its foundation. By this route we came at last to economics and so found ourselves at odds with the prevailing schools of economic thought."[18] I am sure that this accurately described what most of them did think, or believed that they did, but there would seem to be at least two fallacies in the argument. One is the hypothesis that what they most valued about southern community life could not be separated from Agrarian economics. A more realistic appraisal of the situation, even before the depression of the 1930s, would have told them that if what they most valued was to have any real chance of being defended, it would *have to be* separated from the agrarian situation, insofar as any specific economic reference was concerned. Ransom's statement that the "question at issue" was whether the South would permit itself to be totally industrialized at the expense of its community identity, or would "accept industrialism, but with a very bad grace" so as to "maintain a good deal of her traditional philosophy" (22) was another way of saying just this. But instead of confronting this fact and framing their strategy accordingly, the group for the most part preferred to ignore it.

The other fallacy, it seems to me, is that having "come at last to economics," it was either practicable or advisable for them to base their campaign on an economic formulation of what they were about. For if life should determine economics, and not vice versa, as Davidson went on to say and as they all believed, then the starting point and the point of ultimate return alike of their argumentation should have been what was "uppermost in our minds . . . our feeling of intense disgust with the spiritual disorder of modern life,"[19] and not an Agrarian economy.

Such is the wisdom of hindsight. On the other hand, however, one must ask this question: if not agrarianism, then what? Tate later said that he conceived of the book as a defense of religious humanism. The term would, in a general way, fit what almost all of them were doing, but not only is it hardly a symbol for rallying around, it omits the critical identification with the South that lay at the heart of the whole venture. We must remember that one of the strongest impulses behind the origination of *I'll Take My Stand* was that of affording the participants a way of asserting a continuing identification with the larger southern community. To have put forward their program, or even to have thought of it, under any device so general and so intellectual as "religious humanism" would not only have failed to serve their purposes, but exemplified just such a human fragmentation as they wished to deny.

Since so much of the motivation for the volume was, in implication, religious, someone without intimate knowledge of the South might well wonder why the frank avowal of a specific religious community identity might not have served their purposes best. But to ask the question is to answer it. *Which* specific religious identity? Except for Tate, the leading figures were of Methodist stock, but all had, in one way or another, forsaken the old religious orthodoxy, and however much they might miss its ordering potentialities and remain dissatisfied with any thing less than a City Upon a Hill, they could no more have defined their individual identities and common role under a specific Protestant religious allegiance than they could have subordinated their poetry to such an extraliterary authority. Sympathize though they did with the fundamentalists and their spiritual fervor when the Scopes trial brought forth so devastating an onslaught against them by all the forces of eclectic modernity and science, they could not accede to any such credo themselves. Tate, in the opening paragraphs of his "Remarks on the Southern Religion," declared that he began "with almost no humility at all . . . in a spirit of irreligion, and without apologies to those who know better, for there seems to be none, as a class, who have that high qualification." (155) In so saying he spoke, I think, for them all, though each one's emphasis might be different. Not one of the four leading Agrarians was an active Protestant believer, in the orthodox sense of the word (and there is probably no other sense of the word that could mean very much of anything).

Their religion was, in essence, a secular one: the South. Tate recognized that very clearly, for the burden of "Remarks on the Southern Religion" was that there *was* none, as such. He recognized only the social and moral implications *for* belief in a faith which should have been, but was not, something resembling (though Tate did not say it) Roman Catholicism much more closely than any of the standard southern Protestant churches.

What Tate meant, I think, was that social, economic, and political conditions of life in the Old South had resulted in a habit of mind which was essentially suited to a religious ordering resembling that of medieval Europe, but that the evangelical Protestantism the Old South professed in its churches was aggressive and materialistic, a "non-agrarian and trading religion." (168) The inadequacy of such a religion resulted in the denial to the South of a theology that could enable it to resist "the postbellum temptations of the devil, who is the exploiter of nature" (173)—so that what had been a non-materialistic, agrarian society was now swiftly capitulating to the exploitative forces of modern industrial society.

If Tate's diagnosis was correct, then the view that Ransom, Davidson, and Tate himself took toward the older, agrarian South and its history and culture was essentially religious, and I think this is largely true. That is to say, they thought and felt about the South in terms appropriate to religious belief. Ransom's poem "Antique Harvesters," with its explicit identification of the South with "Our Lady," and its depiction of faithful southerners as harvesters garnering her treasure, makes Tate's point admirably. So, too, does Davidson's finest poem, "Lee in the Mountains," with its beautiful closing evocation of General Lee telling the young southern collegians that God "in His might" waits

> Brooding within the certitude of time,
> To bring this lost forsaken valor
> And the fierce faith undying
> And the love quenchless
> To flower among the hills to which we cleave,
> To fruit upon the mountains whither we flee . . .[20]

And so, too, if a good deal less poetically, does the epitaph of the southerner quoted by Stark Young in *A Southern Treasury of Prose and Poetry*, who, according to the inscription upon his tombstone, "die[d] a Christian and a Democrat."[21]

The truth is that the *only* rubric that might serve to cover the various objectives and concerns of the contributors to *I'll Take My Stand* had of necessity to be the idea of the South. It was this identification, going along with the growing distaste for the urban, industrial drive of the 1920s in the United States, that had prompted the group's formation in the first place. They had wanted to "do something" about the South. In retrospect one can say that they would have been well advised to hold their program to that, and not to have proceeded by logic to the specific agricultural economic image. This, I feel, is more or less what Tate wanted: a vigorous defense of the life and values of the traditional southern community, in the face of the forces of change that were bent upon transforming it—positive reaction, as he termed it. In 1927 he had written Davidson that "the chief defect the Old South had was that in it which produced, through whatever cause, the New South. I think the test of the True Southern Spirit would be something like this: whenever the demagogues cry 'Nous allons!' if the reply is 'Non! Nous retardons!' then you may be sure the reply indicates the right values. The symptom of advance must be seen as a symptom of decay."[22] But the group needed something more positive than that, and they were unwilling to have their project be merely an expression of their belief in the old community and dislike of progress. Philosophical and literary resistance was not sufficient; they wished to have something equally specific and practical to offer in the place of the New South ideal of progress and prosperity through industrialization. Thus when Ransom developed the Agrarian identification as the logical result of their discussions, the others accepted it.

The real difficulty, it seems to me, was that the essence of the Agrarian program was not and could not consistently be made to be specific and practical, in the sense of offering concrete alternatives to modernism and industrialism. The only "practical" proposal that could be made was to pursue an agrarian economy, and several hundred years of western European and American history and a long-disadvantaged regional economy militated against any such possibility. The values that the Agrarians wished to preserve and enhance were important precisely because they were *not* "practical," and it was a mistake to have presented them as otherwise. Whenever the philosophical, social, and religious attitudes that the various Agrarians professed were placed in a "practical" context, as in Ransom's attempt in the early 1930s to improve the farm economy, they were either inadequate or absurd. What the Agrarians had to offer, both individually and as a group, was what Tate proposed: a reasoned, intelligent, planned defense of religious values and humane community attitudes as a way of retarding (and in the doing, humanizing) the pell-mell rush of the modern South to adopt the ways, values and practices of industrial America.

There was and is no "practical" alternative to indoor plumbing and rural electrification; nor, I am convinced, were most of the Agrarians really interested in discovering one if it existed. What they wanted was to make people aware that plumbing and electrical appliances were not the be-all and end-all of existence, that there were qualities about community experience that were every bit as important as the securing of plumbing and rural electrification, and that if they did not recognize and look to the preservation of these qualities, a single-minded pursuit of septic tanks and rural electrification at any cost might result in their destruction. That, and not the economic virtues of subsistence farming, is what *I'll Take My Stand* was and still is all about.

A Band of Prophets

It may be remembered that when plans for *I'll Take My Stand* were getting into high gear, Allen Tate wrote to Donald Davidson from Paris to say that, unlike Davidson and some of the others, he was skeptical about the eventual success, "in the practical sense," of the project. He thought "that there is enough value to satisfy me in the affirmation, in all its consequences, including action, of value,"[23] but did not anticipate Nashville agrarianism would be achieving any direct impact upon southern society. Tate also said that he thought Ransom and Warren agreed with that estimate.

It turned out that Ransom, however skeptical about the practical impact of Agrarianism at the outset, became for a time deeply involved in its practicalities once the enterprise became public fact. In reaction to the charges of impracticality leveled against the Agrarian statement, he would seem to have been caught up in the economic argument for agrarianism, and he spent the next several years studying economics, writing about farming, and attempting Agrarian polemics of a quite specific sort. Later, when he began breaking with the movement, he moved rather emphatically to make known his change of mind. But during the early 1930s he was as dedicated and as involved an Agrarian as could be imagined.

Davidson's own involvement, as Tate pointed out, was never less than literal and whole-souled, and it carried over into everything he wrote. He identified the cause of the South with the cause of agrarianism; they were one and the same for him. The literary regionalism of the 1930s fitted handily into his thinking; to stress the cultural hegemony of the region was as natural as to make the case for agrarian, non-metropolitan society. When in 1937 Ransom gave signs of slackening in his advocacy of agrarianism, Davidson was outraged; he wrote to Tate, quoting a remark that Ransom had made: "'Mr. Davidson had always taken a more *Southern view* etc., etc. than the rest of us.'"[24] Davidson couldn't understand how Ransom could make a distinction between Agrarianism and the South, and he felt, correctly as it turned out, that Ransom was backing off from the whole enterprise.

In early 1943 Davidson published an article in the *Saturday Review of Literature* entitled "The 'Mystery' of the Agrarians," in which he criticized a reference by one commentator to "John Crowe Ransom and his Southern Agrarians"—the Agrarians, Davidson said, "were never John Crowe Ransom's property, nor was he or anybody else their manager or high commander." He also suggested that the book that Herbert Agar and Allen Tate had edited in 1936, *Who Owns America?*, in which Tate and Agar had joined into a single volume Agrarian and English Distributist critiques of industrial capitalism, had "rather unfortunately displaced" a sequel to *I'll Take My Stand* in which the Agrarians would have presented "the extensions and amendments of their views, the applications and documentations of their ideas."[25] Tate in reply pointed out to his friend that the Tate-Agar book had come about only because Davidson and the other Agrarians had not themselves acted to get out an Agrarian sequel. He also wrote that "you evidently believe agrarianism was a failure; I think it was and *is* a very great success; but then I never expected it to have any political influence. It is a reaffirmation of the humane tradition, and to reaffirm that is an end in itself. Never fear: we shall be remembered when our snipers are forgotten."[26]

Whether in fact the agrarian enterprise could be considered successful or unsuccessful depended upon how it was defined. It cannot be said to have succeeded in the objective stated in the "Statement of Principles," to persuade younger southerners "who are being converted frequently to the industrial gospel" to "come back to the support of the Southern tradition." (xx) Even in the worst stages of the economic depression the South continued to industrialize, and once the economy went back on the upswing the industrialism proceeded as never before. The economic boom attendant upon World War II converted the region into one in which industry became financially more important than agriculture, and the years that followed saw the South narrow the gap in per capita wealth between it and the remainder of the nation, become predominantly a region of cities, and bid goodbye to much of the political and social apparatus attendant upon its former agricultural life. Subsistence farming dwindled; New Deal legislation had the intended effect of getting marginal farmers off the land to keep food prices at profitable levels; development of mechanical equipment did away with the need for large-scale black farm labor, and the blacks departed for the cities; the nature of southern agriculture thus changed considerably. No one, surveying the South today, can say that the region is primarily agrarian in its economy.

Nor can the South be said to have held to the specifics of its political and social "traditions," insofar as they involved such factors as fealty to the Confederate heritage, one-party democratic rule, white supremacy, and the like. The day passed when a southern politician could get elected by invoking the memory of the Lost Cause. For the generation of southerners who came to maturity with World War II, and whose experience involved no memory of living Confederate veterans, the names of Lee, Jackson, Forrest, and the heroes of the past held little beyond an antiquarian interest. The situation portrayed by Tate's watcher at the cemetery gate in "Ode to the Confederate Dead," pondering his distance from his tradition, did not importantly characterize the actual experience of a later generation; for the younger southerners the Confederate past could be at most a metaphor, rather than a specific, palpable social reality—which was pretty much what the poem had suggested was happening. In politics, no longer does the southern politician get elected by excoriating the ways of the city. Southern politics of the 1970s bears only the most superficial resemblance to that of the years when the Agrarians were formulating their plans.

As for white supremacy, to the extent that it was a southern "tradition" it has eroded to an almost incredible degree. From being the least, the South has perhaps become the most racially integrated of all American regions, with the result that there is probably less racial unrest in the South than anywhere else in the country where race is a factor. The effects on everyday southern life have been complex; and the shift of the center of racial tension from the rural South to the large cities of the

North and the Midwest has meant that the region's political relationship to the rest of the country has dramatically changed. Thus, as the nation celebrated its Bicentennial, it witnessed the spectacle of a rural southerner being elected president of the United States, with a nearly solid black vote providing his margin of victory. The region is by no means a showcase for racial harmony—we have none in this country; but more than one black leader has commented publicly that the problem of the black man in American life may be coming closer to genuine solution in the towns and cities of the onetime Confederacy than in the large northern cities. When school integration aroused public resentment in Boston recently, for example, the students at integrated public high schools in Charlotte, North Carolina, invited the Massachusetts students to come down and see for themselves how well it could be made to work.

Except for Warren's essay "The Briar Patch," as we have seen, *I'll Take My Stand* had very little to say about the presence and place of the black man in the South. In offering the example of the Old South as a society free of the commercial materialism of modern industrial life, of course, the Agrarians had to take cognizance of the fact that Negro slavery lay at the basis of that society. Thus Ransom referred to slavery as "a feature monstrous enough in theory, but, more often than not, humane in practice." (14) Owsley, discussing "The Irrepressible Conflict," had to deal with it; his basic approach was the traditional one, to the effect that the North had used the slavery issue to further its economic imperialism. Neither he nor Ransom saw slavery as essential to southern agrarianism. Generally the black man in *I'll Take My Stand* is viewed as a kind of peasant, an element in southern society fitted to be the hewer of wood and drawer of water, and one that can be accommodated within an Agrarian dispensation without too much adjustment. Only Warren's essay faced the fact that the black man had much to gain, in the way of economic and educational opportunity, from the coming of industrialism, and Warren's solution, as we have seen, was to insist that while the black man would really be better off without industrialism, too, it would be essential for him to enjoy the equal opportunity implied in the "separate but equal" shibboleth. Warren's essay was thus implicitly disruptive of the southern racial status quo, as several of his colleagues at once recognized.

F. Garvin Davenport, in *The Myth of Southern History*, has portrayed the Agrarians as caught in a dilemma over the black man that vitiated their effort at offering a coherent critique of industrialism. To deal with industrialism meant dealing with the black man, but to offer leadership in combatting the evils of industrialism meant offering leadership in solving the racial problem, and the way toward solving that lay in the methods and attitudes of the new social sciences, which were part and parcel of urban industrialism, and which would also have split them apart from the very southern community consciousness that they sought to arouse. This was the historical trap, Davenport contends, from which the Agrarians, as southerners, could not escape.[27]

It is quite true that if one views agrarianism as an attempt to create, or perhaps recreate, an agrarian "garden," a place where man might regain innocence and his society be made simple and nonacquisitive, then there were serious contradictions and confusions within the enterprise, of which the second-class citizenship of the black southerner was only one. Virginia Rock, in her excellent dissertation, "The Making and Meaning of *I'll Take My Stand*: A Study in Utopian-Conservatism, 1925–1939," makes pretty much the same assumption as Davenport: "The Agrarians never admitted in the symposium that a man is as thoroughly enslaved by a discriminatory system perpetuated by laws as by serving the machine; a Negro is degraded as a man by being denied human and political rights no less than is the factory worker who is reduced to a time-clock card. Spiritual death is as certain for one as for the other." Miss Rock's subtitle, "A Study in *Utopian*-Conservatism," shows what is assumed in her argument, and in Davenport's as well. Arguing that the Agrarian hope of restoring a life unspoiled by industrialism was retrogressively Utopian and therefore essentially ahistorical, Miss Rock writes that "through their Agrarian myth, localized in the South before it was—as they believed—infested by industrialism, the Agrarians hoped to destroy the realities of a mechanistic, materialistic modernism."[28]

It is quite in order, of course, to treat the Agrarian movement as if it were a Utopian enterprise; one can find considerable justification in some of the essays of *I'll Take My Stand*, such as Andrew Lytle's impassioned plea for rejection of the machine in favor of old-time subsistence farming, for looking at agrarianism in such fashion. If this is one's approach to *I'll Take My Stand*, then the criticisms advanced by Miss Rock, Mr. Davenport, and others might be said to have considerable validity. The Agrarians did tend to ignore some of the more vexing realities of southern history and experience in urging retention and enhancement of the old agricultural society.

Yet such an approach, however more subtle and reasoned, is ultimately no more central to what *I'll Take My Stand* was really all about, and what it meant and means, than the attacks that came out upon its first publication, in which the Agrarians were depicted as romantic apologists for slavery and nostalgic dreamers who wished to restore plantation life. For all such responses to *I'll Take My Stand* assume what I think ought scarcely to be assumed: that the underlying dynamics of the Agrarian enterprise were ever directed toward the achievement of economic and social reformation, and that the significance of *I'll Take My Stand* lay or lies in the quality of its recommendations for repealing the industrial age.

Such assumptions seem very dubious to me, for if the Agrarian symposium is to be pronounced as deserving our attention because it offered an expedient alternative to industrialism, whether for the South or for the nation at large, then it is hard to fathom how it could be taken seriously at all. It makes no real economic proposals for dispensing with what the machine age can offer; it hardly even defines what agrarianism is, other than something generally involving a society in which farming is of importance; it says a great deal about what is wrong with industrialism, but almost nothing about how to get rid of it or what to establish in its place; it leaves a whole host of practical problems untouched, of which the place of the black man is but one. Furthermore, in this sense it is indeed ahistorical, in that it generally overlooks or oversimplifies why industrialism came and why the Old South fell. Published in the year 1930, it says little or nothing about sharecropping, crop liens, or farm tenantry.

So if the book does have the continuing significance that its continued life for almost a half-century surely indicates, is it reasonable to assume that the basis of such an appeal could possibly reside in its proposed alternative to southern industrialism? The very notion would seem preposterous. One might as soon view the recommendations made by Henry David Thoreau as important for the practical alternative offered therein to industrialism. The feasibility and plausibility of the entire population of Massachusetts taking to the woods in the 1840s, as a way of rejecting the rise of New England industrialization, were hardly more remote than a literal acceptance of an Agrarian economy by the South in the year 1930; and one ought scarcely to attribute *I'll Take My Stand*'s continued life to its practical recommendations, any more than that of *Walden* to the same kind of appeal.

Of course it is quite true that there were those among the Agrarians, particularly Davidson, who saw the enterprise as a practical political and economic program with very real chances of success. But even in Davidson's instance, we must ask of what such a success would have consisted. Surely not the turning away of the South from any further dealings with industrialism; Davidson knew better than that. All that Davidson could have hoped for was a reawakening of southern sectional consciousness to a degree that would have caused the region to chart its own course, resolutely and consciously, in the direction of maintaining its community identity and refusing to let its patterns of daily life be depersonalized and coarsened by a massive urban, industrial regimen. In a letter to Tate in late December of 1929, Davidson suggested that "perhaps our program develops into a program of provincialism in general, not only Southern provincialism, and with it all the values (to be defined and announced) that belong to a country life, decentralized, stable, local, self-sufficient, etc., as opposed to the other thing now rampant but already attacked from various quarters. In that view, the South would be the most obvious historical and contemporary example available, and the most exciting example."[29] Even in thus foreseeing an extension of their enterprise beyond a southern application, Davidson was hardly anticipating an agrarian society as supplanting the American industrial economy; primarily he wanted southern attitudes, values, loyalties, and community ways, which he associated with "country life," defended against the ideological and social values and attitudes of modernism. If this was utopianism, it was so only in a kind of general, negative way; it was certainly not a practical economic program that he envisioned.

Tate' of course, was not prepared to go even that far. Indeed, there was nothing utopian whatever about Tate's attitude toward the Agrarian venture. When he wrote Davidson in 1943, as we have seen, that in his view agrarianism had been and still was a success, since it had been a "reaffirmation of the humane tradition," he was saying no more or less than he had suggested in 1929 when he stated his skepticism about the enterprise's practical importance on the plane of action. From the outset, Tate conceived of the movement only on the terms that constituted its ultimate importance and secured its appeal: its assertion of religious humanism, through offering a vigorous and imaginative rebuke to the dehumanizing, materialistic forces of modern industrialism.

A dispassionate examination of *I'll Take My Stand*, from the "Statement of Principles" that castigated industrialism and had so little to say about agrarianism, onward through the various essays, can only reveal how appropriate was Tate's version of what the enterprise was all about. It was a way of striking out against the deification of the machine, of warning against the depersonalizing forces of an unchecked, unrestrained industrial capitalism. It was not utopian so much as protest literature. The agrarian community which it imaged filled the function not of an economic alternative to the city, but of a pastorale rebuke giving warning of the fragmenting complexity of modern urban society. And like all pastorale, it was written not for shepherds but for city dwellers—for southerners who were already living in urban America.

The literary tradition into which *I'll Take My Stand* fits, therefore, is not that of works such as *The Republic, Das Capital,* or the *Nouvelle Héloïse,* with their proposals and systematic master plans for the reorganization of society along Utopian lines. Rather, it is the tradition of Cooper's *The American Democrat, Walden,* the American Scholar Address—works that censured the abuses of the age. Between the social and theological assumptions of New England transcendentalism and those of Nashville Agrarians there is a considerable difference, but in inception and motivation the movements are quite similar. Both were the work of poets who became alarmed at the complacency and materialism of their society, and who felt an

absence of spiritual concern within the society. The leading Transcendentalists were of Calvinist background,
had become Unitarians, and broke with what Emerson
called the "corpse-cold Unitarianism of Harvard College
and Brattle Street" to reassert the supremacy of human
feeling and warmth over the Protestant work ethic and
the tyranny of the countinghouse. They reasserted the
New England spiritual heritage of the once-vital City
Upon A Hill, not in terms of the old Puritan theology,
which they too rejected, but what Perry Miller calls "a
passionate search of the soul and of nature," in which
they "sought with renewed fervor for the accents of
the Holy Ghost in their own hearts and in woods and
mountains."[30]

In very much the same way, the young Fugitives had
come out of the old social community of the premodern
South, with its religious orthodoxy and its traditional pieties, had found themselves in the urbanizing, industrializing America of the 1920s, and had missed in its "vulgar prosperity that retrogrades ever to barbarism" (as
Emerson had said of Massachusetts of his own day) the
kind of life in which (to quote Ransom of Tennessee)
"man and nature seem to live on terms of mutual respect
and amity, and his loving arts, religions, and philosophies
come spontaneously into being." (7) And like Emerson
and his friends, they felt impelled to express their disagreement with the prevailing mercantilist establishment
and to warn of its dehumanizing potentialities—the more
so since, as southerners, they had come late to industrialism, and had seen some of its destructive potentialities
used against their own community in the not-so-distant
history.

The essential kinship of the impulse behind Nashville
agrarianism with the apprehensive concerns of the New
Englanders of a century earlier is immediately apparent,
I think, if we examine a book like *Walden*, and in particular passages like the following:

The nation itself, with all its so-called internal improvements, which, by the way, are all external and superficial, is just such an unwieldy and over-grown establishment, cluttered with furniture and tripped up by its own traps, ruined by luxury and heedless expense, by want of calculation and worthy aim, as the million households in the land . . . . Men think it is essential that the *Nation* have commerce, and export ice, and talk through a telegraph, and ride thirty miles an hour, without a doubt, whether *they* do or not; but whether we should live like baboons or like men, is a little uncertain. If we do not get out sleepers, and forge rails, and devote days and nights to the work, but go to tinkering with our *lives* to improve *them*, who will build railroads? And if railroads are not built, how will we get to heaven in season? But if we stay at home and mind our business, who will want railroads? We do not ride on the railroad; it rides upon us.[31]

"Simplify! Simplify!" Thoreau counseled the members of a rapidly expanding New England urban society. His journey to Walden Pond and his vigil in the woods were an attempt to discover and describe what was essential, and what was superficial and materialistic, about life in his society. Critics of Thoreau, such as James Russell Lowell, who pointed out the inconsistencies and impracticalities of his undertaking, missed the point. "Thoreau's experiment," Lowell complained, "actually presupposed all that complicated civilization which it theoretically abjured. He squatted on another man's land; he borrows an ax; his boards, his nails, his bricks, his mortar, his books, his fishhooks, his plow, his hoe, all turn state's evidence against him as an accomplice in the sin of that artificial civilization which rendered it possible that such a person as Henry D. Thoreau should exist at all."[32] (In just such fashion, certain critics of the 1930s "refuted" agrarianism by pointing to the fact that the participants were mostly college professors, not farmers.) But Thoreau was no primitivist; nor was he suggesting that his fellow citizens literally adopt his particular example. He was constructing, in highly literary fashion, a metaphoric pastorale, structured upon the image of the rhythm of the seasons, in which he was urging his fellow New Englanders to examine their social, economic, and political assumptions to see whether their involvement in the values and concerns of their society was serving to enhance or impede their confrontation with the essentials of human life. His own close observation of nature was proposed, not as a universal model to be followed, but as a way of showing how the possibilities of consciousness were being glossed over or obscured by the slavish, unexamined bondage to material possessions, by men who "through mere ignorance and mistake, are so occupied with the factitious cares and superfluously coarse labors of life, that its finer fruits cannot be plucked by them."[33] To point out impracticalities or inconsistencies in Thoreau's specific arrangements at Walden Pond, as Lowell and others have done, is irrelevant. To claim that in his handling of the Irish laborers who seemed to represent a lower order for him, he failed in his own human compassion, may be true, but surely the failure must be seen as strictly tangential to the meaning and to the significance of the work of humane affirmation that is *Walden*.

In the same way, I think, charges that the Agrarian enterprise failed to come to terms with the needs of the black southerner are, while no doubt true, not an important invalidation of *I'll Take My Stand*; the book's significance had very little to do with the specific social arrangements it proposed for the South.

The Agrarians, of course, would not have been especially flattered by a comparison of *I'll Take My Stand* with the writings of Emerson or Thoreau (both of whom were abolitionists), and there are some striking differences between the New Englanders and the southerners which cannot be overlooked. For one thing, *I'll Take My Stand* was informed by an intense sense of social necessity. The Agrarians wrote in terms of a community responsibility, not of the individual consciousness, and they were suspicious of the unaided vision that could dispense with tradition and role within society in order to confront natural truth. Men must not lose sight of nature, they insisted, but they also insisted that men were not defined through nature, but set apart from it by the very fact of their humanity. Thoreau's appeal to the Higher Law was abhorrent to them, both socially and morally; they could not envision the human being as perfectible, nor would they trust him to do good without the constraints of social and historical experience to guide him. Nor did they identify simplicity with spartan austerity; they would not starve the body to improve the soul, and they did not see any particular virtue in doing without such amenities as life afforded. They would have scoffed at Thoreau's notion that the ownership of property necessarily involves enslavement to it; theirs was no advocacy of a state of anarchic nature.

Finally, the Agrarian enterprise was steeped in the history of the South, and strongly informed by its historical sense; the best of the past was held up as a model. The New Englanders, by contrast, who did not write out of a heritage of military defeat and had never known the experience of failure, were essentially uninterested in history; they looked to the future, not the past, for guide and verification. The southerners were not optimists; the New Englanders were that, although Thoreau was sometimes whistling in the dark. "There is more day to dawn," Thoreau declared in ending *Walden*. "The sun is but a morning star":[34] a very different matter indeed from Allen Tate's key question, "How may the Southerner take hold of his Tradition?" (174) Indeed, Tate has written that the willingness of Ralph Waldo Emerson to speak for the future at all costs, to discredit the old theology as a constraint upon man's realization of his human potentiality, had the result that he "unwittingly became the prophet of a piratical industrialism, a consequence of his own transcendental individualism that he could not foresee."[35] (Tate's proposition, I think, is just about as ridiculous as censuring the Agrarians, as some did, for unwittingly sponsoring fascism.)

No matter. For all their differences in assumptions and values, it seems to me that so far as their objectives went the Nashville Agrarians were engaged in a kindred enterprise, as distinctively rooted in the American experience as that of the New Englanders of a century earlier, and one that needs constantly to be performed. In a society threatened by the material success of its own economic entrepreneurism, they were asserting the primacy of the human spirit and were rebuking the dependency upon material possessions and the lure of wealth.

And, just as Emerson and Thoreau had called upon their fellow New Englanders of the 1830s and 1840s to examine their assumptions, and not to accept without question what custom and habit informed them was inevitable about their lives, so the essays in *I'll Take My Stand* repeatedly make the point that if southerners would preserve the community in which human beings could live decent lives, it was necessary to think about it, to act consciously rather than to drift indecisively. "Men are prepared to sacrifice their private dignity and happiness," their Statement of Principles declared, "to an abstract social ideal, and without asking whether the social ideal produces the welfare of any individual man whatsoever. But this is absurd." (xxviii) Ransom built his essay on the need for the South to control, consciously and determinedly, whatever industrialism was necessary to their well-being rather than be controlled by it. Davidson stressed the need for the provincial tradition "to be consciously studied and maintained by artists, Southern or not, as affording a last stand in America against the industrial devourer—a stand that might prove to be a turning-point." (59–60) Stark Young insisted that "we can, if we only would, see industrialism as it spreads in the South, and study it, from the vantage point of theory, criticism, and error elsewhere developed from experience and from longer observation. We can accept the machine, but create our own attitude toward it." (355)

As for Tate, he based his whole argument upon the necessity for the South, if it would reestablish and retain its tradition, to proceed by conscious act; it could not be done otherwise. "How may the Southerner take hold of his Tradition?" he asked. "The answer is, by violence"— by an act of the conscious will, and he was skeptical that it could be done: "I say he must do this; but that remains to be seen." (173–74) From the beginning of the enterprise Tate had seen the principal objective as that of getting the South to think about the situation confronting it; as we have seen, his proposed course of action was designed to *"create an intellectual situation interior to the South.* I underscore it because, to me, it contains the heart of the matter."[36] Most of all the Agrarians, perhaps, he saw the movement in its ultimate terms: not the assertion of the need for a farming economy; nor the preservation of a status quo, whether social, racial, political, or economic; but the need for the determined assertion of conscious humane values as a defense of individual human dignity against a depersonalizing materialism. He was not optimistic about the outcome, but he did not doubt the need to make the assertion.

Robert Penn Warren, I think, has given perhaps the most cogent explanation of the ultimate worth of *I'll Take My Stand* and why he and his fellow Fugitive poets became involved in it. At the Fugitives' Reunion in Nashville a quarter-century afterward, in 1956, Warren talked about his own involvement. It came, he said, after he had lived away from the South and the kind of life he had been accustomed to living. He had been talking and thinking about the disintegration of the idea of the individual in modern society and how this problem related to democracy. "It's the machine of power in this so-called democratic state; the machines disintegrate individuals, so you have no individual sense of responsibility and no awareness that the individual has a past and a place." Along with this notion about the present, there were the pieties and loyalties and sentiments of his southern background, including the Confederate heritage—"a pious element, or a great story—a heroic story—a parade of personalities who are also images for their individual values." Thus his involvement in agrarianism was a protest "against certain things: against a kind of de-humanizing and disintegrative effect on your notion of what an individual person could be in the sense of a loss of your role in society." In the writings of Bertrand Russell and others, he encountered the idea that in the power state the individual lost existence, became a cipher. Agrarianism involved the image of a simpler world:

And your simpler world is something I think is always necessary—not a golden age, but the past imaginatively conceived and historically conceived in the strictest readings of the researchers. The past is always a rebuke to the present; it's bound to be, one way or another: it's your great rebuke. It's a better rebuke than any dream of the future. It's a better rebuke because you can see what some of the costs were, what frail virtues were achieved in the past by frail men. And it's there, and you can see it, and see what it cost them, and how they had to go at it. And that is a much better rebuke than any dream of a golden age to come, because historians will correct, and imagination will correct, any notion of a simplistic and—well —childish notion of a golden age. The drama of the past that corrects us is the drama of our struggles to be human, or our struggles to define the values of our forebears in the face of their difficulties.[37]

In Warren's estimate of what he and his friends had really been up to a quarter-century before, then, agrarianism was a kind of pastoral rebuke grounded in the actualities of southern history, designed to counter the dehumanizing tendencies of the present by employing the achievement of human beings in the past to point out the failures in the humanity of the current age. It is noteworthy, I think, that Warren says nothing about reestablishing that past itself, or even safeguarding what is left of it; he assumes that the struggle to be human is the constant element in the tradition, and that the succeeding generations each confront this need, that their success is always partial, and their particular virtues always need redefinition in the light of changing circumstances. The past is the best rebuke because the records of its accomplishments, having already taken place, are visible and definable, and can be protected against sentimentality or oversimplification by the historical evidence itself.

This is very much the same kind of assumption, I think, suggested in Tate's insistence to Davidson that the reaffirmation by the Agrarians of the humane tradition had been "a very great success" because to do so was an end in itself. When Tate told an interviewer in 1961 that he still thought of himself as a southern agrarian, he made the point quite emphatically: "I think that the point of view expressed in [*I'll Take My Stand*] . . . and in the essays by my friends, and in some of the essays by myself, represents the permanent values of Western society. It isn't our fault if our fellow-Americans don't want to adopt them." [38]

The lasting qualities of *I'll Take My Stand*, then, have to do not with its supposed "alternative" to an industrial society, but with its assertion of permanent, ongoing humane values, as a protest against the dehumanizing possibilities of that society. It is this that made the Agrarian symposium read and makes it still readable; and its continuing appeal lies in large part in the critique of modern American urban society from the standpoint of the human spirit, made in 1930 but still very much pertinent today.

The truth is that *I'll Take My Stand*, however outmoded some of its specific recommendations may be (and may already have been in 1930), was a prophetic book. It is not too much to say that the supposedly impractical, romantic neo-Confederate defenders of an Old South that never was (to paraphrase some of their critics) have turned out to be, in the light of a half-century of American experience, a band of prophets. Merely to quote a few passages from *I'll Take My Stand* is to make the point clear. The contemporary relevance of such passages as the following is all too obvious:

It is an inevitable consequence of industrial progress that production greatly outruns the rate of natural consumption. To overcome the disparity, the producers, disguised as the pure idealists of progress, must coerce and wheedle the public into being loyal and steady consumers, in order to keep the machines running. So the rise of modern advertising—along with its twin, personal salesmanship—is the most significant development of our new industrialism. ("Statement of Principles," xxvii–xxviii)

Industrialism is rightfully a menial, of almost miraculous cunning but no intelligence; it needs to be strongly governed or it will destroy the economy of the household. (Ransom, 16–17)

The furious pace of our working hours is carried over into our leisure hours, which are feverish and energetic. We live by the clock. . . . We do not have the free mind and easy temper that should characterize true leisure. Nor does the separation of our lives into two distinct parts, of which one is all labor—too often mechanical and deadening—and the other all play, undertaken as a nervous relief, seem to be conducive to a harmonious life. (Davidson, 34)

The industrial technology which Mr. [John] Dewey exalts so highly is a two-edged sword; theoretically it might appear to be the mechanism by which the ideal collective existence could be consummated; actually it is a form of legerdemain through which a stupendous concentration of wealth and power is achieved, along with a corresponding degree of exploitation of human effort. (Lyle Lanier, 141–42)

Our vast industrial machine, with its laboratory centers of experimentation, and its far-flung organs of mass production, is like a Prussianized state which is organized strictly for war and can never consent to peace. (Ransom, 8)

All relations between groups in the city tend to become formal and impersonal, and such is especially true in those of the two races. (Warren, 262)

The first principle of a good labor is that it must be effective, but the second principle is that it must be enjoyed. Labor is one of the largest items in the human career; it is a modest demand to ask that it may partake of happiness. ("Statement of Principles," xxii)

Since there is, in the Western mind, a radical division between the religious, the contemplative, the qualitative, on the one hand, and the scientific, the natural, the practical on the other, the scientific mind always plays havoc with the spiritual life when it is not powerfully enlisted in its cause; it cannot be permitted to operate alone. (Tate, 173)

The humanities, which could be reasonably expected to foster the arts, have fought a losing battle since the issue between vocational and liberal education was raised in the nineteenth century. Or they have kept their place by imitating the technique of their rivals. (Davidson, 37)

The artist is no longer *with* society, as perhaps even Milton, last of classicists, was. He is *against* or *away from* society, and the disturbed relation becomes his essential theme. (Davidson, 43)

The latter-day societies have been seized—none quite so violently as the American one—with the strange idea that the human destiny is not to secure an honorable peace with nature, but to wage an unrelenting war on nature. (Ransom, 7)

Fresh linen has too often been mistaken for culture by people who scrub all the oil from their skins in the articles of the plumbing industry. (Lytle, 211)

We defend certain qualities not because they belong to the South, but because the South belongs to them. (Young, 336)

It might be objected, of course, that if that is where the significance of Nashville agrarianism lies, then what does it necessarily have to do with the South? Why call the volume *I'll Take My Stand?* What, in short, therefore serves to distinguish it from any number of similarly impassioned protests against the industial age, the power state, the depersonalization of the individual, that have been a constant theme in English and American literature at least since Blake and Wordsworth?

One might reply that the South is just as much a part of America as New England or any other region, and that the experience of southern Americans is as central to that of Western man as the experience of Englishmen or of anyone else. In this sense, the force of *I'll Take My Stand* surely resides in the fact that it *is* central, and that its rebuke to dehumanization speaks to the experience and needs of men without regard for whether or not they fit into the specific southern frame of reference. What *I'll Take My Stand* has to say about man in confrontation with the power state has meaning for northerners and westerners and Englishmen and others in precisely the same way that a novel about a parvenu building and losing a plantation dynasty in nineteenth-century Mississippi can speak to the interests of readers who have never been in Mississippi and know little or nothing about the history and society of the Old South.

But this is to beg, or in any event to slight, the issue. The southern experience is indeed crucial to Nashville agrarianism and *I'll Take My Stand*. It is part and parcel of both the impulse that resulted in the book, and of the form that it took. One can no more imagine its occurring as it did, or taking the shape that it did, without the South being centrally involved, than one can imagine Faulkner's Quentin Compson as a Californian or a New Yorker. The imagination is intricately and inescapably bound up with the historical and social milieu, and the more faithfully the specific situation is explored and interpreted, the more universal is its relevance.

I'll Take My Stand is a book written by young men who came late to modernism, and came to it out of a community experience that was historically apprehended. In the tardy and sudden confrontation of their region with the modern world during their own early years, they were provided with the historical and social situation that en-

abled them to dramatize, out of their own passionate involvement with it within their own sensibilities, the human consequences of that confrontation. It has been said
of the Agrarians, in attempted deprecation, that they
were not farmers, but intellectuals, a band of poets. *Of
course they were.* They were young men who had grown up
in a community in the process of change, but one still
very marked by its historical experience and imbued with
its expectation of community identity, and who had, to
the extent that they were intellectuals, been dislodged
from that community experience by the very nature of
the change that was involved. Out of what they missed in
the new identity that had come upon them, they were
able to identify flaws, dangers, and divisions within that
modern urban, industrial society of which they were now
dues-paying members, and to articulate their rebuke—
what Warren described as the protest "against a kind of
de-humanizing and disintegrative effect on your notion
of what an individual person could be in the sense of a
loss to your role in society."[39]

The South—the historical memory of a community
not yet marked, or just beginning to be, by the impact of
urban industrial society—was still very much with them.
It provided them with both an attitude and a historical
image which they could use to measure and interpret the
world which they inhabited. Certainly that earlier community had its flaws and injustices and its own disintegrative elements. But it also offered its members an intense
community experience—and it was precisely that community experience that seemed to be lacking in, or in any
event endangered by, the dominant forces and trends of
American society of their own time. As human beings,
southerners of a particular time and place, they felt, poignantly and powerfully, the importance of the virtues of
such an experience. As intellectuals, writers, they identified and articulated them, and warned of their erosion.

The result was *I'll Take My Stand: The South and the*

Agrarian Tradition, by Twelve Southerners—which is to say, Americans—of the Twentieth Century who, out of their own historical instance, framed a statement that, in the immediacy and the particularity of its evocation, was a powerful rebuke to their society and ours and I think, in the intensity of its "reaffirmation of the humane tradition," a challenge and a promise.

The day has long since passed when those who took part in it felt any need to apologize for or explain away their participation. For their Agrarian symposium speaks to the problems of today and tomorrow in a way that few documents of its time have done. Tate was right when he told Davidson not to fret, because they and their fellow participants would be remembered when their critics would be forgotten. In all the ways that mattered, *I'll Take My Stand* was no failure; it was, and is, a success.

5 The Descent from the Mountain

Who Owns America?

So far as the Nashville Agrarians were concerned, the publication of *I'll Take My Stand* was intended to constitute only the beginning of their campaign. Although the movement never exhibited much cohesion, and the individual participants carried on with the work with something rather less than uniform dedication and intensity, most of the participants were by no means ready to quit after they had taken their stand in 1930. They never came close to achieving the disciplined intellectual identity that Tate had envisioned in 1929 when he had proposed the formation of a Southern Academy, with a constitution, philosophical rationale, and organs for publication of their views, but most of the group did not slacken their individual fire for some time to come. Throughout much of the decade that followed, they strove to develop their critique of industrialism.

Capitalizing on the controversy surrounding the initial publication of their symposium, they helped to set up and participate in a series of public debates in which Ransom and Davidson took to the platform to champion and defend the cause. Meanwhile they lost no opportunity during the several years that followed to carry on their argument in print. In book reviews, essays, and articles they sought to keep the Agrarian viewpoint before the public.

Because a great deal of the initial response to *I'll Take My Stand* had been aimed at refuting the practicalities of agrarianism as a southern program for economic and social action, they were led, or most of them were, to attempt justifications for the movement as a viable course of public policy. John Ransom in particular began reading up on economics and writing articles about farmers and farming. For a time he worked on a book about it. Davidson quickly moved to associate his position with the growing chorus of regionalist critics of the political, social, and economic domination of New York and the Northeast. In *The Attack on Leviathan* (1938) he published a set of essays that drew the battle lines squarely along regional grounds. Meanwhile in Seward Collins' *American Review* the Agrarians had found an organ for disseminating their views. For a while their essays and reviews appeared regularly there. Ultimately most of them broke with Collins after he moved to identify his cause with fascism. In later years they would be accused of proto-Fascist sympathies, in large part because of the association with Collins. Economic and social conservatives some of them were, but they were also strong believers in personal liberty and in individual conscience; they had nothing to do with the Fascist principle of the subservience of men to the state. The worst that can be said against them is that they allowed themselves to get into bad company and were none too quick to recognize it.* When in 1935 Cleanth Brooks and Robert Penn Warren became managing edi-

* Virginia Rock's discussion of this point in "The Making and Meaning of *I'll Take My Stand*" is very much to the point (401–12).

tors of a new publication, *The Southern Review*, at Louisiana State University, the Agrarians had another and better outlet for their writings.

There was talk, in the early 1930s, of putting together a second Agrarian symposium in which they would set forth their cause in more practical terms. Nothing came of this, however, and after waiting several years for something to materialize, Tate joined Herbert Agar in organizing a project in which the southern Agrarians joined with other critics of big business, including several English Distributists, in an attack on large corporations and centralized power.[1] Entitled *Who Owns America?* it is as close as they ever came to a sequel to *I'll Take My Stand*. Davidson and Frank Owsley were unhappy with the volume, however; they felt, justifiably, that it weakened the Agrarian enterprise.

Unlike *I'll Take My Stand*, the new volume had no statement of principles and was not a group effort; it was edited by Agar and Tate and the contributors selected by them and essay assignments allocated. The volume attracted little attention; it lacked not only the unity and coherence of *I'll Take My Stand* but also its excitement. For it was directed at economic reform of American society, and its perspective was national. By eliminating or minimizing the southern identification, the project, as far as the Agrarians were concerned, lost most of its strength, since there was no concrete social entity involved. Unlike the essays in *I'll Take My Stand*, its contributions were not written out of a shared identity which gave to the individual essays a tangible foundation of belief and made the arguments not merely vigorous assertions of ideas but disciplined emotional declarations. The central image in *I'll Take My Stand*, the impassioned quality of pastoral rebuke, is largely missing in *Who Owns America?* because there is little or no imaginative dialectic involved in the writing. The contributors are not attempting to come to grips with their own identities in terms of their social and economic stake in a community; they are arguing for intellectual positions, and it is ideas, and not attitudes, customs, and pieties, that are at issue. Ransom's essay on farming, for example, entitled "What Does the South Want?" is all logical deduction; he is not, as in *I'll Take My Stand*, defending the metaphor of a religious community, with all his emotional involvement in its institutions and attitudes, but merely presenting a case for subsistence farming as against big business. Only logical ingenuity, not dialectic passion, is offered, and the result is the Ransom prose style achieving empty triumphs in a vacuum, not employed as it usually was to discipline passionately felt belief.

Davidson's "That This Nation May Endure—The Need for Political Regionalism" is weakened by the necessity of his having to cloak his impassioned identification with the South in a façade of concern for a representative regional political balance as such; and this is not Davidson's true objective. He isn't primarily interested in seeing that all the various sections, including the South, have their just share of influence in a national government; primarily he wants to denounce the injustice perpetrated by the Northeast upon the South. But the format of *Who Owns America?* forces him to disguise his objectives, and unlike Ransom, Davidson was never much at home with an oblique strategy.

Tate's essay, "Notes on Liberty and Property," is an attack on the idea that corporate capitalism is true property ownership. He wishes to show that the original American concept of property as the bulwark of liberty has been perverted to the extent that giant corporative ownership and big business farming are inimical to personal liberty. But the essay, however logically argued, is flat; it is well that Tate has not seen fit to republish it in his later collections of essays. The trouble is the same as with most of the other essays in *Who Owns America?*: the author is not emotionally involved. Dealing as he must in terms of economic ownership, and possibly not totally believing what he is saying anyway, he must write only at the level of abstraction, and cannot draw upon the moral indignation that infuses his imagination when he deals with the individual in modern society. He is forced to simplify, when the whole bent of Tate's talent is to delineate complexity.

The one essay of any of the four leading Agrarians published in *Who Owns America?* that comes anywhere near to the level of their best work is Robert Penn Warren's "Literature as a Symptom." Like Tate, Warren had the instinct for complexity, and also like Tate, Warren was no man to subordinate his critical taste to a social thesis; but in this instance, unlike Tate, Warren had a subject that enabled him to get involved in it, and one that enabled him to use what he knew. (Tate's choice of subject was almost uniquely calculated to achieve the opposite result.) Just as with *I'll Take My Stand*, Warren's approach was implicitly subversive of the more simplistic assumptions of the project at large. In the first symposium he had shown how the black man's stake in the nonindustrialized, traditional community depended very much upon his being accorded full human status. Now he set out to show how the modern American writer was dislodged by his time and place from the advantage of enjoying automatic, unconscious possession of a social or moral theme, and how the two leading movements of the 1930s, regionalism and proletarian writing, each offered to the lazy, facile writer the excuse for avoiding the need to confront the gap between received social assumptions and his own private integrity. In each instance the writer is enabled to associate himself with a set of values that can bring author and audience together, so that he need not search out the implications of the separateness either for himself or for his society.

Warren ticks off the spurious comforts afforded both the regionalist and the proletarian writer by this evasion, at the expense of ultimate artistic integrity, and though

he sees the regionalist escape hatch as perhaps less suffocating than the proletarian escape, he makes it clear that
the genuine American artist must choose neither, and
that he can ground his art in social justice or regional experience only so long as he brings to bear on his subject
the most mature and deep powers of thinking and understanding that he can command. Such an artist does
not need an externally received set of illustrative values;
he can find his own illustrations in the human experience
he knows. Warren was thus able to adapt the objectives of
Who Owns America? so that they served his own "great
theme"—the private sensibility in confrontation with the
public, social responsibility—in a way that Tate and Ransom, for different reasons, were kept from doing.

Who Owns America? did not attract the attention that *I'll
Take My Stand* did, and neither has it survived in the same
way. One sympathizes with Davidson's complaint that the
appearance of the book preempted a possible Agrarian
volume, but at the same time Tate was probably correct
when he told Davidson that it was such a book or no book
at all in the foreseeable future, since the Agrarians had
shown no signs of ever getting a second symposium under way.

Davidson: The Defense of the South

The truth is, however, that of the four principal Fugitives
who became Agrarians, only Donald Davidson had not
said just about all that he had to contribute to the subject
in *I'll Take My Stand*. This was because only Davidson was
truly committed to the ostensible objective of the enterprise, as expressed in the "Statement of Principles" to *I'll
Take My Stand*: that is, to reform public opinion so that
"the younger Southerners, who are being converted frequently to the industrial gospel, must come back to the
support of the Southern tradition" and "look very critically at the advantages of becoming a 'New South' which

will be only an undistinguished replica of the usual industrial community."[2] This was Davidson's hope and his goal; for him the Agrarian involvement was not a poet's vision of the ordered society extended logically into everyday life, as it was for Ransom; nor a way of reaffirming the humane tradition amid the modern wasteland, as it was for Tate; nor yet a protest against the disintegration of the importance of the individual in modern society, as it was for Warren. Nashville agrarianism for Davidson was the defense of the South and its values, as he saw them. He was able to order his poetry, his polemical writings, his life itself by that goal, and he never wavered from it.

Thus in his later years he could, in his disapproval of the New Deal, the Fair Deal, and the liberal wing of the Democratic party in general, completely turn his artillery to face in that direction, and write pamphlets to be published by the Southern States Industrial Council, which was not exactly a pro-Agrarian, anti-industrial force in the South. The federal government, not big business, was now the enemy of the South, he had come to feel by the late 1930s; and after the promulgation of civil rights legislation by the Truman administration, and then the *Brown* v. *Board of Education* decision in 1954 and its subsequent enforcement by both Republican and Democratic administrations, he was in the vanguard of the campaign of resistance to integration, heading up something known as the Tennessee Federation for Constitutional Government, in which he plotted strategy and tactics with segregationists of all stripes. Even his closest friends, such as Tate and Lytle, deplored the company Davidson had been drawn into at this juncture. It was not that Tate himself approved of court-ordered racial integration; though not a segregationist, he was very much against federal interference with the South and its institutions. But he deplored what he felt was his old friend's indiscriminate allegiance with anyone who shared his tactical objectives.

The gradual slackening of interest in agrarianism on the part of Davidson's friends during the middle and late 1930s both puzzled and pained him. He could not understand why the others were, as he saw it, abandoning the cause. In late 1936 it began to appear that John Ransom was having second thoughts about the enterprise. Davidson noted in a letter to Tate the following March that Ransom had made a distinction between his and Davidson's views on the grounds that Davidson's were the more "Southern." Davidson told Tate that Ransom's "view of American affairs, I believe, is economic and aesthetic, not political-historical; he doesn't read history." Thus Ransom was "psychologically prepared for New Dealism when other things seem hopeless."[3] It soon transpired that Ransom was offered a position at Kenyon College, and when Vanderbilt made, as Davidson and Tate indignantly declared, an insufficient effort to hold him, he left. When Tate departed for North Carolina the year following, Davidson wrote that "There is an awful gap. I am beginning to feel as I did in army days when my closest associates began to be transferred from the old company & regiment to go into the army of Occupation, or to go home to be discharged. . . . It is an uncomfortable let-down after the stirring battles of the past 12 or 15 years. I am beginning to see myself as Ransom's Captain Carpenter. . . . It is unthinkable that the communion should cease, and it won't. As long as any of us are living, some of us, whether of the older generation that we are becoming, or of the younger generation that succeeds us, will be hereabouts to keep the sacred vows, to keep the flag flying."[4]

Two years later (February 23, 1940), upset by some remarks of Tate's in a letter, he expressed his genuine bewilderment at what he thought was happening. It is a painful letter, which any admirer of Donald Davidson must find touching to read.[5] He had apparently objected to Cleanth Brooks's publishing Delmore Schwartz's essay on Tate's poetry in the *Southern Review* because, though favorable, it had not been written by a southerner with the proper sympathies. The same issue (winter, 1940) had contained a review of Davidson's "Lee in the Mountains" by Morton Dauwen Zabel which noted a split between Davidson's critical self-consciousness and his use of historical tradition. "Here is another case of an unresolved division of tendencies," Zabel wrote. "The one recreates the past while the other objectifies the local, personal, and immediate present. Such an opposition can usually be resolved only through a style that captures the tensions explicit in the divided nature of the modern man. And Davidson's style is too relaxed and confidential to carry over to his reader what is doubtless a strong personal intelligence of this problem. His poetry may be strongly felt in his emotions and personal contacts, but it is only partially and vaguely realized in what reaches print."[6] This was very close to what Tate had said upon seeing the early version of *The Tall Men* in 1927. Also in this issue of the *Southern Review* was an essay, "For the Preservation of the Land," by Russell Smith, which discussed the dire poverty of the rural South and called for its rectification by federal policy to get more rural southerners into industry and governmental purchase of unused land to set up farming cooperatives.

Davidson must have expressed his strong disapproval of what Brooks and Warren were doing with the *Southern Review*, in effect seeing the magazine's inclusiveness as a betrayal of Agrarian objectives. Tate in reply would seem to have chided Davidson for his parochialism, commented on Davidson's poetry in terms of its southern bias, and linked it to romanticism.

Davidson retorts that "what you write of my poetry, while it may be plausible on the external critical side, is as far off from the truth as Schwartz's essay on your poetry. You say I conceive myself as the 'spokesman' for a culture & a people! What foolishness! You talk like a New

York *Times* reviewer, not like yourself." He goes on to say that "I would not mind your calling my poetry 'romantic' if you did not also imply that yours is not. And knowing how the word 'romantic' has been used in your critical essays and John's, I know that you mean to say (though not quite, I hope, with John's cruelly polite snobbishness) that the non-romantic is of the superior, the winning order, and mine is (with exceptions) of the inferior and losing order. I have never understood why you think that your poetry is not romantic—or why John's, or Red's or T. S. Eliot's is not in the 'stream of the romantic movement' while mine is, all wet, right in that stream."

Davidson was deeply concerned, and the exchange gave him an opportunity to express it. "We have not understood each other," he wrote. "Let me remind you that in the past four or five years we have hardly had a serious conversation on such topics. What makes you think you know my purposes and beliefs when you have never—or rarely—asked me what they are? I don't like to be dismissed by a friend with a speculative generality." Tate must have remarked that Davidson was isolated from what was going on. "Well, I certainly am isolated," Davidson wrote. "No doubt of that. I do not grieve, however, over the kind of isolation that may occur from the disregard of Mr. Zabel or of the Communist reviewers of New York. . . . I mean that I find myself suddenly at a disagreeable intellectual distance [from my friends] for reasons that I do not in the least understand. You put me there, in your recent letter, by accusing me of being 'contemptuous of art'—a hard saying, but not the only hard saying in your letter." Then followed a rending paragraph:

It is this intellectual isolation, this lack of communion, which I feel the most. And it began before any of you left these parts. Why, is a mystery I can't solve. What fault was I guilty of? Did I just fail to keep up with the pattern of your thinking, and, though once worthy, thus became unworthy? I felt, more than once, that there was a cloud between me on one side and you, J. C. R., Andrew and perhaps more, on the other. We were all apparently as good friends as ever, yet there was this cloud. I am not speaking, of course, of mere personal differences of opinion about this or that, at any given time, but of something more impalpable. But since I can't solve the mystery, I am going to stop thinking about it, and don't propose to return to the subject.

If Tate replied to the letter—he must have done so—his response does not exist. In July he wrote to Davidson from Princeton, where he was now teaching, to say that the Tates were coming to Bread Loaf, Vermont, where Davidson spent his summers, and that the Lytles would probably accompany them. Ransom was teaching at the Bread Loaf School of English that summer. "Since John is there, we can have a real reunion which ought to do all of us a great deal of good. Separation and isolation breed misunderstanding."[7]

But what could Tate have said to Davidson, other than assure his old friend of his longtime personal affection and his personal admiration for what Davidson stood for? There *was* a barrier between Davidson and the others, and the departure from Tennessee of Tate and Ransom for other parts was not what had created it. It had been there, to a degree, as early as the 1920s, when the dispute between Davidson and Tate over *The Tall Men* and the "Confederate Ode" occurred. The enthusiasm of the Agrarian enterprise had patched it over, but even in those years it was latent. Davidson, from the middle 1920s onward, was a southerner who wrote poetry. Tate and Ransom were men of letters who were deeply interested in the South. In the final analysis Davidson judged literature in accordance with its social and political orthodoxy. His position was essentially Platonic. Tate and Ransom (and Warren), however much they might get involved with the South in their lives and in their polemical writings, were poets and critics first, and southerners second.

It was a distinction that Davidson could not accept, and since poems and poetry were the central interest in these men's lives, the chasm could not be bridged.

Tate's remark that Davidson was "contemptuous of art" was perhaps excessively worded, but by his and Ransom's standards it was more true than false. Davidson was ever willing to bend literature to extraliterary needs. We saw Tate cautioning him about this in his strictures on Hemingway, in 1929: "I don't think we can afford to give the opposition the slightest chance to say that we aren't as disinterested as to literature as any critics can possibly be. Shouldn't we keep the two things distinct?"[8] Significantly, in his essay in *I'll Take My Stand* Davidson tells the regional artist that he "cannot wage this fight by remaining on his perch as artist. He must be a person first of all, even though for the time being he may become less of an artist."[9] In 1933 Davidson was proposing to Tate that "I think we who write poetry (I say *we*, boldly including myself) would be fools to neglect the strongest weapon in our armory. A book like I'll Take My Stand has to be 'proved.' Poetry doesn't. We should do our damnations in satirical verse, our heroics in heroic verse."[10]

When Tate published his novel *The Fathers* in 1938, Davidson was highly complimentary, but he objected to an episode in which a mulatto slave attacks a white woman who is his half-sister: "You seem here to play into the hands of our Yankee torturers just a little." Tate replied that he "knew that you would question at least the Yellow Jim aspect, and I feared you might not like any of the book." He explained that the incident had happened in his family, though the slave had not been a half-brother but at least a first cousin of the lady he attacked. "I followed that tale pretty literally because I knew that it contained a profound truth of the relation of the races," he said. Yellow Jim was to show the worst effects of slavery, and two other black characters, the best and the average.[11] The idea that Tate might, in a novel about the antebellum South, desire to portray the worst as well as the best effects of slavery upon the slave was inconceivable to Davidson. His view on the proper treatment of slavery in literature was more or less that of southern newspaper editors of the 1850s: It must not be criticized, for it would aid the attack on the South. And so on. Davidson *was*, from Tate's and Ransom's standpoint, "contemptuous of art," in that he would put it at the service of a social objective, and Tate's and Ransom's view of art was that for a poet, everything else, including social objectives, was at the poem's service, for poetry was a way not of achieving action but of viewing the world.

Davidson's feelings again surfaced in 1942 when he prepared an essay on "The 'Mystery' of the Agrarians: Facts and Illusions about Some Southern Writers," for the southern issue of the *Saturday Review of Literature*. In corresponding with Tate about the article, Davidson intimated that the other Agrarians having abandoned the field, he alone was left to continue the fight. Tate pointed out that in the instances of both *I'll Take My Stand* and *Who Owns America?* he had been forced to act, or else publication would have been indefinitely delayed. "Don, you have a gift for persecution and martyrdom," he wrote. He also told Davidson that where the latter had a steady job and security and considerable royalty income, while he had known only temporary jobs and insecurity, Davidson had been unwilling to concern himself with Tate's circumstances when Tate had "mildly alluded to my predicament" in a conversation the previous fall, even though Davidson had gone at great length into his own troubles and anxieties. "So far as I can see you have not made any material sacrifices for agrarianism, while others certainly have." [12]

Davidson was shocked. He cited the record: "From 1936 to 1940 I published 17 articles and several reviews which bear rather specifically upon agrarian matters, as I understand them. In the same years I published *The Attack on Leviathan*. During this same period nearly everybody else in the group turned to purely literary articles or historical specialties." He also noted his numerous public appearances, the fact that he taught in his classes the work of Tate, Ransom, Warren, and other Agrarians and their friends, and that in his textbook, *American Composition and Rhetoric*, he took care that the same group of people "should be fairly & favorably represented," even though this would injure its chances of adoption. He did not, he said, criticize Tate for devoting himself mainly to poetry and literary criticism or fiction. As for his indifference to Tate's personal financial situation, "What you refer to as a 'blank stare' was simply the inexpressiveness that, I am afraid, is a family failing—a Davidson muteness which you would recognize if you knew many of my people."[13]

The quarrel was smoothed over; the quarrels between Davidson and Tate always were, such was their mutual affection. But in the years that followed the break-up of the Agrarian movement, Davidson was, as he admitted, isolated in Nashville, and the old camaraderie was never recaptured. Tate continued to send Davidson copies of some of his new poems, and Davidson usually responded with quite sensitive readings of them. When it came to understanding Tate's work, he was usually equal to whatever demands were made on him; but it was not his kind of writing, and in his own criticism he showed little sympathy for modern poetry. At the Fugitives' reunion in Nashville in 1956 he started off arguing for the importance of the oral, lyrical tradition of poetry against Tate's and Ransom's preference for the written intellectual art. Yet when William Yandell Elliott and others of the former Fugitives who had not become professional poets began attacking the Fugitives for their failure to have produced epic poetry,* Davidson switched sides and was defending the modern poetry of his own day, along with

* Needless to say, *all* the Fugitives had failed to write epics, so that as epic poets they were all of the same rank, whereas only *some* of the Fugitives had failed to become important lyric poets.

Ransom, Tate, and Warren. It was, for those who were in attendance, a touching and saddening demonstration of what the departure of the other leading Fugitives had meant to Donald Davidson's own achievement as a poet.

When in 1962 Harper & Row set out to republish *I'll Take My Stand*, with an introduction by the present writer, Davidson wrote to Tate that the introduction "is soft and nice and 'moderate' and praises us to the skies as literary persons, etc., etc., but on the whole seems to me defensive in a way that I can't much like."[14] (He also expressed his dissatisfaction directly to me. Davidson had no way of knowing, of course, nor did I tell him, that I had sent the draft of the introduction to Tate for his approval, and that only when Tate had responded that it was exactly what he thought should be said about the book was it forwarded to the publisher. I should add that upon publication, Davidson wrote me to say that upon seeing the introduction in print he was pleased with it and wished to retract most of his earlier criticism. Whether he really meant this, or merely wished to be kind as always to a young friend, I cannot say.)

In the middle 1950s, after a hiatus of some years, Davidson began writing poems again. They are among his more attractive, gentler in tone and less ideological than much of his earlier work, and though perhaps they do not come up to "Lee in the Mountains" or "Hermitage" in their elegiac beauty, they represented a surprising late flowering of talent in a poet who had generally been thought to have finished his career with the 1930s. They showed what Davidson's polemical activities had tended to obscure: that he was a craftsman of language, deft and articulate, when he chose to be. The Vanderbilt University Press published a collection, *The Long Street*, in 1961, and Lytle, who was now editor of the *Sewanee Review*, arranged for Tate, Ransom, and John Donald Wade to write about them. Davidson was grateful, though I rather imagine that privately he had mixed feelings about Ransom's offering, which made the same distinction about Davidson's southernness that had so irked him a quarter-century earlier, this time likening him to a sturdy Scotsman walking a city street "and making harsh melodies on his bagpipe. But my admiration does not quite become emulation; there is a defect in my temper. It always occurs to me that our heroic days are not recoverable." Tate, in his review of the book, was less equivocal, and Davidson was deeply grateful.[15]

A few years later Tate tried unsuccessfully to get Scribner's to publish Davidson's collected poems, then arranged to have them brought out with the University of Minnesota Press. *Poems 1922–1961* was published in 1966, but received very little national attention except for a sneeringly condescending paragraph by Karl Shapiro in the *New York Times Book Review*.

The poems were, alas, "out of fashion." While shoddier and far more didactic verse was praised for its social "engagement," Donald Davidson's carefully constructed, often beautifully executed poems went ignored by most reviewers. Even so, the volume would appear to have sold well, and Davidson was pleased.

It was Tate's last service to his friend; each had done so much, despite their occasional ideological disagreements, to support the other's work. Davidson died in Nashville on April 25, 1968.

In 1959, on the occasion of Tate's sixtieth birthday, he had penned some lines to his old companion. They can serve at least as appropriately for himself. They ended as follows:

> No marshals but the Muses for this day
> Who in other years did not veil their sacred glance
> Or from you look askance
> And will not cast you off when you are gray.[16]

Ransom: Art as a Career

Whatever private reservations John Crowe Ransom might have entertained concerning the practicality of agrarianism in the years while *I'll Take My Stand* was being assembled, once the book was out he plunged into a thoroughgoing involvement in the enterprise as a viable, expedient program for the South. It was Ransom who debated Stringfellow Barr before an audience of several thousand persons in Richmond in late 1930. Twice more in the succeeding months he defended the Agrarian cause in public debate, and since the chief weapon that his opponents used against the movement was the claim that it was visionary and impractical, Ransom concentrated upon the attempt to demonstrate its utility.

To do this, he was drawn into economics to a much greater extent than ever before, and he responded by undertaking a determined study of farming, politics, and finance. In 1931–1932 he received a Guggenheim Fellowship and went to England with the intention of writing a book to be entitled *Land!*, in which he would set forth the case for agrarian self-sufficiency for America. The manuscript was rejected by various publishers, however, and Ransom concluded that he did not know enough about advanced economics to be able to write authoritatively on the subject. But his interest in what the South should do with its economy and its life did not wane just yet; he published a number of articles, reviews, and essays which focus upon that concern. The titles alone are indicative of how seriously he viewed the problem: "The State and the Land"; "Land! An Answer to the Unemployment Problem"; "Happy Farmers"; "A Capital for the New Deal"; "Sociology and the Black Belt"; "What Does the South Want?"; "The South Is a Bulwark."

During those years Ransom published almost no poetry. His career as a poet pretty much came to an end with the late 1920s. There is no government regulation, as Ransom once observed wryly, that requires a man to continue to write poetry all his life, and it may be that his forsaking the muse while still in his middle-40s was a conscious decision. Yet one is not disposed to leave the matter there. Why did this highly accomplished poet, once so productive of verse, and still, for the rest of his long life, greatly interested in poetry and poetics, cease almost overnight to write poems? What did it have to do with his Agrarian interests? Finally, why, when he ceased to write about agrarianism and the South, did he do so with such abruptness, and feel it obligatory to repudiate his previous positions?

In an earlier chapter I have attempted to make some conjectures about the way that Ransom dealt with ideas. He was a man of great logical powers and prided himself upon logical consistency. But the logic was not open-ended; he started with some rather formidable assumptions, to which he was drawn with powerful emotion, and dialectic and argumentation for Ransom were a way of disciplining and ordering his passionate emotional experience. If the conclusions toward which his thinking led him were sometimes oddly logical and abstract, the emotional and psychological need that those conclusions played in structuring his life was deeply felt and passionately apprehended. Logic systematized his emotions; he did not, as Frank Owsley said, so much reason himself into agrarianism, as formulate a rational system, which involved a program, that would rationalize and objectify strongly felt loyalties and spiritual necessities. In poems such as "Antique Harvesters," "Amphibious Crocodile," "Conrad in Twilight," and "Armageddon," written before agrarianism had emerged from his thinking as a programmatic system, he had articulated his feelings about man's (including John Crowe Ransom's) proper condition in the universe. The ensuing theorizing, in *God Without Thunder* and the essay "Reconstructed but Unregenerate" that led off the Agrarian symposium, was his way of systematizing and formalizing his conclusions. This was very necessary to Ransom; he was not a man for whom an implicit, blurred intellectual situation was acceptable. He had no taste for leaving things on the surface; he demanded exploration, explication, and was not content until or unless his apprehensions were linked up in an ordered and rational system.

Yet here we have a paradox. For philosophically Ransom was not only a dualist, but his philosophy, his aesthetics and his poetics alike were predicated upon the inadequacy of intellectual formulations and philosophical systems, and the falsification of reality that resulted when they were imposed upon the complexity of human experience. The most fiercely opprobrious term he could apply to any intellectual or aesthetic position was to say that it was Platonic. In Ransom's aesthetics, Platonism was as villainous a force as industrialism was in his economics. He even wrote a poem about it, entitled "Survey of Literature," beginning, "In all the good Greek of Plato / I lack my roastbeef and potato."[17] *God Without Thunder*, which started out as a book on aesthetics, had developed the argument that Western society, in turning to the Platonic worship of the *Logos* rather than the Old Testament God of awe and mystery, had deified reason and opened the way to the worship of science, thus losing the sense of wonder and dependence of a God who can be feared and loved. The absence of such supernatural authority as restraint had made possible the limitless exploitation of nature in terms of its material usefulness, through industrialism, the economic method of applied science. In devouring nature, predatory industrialism also used men, degrading and brutalizing labor. The modern city was industrialism incarnate; shielding its inhabitants from any sense of the infinitude and mystery of nature, it gave men the illusion of mastery over nature, and at the same time forced them into the status of production units designed to produce and consume material goods. They were thus prisoners of an ever-expanding, ever-devouring industrial system that dehumanized their lives and pressed them into joyless labor on behalf of a never satiated big business establishment. Under such an always-driving industrial dispensation, neither religion nor art is possible, since both depend upon the sense of reality as something ultimately mysterious. Without ritual and contemplation, there can be only naked human aggression.

So the Agrarian community, for Ransom, is that in which, because the savage industrial drive toward mastery over nature has not been permitted to destroy the human sense of mystery and finiteness in the face of that nature, religion and art *are* possible. Aggression—the desire for possession—has been halted, or at any event domesticated and controlled, through ritual and contemplation. We have seen how all these images were fused in the poem entitled "Antique Harvesters," in which the harvesters till the earth and gather the bronze treasure for the Lady, while the hunters, "keepers of a rite," ride by in pursuit of "the fox, lovely ritualist." [18] Art, religion, agriculture, and the South are made into one coherent image.

Agrarianism, therefore, is the policy for poets. The Agrarian South is again and again presented in Ransom's *I'll Take My Stand* essay as a work of art. "The South took life easy, which is itself a tolerably comprehensive art," Ransom declares in summation. He defines the true farmer as one who "identifies himself with a spot of ground, and who would till it not too hurriedly and not too mechanically to observe in it the contingency and the infinitude of nature; and so his life acquires its philosophical and even its cosmic consciousness." Ransom thus advocates "the clean-cut policy that the rural life of America must be defended, and the world made safe for the farmers." [19] It goes without saying that this is the situation for a poet, too. As the "Statement of Principles" for *I'll Take My Stand*, which Ransom wrote, declares, "Art depends, in general, like religion, on a right attitude to nature; *and in particular on a free and disinterested observation of nature that occurs only in leisure.*"[20] But not only for the farmers. For if poetry depends upon the "right attitude to nature," the free and disinterested observation that comes only with a leisure denied to an industrialized society, then to make the world safe for farmers is also to make the world safe for poets—in which category may be numbered, among others, John Crowe Ransom.

The point is that Ransom saw industrialism and urban society as inimical to the nature of poetry, and agrarianism and rural society as essential to it, and if we search out the delineation of his ideal Agrarian society, it is obvious that he viewed himself, in no exclusive sense, as its poet—as, if we examine the topics and imagery of the poetry he wrote, he had every right to do. He also saw his poetry, and poetry in general, as drawing upon the same impulses and assumptions as religion, involving a sense of mystery and awe, the product of ritual and contemplation, and inimical to the aggression and exploitation of an industrial society. We recall that, back in his young manhood, he had written to his clergyman father to identify the artist with the moralist: "he is interested in humanity, its vivid passions, its subtle refinements, its slow fires: he communicates the fascination of the study and thereby becomes a moral preceptor."[21]

When Ransom mounted his campaign for agrarianism in the late 1920s and the early 1930s, therefore, he was also waging a campaign for poetry and religion, and for a passionately logical mind like his, the congruence of the activities was not only explicit but essential. He wasn't, in his own mind, engaged in the one activity instead of or in addition to others; they were part and parcel of the same enterprise, and what was involved in the early 1930s was an emphasis upon the economic aspect of a single human predicament.

So when the critics of agrarianism began taking the approach, as they customarily did, that it was a visionary, impractical enterprise which failed to take account of the actual needs of the southern agricultural situation, Ransom's response was predictable. He undertook an intensive study of economics in order to demonstrate the utility of Agrarianism, and he wrote articles based on his study. Of all the charges that might have been brought against the enterprise, surely the notion of its being a visionary, theoretical scheme, an idea that failed to take account of the economic actualities, must have irked him most. For if true, that would make it nothing less than a Platonic affair, an abstract design: one which imposes its holder's heart's desire upon recalcitrant human experience, to shape it to his liking through an act of the will. Clearly this would not do at all; agrarianism *had* to be practical, it had to fit the human, economic facts and not ignore them, and Ransom was not about to countenance the possibility that it didn't. Thus his economic studies and his essays of the early 1930s. For if agrarianism, like the good Greek of Plato, left out the roast beef and potato of the agricultural situation, then it was nothing that a poet ought to be engaged in promoting.

It was in the period 1931–1932, when Ransom was abroad on a Guggenheim Fellowship studing economics in England, that he wrote a long, two-part essay entitled "A Poem Nearly Anonymous," which he published in the *American Review* and later, under that title for the first part and "Forms and Citizens" for the second, incorporated into his book on poetry and aesthetics, *The World's Body*.[22] This was Ransom's first really major essay on poetics. *God Without Thunder* had started out as a book on aesthetics, to be entitled "The Third Moment," but had moved into theology and agrarianism. The new essay was a brilliant piece of theorizing, in which Ransom used the poet John Milton and "Lycidas" to develop a complex aesthetic theory. He followed it the next year with "Poetry: A Note on Ontology," one of the seminal critical writings on the nature of poetry for the next several decades; no discussion of twentieth-century poetic theory can omit a consideration of this essay. The year after that, 1935, he produced three more major essays on poetry and aesthetics, "Poets Without Laurels," "The Cathartic Principle," and "The Mimetic Principle." These essays established him as one of the important literary thinkers of his time. Until they appeared his reputation had been that of a distinguished lyric poet who had also produced some interesting but narrowly focused prose having to do with regionalism and tradition. Now he was a major critical theorist, whose views were discussed on two continents.

In 1937 came a crisis in Ransom's career.[23] He was approached by the new president of Kenyon College, Gambier, Ohio, and invited to come there as professor of poetry. Having spent all but eight years of his life since 1903 at Vanderbilt, the notion of seriously considering a permanent move elsewhere came as a shock. But he was weary of the heavy burden of committee work at Vanderbilt, and the Kenyon salary was decidedly better than his present Vanderbilt stipend of just over $4,000. When it became evident that Ransom was seriously considering leaving, Tate wrote an open letter to Chancellor James C. Kirkland of Vanderbilt, sending a copy to the Nashville *Tennessean*, in which he savagely denounced Vanderbilt's failure to appreciate the international distinction that Ransom and his activities had brought to it.

The question of Ransom's status quickly became a cause célèbre. *Time* magazine sent a reporter to investigate. The position of Kirkland and of Edwin Mims, chairman of the Department of English, was that Vanderbilt could not give Ransom a higher salary than others at the same rank. Donald Davidson was enraged; in a face-to-face confrontation with Mims he asserted himself as he had never before been known to do. The newspapers were full of the situation. The Vanderbilt Board of Trust was approached. A testimonial dinner was organized for Ransom. Distinguished literary figures from America and Europe sent telegrams.

Apparently Kirkland did finally consent to place the matter before the Board of Trust, with the understanding that a $500 yearly increment would be forthcoming from the alumni association to supplement Ransom's $4,200 salary, through an anonymous gift—if Edwin Mims wished it done. Mims, however, would not agree. He was not willing for Kirkland to propose special arrangements for Ransom, and he "never thought that Vanderbilt should match the Kenyon College offer." So no action was taken, Ransom announced his resignation at the testimonial dinner, and Edwin Mims, who had built his Vanderbilt English department into one of international prominence, had now pretty much contrived at its being wrecked. Only Donald Davidson, of all those who had made *The Fugitive* into the magazine it was and had then unloosed the Agrarian jehad, was left. That autumn Ransom began his tenure at Kenyon College.

Why did Ransom decide to leave Vanderbilt after so many years? It could not have been money, since the sum finally authorized by Vanderbilt, though never actually offered, was, as Thomas Daniel Young says, certainly competitive. Ransom had become tired of his work on curriculum revision. To a newspaper reporter in Boulder, Colorado, he declared, "I think in a smaller college I'll have more time for writing. In a large community there are so many demands upon a person's time—committees and curriculum reform and paper work and all of that." He liked the idea of being professor of poetry rather than professor of English, he said. I imagine he was also impressed with Gordon Keith Chalmers, the new Kenyon president, and had some encouragement that such developments as the *Kenyon Review* and the Kenyon School of English were to be possible.

Yet more than this was involved in John Ransom's decision to leave Vanderbilt and Nashville. It had more than a little to do with agrarianism, or rather, with Ransom's loss of interest in it. I think Ransom *wanted* to leave Nashville. He had pretty much come to feel that as long as he remained there he would be caught up in and identified with agrarianism, and by 1937 he had had all the agrarianism he wanted. He wanted to get back to poetry—if not to the writing of it, then at least to writing about it.

With this in mind, I propose now to look at the essay "A Poem Nearly Anonymous" and its sequel, "Forms and Citizens," which he wrote while the Agrarian interest was still apparently in full swing, and which turned out to be the first statement of the new preoccupation with poetry and poetics that would come to the forefront in the middle 1930s and thereafter become his chief attention for the remainder of his life.

The "Poem Nearly Anonymous" is "Lycidas," which Ransom describes as a work of "an apprentice of nearly thirty, who was still purifying his taste upon an arduous diet of literary exercises." (1) Throughout most of the poem the personality and the direct autobiographical concerns of Milton the man are suppressed in favor of Milton the poet; "Milton set out to write a poem mourning a friend and poet who had died; in order to do it he became a Greek shepherd, mourning another one." (2) Surveying the stanzaic form and rhyme scheme of the poem, however, Ransom finds certain irregularities that violate the classical model, and decides that these must have been *intended* by Milton, not because they make points within the form of the poem but because it was Milton's way of asserting his own superiority to the established forms. "They are defiances, showing the man unwilling to give way to the poet; they are not based upon a special issue but upon surliness, the general principles." (11) This assertion of personality, he declares, makes Milton a modern poet, asserting his rebellion against the traditional forms. He suggests that Milton first wrote the poem in regular stanzas, then went back and deliberately roughened it.

Forms and ceremonies, Ransom says, constitute the pure artistry, but the modern poet, fearful of monotony, would violate them enough to call attention to himself as artist. Milton is master of many forms within the poem and uses them all with great virtuosity, but at times he refuses to remain within them, and asserts himself directly, as in his censure of the English clergy. Though it is done in the speech of St. Peter, he "drops his Latinity for plain speech, where he can express a Milton who is angry, violent, and perhaps a little vulgar. It is the first time in his career that we have seen in him a taste for writing at this level." (23) In the years immediately following he would write other poems displaying such anger, and prose as well, before returning for good to the formal anonymity of the great epics, composed in the unique Miltonic style.

Ransom makes one more conjecture. He notes that after the speaker of the poem expresses his bitter thoughts on the futility of art—"Alas! what boots it with incessant care/To tend the homely slighted shepherd's trade,/And strictly meditate the thankless Muse?"—and asks whether it were not a better idea to do as others do and pleasure oneself, Milton violates the monologue convention of the poem for the only time. Having said that "Fame is the spur" and pointed out that instead of fame, there comes Death, "the blind Fury with the abhorr'd shears," to nullify it, he interrupts the monologue with a speech by Phoebus. "'But not the praise,'/Phoebus replied, and touched my trembling ears"—Phoebus goes on to speak of Fame as residing in immortality. Milton then resumes the monologue and concludes his poem.

In violating the elegiac form here, Ransom says, Milton again asserts his individuality, and not without accident is it with a passage having to do with fame: "in his disrespect of [the form] . . . he can be the John Milton who is different, and dangerous, and very likely to become famous." (26) In this instance Milton is again the modern poet who "does not propose to be buried beneath his own elegy." The danger is that in so asserting his personality the poet will overreach himself. He violates the artistic illusion, and if he is not careful, we become aware that "he has counterfeited the excitement" and are "pained and let down." (27–28)

"Lycidas," Ransom says in conclusion, is, though mostly a work of great art, "sometimes artful and tricky," and we are made "disturbingly conscious of a man behind the artist." (28)

The second essay, "Forms and Citizens," was originally designed as the second part of a single essay, and I want to summarize it as well. Ransom begins by leaving the subject of Milton in order to discuss forms and rituals, in poetry and society. Poetry is one of the aesthetic forms that a society hands down. Unlike economic forms, these "do not serve the principle of utility." They are "play-forms," not "work-forms." (29) The economic forms, by contrast, are of "intense practicality," and are "the recipes of maximum efficiency, short routes to 'success,' to welfare, to the attainment of natural satisfaction and comforts." (30) In earlier societies, "play-forms" were as important as "work-forms." The aesthetic forms were "techniques of restraint," standing "between the individual and his natural object" and imposing "a check on his actions." Modern society [here read industrialism], with its horror of "empty" forms and ceremonies, may well be exposing its social solidarity "to the anarchy of too much greed." (31)

Art, like manners, Ransom continues, imposes an aesthetic distance between individual and object; it proposes a form. Without the form, we have desire directly acted upon, as in the savage who covets the woman. But manners require that the social man approach the woman "with ceremony, and pay her a fastidious courtship." The woman, contemplated under restraint, becomes "a per-

son and an aesthetic object; therefore a richer object."
(33) The function of a code of manners, therefore, is to
civilize, and therefore to enrich, thus making us "capable
of something better than the stupidity of an appetitive or
economic life." (34)

In the same way, Ransom says, a religious ceremony,
by forcing the bereaved to contemplate his loss through
ritual and form, both expands and lightens the grief,
mitigating its explosive or obsessional quality, and giving
him the "grateful sense that his community supports him
in a dreadful hour." (35) The pageantry dispels his preoccupation with the deadness of the body.

Society, through its forms, rituals, ceremonies, and conventions, chooses "to graft upon the economic relation a
vast increment of diffuse and irrelevant sensibilia, and to
keep it there forever, obstructing science and action."
(36) It stands between the animal and his desire; it makes
possible contemplation, aesthetic pleasure. It is, therefore, our civilization. The function of art is thus to "frus-
trate the natural man and induce the aesthetic man." Art
"wants to enjoy life, to taste and reflect as we drink," (39)
rather than to gulp it down, and so its technique must be
artificial, as the techniques of manners or rituals are. The
poet, having to take account of his form, is delayed and
hindered in describing the object, and is thus able to ap-
prehend its existence in its own sake and not merely as an
object to be unthinkingly possessed. Art rests on formalism, as do religion and manners, so that "a natural affili-
ation binds together the gentleman, the religious man,
and the artist—punctilious characters, all of them, in their
formalism." (40) Ransom takes up Eliot's famous pro-
nouncement, "In politics, royalism; in religion, Anglo-
Catholic; in literature, classical," and suggests his own
version: "In manners, aristocratic; in religion, ritualistic;
in art, traditional." (42) He urges his generation to em-
phasize the "formal" emphasis as a way of humanizing

the natural man: "The object of a proper society," he says, "is to instruct its members how to transform instinctive experience into aesthetic experience." (42)

Ransom goes on to say that religion exists for its ritual, not its doctrine, for the doctrinal issues are "really insoluble for human logic," and "the only solution that is possible, since the economic solution is not possible, is the aesthetic one." (43) He describes some of the occasions of human experience in which the aesthetic experience is appropriate—occasions in which contemplation rather than economic possession is desirable. Then he distinguishes between two kinds of contemplation, the scientific and the artistic. The scientist would study the object to control it; he is like the caveman, the economic man, in the sense that his ultimate objective is possession. The artist, by contrast, would contemplate the object neither for immediate nor future possession, but only to know it for its own properties. His knowledge of the object is therefore a kind of "knowledge so radical that the scientist as scientist can scarcely understand it, and puzzles to see it rendered, richly and wastefully, in the poem, or the painting." (45)

At this point—before Ransom gets back to Milton—we might pause to note several things. One is that Ransom has contrasted religious and aesthetic knowledge with scientific and economic knowledge, in that they are not aimed at useful possession but at formal contemplation. He has furthermore equated civilization with that contemplation; the raw economic desire to possess, or the
. more sophisticated scientific knowledge which is nonetheless aimed at just such efficient economic possession, are at the service of the animal, but only the civilized man can enjoy the formal, ritualistic, aesthetic or religious knowledge, which is nonpredatory. What is especially interesting, if we think of the possible relationship of this discussion to his Agrarian interests, is that he chooses to

use the word *economic* to designate practicality, "short routes to 'success,'" "to the attainment of natural satisfactions and comforts." (30) The implication is that insofar as a society must be economic, must concern itself with economics, it is to that extent therefore *not* aesthetic, *not* artistic—not civilized. It goes without saying, therefore, that to the extent that economics must be considered in an Agrarian (or any other) program, the program is to that degree unaesthetic, even opposed to the aesthetic forms. And it also appears pretty much self-evident that someone who happens to be chiefly concerned with aesthetic forms will not be rendering his own true account by continuing to concern himself with the economic forms. In short, Ransom has put culture and economics at opposite poles, and there can be little doubt where his own sympathies lie.

To continue now with Ransom on Milton, which I intend to suggest is also Ransom *as* Milton, or Ransom on Ransom. The man Milton, Ransom says, "is a strong man, and has intense economic persuasions, if we may bring under that term his personal, moral, and political principles." (46) Although his poetry deals with these principles, it does not do so as poetry; for as poetry the situations dealt with are "fancied ones which do not touch him so nearly." Milton may be found to have dealt with his economic persuasions "more precisely or practically somewhere in his economic prose; that is, in the ethical, theological, political tracts." (47) In "Lycidas" he was the poet, though sometimes he found it difficult to repress the economic man, and these are the less artistically successful elements of the poem. But though he felt the economic considerations of his time strongly, and was naturally inclined to deal with them and sometimes did so very strongly indeed, "he knew of this tendency in himself and repressed it." (48) He did not choose finally to define himself as a man, but as an artist. "As a man he was too much like any of us; if not too appetitive in the flesh, at least too zealous in intellectual action, which comes aesthetically to the same thing." (49) But as an artist he was John Milton.

Milton did, as a man, have one blind spot. Like many a modern he was suspicious and truculent toward ritual. Had he been a Catholic rather than a Protestant, Ransom suggests, or perhaps an Anglo-Catholic, he would not have felt such suspicion and truculence. "So inveterate and passionate did this resistance become that it took him into the extremist Protestant camp to write hard doctrine, and actually to set up his own religion as a project in dialectic," even though "all the time he 'knew' better." (50) (Here we might keep in mind that the author of that observation was also the author of *God Without Thunder: An Unorthodox Defense of Orthodoxy*.) But as it turned out, this did not matter, for as a poet he used ritual and understood it well, even though in its public, political form he resisted it. Milton made his choice and became the artist.

There then follow in Ransom's remarks on Milton sentences so striking that I would quote them in full:

We do not regret his decision when we have to follow him during the ten or fifteen years after 1640, the period when he felt obliged as a citizen to drop the poet and become the preacher, the tractarian, and the economic man. During that period we remember gratefully that he shares our own view of his intractable nature, in which so much of the sin of Adam resides; that he understands his predicament. The formality of poetry sustained him, induced in him his highest nobility, and his most delicate feeling. The ding-dong of contemporary controversy brought out of him something ugly and plebian that was there all the time, waiting. He took care that the preacher should be the Miltonic rôle for but a period; the artist came back, and may have been the better artist for the ignominy which he had suffered; though I shall not try to argue that. (52–53)

And Ransom concludes with a justification of the rightness of Milton's decision to be the artist, saying that art "is a career, precisely as science is a career. It is as serious, it has an attitude as official, it is as studied and consecutive, it is by all means as difficult, it is no less important." The Milton who matters is the poet; "Milton is the poetry." (53–54)

What I propose, of course, is in these two essays on John Milton's poetry, written in England in 1931–1932 while on temporary leave from Vanderbilt, Ransom was very actively pondering his own situation. Whether or not "Lycidas" is "a poem nearly anonymous," it seems clear that in their authorship these essays are only partly anonymous, and that John Ransom the man is, I think quite intentionally, declining to give entire precedence to John Ransom the critical explicator of Milton. For Milton is not the only poet in the English language who had as poet taken a pastoral role to deliver himself from "the scrivener's son, the Master of Arts [from Oxford, not Cambridge, to be sure], the handsome and finicky young man." (3) Not merely Milton has been suspected of going over a smoothly written poem and deliberately coarsening it. Not merely Milton, having concluded the poems of his apprenticeship, had found himself "uneasy, skeptical, about the whole foundation of poetry as an art." (11) Not merely Milton discovered that the "point of view of . . . shepherds, as romantic innocents and rustics, is excellent, and offers a wide range of poetic discourse concerning friendship, love, nature, and even, a startling innovation . . . the 'ruin of the clergy.'" (19) (Cf. "Armageddon.") John Ransom too tried sonnets, also the ballad form (Cf. "Piazza Piece," "Captain Carpenter.")

Milton was not the only "artist capable of perfect logic." (26) Ransom too was a strongly passionate man, with "intense . . . personal, moral and political principles," who treated the major concerns of his poetry at other times in "his economic prose; that is, in the ethical, theological, political tracts." (46–47) Like Milton, Ransom was "a man of his times and held strong views upon the contemporary ecclesiastical and political situation, in a period when the church and the political order were undergoing revolution." He too had "a natural inclination to preach, and display his zeal; to preach upon such themes as the reform of the clergy, and the reform of the government," and "knew of this tendency within himself and opposed it." It can probably be assumed that this son and grandson of Methodist ministers "went so far as to abandon that career in the church which his father had intended for him and to which he seems at first to have consented." (48) Ransom the dialectician was "if not too appetitive in the flesh, at least too zealous in intellectual action, which comes aesthetically to the same thing." (49) And so on, even down to Ransom having for a period of some years "felt obliged as a citizen to drop the poet and become the preacher, the tractarian, and the economic man." (52) I am not at all convinced that Ransom's depiction of Milton corresponds to the biographical John Milton; but beyond a doubt it corresponds to the situation of John Crowe Ransom in the early 1930s.

He had gotten involved in agrarianism because by the late 1920s he had come to the stage at which he could no longer, in his own mind, separate the writing of poems from theorizing about the nature of poetry and of art, and his aesthetic thinking had led straight into more thinking about religion and the good society. I have suggested that long before Ransom became an Agrarian in any conscious sense, he had written certain poems, notably "Armageddon," "Conrad at Twilight," and "Antique Harvesters," in which the ideas and attitudes in *God Without Thunder* and his Agrarian writings had been pretty much worked out as images. After Ransom reached those conclusions, he had ceased to turn out much new verse. Where in the early and middle 1920s he had produced new poem after new poem, we will find that in particular after "Antique Harvesters," which appeared in the *Southwest Review* for April, 1925, he wrote comparatively few poems.

It is interesting that this poem, in which, as I have noted, he unites for the first time the themes of the South, religion, ritual, and agriculture in a single poem, is quite unlike most of Ransom's poetry in that it lacks the customary qualifying of the speaker's position. It takes a stand from the outset, and does not proceed to develop any kind of ironic counterpoint between meaning and language. As Vivienne Koch remarks, the poem "shows Ransom triumphing on purely poetic grounds over his own critical notions concerning poetry and belief." She proclaims it "a conquest of structure by texture"—meaning that the language requires the reader to accept the idea content, rather than scoring points off it as Ransom almost always does in his poems, and as he says is essential to the nature of poetry.[24] In its assertion of belief, and its unqualified identification of the speaker with the assertion, it is as "patriotic" a poem as any that Donald Davidson ever wrote.

I do not think this is an accident. I believe that the writing of "Antique Harvesters" signifies Ransom's arrival at a point in his career at which he had pretty much decided where he stood in the cosmos. He has made his allegiances, and elaborated the ceremonies. The long exploration for the meaning of his experience that he had begun in his poetry back with the early lyrics of *Poems About God* is just about concluded. Given Ransom's particular kind of sensibility, he could not dissociate what he did while writing a poem from what he did as thinker and logician. The logic, the poetry, the religious and social belief had to operate together. Having reached the position in his poetry, he now had to work it out logically, in prose, and this he did. Another kind of poet—Davidson, for example—might go right on writing poem after poem designed to promulgate his belief. But not Ransom; except for "Antique Harvesters," he was not that sort of poet.

So, with several brilliant exceptions such as "Painted

Head" and "Prelude to an Evening," Ransom had all but finished his work as a poet when he had reached the position in his thinking denoted by "Antique Harvesters." He plunged into agrarianism, and for the next half-dozen years and more he was "the preacher, the tractarian, and the economic man."

Yet if Ransom had come to agrarianism as the *locus* of art, the image of the country where the ceremony of poetry is possible, as in a predatory industrial society it was not possible, it would follow that there should not be any conflict between agrarianism and poetry, but rather the reverse. What he found, however, was that in responding to the attacks on *I'll Take My Stand* as an impractical affair, he had to immerse himself in the study of economics and the writing about economics. It turned out, therefore, that one could not have the vision of the Agrarian society as the place for poetry and ritual, if the economics was unrealistic. So the economics came under logical scrutiny. And when Ransom, with that very logical and dialectical mind of his, began examining the economics, what he began finding, however reluctantly, was that the agrarianism didn't really make too much sense as a literal economic prescription for the South.

Well before the time of the publication of *Who Owns America?* in 1936, we find Ransom changing his position. In his contribution to that symposium, "What Does the South Want?" we find him asserting that "there are business men and laborers, equally with farmers, to be defended," and there is "practically nobody, even in the economically backward South, who proposes to destroy corporate business. Least of all, it may be, in the South, which wants to see its industries developed, so that it may be permitted to approach closer to regional autonomy."[25] It turns out that what is wrong is not corporate business, not industry as such, but big business, predatory industry.

It also turns out that farming is, after all, appropriately viewed as a business, not an aesthetic ceremony, and its difficulty is that it "is an over capitalized business, therefore an overproductive business, and therefore an unprofitable one."[26] Unlike the industrialist, the farmer cannot destroy his excess of fixed capital, since his capital is the land. Therefore the thing to be done is for the farmer to strive for self-sufficiency, and for the federal government to come to his aid by lowering and even eliminating his taxes, and provide a great deal more services for him than it now does, such as rural free electrification. As for the laboring man, he should have his job tenure made secure, and unemployment insurance if he is out of work. The standard of living should be raised in industrial communities, with indoor plumbing, pavements, playgrounds, parks, adequate medical and hospital services, and so on.

By the year 1936, in other words, John Ransom has become no economic conservative at all, but a good New Dealer, and such, I believe, he remained for the remainder of his long life. Davidson was quite right when he wrote to Tate in early 1937 that Ransom "seemed to me (when I talked with him) definitely to be giving the signal for a crossroads at which he takes a turn to the left."[27] What happened is that Ransom's essential economic and political realism won out over his poetic view of the Agrarian South. The agrarianism, and the South, therefore no longer fit into his image of the only proper country for poetry, which is to say, the place for ritual and ceremony and belief. For if the South is industrializing, and *should* industrialize because economically it must, then it isn't the South that can provide the place for the aesthetic ceremony any better than some other place could—preferably some small place, politically liberal, but with the fine arts and the humanities very much honored there. A place, let us say, such as a small liberal arts college, not located in a big city but in the country, and where there is a definite commitment to ritual and ceremony—a small Episcopal college it might even be.

Of course I do not suggest that it happened nearly so logically and consciously as that. This would leave out fortuitous circumstances, and finances, and numerous other considerations. The truth is that Ransom was tired of southern agrarianism, weary of writing articles on economics, and he wanted to get back to poetry—if not to writing it, then in any event to writing about it. So long as he stayed in Nashville and at Vanderbilt, the old allegiances and associates would be very much present, and to turn away from being "the preacher, the tractarian, and the economic man" would be all the harder. Therefore the prospect of a clean break, at a small college "of the Ohio the bank dexter" rather than the "bank sinister," where he could be professor of poetry and only that, came to seem very attractive indeed. Whereupon he joined the faculty of Kenyon College.

Being John Ransom, however, even that was not enough. It was necessary for him to bring his logic into order, to work out the matter in accord with the fullest extension of the logical implication. Ransom was no one to leave inconsistencies unresolved, to permit areas of thought within the logical framework to remain unexamined. So it was not sufficient that he give up his Agrarian allegiance; he also had to repudiate it. What is interesting are the terms on which he goes about doing so. In the *Kenyon Review* for autumn, 1945, he published an essay, "Art and the Human Economy," commenting on two other essays in that issue on religion and poetry. He remarks of one of them that the author, W. P. Southard, "taxes the Southern agrarians for not having practiced what they preached," by being unwilling to live an agrarian life as well as write about it. Ransom remarks that "without consenting to a division of labor, and hence modern society, we should have not only no effective science, invention, and scholarship, but nothing to speak of in art, *e.g., reviews* and contributions *to reviews*, fine poems and their exegesis." The various branches of knowlege, and the products of civilization, constitute science, "and are the guilty fruits" of our society. "The arts are the expiations, but they are beautiful. . . . They seem worth the vile welter through which homeless spirits must wade between times, with sensibilities subject to ravage as they are." Such are the only practical terms on which the human economy can now operate.

The Agrarians, he admitted, "did not go back to the farm. . . . And presently it seemed to them that they could not invite other moderns, their business friends for example, to do what they were not doing themselves." He found it ironical that the recently announced Declaration of Potsdam proposed that when the war was won Germany should be deindustrialized and the German people forced to take up an agrarian economy. "Once I should have thought there could have been no greater happiness for a people, but now I have no difficulty in seeing it for what it was meant to be: a heavy punishment."

Ransom went on to declare that the "agrarian nostalgia" had been valuable to the participants, and that he found it interesting that now, whatever the politics of the individual Agrarians might be, "I believe it may be observed that they are defending the freedom of the arts, whose function they understand. Not so much can be said for some intemperate exponents of the economic 'progress.'"[28]

As might have been expected, Donald Davidson was outraged, the more so, as he wrote to Tate, that Ransom had sent him a copy of the *Kenyon Review* "the only copy I have ever received from John since he began editing it, except for one copy I earned for my one and only review contributed." Clearly Ransom had wished to notify his former colleague and fellow Agrarian of his recantation. What most annoyed Davidson was that "John accepts as a valid interpretation of our principles the silliest and meanest version of our ideas that our critics gave. . . . He even accepts the 'nostalgia' part as authentic. . . . I can only say, what devil has got into John Ransom?"[29]

Ransom's version of what agrarianism had been all about did indeed make the assumption that the Agrarians had wanted the South to remain agricultural in order that they might enjoy the fruits of such a society as a place for writing poetry. And of course there was a great deal more to agrarianism that that; the whole thrust of the movement as a protest against dehumanization is left out of such a diagnosis. But from the standpoint of Ransom's own involvement in *I'll Take My Stand* and the ensuing enterprise, there was, to make a bad pun, more truth than poetry to what he said. He *had* gotten involved in agrarianism by the route of aesthetic theory and his southern allegiance; and his agrarian activity had been a way of asserting, in social and economic terms, the need for the society of ceremony and belief. When he had been forced to examine his economic assumptions, to face up to what for him was the actuality of an agrarian society, he had found that—*in the terms that he had conceived of it*—agrarianism had been only a romantic dream after all, a heart's-desireland where the ceremony of poetry could be possible, and which was not the twentieth-century South he lived and worked in at all. The fusion of ritual and religion, art and religion that he had set forth in the poem "Antique Harvesters" was only, after all, the image for a poem. The poetry was not the South; in that case he would go with the poetry. Thus the *Kenyon Review*, and the New Criticism. He even went so far as to propose to omit "Antique Harvesters" from his 1945 collection of poems; Tate, to whom he sent the manuscript, had to insist that so fine a poem not be victimized for the sake of "logical consistency."

There was still one more exploration necessary, however, and Ransom soon made that one. If agrarianism was not a reality, and a poet had to live and work in twentieth-century industrial society, what did that make of the poet's place in society? As the keeper of ritual, the creator of ceremonies, of course, using the forms to infuse into the consciousness the kind of knowledge that only the arts could provide, which is to say, knowledge without desire, knowledge of the world's body, the object for and of itself. He wrote a number of essays to enforce this poet, of which "Poetry: A Note on Ontology" was the first and perhaps always the best. But a poet had to live somewhere. So he developed another theory, which he elucidated in the essay entitled "The Communities of Letters," published first in 1952. The kind of knowledge of the world that the poet offers, knowledge without desire, can *only* be apprehended aesthetically; it cannot be translated literally into the public world. But if the vision of the poet is wise and true, he acquires readers who will share with each other the enjoyment of the knowledge of the world he offers, and who will thus constitute a community of letters. "How much more tolerant, and more humane, is this community than the formal society!" The public of each and any important writer constitutes such a community; "it is one of those minority cultural groups which have their rights in a free society as surely as individuals do." And though this community of letters has no corporate boundaries and no economics, it is real, and together with the other communities of letters makes up a kind of "secondary society branching off from the formal or primary society."[30] To use another metaphor which Ransom has used, we thus have "pockets of culture," with the hope that they may become more numerous and more widespread. This is a long way from the vision of the southern agrarian community, with its farmers being philosophers. But it is nevertheless a community, and so we might say that Ransom still managed to find a community role for his poets.

If in writing about John Milton returning to his muse after a tractarian and economic period, Ransom did envi sion himelf being able to do the same, then his expectation was not borne out. After leaving Vanderbilt he published no more poetry save for his Harvard Phi Beta Kappa poem, "Address to the Scholars of New England," in 1939. In the 1960s, following his retirement as editor of the *Kenyon Review*, he began revising a few of his earlier poems, with results that can only be termed appalling. Happily, his publisher declined to excise the earlier versions from the several editions of his *Selected Poems*; both the older versions and the revisions were included. Why it was that Ransom decided to do this, I have no idea. But doubtless he did; however illogical anything John Ransom did, he always had a logical reason for it. Allen Tate is accurate in describing "his compulsive revisions as a quite consistent activity—as an extension of his reliance on *logic* as the ultimate standard of judgment."[31]

Similarly, any explanation of why it was that Ransom did not, after the 1920s, write much in the way of new poetry must remain in the realm of conjecture. My own theory is that when Ransom insisted critically that poetry was *knowledge*, he was describing its function for himself; when he wrote a poem, it was an organic, functioning part of a reasoning process that was going on in his mind, and what happened by the late 1920s was that he had pretty much figured out for himself what he wanted to know. When he described poetry as civilizing desire by forcing formal expression upon it and thus changing it from animal appetite into knowledge without desire, he was saying something about his own complex nature as man and poet. I think that the ceremony of poetry had the result of making Ransom see the world and his place in it differently, making possible a kind of disciplined mastery over himself and his mind, so that he could thenceforth be content with the rational method of logic as his way of ordering his experience. There was therefore no role, for Ransom, for the poetry to perform. Through writing poetry he wrote himself out of the need to write it.

In this context I would note a remark of Ransom's in the essay entitled "The Tense of Poetry," which was first published in the *Southern Review* in 1935. Ransom is postulating a history of the human race in respect to language. First is the Golden Age when prose and poetry were one. Then came the historical epochs when the two kinds of discourse diverged, with prose becoming the language of business, morality, and science, and poetry set itself up to stand against these. The third, the modern age comes when prose has taken over all the objects it thinks worth claiming, and poetry must become difficult and strange, torturing itself in order to be poetry at all. The prose, he concludes, "is located, if we prefer, in our own minds, *which have acquired such a prose habit that those parts which are not active in prose are thoroughly suppressed*, and can hardly break through and exercise themselves." [32] The key word, I think, is "suppressed." It is almost as if the poetry has been kept throttled and under control in order that the prose could keep on doing its job.

If so, we can only say that however much the suppression may have deprived us of more poetry, it was in a very good cause indeed, and we are more than willing to accept the deprivation, if such it was, in return for the distinguished critical writing and editing that this man performed during the several decades after his fiftieth year. If he forsook the muse, or vice versa, he did not, as writer of criticism, abandon the ceremonious language. "For John Ransom," in Allen Tate's words, "wrote the most perspicacious, the most engaging, and the most elegant prose of all the poet-critics of his time." [33]

He died July 3, 1974, at the age of 86. One might quote from his own poem for an epitaph:

> I thought him Sirs an honest gentleman
> Citizen husband soldier and scholar enow
> Let jangling kites eat of him if they can. [34]

Tate: The Seasons of the Soul

When Allen Tate and his wife and daughter had come back to Tennessee from France in January of 1930, it had been not merely with the thought of getting involved in agrarianism and *I'll Take My Stand*, but of establishing his permanent home in the South as well. Indeed, the two motivations were synonymous; Tate was for the first time in his life "settling down," as far as he was concerned, and the decision to move to Tennessee carried with it the commitment to what he saw as the intellectual and social implications of that decision. He was going to make his residence in Tennessee, and he was also going to center his art and thought upon the meaning of that identification.

As we have seen in an earlier chapter, there was much about Tate's personal situation that was likely to make such a move attractive to him. Never before had he lived permanently in a house of his own. The years of his boyhood had been spent in constant impermanence, first as his father's business interests shifted from place to place, and later as his mother, after the partial rift with his father, located herself in various places. Each summer he was carried on a tour of the Virginia resorts. When his older brothers enrolled at Vanderbilt his mother had moved there for several years. Later, he himself had been a Vanderbilt undergraduate, and as we have seen, following graduation he went to New York to pursue a literary career, living in the city or just outside it, never in permanent quarters. After the European stay it was a question of whether to return to the financially precarious literary existence in New York, which was now caught up in the growing economic depression, or else to go back South. He chose the latter, not merely because of precarious economics and his distaste for more metropolitan "cliff-dwelling," but also because the ideological currents of literary New York had grown less and less to his liking. The deepening economic crisis had resulted in a move toward Marxism on the part of many of the young intellectuals, including his own closer friends such as Malcolm Cowley and Edmund Wilson. The Lost Generation had become politically militant, and in a way that Tate found deeply uncongenial. If he had been unable to define himself satisfactorily as a literary modernist without a social and economic role, the prospect of intellectual Marxism was an even less plausible alternative. If a social and economic allegiance had to be asserted—and events had been propelling him as well as his friends in that direction—then agrarianism and a commitment to the land and the southern tradition were far more to his taste.

There was the additional fact that while he had been in France, his mother had died. A strong-willed, assertive woman, she had furnished her youngest son with a kind of identity, if only at first through iconoclastic reaction; her death left him feeling even more rootless and adrift than before, and he felt the need more strongly than ever to search out and establish a foundation for his own life. We have seen how, during the late 1930s, he had been moving to assert his southern identity, writing Civil War biographies, exploring the distance between himself and his familial past in "Ode to the Confederate Dead." Now he would make the assertion formal and geographical, through establishing actual physical residence. So when his brother Ben, who was among other things a prosperous coal dealer in Cincinnati, offered to purchase a home for him near Clarksville, Tennessee, where Caroline Tate's people had lived, Tate accepted the offer, and the family moved into a handsome antebellum farmhouse, which they christened Benfolly. (A description of the home may be found in Caroline Gordon's novel *The Strange Children*.)

I have suggested that it was the Agrarian venture, and what it meant, that made it possible for Tate to return

to Tennessee in 1930. It was a way of focusing his literary, intellectual, and personal concerns. The premodern
southern mind, he wrote many years later, "was an extro-
verted mind not much given to introspection.... Such
irony as this mind was capable of was distinctly romantic;
it came out of the sense of dislocated external relations:
because people were not *where* they ought to be they
could not be *who* they ought to be; for men had missed
their proper role, which was to be attached to a place."[35]
Tate's own mind was certainly not premodern; as we
have seen, his poetry was the product of an intense introspection. At the same time, however, he did feel the need
for a strong attachment to a place, and he felt that without such an attachment, his own life suffered from the
intense dislocation and rootlessness of the modern intellectual. To live "out of place, out of time" was to be a spiritual as well as a physical nomad.

We have seen how, in the late 1920s, he had been
strongly drawn to Catholicism, and how in the poem entitled "The Cross" he had seen the religious experience
as "world-destroying"—in its implications antithetical to
the concerns and values of mortal life. Interestingly
enough, that poem begins "There is a place that some
men know"—as if the meaning of Calvary and of the
world-destroying belief in the actuality of God were itself
central upon a location, a precise area: "in so severe a
place."[36] In rejecting, for a time, any overt religious definition for his experience, he turned to agrarianism; and
he returned to a place which could, he felt, give him and
his art the definition he felt was necessary. If one looks at
the poems that Tate wrote from the late 1920s onward,
there is scarcely a one that does not in some way or another delineate a sense of place or land, and many of
them portray what is happening as taking place within a
specific house. His imagination is strongly spatial and
geographical.

Settled now in an antebellum house near a small southern city, he hoped to find the anchor and identity that he felt he had been missing—missing, for that matter, throughout all his previous life, for it will be recalled that as a child he had moved from place to place with his mother, as he later wrote, so that "we might as well have been living, and I been born, in a tavern at a crossroads." He has also recalled that it was not until 1930, while he was traveling with his father in Kentucky, that he realized that he had been born not in Virginia but in Kentucky— his father, he wrote, pointed out a house in Winchester, Kentucky, as his birthplace; "had we not taken that trip I should be thinking to this day that I had been born in Fairfax County, Virginia, for that was where my mother said I was born, and she always bent reality to her wishes."[37]

Whether this was literally true or not, symbolically it is of considerable importance, for it points up a problem that was central to Tate's intellectual concerns of the early 1930s. His mother had not merely been a Virginian herself, but had constantly impressed upon his consciousness her family's antebellum Virginia past. Her dependence upon her Virginia ancestry as a mode of self-definition, and the image of aristocratic decline and fall involved in the fact that they now lived in Kentucky, not Virginia, and thus were alienated from their true birthright, had been of great import upon her youngest son's thinking. Had the Yankees not come, and the inheritance that was rightfully theirs not destroyed, then things would have been different, and infinitely more satisfactory.

Tate had long since become convinced of the heart's desire element in all this, and had learned not to view himself as the dispossessed heir, but so immense a psychological and genealogical burden was not something that could be laughed off. In his biography of *Stonewall Jackson*, as we have seen, he noted that if Jackson had lived to the year 1900 he would have seen "a whole people, some of them deprived of their birthright, but all of them sorely afflicted with the delusion of ancient grandeur."[38] If Tate had his mother in mind, he is nonetheless ambivalent as to the putative authenticity of the claim.

It is interesting that the subjects of both the Confederate biographies that he wrote during the late 1920s bore only an oblique relationship to the antebellum Virginia plantation gentry. Stonewall Jackson was a western Virginian, of middle-class, Scotch-Irish stock; he was raised as a Methodist and after a spell in the Episcopalian Church became a Presbyterian. Jefferson Davis was a Mississippian, born in a log cabin and come to wealth and planter stature in his own lifetime. His claims to gentility were never quite accepted by the Virginians: he was a "westerner." Thus while both Jackson and Davis were undeniably southern types, and authentic heroes of the Lost Cause, neither was a Virginian to the manner born, and so as subjects neither involved the element of self-definition for a biographer who as poet had produced a poem which scrutinized the barrier to any easy establishment of an identity with men of a past day. For this and other reasons, perhaps, Tate had been able to throw himself into the composition of the Jackson and Davis biographies with a minimum of self-scrutiny; he had "experted," fought the war over again to show all the Confederate military mistakes, and confidently demonstrated how Jefferson Davis had allowed the Confederacy to fail because of his lack of ruthless logic and his sentimental inability to face the real issues. As I suggested earlier, in both these two books he did swiftly and in rather facile fashion what in "Ode to the Confederate Dead" he had shown was extremely difficult to do.

Now, settled in Tennessee, he set out to produce a third Confederate biography, this time of Robert E. Lee. There was, however, a difference that I think turned out to be of importance. Lee was a Virginian. An authentic gentleman, he had nothing to prove about his status; he was an aristocrat, a man of principle, and he had also been a man of action, effective in battle. In 1861 he had "gone with his native state," even though not a secessionist. In the biographies of Jackson and Davis, Tate had been inclined to deal with some severity with Lee's lack of ruthlessness, his scrupulous insistence upon not transgressing the line between military mission and civilian authority. But such putative defects, however much they might have detracted from his ultimate effectiveness as the embattled Confederacy's military leader, were nonetheless traits of the disinterested Virginia gentleman. Lee was the authentic Virginia hero. If Tate were to examine Lee, he would be brought up against many of the virtues and attitudes that he most cherished as the hallmark of the self-contained, humane, classically proportioned society that he saw as exemplified in antebellum Virginia life at its best. Did they hold up under scrutiny? If not, then what were they ultimately worth? If these virtues, in the character of the foremost Virginia hero, had caused the war to be lost, when more ruthlessness and greater personal ambition would have achieved a different result, what did that say about the "virtues"? Yet without them, would the winning of the war and the preservation of southern antebellum society have really been worthwhile after all?

So a biography of Robert E. Lee involved, for Allen Tate, problems of definition and of value that came much closer to home than had the two previous biographies. The relationship of author to subject was much more complex, more personal. For Lee and what he supposedly exemplified were in effect Tate's "tradition," and if the defeat of the South, the rise of industrial America, the coming of modern society had dispossessed him of that tradition, then the problem was indeed that which he had set forth in the Confederate Ode: "what shall we do who have knowledge/carried to the heart?" Tate might possess the assumption that the private integrity *should* be grounded in the public and social forms, and the conviction that the individual was out of his proper place when he could not discover in the values and institutions of his society the secular equivalent of his private moral and aesthetic convictions. But how to regain these? How to take with complete seriousness of belief the personality of Robert E. Lee and his response to his times, with neither the destroying irony nor pious sentimentalizing of the modern imagination? How, in other words, to make Robert E. Lee a believable, credible human being in a biography?

To put the problem in terms of the writing of books, if Tate, as a southerner come back to the South and prepared to live there and make his life work out of its human lineaments, could not "make sense" of Lee, then what did that signify about the identification he was proposing for himself? He presented the situation in a poem written during the first year of his stay at Benfolly. "Maryland, Virginia, Caroline," it begins—from that place and time his "furthest blood/runs strangely to this day"; now he lives west of the mountain range, away from the ground where his forebears are burisd:

> Far from their woe fled to its thither side
> To a river in Tennessee
> In an alien house I will stay
> Yet find their breath to be
> All that my stars betide—
> There some time to abide
> Took wife and child with me.[39]

In a sense, Tate, as a modern southerner, was attempting to do in his own life just what he asserted in "Remarks on the Southern Religion" that the modern southerner must do if he would regain his tradition: take hold of it "by violence."[40] His move to Benfolly can be seen as his own considered act of the will whereby he had placed himself as writer and as man in a habitation and situation in order to "re-establish a private, self-contained, and essentially spiritual life"—in order, that is, to write his books.

He did not complete his biography of Lee. There is no doubt that so far as putting words down on paper and developing a publishable narrative, he could have finished it. For another writer that might have sufficed. But Allen Tate's is a fastidious muse; to write a book, whether of biography, fiction, or poetry, on a subject which he thought was of absolute importance (as I think he did not really envision the first two Confederate biographies), without being able to shape it as he wished it to go and make it completely believable to himself, was beyond his powers as a writer. He was incapable of setting things approximately in order and then going on to the next paragraph or stanza or chapter to see how they turned out. Whatever the nature of his artistic impulse, it clearly required a kind of unity of language, tone, and content that had to be present if he was to write and to continue writing until done. If it began to go wrong, and his control of one or more of the elements faltered, he was unable to continue. Ernest Hemingway once remarked that the basic tool of the good writer was a "built-in shit detector." Tate, one would guess, had a very good one—if anything, one that was sometimes a bit too sensitive in the fastidiousness of its registry. His own writing was so thoroughly attuned to his personality that the slightest falseness, the merest hint of insincerity, caused him to draw off from the project.

In his way of approaching his craft he was very much unlike his friend Robert Penn Warren, whose relationship, one gathers, to what he was writing was entirely different. Warren could become fascinated with a project, and could work it through to its conclusion completely on its own terms; the element of its personal relevance to him, of its possessing the psychologically correct "tone" for him, did not necessarily operate. Warren was able to objectify and externalize his personal response to his own writing, where with Tate the sense of the total relationship of what he was writing to his own personality and sensibility was absolutely essential.

Somehow, in any event, the Lee biography went wrong for Tate, and he could not force it through. My own guess is that it had to do with Tate's finding that in order to show Lee as having the knowledge and awareness that would make him a believable, interesting Virginia hero, it would be necessary to give Lee the kind of self-conscious irony and habit of cerebration that would violate what Tate felt that Lee was and what he represented. If he could not see Lee as genuinely possessing such attributes, then he would have to wind up presenting Lee as much more a positive failure in his role as the South's military hero than Tate was willing to accept. What would have resulted might be almost a 'debunking' biography, after the manner of Lytton Strachey, and that was not what Tate wanted to do, for it would be contradictory and antithetical to what had gotten Tate involved in the southern equation in the first place. Or so it would appear to me.

The true explanation doubtless lies in the fact that during those early years of the 1930s, Tate was moving toward a new focus for his thinking about the South. The return to Tennessee and the attempt to write the Lee biography may have impelled him in that direction, but the biography would not be the appropriate vehicle for its exploration. It wasn't the nature of the Old South as exemplified in its official hero that Tate found himself pondering, but his own ultimate relationship to the tradition. *Why* couldn't he fit tidily into it? What had happened to the tradition that had made it unavailable?

I find it most interesting that, according to Tate, it was *his father* who informed him that he was not Virginia-born, as his mother had willed him to believe, but a native Kentuckian. His father's family was not of the old Virginia planter lineage. The first American Tate, a

Scotch-Irishman, had come to Maryland, served as an apprentice cabinet maker in Annapolis, then made his way southward. Subsequent generations had lived in Virginia and North Carolina, then come west to Tennessee and Kentucky. The family had prospered, owned much land at one time, but it was never of the planter aristocracy. His father, in pointing out to him his Kentucky birthplace, had more or less reminded him of that. To reexamine the meaning of all this, and its relationship to his ideas about the South and his own relationship to it, was what he felt increasingly impelled to do, now that his mother was dead and he was again living in the South—his father's part of the South rather than his mother's.

What Tate did in the early 1930s, in effect, was what none of his fellow Agrarians really attempted to do: turn the Agrarian concerns inward, and undertake, in his more important writings, an intensive search into their meaning so far as his own personal identity was involved. Agrarianism became not only a program or even a defense of religious humanism, but also a complex problem in history, society, family ties, and personal allegiance. The question "What should the South do?" became "Who am I?"

In 1931 he wrote a series of nine "Sonnets of the Blood."[41] Addressed to his brother, they constitute an inquiry into the cost of their twin heritages. The theme is that in their blood there is a hard, driving rage, "a canker of perennial flower." How it got there and what it means is the burden of the commentary. The inherited passion

> is a flame obscure to any eyes,
> Most like the fire that warms the deepest grave
> (The cold grave is the deepest of our lies)
> To which our blood is the indentured slave . . .

The paradox is that each considers the fire his own secret, yet it "consumes not one, but two–/Me also, marrowing the self-same bone." The common rage they share makes the conditions of life itself inadequate and unsatisfactory, "Flawing the rocky fundament with strife."

To allow the secret rage to drive them to battle with the world as it presents itself, he argues, is perilous. In the past it had taken the form not of open rage but of the private will to act upon one's convictions as one saw fit, as in the instance of the "Virginian/Who took himself to be brute nature's law,/Cared little what men thought him . . ." This man had

> meditated calmly what he saw
> Until he freed his Negroes, lest he be
> Too strict with nature and than they less free.

He addresses their elder brother who had been "sent by the shaking fury in the track/We know so well, wound in these arteries," out to the West. Like the other two, this brother too has been brought up sharply by the death of their mother, "one who of all persons could not use/Life half so well as death." He suggests that they

> Look beneath
> That life. Perhaps hers only is our rest—
> To study this, all lifetime may be best.

It is their mother, the strong-willed person who had so marked her sons' lives by her unwillingness to accept the conditions of her life, who most embodied the rage within them. With her death the fire, which had burned hottest within her because nearing its end, "is all but spent." They had seen "the sacred fury's height" in her, "Seated in her tall chair, with the black shawl/From head to foot, burning with motherly light . . ." It is left for her sons to question what it meant, in their own time, and to see how it operates, in separate ways but with the same passion, within them. His brother is a business man, and the final sonnet of the sequence urges him, as one of the "captains of industry," to "be zealous that your numbers are all prime," lest his urge to force his will upon life destroy those human qualities they most cherish in an effort to get at the ultimate unknown secret. In so doing he will only doom himself, for "that bulwark of the sea" he hopes to remove will when breached

> turn unspeaking fury loose
> To drown out him who swears to rectify
> Infinity, that has nor ear nor eye.

In ascribing the "fire" of discontent to his and his brothers' "blood"—an inheritance from their Virginia mother whose will had sought to bend reality to her desire—Tate was placing *within* the Virginia legacy the potentiality for disorder and individual fury of will that, when undisciplined by the social and religious forms, could produce such disruptive and predatory forces as industrialism. He was equating his brother's zeal for business success with his own rage for literary definition, as being alike fired by a hereditary dissatisfaction. So if the South of his own day was separated from its tradition, and the modern southerner felt the absence of "a private, self-contained, and essentially spiritual life"[42] such as had once been his birthright, it would be appropriate for him to look within his own history, and at his own response to that history, to discover why his tradition had failed to guide and order his conduct.

In his essay in *I'll Take My Stand* Tate had identified the culprit as the religion, or lack of one, of the antebellum South; it had been mercantile, Protestant, rational, unfitted to the self-sufficient, feudal, spiritual basis of its social and economic attitudes, and therefore unable to provide a spiritual base for secular life when the postwar temptation of industrialism presented itself. The only way for the modern southerner to regain his tradition, he had asserted, was through an act of the will—a method that was "political, active, and in the nature of the case, violent and revolutionary. Reaction is the most radical of programs."[43] But if the failure that had caused the tradition to crumble had been ultimately religious rather than secular, then was the proper way to reassert that "private, self-contained and essentially spiritual life" through secular or religious terms? *I'll Take My Stand*, agrarianism, the southern past—all these were secular referents, and took their form from history. Would they suffice?

In coming back to the South to live, Tate was placing his reliance, one might even say his faith, in the historical identity. Yet even so, we find him writing about it in religious terms, as in his letter to Donald Davidson from Paris in December, 1932. Caroline Tate had received a Guggenheim Fellowship, and the Tates had rented out Benfolly and gone abroad for the 1932–1933 year. Davidson had written to say that none of the leading Agrarians was sufficiently crusading in his willingness to sacrifice all his material prospects for their cause: "We like to think of ourselves as crusaders; in our minds' eye, we can see ourselves doing a kind of Pickett's charge against industrial breastworks, only a *successful* charge this time. But we don't actually do the crusading. We merely trifle with the idea a little." Tate replied that "The trouble with our agrarianism is not that we don't believe in it enough to make sacrifices; it is rather that we don't believe in it in the way that demands sacrifice. In other words not one of us has a religion that any of the others can understand. That sort of understanding is necessary to fire the enthusiasm of a group; it is reciprocal in its action. *Vide* my Remarks on the Southern Religion."[44] The implication would seem to be that agrarianism itself, without a proper religious foundation, was inadequate to kindle enthusiasm and produce meaningful action, and Tate had already pointed out in his essay that the historical southern experience lacked any such explicit religious formulation. At this point Tate may well have asked himself whether, if it was the religious foundation that was essential, the problem he was grappling with was really uniquely or even importantly southern in its implications at all.

The Tates were in Europe for a year. During that period Tate worked for a while on his Lee biography, but made little progress. He spent considerable time with the poet John Peale Bishop, and he wrote several poems. "The Mediterranean" was composed following a picnic on a beach at Cassis and is one of Tate's very best short poems. He portrays the vacationers as repeating the voyage of Aeneas, reenacting the arrival of the Trojans. Feasting on that shore,

> We for that time might taste the famous age
> Eternal here yet hidden from our eyes
> When lust of power undid its stuffless rage;
> They, in a wineskin, bore earth's paradise.

They imagine themselves as men of the long ago, before the discovery of America; here, still at the dawn of European civilization, they rest from their voyages. What country shall they seek next for their kingdom?

> We've cracked the hemispheres with careless hand!
> Now, from the Gates of Hercules we flood
>
> Westward, westward till the barbarous brine
> Whelms us to the tired land where tasseling corn,
> Fat beans, grapes sweeter than muscadine
> Rot on the vine: in that land were we born.[45]

They will go westward to the New World; the settlement of America was one more move in the exploration journey westward and outward to new lands and places.

By turning back to Europe and the classical heritage, the poet regains his identity as American, and a particular sort of American at that—one who lives in a "tired land," blessed with agricultural plenty. This is a very different poem from the "Message from Abroad" that he wrote in 1929, when in Europe for the first time. In the earlier poem he could not find the image of his own home and its people in the European situation:

> The man red-faced and tall
> Will cast no shadow
> From the province of the drowned.[46]

But in "The Mediterranean" the image of the European, classical past enables him to see his homeland and his own relationship to its life as the extension of the classical Western heritage, in a new time and place. The Old South, imaged in the description of the "tired land," becomes less exclusively the product of American historical identity, and more an aspect of Western, European culture in general.

The same transaction occurs in "Aeneas at Washington." Here the poet imagines the Trojan hero as recalling the days of battle at Troy and his flight when his city fell. The fall of Troy is likened to the fall of the Old South:

> That was a time when civilization
> Run by the few fell to the many, and
> Crashed to the shout of men, the clang of arms

Fleeing from the wreckage of his home, Aeneas "made by sea for a new world," bearing with him the remnant of civilization:

> a mind imperishable
> If time is, a love of past things tenuous
> As the hesitation of receding love.

Having gained the knowledge of time, he can see the past and the present as connected, so that "the glowing fields of Troy" and "the thickening Blue Grass" of Kentucky are alike "lying rich forever in the green sun." Unlike the Confederate soldiers in the "Ode to the Confederate Dead" who had expected to resolve their desires in a day's battle, Aeneas has learned, with the passage of the centuries, to accept the recurring defeat of high hopes, to contemplate meaning without desire. Now

> I stood in the rain, far from home at nightfall
> By the Potomac, the great Dome lit the water,
> The city my blood had built I knew no more

Another civilization formed along classical principles has fallen; once again the aspirations of men for something better than mere animal survival have gone for naught:

Stuck in the wet mire
Four thousand leagues from the ninth buried city
I thought of Troy, what we had built her for.[47]

The fall of the Old South and the fall of Troy are linked as defeats of traditional societies. In defeat, the vanquished retain their dignity, preserve their integrity, untouched by the public clamor, but the knowledge is private, the personal property of the individual. He can make what he will of it, in accordance with what he is. If the refusal to accept spiritual defeat is admirable, it is also steeped in irony, since nothing more than such private realization is possible.

Living in Europe for a year, away from the Agrarian battle scene, Tate was having second thoughts. He wrote Davidson that the emphasis in *I'll Take My Stand* on the English tradition (for which Ransom had been most responsible) had been a mistake: "Any school-boy who has read his Jefferson knows that as early as 1770 we had something very different. Our program stood or fell by virtue of its standing-on-its-own-feet-ness. There was too much Anglo-nostalgia in it to achieve that."

He even doubted the wisdom of having referred to a "tradition" at all; "we should have stood flatly on the immediately possible in the South." This might seem odd, as coming from one whose essay had made much of the firmness of the Old South tradition, and had ended with the assertion that the modern southerner could regain that tradition only by an act of the will. Was Tate saying in effect that no such recovery was either desirable or possible? I do not think so. He was referring, I think, to tactics—*I'll Take My Stand* had been weakened, he was saying, because it had had much too much to say about "tradition" and "gentlemen" and other such fond abstractions, and too little to say about the actualities of the South as it now was, in terms that southerners who were not scholars and intellectuals could take seriously. The failure of the Agrarians to deal with the here-and-now, to view their enterprise as other than a little academic game involving the manipulation of ideas, irked him. "I get a little bitter about all this. I came back to live in the South, and I've been let down."[48]

In what sense, one might wonder, did Tate feel he had been "let down"? Surely not because agrarianism had proven to be less than a politically and economically successful program; he had never thought that was likely to happen. I think it comes down to the fact that he had believed that his colleagues were prepared to engage in a unified, cooperative intellectual venture, a concerted effort to assert a philosophical and social position and to expend their energies in a focused, disciplined program of actions designed to further their position. Instead, however, individual Agrarians had each followed their own pet projects, indulging themselves in whatever interests that appealed to them, and had been generally unwilling to subordinate their personal and professional needs and desires to the claims of a common enterprise. Agrarianism had meant, for each of them, a device for expressing subjective concerns and interests; they constituted no disciplined intellectual movement, no ideological phalanx. Tate had come South expecting to participate in a joint intellectual venture, an "academy" with a program. He had found nothing of the sort: only a group of friends, mostly scholars, who shared some of the same views and were content to assert them from time to time in their own individual ways. Without the discipline and planning of a concerted operation, their assertions could amount to little more than pious gestures. In other words, no "Agrarian strategy" had emerged, and without it, no lasting impact on the region's intellectual identity was likely to be made. However pleasant living at Benfolly might be, for all intents and purposes Tate might just as well have continued to reside in New York or in Europe, so far as being enabled to join with his friends on any concerted project to "do something about the South" was concerned.

Returning to the United States in February, 1933, the Tates settled in at Benfolly late that spring. Without any income to speak of except from writing, however, it proved to be tough financial going, and when Robert Penn Warren left his teaching post at Southwestern University in Memphis, Tate took Warren's place on the Southwestern faculty and moved his family into a rented house in Memphis. By this time he had pretty much given up the idea of writing the Lee biography. He had, he said later, come to "detest" Lee—by which I take it that he meant that the qualities of character he saw in Lee represented many of the elements that rendered the South inadequate to prosecute its war for independence successfully. Lee's scrupulosity, his concern for personal honor —in early 1861, before Virginia had seceded, he had written to his son that he thought the dissolution of the Union would be a calamity, and that he was "willing to sacrifice everything but honor for its preservation"[49]— and his unwillingness to enforce his will upon others were emblematic of the aristocratic Virginia virtues, but what the Confederacy had needed to survive was the single-minded will to win at all costs, or else the society that made possible the exercise of those patrician virtues was doomed.

I have already suggested how closely the problems involved in that situation were interwoven with Tate's own personal problems of self-definition and therefore of a creative focus for his writings. The upshot was that, after a period during which Tate did very little writing and underwent considerable depression of spirit as well as of finances, he began writing the novel that would become *The Fathers*.

It was not Tate's first excursion into fiction; he had previously done some work on a novel to be called "Ancestors of Exile," a section from which was published as a short story in *The Yale Review* in 1934 under the title of "The Migration."[50] Although not impressive as a short story—it has little or no development or plot—it is an interesting first-person narrative of the travels of a family much like the Allen branch of Tate's father's people from their arrival in the New World in Maryland in 1779, through life in Virginia and North Carolina, and then westward to Tennessee. The narrator, Rhodam Elwyn, seems to be closely patterned after Tate's own great-great-grandfather Rhodam Allen. (Tate's father's death in October, 1933, at the age of 71, seems of some significance.)

As portrayed in "The Migration," the Elwyns are pioneering Scotch-Irish who become pious Methodists. They are sober, industrious, not particularly imaginative, and they represent a very different and more adventurous element of southern society than the patrician Varnells of Tate's mother's side. Tate intended in "Ancestors of Exile" to show how the twin strains of his inheritance, the Scotch-Irish pioneers and the Virginia planters, combine to produce the modern situation. He threw over the idea, he wrote to John Peale Bishop, because "the discrepancy between the outward significance and the private was so enormous that I decided that I could not handle the material in that form at all, without faking either the significance or the material."[51] I take this to mean that Tate had been trying to make of the different histories of the two sides of his inheritance a pattern which would exemplify and embody the relationship of a modern southerner to his regional and familial past and to the impulses of the changing present—which is to say, pretty much the situation of the Confederate ode. To make this function, he had to show, in what *had* happened, the explanation for what he now *was*. The trouble, one suspects, is that when he came to look at his own father's life and character and at the pioneer Scotch-Irish experience that had preceded it, he could not really recognize the survi-

val of the old hard-driving, pioneer realism that produced the forces of change and disruption and new opportunity that exemplified one part of the southern
situation. The "shaking fury in its tract," the fires of discontent seemed, as we saw in "Sonnets of the Blood," to
have been somehow centered in his mother's people,
equally along with the old social stability and eighteenth-
century formality of the antebellum patrician Virginia
heritage. If this was so, then to have ascribed the disruptive force, the restlessness of "modernity," to the pioneering blood would have indeed meant "faking" the actual
material to provide public significance.

Tate taught at Southwestern University for two years.
After that he settled back in at Benfolly and sought to
support his family by his writings and by summer teaching stints at Olivet College and Columbia University. It
was while he was at Benfolly that the controversy erupted
over John Ransom's departure from Vanderbilt to Kenyon College. As we have seen, Tate was heavily em-
broiled in the incident, for he saw in Ransom's departure
not merely the loss to Vanderbilt of the South's most distinguished poet and critic, but an ominous reenactment
of the long-held dictum that there was no place for the
truly professional man of letters in the South. The fact
that Vanderbilt seemed unwilling to make the relatively
minor financial arrangements needed to hold Ransom in
Nashville, and utterly unable to recognize the tremendous blow to its intellectual prestige that Ransom's departure would constitute, seemed to be yet another manifestation, in his own time, of the same imperceptivity that
had sent Poe, Cable, Stark Young, and many another
southern literary artist northward in search of a more secure living. If there was no place for John Ransom at a
leading southern university to which he and his students
had brought international literary renown, then what did
that signify about everything that Ransom, Davidson,
Warren, himself, and others had said about the relation-

ship of culture and society during the previous decade?

Tate had discussed the problem of the writer in the South in an essay written for the *Virginia Quarterly Review*'s tenth anniversary issue, in 1935. Entitled "The Profession of Letters in the South," the essay examines the role of the committed man of letters to southern society. Beginning with the premise that under modern finance-capitalism the writer is isolated from his society, which desires only best-selling commercial wares designed to divert readers but not to question that society's underpinnings, he points out that the aristocratic feudal community of the Old South should have made possible a literature that was organically representative of its culture. But the political obsession of the embattled antebellum South worked against a genuine literary professionalism, and the existence of Negro slavery interposed a barrier between the ruling class and the land. All great cultures have been rooted in peasantries, but the presence of black slavery broke the gradations of class that could have nurtured the writer in the image of the man of the soil. The result was a literature of genteel romanticism, formless, rhetorical, unreal. Because the old society was a better place to live in than acquisitive industrial society, the southern intellectual is tempted to defend its literature: "It is a great temptation—if you do not read the literature."[52]

If the committed modern southern writer is to live and work in the South, Tate maintained, he needs to force upon the region a literature that can ground itself in its deepest needs and forms, and this can be possible only if a genuine profession of letters can sustain itself there. This means magazines, criticism, a publishing industry of its own, not subservient to the commerical demands of the Northeast. But such a literature cannot be provincial; it cannot be written for the tastes of the average southern reader alone. "Like his Northern friend [the southern publisher of books] would, for a few years at least, sell the southern article mostly north of the border. Until he could be backed by a powerful southern press he would need the support of the New York journals for his authors, if he expected them to be read at home."[53]

The achievement of the contemporary southern literary renascence, he warned, is only momentary, coming from the change going on in southern society as it becomes more urban and industrial, "the curious burst of intelligence that we get at a crossing of the ways." But as the change proceeds, the survivals of the Old South organic community that might even now make possible the basis for an important literature grow ever more weak. In defense of that swiftly crumbling community the serious southern writer is inevitably drawn toward politics; he is led to oppose the economics-dominated society of capitalism. The emergency becomes a pretest for ignoring the arts. Thus "we live in the sort of age that Abraham Cowley complained of—a good age to write about but a hard age to write in."[54]

Tate was, of course, writing about his own situation and that of his fellow authors. Agrarianism was just such a political program. *Who Owns America?*, the symposium he and Herbert Agar were in the process of editing, represented exactly the diversion into economics and politics that forced himself and his friends to ignore the arts. The situation Tate spelled out in his essay was that with which he had been grappling. To make the South a community in which the writer could genuinely participate, it was necessary to safeguard the old community against the dehumanizing, depersonalizing impact of industrialism. Thus in order to arouse southern opinion to an awareness of what it was allowing itself to become, it was necessary to create "an intellectual situation interior to the South," to mount a disciplined intellectual attack designed to capture informed southern opinion. But the only way to do that would be by "violence"—through a determined act of the will—and the very continuance of the act itself ran counter to the social and philosophical assumptions inherent in the social attitudes it would defend. It was theoretical, conceptual; it was an idea, an abstraction, an affair of the intellect. Southerners did not go in for such an approach to the complexity of their experience—and yet the fact that they did not, and what that meant, was precisely *why* Tate and the others approved of their ways.

So there was a real dilemma involved, and what it came down to was that seven years after Tate had come to the South to live, and almost as many again since he had first left Vanderbilt for New York, he was seemingly no closer than before to resolving the question he had posed in his Confederate Ode—"What shall we do who have knowledge / Carried to the heart?" How does the modern southern writer, informed by the self-conscious insights that are characteristic of the modern dissociation of sensibility, reconcile his capacity for those insights with his assumptions about the need for an ordered, traditional society, bequeathed him by his regional heritage? Out of the tensions involved in that dilemma Tate had managed to create a number of quite distinguished poems and some excellent essays, which was one kind of practical solution. Yet it was one thing to make literature out of the contradiction—as a writer, I believe Tate once remarked, though I do not recall just where, he *had* no experience—but to handle the problem as a man, a man of letters, was another thing. For part of the nature of the art lies in the thwarted expectation that a man *should* be able to function within a society, and so however fruitful the search for such a reconciliation might be when faced poetically, it was not and could not be handled merely as a literary theme. Literature was not life, it was *about* life; and the life it was about was the author's.

John Ransom had grappled with the problem symbolically, in terms of the conflict between the religious community, the community of ritual and therefore of art, and the industrial society of sheer predatory appetite. When he found that the Agrarian identity did not serve to reconcile the dilemma, because to deal meaningfully with the society in realistic social terms one must work in terms of the appetite and not the ritual, he decided that he preferred the ritual of art to the society of appetite, turned away from the South both intellectually and geographically, and became the formalist critic. Donald Davidson chose a fierce identification with the society itself over its use as literature. As writer he turned away from the recognition and exploration of self-consciousness in order to function as man within the community, and identified himself with what he felt the South *had been* and thus *should be*, to the exclusion of any concession to much that it manifestly *was*, as exemplified within himself. Allen Tate wrote a novel.

The Fathers[55] is related by Lacy Buchan, who at the time of telling is an elderly man living in Georgetown, across the Potomac River from Virginia. He had served in the Confederate Army during the Civil War, then had studied medicine and practiced it for many years, and is now retired. The story he recounts is of events in the Buchan and Posey families during the several years just before and after the coming of the war. He tells what he saw and what he thought about at the time, but as he says, "in my feelings of that time there is a new element—my feelings now about that time: there is not an old man living who can recover the emotions of the past." He can only summon up the memory of the objects around which the emotions had ordered themselves, and these become "symbols which will preserve only so much of the old life as they may, in their own mysterious history, consent to bear." (22) Thus Lacy Buchan's account of his long-ago experience contains the meaning that he has come in time to attach to that experience.

The story that Lacy tells is of the breaking up of the Buchan family, including the deaths of his father Major

Lewis Buchan and of his brother Semmes, and the burning of the family place, Pleasant Hill, by Union soldiers in 1861. It was the events of the war that ended the Buchan establishment, but—and here is where *The Fathers* differs so importantly from Stark Young's *So Red the Rose* and many another historical romance of the fall of the Old South—these events came from *within* the family as well as without, and were ultimately made possible by a social and moral situation interior to the society. Through the agency of George Posey, Lacy Buchan's brother-in-law who, as Lacy imagines his long-dead grandfather saying to him, had no "intention to do evil but . . . does evil because he has not the will to do good," (267) the family and the society encompass their own dissolution. Yet—such is the wisdom of this complex and profound novel—George Posey is no villain in Lacy's eyes; the young Lacy admires him and declares at the close that "if I am killed [in the war] it will be because I love him more than I love any man." (306)

If George Posey had been a rogue, a scoundrel, he would have been capable of being dealt with, but he was not. He *meant* well (the proverb concerning the pavement of the road to hell is appropriate here). He was generous, impulsive, personally brave, warm-hearted; yet his advent into the Buchan family precipitated the collapse of that family and the traditional society it exemplified.

Why Lacy Buchan feels impelled to tell his story is explained early in the novel: "Is it not something to tell, when a score of people whom I knew and loved, people beyond whose lives I could imagine no other life, either out of violence in themselves or the times, or out of some misery or shame, scattered into the new life of the modern age where they cannot even find themselves? Why cannot life change without tangling the lives of innocent persons? Why do innocent persons cease their innocence and become violent and evil in themselves that such great changes may take place?" (5)

The Fathers has been admirably written about by such commentators as Arthur Mizener and Radcliffe Squires, the latter of whom in particular does an illuminating job of showing how Lacy Buchan, as the member of his family who survives the holocaust, can recognize the limitations and liabilities of both his Buchan heritage and of the approach to experience exemplified by his brother-in-law.[56] Major Buchan's world is founded upon order, dignity, social role; he is so thoroughly a creature of that northern Virginia planter society he represents that he can completely define himself within its forms and thus be spared the need to search within himself for the meaning of his behavior. Pleasant Hill, his estate, is appropriately named: it provides a civilized, dignified home for himself and his establishment, leisured and mannered, "a house where all's accustomed, ceremonious." There are slaves, but they perform only a modicum of work and pretty much come and go as they please. (In his biography of John Brown, Robert Penn Warren reported the reply of a Mr. Byrne, a slaveowner in the northern Virginia area not too far from the scene of *The Fathers*, when one of Brown's men demanded that he produce his slaves: "Mr. Cook, if you want my slaves, you will have to do as I do when I want them—hunt for them. They went off Saturday evening and they haven't gotten back yet."[57]) Major Buchan reads his history and rides to his hounds. Such humane virtues as are provided by a comfortable establishment, a conviction of identity, a network of social forms and established ritual and ceremony, a life of moderation and reason, a code of honor, a known ancestral past and seemingly secured future, are his—and these, without ostentation or self-consciousness, are clearly set forth by the author as pretty much the most that a civilized life can provide. In terms of *I'll Take My Stand*, surely this was the Agrarian ideal at its most desirable.

It might have gone on thus, for Lacy and his descendants—as another novelist, a friend of Tate's, once wrote about an imagined life of heart's desire, it would be "pretty" to think so. Into this seemingly changeless and self-contained world, however, comes George Posey. His people were Marylanders who had moved from the countryside into Georgetown. The Poseys are queer, unstable, without balance. George, who marries Lacy's sister Susan over the helpless objections of her father, is a shrewd businessman. He is attractive and kind, and the young Lacy Buchan admires him immensely, as does Lacy's older brother Semmes, through whom Posey is introduced into the family. In his openness and his lack of any guiding tradition and forms, George Posey is the modern man; he possesses no code or social standard against which to measure his actions. He is impervious to Major Buchan's freezingly polite disapproval because he has no sense that it *is* disapproval. Each experience that Posey encounters is without precedent, because he has no tradition of social or moral behavior to inform his response. He can be capable of great generosity, yet at the same time can sell a Negro slave out of the family in order to buy a new horse. He feels no necessity to unify his personal actions with his beliefs, for he is oblivious of contradictions. The world seems open and available to him, because he operates without any sense of social necessity or obligation. In the same way, the idea of death is terrible and threatening to him, since he cannot imagine it as gentled by ritual. Thus he can only try to ignore it; he will not attend Mrs. Buchan's funeral; he will not visit his dead mother's room. Unprotected by moral forms or social ceremonies, he is exposed to the brute force of raw, elemental nature, to master it or be mastered as he must be.

Because Lacy's older brother Semmes Buchan realizes that his father is allowing the family estate to slip into economic ruin, he arranges with Posey to save it by having George sell the slaves sent to him by Major Buchan to be freed; Posey also takes over power of attorney for Pleasant Hill and sees to it that the overseer gets work out of the remaining slaves, through use of the lash if necessary. Slaves are manpower as far as Posey is concerned; all such problems are economic, not human.

Posey is the agency of the tragedy that strikes the Buchans. Each of the cataclysmic events that destroy them can be attributed to him. His wife goes insane. His brother-in-law Semmes kills the slave Yellow Jim, who has been driven to cause the disgrace of Jane Posey, George's sister who is to marry Semmes, by entering her room; whereupon George kills Semmes for killing his half-brother. He did not "mean" to do any of it; but he did all this and more, often enough from motives that were quite innocent. Without a code of behavior and without social forms to discipline it, his very innocence is fatally disruptive. As Radcliffe Squires says, "he is at the mercy of phenomena, and to this condition may be attributed his ruthlessness and violence. For the man who has no ordered world will try to create a different world. He will never know exactly what he will do in the real world from one moment to the next, for while the real world is the world in which he acts, the world in which he conceives his acts is one of fantasy."[58] At the end, he kills the Confederate officer who viciously insults him, and must leave the army and flee—to Georgetown—to the city, to the west, to the end of the world—while Lacy returns to the army to fight for both of them in the war, the war which has already leveled Pleasant Hill to the ground and will utterly ruin what is left of the society in which Lacy was born and has known.

Yet it will not suffice to see George Posey simply as a restless element who forces his way into a traditional society and wrecks it. Posey's impact is possible only because the society itself contains the potentiality for self-destruction. Major Buchan, the man of taste and reason, could not withstand Posey's entrance because he was insufficiently able to cope with what he did not understand —and he did not sufficiently recognize that there *were* forces that he could not understand. There was, in his sense of role and tradition, a kind of abstraction, a reliance upon his forms and standards and his concept of "honor" that failed to take account of the irrationality and ungovernable quality of human life. If the social forms can provide a means of apprehending experience so that each event in one's life is not a new and unprecedented phenemenon, they are *not* the totality of the experience itself, and to rely upon them to the utter exclusion of the individual moral judgment can be perilous. Major Buchan is a Unionist, and so sure that men of reason will settle the sectional conflict that he is not able to comprehend the passion of unreason that causes war and destruction. When his son Semmes chooses to join the secessionist side, the major thereupon informs him that he is no son of his; and this abstract, ideologically based action helps make possible the catastrophic events that wreck the family. The major believes in honor to the extent that it becomes a concept, divorced from the love and passion of the family situation itself. Instead of giving moral strength and dignity to the life he knows, it finally distorts and wrecks it.

The comfort and dignity of life at Pleasant Hill are dependent, ultimately, upon slavery, and slavery is in crucial respects an economic institution. When the major sends his slaves to George Posey to be freed, he is performing a morally noble act, but it is an act that is separated from its economic consequences, and the major's heirs cannot overlook such matters—it is they, and not the major, who will have to pay the ultimate cost of the major's moral nobility. Semmes Buchan knows all too well that the establishment of Pleasant Hill is failing economically; "Good God, boy, look around you," he tells Lacy; "there hasn't been any tobacco in the barns for nearly ten years! And how much corn do you think papa makes? Fifteen bushels to the acre!" (19–20) The implication is that the humane master-slave relationship of

Pleasant Hill is being purchased at the price of Pleasant Hill itself. It is slavery almost without enforced labor, but slavery exists as a means of enforcing labor. Without the ownership of slaves and the using of them *as slaves* there can be no Pleasant Hill, and no such planter society as it exemplifies. The major may shut his eyes to the fact; Semmes Buchan cannot, and so George Posey is called into the situation to protect his wife's and his in-laws' property. The existence of slavery, therefore, implicitly demands the economic ruthlessness, the shrewdness to sell the slaves when unprofitable, and the insensibility that permits such shrewdness, of George Posey. Without the willingness to use slave labor there would have been no Pleasant Hill in the first place, and when there is slavery it is always possible for a George Posey to sell his half-brother for a new horse. Major Buchan's high-minded sensibility and generosity are indulged at the price of unreality, and depend upon an unwillingness to face reality. Thus the agrarian planter society is doomed not only because a George Posey is possible, but because he is *inevitable*.

Lacy Buchan, born into that society, growing to manhood just as the war commences that will destroy it, sees this happen, and as an old man looking back upon the time of its dissolution can begin to understand why it came about. But why, one might wonder, since George Posey was the instrument of his family's collapse, does Lacy remember himself as feeling that he will stay with the army to fight for both George and himself, and that if he dies in the war it will be because he loves him more than any man? Surely it is because George Posey, in all his naïveté and destructiveness, who could "never have anything to do with death," represents life, the striving human being trying to make sense of things, caught in his own fallibility and yet meaning well. Lacy will go with George Posey because George is a modern man and because modernity is part of his own birthright, too. The traditional society that his Buchan heritage represents is dying, will soon be gone—it is not merely the war that Lacy has in mind when he says at the end that "I'll go back and finish it. I'll have to finish it because he could not finish it." (306) The title of the novel is *The Fathers*, and George Posey is, equally with Major Buchan, Lacy's spiritual father. Had the traditional society of Major Buchan been sufficient to define the experience of his children, Lacy would never have been drawn to George Posey, any more than would his sister Susan, who married him, or his brother Semmes, who connived with him to convert Pleasant Hill into a profitable economic unit. The society of Pleasant Hill, though it had appeared invulnerable to time and change, fit to provide its family with the best that civilized life might afford, was not lasting. The very conditions that made it possible doomed it. The advent of George Posey was inevitable; and for Lacy Buchan there was finally no choice but to accept George's burden, and face the world in whatever guise it presented itself.

Yet though Lacy loved George Posey and shares in his humanity with George, he is *not* George. There remains for him the Buchan heritage, or more properly, its vivid memory and its assumptions and expectations. Thus the aged physician in the Georgetown of the early twentieth century ponders the why of the tale. It is the next generation—the generation of Allen Tate—who, without the memory of Pleasant Hill and inheriting only the assumptions and expectations, are the southerners of the twentieth century, separated from a tradition by time and history, searching for a way of locating, embodying "knowledge carried to the heart" in the life and the institutions of their own time and place.

Precisely that, it seems to me, is what agrarianism came to signify for Allen Tate. And if so, the conclusion seems inescapable that it did not, finally, suffice. There *was* no way that he found for creating the kind of intellectual situation interior to the South that would bring about the reclaiming of the tradition through the determined, concerted action of the public will. The writing of *The Fathers* only went to show why it could not be done.

When Tate completed *The Fathers* he was no longer living at Benfolly; he had been offered a position at the Women's College of the University of North Carolina at Greensboro, and had moved his family there in what turned out to be a permanent departure from the house his brother Ben had given him. A year later he had accepted a position at Princeton University, and then at the Library of Congress. In 1944 he became an editor with Henry Holt and Company in New York. After that came a year as lecturer at New York University and another as visiting professor at the University of Chicago, and in 1951 he accepted an appointment as professor of English at the University of Minnesota. At the age of fifty-two, for the first time in his life, he had an academic position with tenured security. He kept it until his retirement seventeen years later, in 1968, when he moved back to Tennessee, where he has since resided.

Tate did not find it necessary to follow Ransom's example and "repudiate" agrarianism, for the reason that he never abandoned either his southern loyalties or his desire to defend the religious humanism that he felt agrarianism had been a means of doing. In this sense he remained an Agrarian. What he did was to broaden and extend its meaning and shift the terms of reference from te Old South to Western society in general, with its tradition of classical humanism and Christian faith. We have seen how as early as 1930, in "Remarks on the Southern Religion," he had felt that the Old South had developed a preindustrial, precommercial society, but could not "create its appropriate religion" to provide the appropriate foundation for the secular economic image of its religious attitude. Clearly he thought that religion should have been Roman Catholicism. In the same way we have

seen how in the early 1930s, in poems such as "The Mediterranean" and "Aeneas at Washington," he had depicted
the society of the Old South as an extension into the new
world of the antique classical heritage of western Europe.

In *The Fathers* he had explored the breakdown of the
society of the Old South before the forces of incipient industrialism. At the moment when the tragedy has struck
the Buchan and Posey household in Georgetown and
Jane Posey had been violated, spiritually if not physically,
by Yellow Jim and by her crazed heritage, a priest and
nuns come to look after the Poseys, who are Catholics.
Lacy looks at the priest, who is named Father Monaghan:
"As he passed me I saw heavy beads of sweat on his forehead. He looked at me: man to man. 'I know you are not
one of us, young man,' he said. 'We've got to keep life
simple. That is a practical reason for saving the human
soul.' He put his hand on my shoulder. 'God bless you,
my son.'" (236)

So in addition to Major Lewis Buchan and George
Posey, there is one more father figure in this novel. I do
not think he is there by accident.

In 1943–1944 Tate wrote a long four-part poem, "Seasons of the Soul," in which he depicted a world at war
with itself, torn by its own greed and lust, starved for love
and bereft of belief. In the fourth section he addressed
himself to "the mother of silences," who may be death,
and may be life:

> Then, mother of silences,
> Speak, that we may hear;
> Listen, while we confess
> That we conceal our fear;
> Regard us, while the eye
> Discerns by sight or guess
> Whether, as sheep foregather
> Upon their crooked knees,
> We have begun to side;
> Whether your kindness, mother,
> Is mother of silences.[59]

In 1951 Allen Tate joined the Roman Catholic Church.

Queried in 1952 about what agrarianism had been all about, Tate wrote to the editors of *Shenandoah* magazine that he had never seen it as a restoration of anything in the Old South, but as something to be created. In the long run, he said, he still thought it would be created, as the result of a profound change not only in the South but in the moral and religious outlook of Western man. "The South is still a region where an important phase of that change may take place; but the change will not, as I see it, be uniquely Southern; it will be greater than the South. What I had in mind twenty years ago, not too distinctly, I think I see more distinctly now; that is, the possibility of the human life presupposes, with us, a prior order, the order of a unified Christendom." Although the Old South had perpetuated many of the virtues of such an order, to try to revive it now "would be a kind of idolatry; it would prefer the accident to the substance."[60]

It was on terms such as these that Tate conducted his literary career in the years after the waning of the Agrarian enterprise. He viewed himself and his fellow writers in the role of the "Man of Letters in the Modern World," the title of an essay of 1950 in which he set forth, as he saw it, the responsibility of the modern man of letters to keep language alive and pure in his time, and to warn when it ceases to forward the ends proper to man. "The end of social man is communion in time through love," he concluded, "which is beyond time."[61] It was to this literary theme that he addressed his work over the course of the years that followed.

6 Robert Penn Warren: Love and Knowledge

A Vanderbilt Apprenticeship

Robert Penn Warren's involvement in the Agrarian venture—not merely *I'll Take My Stand* itself, but the several years of planning that produced it and the subsequent period of disengagement—was essentially different from that of his three fellow Fugitive poets, and, from the standpoint of Warren's career, of lesser literary importance. For the others it represented an important crossroads in their literary careers. For the oldest, Ransom, it coincided with the virtual end of his rôle as an active poet, and when after the years of involvement in cultural and social matters he turned back to literature, it was as critic and editor. For Davidson, on the other hand, the Agrarian enterprise provided him with historical anchor and geographical definition; through it he entered upon his characteristic mode as a poet, and thereafter wrote his poetry and ordered his life out of the Agrarian social assumptions. As for Tate, agrarianism provided him with the issue and the image to assert his belief in religious humanism, and to create poems out of his relationship to Agrarian social and moral assumptions. Much of his best poetry came out of the Agrarian allegiance, and when later he moved on to a different allegiance, overtly religious in identity, it was not a matter of changing, so much as of extending his cultural and social assumptions. One cannot imagine either the major writings or the subsequent careers of these three men being what they were without the Agrarian episode.

By contrast, Warren was still very much in the apprentice stage of his literary career when agrarianism was formulated and *I'll Take My Stand* published. It was not until the mid-1930s, when the Agrarian activity was coming to a close, that he began to produce his more mature work. Agrarianism never became the central allegiance for him, either as man or writer. In important respects he was of a different generation of southerners from that of his friends. The Agrarian venture had its significance for him, but far more important was the Vanderbilt milieu as such, and the personal associations with Tate, Ransom, and Davidson. Had Warren never been invited to contribute to *I'll Take My Stand* at all, it is doubtful whether his subsequent writings would have been greatly different from what they are. I do not mean by this that either his views or his writings became antithetical to his rôle as Agrarian. It is rather that his own creative imagination sought and found other and different forms.

Warren was born in Guthrie, Kentucky, across the state line from Tennessee, April 24, 1905. In the years just after his birth the locale was the scene of considerable unrest and violence, for it was the area in which black leaf tobacco was grown. When in the early 1900s, as the result of the American Tobacco Company's market monopoly, tobacco leaf prices dropped below the cost of growing crops, farmers had formed a protective association to keep prices up, and when that failed, bands of night riders took to scraping tobacco beds, burning barns and warehouses, using physical terrorism and even murder to force compliance with their program. Ultimately martial law had to be declared and the National Guard was called out to preserve order.

Although nominally Methodist, Warren's parents were not especially religious in outlook or interests. He attended elementary school in Guthrie and high school there and across the line in Clarksville, Tennessee. Most of his summers were spent in the country, on the farm of his grandfather, a Confederate veteran. As a child he did a great deal of reading, especially in history, and by the time he arrived at Vanderbilt University as a freshman in the fall of 1921 he was more than ordinarily well prepared to take advantage of the intellectual situation. His freshman English teacher was John Ransom, who was sufficiently impressed with his writing talents to invite him to enroll in his advanced composition course the next term. Donald Davidson taught him sophomore English literature. Soon he had made friends with another, older student, Allen Tate, and was writing poetry and being taken to Fugitive meetings. He began publishing poems in the magazine and was made a member of the group. Rooming with Tate and Ridley Wills in Wesley Hall he was introduced to—among other things—the work of Eliot, Pound, the French Symbolists, and the burgeoning literature of post-World War I modernism. Most of the older Fugitives, in particular those who, like Sidney Hirsch, were essentially dilettantes so far as literary activity was concerned, he found rather uninspiring. Writing poetry was no gentlemanly avocation for him.

Like many another talented young man, I think, he was considerably more sophisticated intellectually and literarily than socially and emotionally, and doubtless he found the intellectual and social assurance of the older and more worldly wise Tate enviable, and Tate's interest in him both flattering and encouraging. Tate for his part quickly discerned that this rather awkward young man was perhaps the most gifted and quietly but fiercely dedicated writer of them all. He still had some painful growing up to do, but when in June of 1925 he was graduated from Vanderbilt, he was determined to have a career in writing and teaching. He had little emotional attachment to the town where he had grown up, though he had always greatly enjoyed his summers on the farm. What he wanted to do was to go abroad, but since that was financially impossible he began graduate study at the University of California in Berkeley, and after receiving his Master of Arts degree there in 1927 went on for more advanced study at Yale University. In 1928 he was awarded a Rhodes Scholarship, and that fall sailed for Oxford. Thus he was absent from the Nashville scene during all the time that the Agrarian enterprise was being shaped, and maintained his ties with the group only through correspondence and occasional visits with Tate, in New York and later in Paris.

The poems that Warren was publishing in the *Fugitive* and elsewhere were apprentice works for the most part, but from the outset he showed a remarkable way with language. Eliot was his earliest and most pervasive influence, as one might expect of a friend and roommate of Allen Tate. The influence, however, was mostly in technique; Warren's early poetry is not much affected by a sense of cultural Decline and Fall. It is rather gloomy work; however, the pessimism is not social but metaphysical, involving a preoccupation with death, the flight of time, the inadequacy of romantic love. Sometimes Warren draws upon the rural Kentucky and Tennessee scene for subject matter, usually in order to make points about the brevity of human life when contrasted with seasonal diuturnity, as in the sestet of "Autumn Twilight Piece" (1924):

> Autumn, we know, is twilight of the year.
> The bronze and amber rumor of our death
> Stains the far hills and soon to us will bring

> The caverned sleep of winter, when beneath
> The fennel's frigid roots we do not hear
> Again the bright amphigories of spring.[1]

This is pretty stern stuff for a nineteen-year-old under-graduate poet. The model is obviously Eliot. One has the feeling that for Warren, at this early stage of his career and for some years to come, the office of poet was seen as that of commenting upon the futility of life in time, rather than getting involved in it himself. There is very little evidence of Red Warren the ambitious young author and student, delighting in his work and friendships, gratefully placing Guthrie, Kentucky, behind him and voyaging out, eager for knowledge and experience.

Oddly, almost nothing of his passion for history, which would be lifelong, gets into the early work. It is as if he felt the obligation not to concern himself with local, temporal, personal human process, lest he betray his own vulnerability, but to view everything *sub specie aeternitatis*. Nor does one find any of the remarkable insight into personality that would later help to make him so fine a novelist. Only his talent for language saves the early poetry from being merely lugubrious—but that talent, however employed in a fashion not calculated to give it full scope, manages to infuse even the most doleful and least promising poetic situation with vitality and intensity of feeling. In a poem entitled "August Revival: Crosby Junction" (1925), for example, the preacher conducting the revival is advised to desist from talk of salvation, since the corn crop remains to be harvested and the dull congregation would be better left undisturbed to conduct its mortal labors. Let nature work out its seasonal progressions without their being remarked:

> But let the serpent coil in the dark winepress,
> The lank hare's foot disturb the withering grass,
> Let young foxes be gnawing the hare's worn skull
> And the owl hoot from the olive tree on the hill![2]

The stanza, it seems to me, menaces the whole direction

of the poem. For Warren imbues the objects designed to convey the desuetude and animal repetitiveness with so singular a vividness and linguistic excitement—drawn mostly from Old Testament imagery—that it is difficult to feel that they can remain unnoticed by the supposedly torpid congregation. They throw the reader's attention upon the speaker, the poet who is telling him this. One has the feeling that the poet-speaker is enforcing a personal commentary upon the subject.

Yet it would appear to me that the poetic strategy that Warren has adopted, and that characterized the poetry of his friend Tate, is such that it cannot permit or tolerate that kind of rôle for a poet. The poet himself is not to be present in the poem as overt interpreter, for the poem should be a quasipublic utterance, objective and complete in itself, and not an expression of personality. For Tate, I think, such a strategy worked out very effectively indeed; as poet he approached things dramatically, and took roles in his poems not as interpreting poet but as participant in the situation. Warren, however, was from the outset the sort of poet (Wordsworth was another) for whom poetry was not only emotion recollected in tranquillity, but for whom the *act* of the recollection and reflection *was* the poem. Tate's poet-participant strategy was not his role, and neither was Ransom's way appropriate for him. He could not as poet separate the act of poetry from the imaginative process of working out the meaning, and concentrate as poet upon elaborating the ironies and ambiguities of the already-perceived situation.

Warren as poet was not a classicist, but a romantic. Yet at this stage in his career, one feels, he was unwilling to thrust himself as poet onto centerstage, so to speak, to let his readers observe and join him in the act of seeking out his meanings. Poetry, he had been instructed and himself believed, was an impersonal activity—as Eliot had put it, an escape from personality. So he sought to work through rhetoric—*i.e.*, through imposing upon the objective material of the poem an intense emotional burden located in the presentation of the material itself.

What the young Warren could manage under this dispensation can be seen in the long, seven-part poem "Kentucky Mountain Farm," the various segments of which were written in the middle and late 1920s and early 1930s. It is a fine poem. The mountain farm is depicted against a backdrop of time and the seasons. The rocks outlast the land, the crops, the wildlife and the farm animals, and the men who now live there. On this farm all things constitute reminders of mortality and impermanence; even the bluejay, "blue cuirassier and summer's lost vidette," is "bright friend of boys, troubler of old men."[3] And in the final section, "The Return," the speaker, who has come back to the scene of his boyhood, realizes that even then, he had before him the augury of change, in that his mother, now dead, had been unable to recognize his changed identity as he had grown.

Yet one is led, in the light of what Warren was later to achieve in his poetry, to speculate on how much more interesting a poem might have resulted had he been willing to accept the logic of what the poem was about, which was not the mountain farm itself as scene and indication of time and change, but the poet's remembered experience of achieving that perspective. Only in the last section, and then only obliquely, does the sensibility appear for whom the image of the mountain farm represents the meaning. The poem is written as if it were concerned solely with *what* he remembers, when what really makes the poem effective is the developing *act* of memory and meditation, viewed in its seven-part sequential development.

In the section entitled "History among the Rocks," for example, the Civil War dead are described in the mountains. The center of the experience lies in the poet's thinking about why the soldiers fought there, and finding it impossible to arrive at a reasonable explanation when he considers the other ways they might just as easily and more naturally have died. The orchards continue to bear their fruit without reference to human time and concerns:

> In these autumn orchards once young men lay dead . . .
> Gray coats, blue coats. Young men on the mountainside
> Clambered, fought. Heels muddied the rocky spring.
> Their reason is hard to guess, remembering
> Blood on their black moustaches in moonlight.
> Their reason is hard to guess and a long time past:
> The apple falls, falling in the quiet night.[4]

Yet instead of locating this meditation openly in the viewpoint of the commentator—"I could not guess their reason," as it were—and permitting himself to perform overtly as the contemplative poet who is viewing the scene in an act of speculative memory, he seems obligated to work around what for him is the most significant aspect of the experience: its impact upon his own reflective consciousness. Tate, in "Ode to the Confederate Dead," might dramatize the modern man at the cemetery gate as participant, viewing the graves of the soldiers and seeking desperately to identify his consciousness with theirs. But for Warren the implied narrator could not be a participant, for as poet he is recollecting, not acting upon his own. He thus had two options: either to focus upon the poet-speaker and show him meditating, or else let the poem be the product of his meditation, in which event only the results could be chronicled. The Warren of the 1950s and thereafter would not have hesitated to choose the first option, knowing that it was the remembering experience that mattered most to him. But for the young Warren, I think, such a procedure would have seemed a romantic insistence upon his own personal experience, an illegitimate intrusion of personality into art. The wonder to me is that, writing out of a strategy that so restricted his own talent, he was able nevertheless to write so well. For "Kentucky Mountain Farm" is an interesting and accomplished sequence.

In the balance of things, when viewed from the perspective of Warren's fifty-year career as poet, his Vanderbilt apprenticeship can only be seen as extremely fortunate. For if the poetics of Ransom and Tate, and through Tate of Eliot, were not in the long run calculated to allow Warren to be fully himself as poet, the discipline of composing poetry to a strict form, with a very precise and even recondite language convention, and with the poet's ego kept carefully suppressed, was far more beneficial than inhibiting. There would be time later for Warren to move into a strategy more appropriate to his own restless, introspective, personally meditative bent. The Fugitives taught him to make his language firm, to control emotion with intelligence, to distinguish between sentiment and sentimentality. They showed him the difference between genuine passion in language and easy rhetorical fustian. They taught him to separate poet from poem, so as to make certain that the result of his labors in verse, whatever else they might involve, would always be *poems*. Later he could move toward working more of himself into his poems, after first mastering the requirement that what he was writing was first of all a poem, and not merely the cadenced representation of an idea or an emotion.

When after his graduation from Vanderbilt he went out to California for advanced literary study, he found that all the talk there was about ideas, not poetics and poems. At California, he remembers jokingly, everyone seemed to know all about Marx and Freud and to consider Witter Bynner and Edna Millay great poets; at Vanderbilt the talk had all been about poetry and related things while the name Marx was familiar only as that of a clothing manufacturer and Freud was a dirty rumor.[5] There would be ample opportunity to study and master ideas, but for a young apprentice poet the privilege of beginning his career with expert tutelage and example in the cultivation of language was invaluable. Without the Fugitive experience Warren would doubtless have gone on to become a powerfully emotive writer. Vanderbilt taught him to be a literary craftsman.

Warren as Agrarian

If Warren's interest in history found so little expression in his poetry—the soldiers in the lines cited earlier are only instances of men in time, not men engaged in a particular war at a particular historical juncture—the same is not true of his first published book. While he was a graduate student at Yale he signed a contract, through Tate's good offices, with Payson and Clarke for a biography of John Brown. Published in 1929, *John Brown: The Making of a Martyr* is rather better work than either of Tate's two Civil War biographies, for Warren made a genuine effort to understand what made Brown what he became in his time, whereas Tate, as we have seen, was principally concerned with using Stonewall Jackson and Jefferson Davis to make cautionary points about the failure of the South to protect its own interests in the past. There is no question as to where Warren stood on the question of John Brown: the old man is a fanatic, for whom abolition is the rationale for failure and excuse for violence, and he and those New England financiers and intellectuals who supported him are both irresponsible and criminal in their willingness to wreck the peace and destroy the republic. But Warren does his best to see Brown's side of the matter, and respects his determination and strength of will even if he thinks the outcome a tragedy for almost everyone concerned.

Nor does Warren allow his disapproval of Brown to blind him to the evil of slavery. Though he depicts the actuality of the peculiar institution as it existed in northern

Virginia as less monstrous and more humane than the theory, he does not neglect to point out the role of the domestic slave trade in Virginia's economy, and he sees the moral issue that confronted the nation as one of how an evil is to be ended, whether through violence and bloodshed or through compromise and patience. Brown's actions, he feels, made the latter solution impossible and the former inevitable.

In retrospect it is easy to see why Warren chose John Brown for the subject of his biography. What fascinated him about the old man was what would constitute the stuff of each of his first five novels: the relationship of private, subjective moral idealism to complex social fact, and the corrupting psychological temptation of power. A biography of John Brown was not, however, an ideal vehicle for Warren to explore his insights along this line. As a historical figure Brown was too well documented, and the factual requirements of straight biography too restrictive, to permit Warren to let his imagination go fully to work. Furthermore, the man was too narrowly religious, too unimaginative, and clearly not sufficiently aware of his motives to permit any conscious moral struggle to be developed within his own mind. But midway through the biography, while describing Brown's Kansas activities, Warren introduces a character who offers considerably more possibilities:

In "Whipple's" [Aaron Dwight Stevens'] company was a young man of twenty-one, named John Henry Kagi. He was a studious fellow, rather slight and stooped in figure, with thin brown hair and lean face. Under well-arched brows his cold, veiled eyes, hazel-grey in color, indicated the reserved, unemotional nature. After a schooling in Virginia he taught at Hawkinstown in that state until too many discussions on the subject of slavery made it best for him to leave for his home in Ohio. He studied Latin, law, and history, wrote for newspapers, and went West to Nebraska. There he was admitted to the bar. On July 4 he saw Colonel Sumner's dragoons drawn up before the meeting house of the Legislature at Topeka, and that sight caused him to join the militia which "Whipple" commanded. From that day on he was ready to fight as well as write for the Free State cause. He was a man with convictions but with no enthusiasms; furthermore, he possessed a strong logical sense. It was that logic which made him argue and write tirelessly, somewhat arrogantly but without passion, made the schoolteacher leave slaveholding Virginia, converted the young lawyer into the militiaman and raider, and which, in the end, carried him stoically, indifferent to success or failure, to his death at Harper's Ferry.[6]

There, a decade before publication of Warren's first novel, is the prototype of Percy Munn in *Night Rider*, as well as of Jerry Calhoun, Jack Burden, Jeremiah Beaumont, and many another Warren fictional protagonist. To his credit as biographer of John Brown, Warren kept Kagi confined to the minor role he played in the events in Kansas and at Harpers Ferry, but his fascination with the character's possibilities is obvious. The description is out of proportion to the needs of the biographical narrative. For here is the young man of education, ambitious, capable, hungry for real impact in life through action, and open to the corruptive potentialities of power under the rationalization that the end will justify the means.

Warren's biography of John Brown was published while he was at Oxford. It was during this time that *I'll Take My Stand* was being planned. Tate, who was in France on a Guggenheim Fellowship, kept him posted on developments. When the various essays were assigned, Warren's subject was the situation of the black southerner. As we have seen, Donald Davidson and some of the others considered his essay to be less than satisfactory because it had little to say about agrarianism as such, and, arguing that the southern black man should remain on the land, proceeded to insist that his opportunities there would have to be made more attractive than they presently were. Although not challenging segregation, Warren insisted that "separate but equal" must mean what it said: the black southerner must be educated if he is to farm successfully, and must have ample opportunity to make a decent living: "The strawberry or the cotton bale tells no tales in the market concerning its origin." [7]

Like Tate, Warren was unhappy with the strong southern agricultural identification implied by the symposium's title. Yet to judge from his essay itself, he did not at first view agrarianism primarily as a kind of pastoral metaphor, an assertion of religious humanism through evocation of the southern rural ordering. On the contrary, his essay approaches its subject quite literally and in very practical terms: he points out the risks that industrialization holds for the black southerner through placing him in direct economic competition with lower-class whites; he argues the case for the black man as farmer; and he stresses the need for practical training in agricultural methods and the necessity of greater marketing opportunities. What seems obvious is that however far removed Warren may have been from the southern scene, living as he was in England when he wrote his essay, his view of farming and the rural South was not remotely to be gentled by metaphor; he had lived and worked on a Kentucky farm too recently to be able to idealize the sturdy yeoman. Furthermore, the memories of the Black Patch Tobacco War, which he was beginning to use in fiction, were vivid enough to remind him all too forcefully of the economic dimension of farming and of its relationship to price levels and marketing problems in a society which had long been closely tied to industrialization insofar as tobacco-growing and marketing were involved. he could not envision agrarianism apart from its economic and social manifestations, could not separate the cultural ideal from the factual documentation.

Why, then, did he take part in *I'll Take My Stand*? It seems to me that he saw his role in the enterprise as a method of *action*. It was a vehicle for protest, and not merely a general, metaphorical rebuke to dehumanization and the society of scientism and mass culture, but a specific, tangible strategy for assailing what seemed so vast and unassailable—not industrialism alone, but all that must have appeared, to a young southern poet in the late 1920s, to go along with it: finance capitalism, the cultural dominance of New York City and the commercialism of the literary marketplace, the debasement of language as practiced in advertising and social science, the defeat and impoverishment of the South, the glib parlor Marxism of the period that was already being mouthed in advanced metropolitan intellectual circles, the self-serving Babbittry of American business, the sense of dislocation, the breakdown in manners and forms, the threat that naked, unchecked economic power posed to democratic society. Here was a way of hitting back. Whether it was practically feasible didn't really matter as much as the opportunity to have an impact. Poets, scholars—the alienated, the cut-off—were together acting *in* the realm of economics and political power.

Moreover, writing his essay from a distance—Oxford —he was able to rationalize away certain unpleasant and contradictory factors that might otherwise have prevented him from being able to enter into the operation—not only its economic impracticality, but the amount of defensive chauvinism involved, the knowledge that what he meant by agrarianism was different from what certain others in the group had in mind, the less than democratic implications of some of the group's premises about the ordered society, his discomfort with the notion of the dirt farmer as sturdy yeoman exemplar of the civilized virtues, and his apprehension that black southerners weren't really going to have their own human needs and ambitions fulfilled if they were to be kept in the rôle of a peasantry. As Warren said of agrarianism many years later, "it hit me at a time when I was first away from this part of the country for any period of time, having lived in California two years, and a year in New Haven in the Yale Graduate School, and then in Oxford. And I had broken out of the kind of life I was accustomed to in that part of the world I knew. And there was a sentimental appeal for me in this."[8]

To a certain extent, I feel, Warren went into the venture in something like the way various of his intellectually alienated protagonists get themselves involved in real life —as a way of attempting to combat the sense of intellectual superfluousness through a commitment to a cause that involved action in society, and at the cost of suppressing other and contradictory aspects of one's own personality.

If so, it did not take very long for Warren to recognize what he was doing and why. In the summer of 1930 he returned home from England to be assistant professor of English at Southwestern University in Memphis. While writing the essay for *I'll Take My Stand* at Oxford, he recalled later, he had also begun to write fiction: "The two things were tied together—the look back home from a long distance. I remember the jangle and wrangle of writing the essay and some kind of discomfort in it, some sense of evasion, I guess, in writing it, in contrast to the free feeling of writing the novelette *Prime Leaf*, the sense of stirring up something fresh. . . . In the essay I was trying to prove something, and in the novelette trying to find out something, see something, feel something—exist. . . . Well, it wasn't being outside the South that made me change my mind [about racial segregation]. It was coming back home again. In a little while I realized I simply couldn't have written that essay again."[9]

But it was not only the racial situation that was involved. Warren drew back from the programmatical aspects of agrarianism. He wrote no more essays like "The Briar Patch," in which he treated Agrarian concerns as a literal or practical matter. His fiction and his poetry manifested his thinking about society, the South, and the situation of modern man, but never *as* Agrarian doctrine. As he wrote in the essay entitled "Literature as a Symptom" for *Who Owns America?*, "at no time, not even the happiest, was the novelist or poet relieved of the responsibility of inspecting the aims of the society from which he stemmed and in which he moved, and of pondering the inevitable puzzles proposed to him by the spectacle of human existence." But such responsibility, he insisted, was properly discharged through his performance as an artist, and thus as "a phase of his own conduct as a human being and, as a matter of fact, a citizen." [10] The artist, he maintained, whether his allegiance be regional or proletarian, who used an ideological position in order to avoid working out the meanings for himself in his fiction and poetry, became the propagandist and the inferior artist. The Agrarian allegiance, as far as Warren was concerned, was not a plan of action but a humanistic view of man in nature and in society. To the extent that the term *Agrarian* implied any explicit program or ideology, any conscious adherence to a theme, it was not part of his activities as a writer; and indeed, because the term seemed automatically to thrust that sort of identity upon its adherents during the 1930s, we find him drawing ever further away from it.

Thus when in 1935, shortly after he began teaching at Louisiana State University, he became associated with Cleanth Brooks and Charles W. Pipkin in editing the *Southern Review*, there was nothing programmatical about the essays on society and literature that were selected for publication. The southern allegiance was there, but not as an ideology—with the result that within a few years Davidson was expressing to Tate his displeasure with the failure of the magazine to function as an organ of the cause.

Modes of Discourse

In 1938 Brooks and Warren published the first edition of a textbook anthology, *Understanding Poetry*, which in the years that followed would be the spearhead of a virtual revolution in the teaching of literature in American colleges and universities. Two years earlier the two of them, together with John T. Purser, had published a general literature textbook, *An Approach to Literature*, and in 1943 Brooks and Warren brought out *Understanding Fiction*. The latter two volumes, as well as their 1949 composition textbook, *Modern Rhetoric*, have been highly successful and widely adopted; but *Understanding Poetry* was their most significant and influential pedagogical collaboration. For what this volume did was to direct the attention of the teacher, and therefore of the student, to the text of the poem, and away from the reading of poetry principally as an aspect of authorial biography, or as an artifact in the history of ideas, or as a vehicle for ideological or inspirational exhortation, or as any other kind of document to be interpreted in terms of a scheme of reference exterior to itself.

The method of Brooks and Warren was highly controversial in its time. Those who used it—and who came to be known as New Critics after John Ransom's book of that title was published—were widely considered as academic radicals, bent upon undermining the foundations of literary scholarship. In many a graduate English department, to be a New Critic was to be considered as antiestablishment, antiacademic, even anticultural in bias. A taint of New Critical zeal was enough to cause many a young man to be disqualified for a teaching position in more than a few distinguished English departments. For it struck at the whole apparatus of historical paraphernalia that had accumulated in the wake of the Teutonic source-hunting imported into American graduate education in the later decades of the nineteenth century. No longer was the expertise of a scholar to be judged in terms of how many "influences" of earlier work he could track down in a poem. No longer would it be sufficient for a teacher to "place" the poem in the poet's life, cite its relationship to historical, social, and philosophical currents, read it aloud in a husky voice, and remark, "The man can write!" or "Gentlemen, I trust you are not blind to the beauties of this passage." [11] For what Brooks and Warren were doing was insisting that although it was perfectly all right for the teacher to discourse upon "influences" and historical, social, and philosophical relationships, his first step must be to guide his students in considering what *was* the poetry, or more specifically, what the *poem* was, and the only way to do that was to examine the actual language, look closely at the imagery, and see how the various component parts—words, metaphors, phrases, images—of the poem related to one another and to the poem as a whole. As Brooks wrote later, "the task of criticism is to put the reader in possession of the work of art." [12]

The publication of *Thirty-Six Poems* in 1935 brought Warren considerable recognition for his own poetry. This volume contained "Kentucky Mountain Farm" and some of his other early poems, and a number of lyrics constructed along pretty much the same model, though demonstrating an ever firmer control over language and an intensification of the theme first developed in poems such as "Kentucky Mountain Farm," of human solitude in nature. The influence of Eliot, which in his earliest work was so pervasive, was thrown off, in the sense that no longer do lines, phrases, and images seem to come almost directly from "Gerontion" and "The Hollow Men." But Warren was still writing the tightly constructed, thickly textured "external" poem, with the personality of the poet playing no overt role in the telling of the poem and manifesting itself only from outside and above. All lyric poetry is by definition first-person utterance, to be sure, and the poet's personality need not figure directly in the telling, as the *I*, to be part of the transaction between poet and reader. But there is a kind of poem in which the persona of the poet enters into the telling not in a dramatic rôle, as participant, but as the reflective, interpretative commentator. As we have seen, Warren's earliest work was not of this sort, and neither for the most part is the poetry he was writing in the 1930s, though it begins to change somewhat early in the decade.

Toward the end of the decade, however, Warren begins to write a formally different kind of poem. This was the period during which he was busily engaged in writing fiction, and which culminated in publication of his first novel, *Night Rider*, in 1939. It may have been that the experience of writing prose narrative, with its necessary level of documentation and its reliance upon dialogue, had something to do with the new strategy with which he now began approaching the writing of poems. For whatever reason, the poetry approaches much closer to the condition of direct address to the reader. The second-person pronoun begins to appear much more often, as in the opening stanza of "Terror":

> Not picnics or pageants or the improbable
> Powers of air whose tongues exclaim omission
> And gull the great man to follow his terrible
> Star, suffice; not the window-box, or the bird on
> The ledge, which mean so much to the invalid,
> Nor the joy you leaned after, as by the tracks the grass
> In the emptiness after the lighted Pullmans fled,
> Suffices; nor faces, which, like distraction, pass
> Under the street-lamps, teasing to faith or pleasure,
> Suffice you, born to no adequate definition of terror.[13]

But the "you" in the lines above is not the reader so much as the author's assertion of an identity between himself and the reader, a universalizing of the experience, which is both reader's and poet's, with the poet using his own actual or fictional experience to stand hypothetically for the reader's. That is to say, the poet assumes that the reader, like himself, will recognize what he means when he speaks of "nor the joy you leaned after . . . suffice," whether or not the reader may have experienced the particular version of it described as watching the passenger train go by at night. Thus the poet is using his own personality more directly, in the way he tells his poem.

At first glance this might not seem to be greatly different from what, for example, Allen Tate does in his "Ode to the Confederate Dead," when he writes:

> The brute curiosity of an angel's stare
> Turns you, like them, to stone,
> Transforms the heaving air
> Till plunged to a heavier world below
> You shift your sea-space blindly
> Heaving, turning like the blind crab.[14]

Just as Tate is addressing a hypothetical reader who, like himself, participates in the experience of alienation from the Confederate past, so Warren is identifying with his own sensibility the experience of emptiness and unreality which in the poem is shown sending men in search of violence and death.

But there is a difference, which in Warren's later poems will become even more pronounced. With Tate the event and the meaning are as one; he is a participant in both. For Warren the search for the meaning of the events is the strategy of the poem, and the reader is invited to join in the speaker's search, which is the poem. Warren's poem is finally far more personal than Tate's, for he is making the poem consist of his meditations, while for Tate the poem is a rehearsal of a common situation for the benefit of the reader. Thus Tate's poem is closed, complete, while Warren's is more open-ended, with the meaning advanced only tentatively as a suggested conclusion of the search for it, a search that the poet conducts with the reader's assent. Warren's poem, though composed in seven ten-line stanzas each concluded by a couplet of which the final line contains an additional metric foot, is far less "finished" than Tate's, for both its meaning and its way of presentation demand that it be much more tentative and less thoroughly resolved.

"Terror" appeared in a volume entitled *Eleven Poems on the Same Theme* (1942). Within two years he published his *Selected Poems, 1923–1943* (1944), containing a group of newer poems including "The Ballad of Billie Potts." This poem, while not one of my own favorites, is, I think, vital to Warren's developing style and strategy. It is divided into two contrasting modes of discourse. The account of the way in which big Billie Potts would lure early Kentucky travelers to their death, and how his son, caught trying to do the same, fled westward, made his fortune, then returned east to surprise his parents, only to be murdered unknowingly by them, is recited in a colloquial, folk ballad-like diction. Along with the narrative, however, goes a parenthetical commentary, in which the poet addresses the reader specifically as "you" and discusses the moral significance of the events of the story, pointing out the archetypal nature of the westward journey into space and time and the return eastward in search of a definition not available in time and change.

Thus in the poem Warren formally separates the experience—the situation, the plot, the objective occasion —from the meditation on meaning, and deals with them alternately, first one then the other. The latter element, freed of any requirement of being objectified and grounded in the language of the experience, can now take off on its own, move in any direction and for whatever purpose the poet desires, and return only to close the poem as a completed artifact. But not necessarily as a completed, logically developed assertion of meaning; the meditative inquiry itself can remain open-ended. Moreover, the story of Billie Potts himself is related primarily in regular, folksonglike couplets:

> They had a big boy with fuzz on his chin
> So tall he ducked the door when he came in.
> A clabber-headed bastard with snot in his nose
> And big red wrists hanging out of his clothes . . .[15]

For purposes of contrast Warren allows the parenthetical

commentary, written in a much more formal, literary diction, to become more and more irregular as the poem develops, in order to avoid monotony:

> Therefore you tried to remember when you had last had
>   whatever it was you had lost,
> But it was a long time back.
> And you decided to retrace your steps from that point,
> But it was a long way back.[16]

When the poem is done with the story of Billie Potts, there follows a formal, literary comment likening the human urge for return and definition to the ways of nature, and this is in turn followed by lines that are much less regular, in which there seems to be a fusion of language, so that the colloquial simplicity of the folktale-telling style is joined with the much more formal diction of the commentary. The result is that the poet seems to combine the two language conventions, retain the earlier, more irregular lines, and to end up speaking in his own voice, neither sustained as formally literary nor turned quaint and folksy:

> To kneel
> Here in the evening empty of wind or bird,
> To kneel in the sacramental silence of evening
> At the feet of the old man
> Who is evil and ignorant and old,
> To kneel
> With the little black mark under your heart,
> Which is your name,
> Which is shaped for luck,
> Which is your luck.)[17]

It seems almost as if Warren were now free to move in and out of his poem as he desires, using the language that best fits his meaning, but with a new directness of address. Whereupon he wrote no more lyric poems for a decade or more. It is as if, because he now had for his poetry the same freedom of discourse that fiction afforded him, it seemed best to him to exercise that freedom in fiction alone. There were things, however, which poems could do that fiction could not, but these would require the direct insertion of personality into the poem—a condition toward which the verse had seemed to be moving all the way along. If so, he would appear not to have been ready to do that just yet.

The Freedom of Fiction

Warren's first venture into fiction, "Prime Leaf," appeared in *American Caravan* for 1931, edited by Paul Rosenfeld, Van Wyck Brooks, and Lewis Mumford. It was written at Rosenfeld's invitation, while Warren was at Oxford. The novelette was in effect a trial run for Warren's first published novel, *Night Rider*, in that it dealt with the Black Patch Tobacco War of his boyhood. "Prime Leaf" is told from the viewpoint of a small boy who watches as his father gets involved in the farmers' association aimed at forcing the buyers' monopoly to pay decent prices. When the night riding activity begins, the father shoots one of the riders and is in turn ambushed and killed. As Charles Bohner says, "Prime Leaf" is an extremely well-done work, with many fine scenes drawn from the farming life Warren had known during his boyhood summers at his grandfather's farm.[18] *Night Rider* is far more ambitious. Its protagonist, Percy Munn, is a young lawyer who becomes involved in the farmers' protective association, rises to a position of power, gives his assent to night riding and soon becomes directly involved in it, and at the last is shot and killed. As noted earlier, Munn's characterization is reminiscent of the description of John Henry Kagi, the accomplice of John Brown, in Warren's first book. He is an educated, intellectual, alienated young man, who accepts the public role and the power afforded him through involvement in the association in order to externalize his own emptiness and to allow him to act in the "real world." The attempted suppression of his own doubts and mixed motives through allegiance to a rationale outside of himself, the temptation to violence, the suspension of his private moral conscience at the behest of a "just cause," bring about the erosion of his own integrity, lead him to commit crimes as reprehensible as any he is ostensibly seeking to rectify, and result finally in his own death by violence.

For his second novel, *At Heaven's Gate* (1943), Warren turned to the contemporary scene. Its setting is the world of Big Business: Bogan Murdock, financier and banking tycoon, constructs his empire through shrewd manipulation of others, seeking in power over others the assuagement of his own emptiness of spirit. Young Jerry Calhoun, star athlete at the local university, enters into Murdock's operations to fulfill his own personal ambition, suppresses his private moral and ethical qualms for the sake of advancement, wins the hand of Murdock's daughter, then is rejected, and when Murdock's corrupt financial empire collapses, is jailed as the scapegoat. Sue Murdock, for her part, despises her father, seeks in promiscuity the identity she cannot find in rebellion, ultimately takes up with a poet, Slim Sarratt, because he represents everything her father supposedly despises, then jilts him and is eventually killed by him. As for Sarratt, he too seeks power, though in the field of art rather than business, and for all his glib ability to diagnose Bogan Murdock's malaise, is as equally empty and lost. When his own falseness and corruption are revealed, he too is destroyed. In all of the major characters there is the sickness of the age, the failure of personal responsibility which leads to the attempt to externalize emptiness and moral schizophrenia in the life outside oneself, resulting in violence, ruin, and self-destruction. Those characters who, like Calhoun and Sarratt, think they see and understand themselves, and believe that through such knowledge they are really in control of their own divided sensibilities, are all the more corrupted by their intellectual evasion. Warren based the business situation in *At Heaven's Gate* in part on the collapse, in 1930, of the banking and securities firm of Caldwell and Company, involving the World War I hero and newspaper publisher Colonel Luke Lea, which ruined more than a hundred banks in Tennessee and elsewhere and almost sent the State of Tennessee itself into bankruptcy.

It was with his third novel, *All The King's Men* (1946), that Warren won major stature as a writer of fiction. By now he had left the South, going to the University of Minnesota as professor of English in 1942 after the demise of the *Southern Review*. Begun as a verse play, *All The King's Men* had developed into a novel. Its central character, Willie Stark, was obviously inspired by the life and personality of Huey P. Long, the colorful and popular governor of Louisiana and afterward United States senator until his assassination in 1935. In order to tell the story as fiction, however, Warren developed another character, Jack Burden, a young newspaperman from one of the most respected families of the state, who, out of his own dissatisfaction and his failure to discover a purpose for his own life and career, goes to work for Willie, seeks to avoid making his own moral choices by doing the boss's bidding, and ultimately plays his part in the political, social, and moral debacle that results in Willie's death and in personal tragedy for all those who are involved.

The story of *All The King's Men* is too well known to require summation here. Suffice it to say that Warren's preoccupation with the problems of public purpose and personal ambition, the nature of democracy and popular leadership, and the cost of evasion of ethical and social responsibility, were joined with his fascination with the modern political and social scene and his insight into human motives to produce one of the most respected and widely acclaimed works of twentieth-century American fiction, which after three decades has lost little or none of its appeal to new readers. The use of Jack Burden, both as commentator upon and participant with Willie, not only gave Warren the reflective point-of-view character who could comment and speculate upon meaning, but added dramatically and thematically *to* the meaning of the novel, because Burden's efforts to understand and explain the personality of Willie and why he went to work for him spoke directly to the political and ethical concerns of the novel. *Why* is The Boss what he is, both for Jack and for everyone else? And what is signified by his being that? The meaning is both personal for Jack and public for the society. In *All The King's Men* Warren produced what is by far the most successful novel ever written on American political life—which especially to readers who are citizens of a republic founded upon the individual's ability to choose his leaders and thus govern himself, surely constitutes a notable literary and social accomplishment.

The relationship of these novels to Warren's earlier Agrarian concerns, though oblique, is clear. The novels are set in an industrial, postagricultural South. Although *Night Rider* takes place in a rural community, the tobacco economy is directly tied in with and dependent upon large-scale marketing and monopoly. In *At Heaven's Gate* the city is obviously Nashville, and though most of the characters are of rural origin, they live and work in the urban, commercial South of the 1920s. *All The King's Men* for its part deals with the realities of power and the dynamics of leadership in a southern state that has moved unsteadily but irrevocably into the modern industrial world. Thus in all three novels the rural ordering lies in the past, and in each novel the problem that the protagonists confront is that of discovering how to translate into new times, changed institutions, with different social needs and wider human aspirations, the imperatives of moral responsibility that in the past had assumed simpler, more familiar forms. Faced with the fact of change—economic, social, political, even religious—Warren's people are cast loose, as it were, without familiar landmarks to guide them, and must therefore work out for and in themselves their relationship to the values they supposedly hold. This is a difficult task indeed, and the human beings forced to undertake it attempt to evade the absolute responsibility for choosing and judging. But in each instance the necessity is inescapable, and the failure to accept it produces personal tragedy and social chaos.

In his fourth novel, *World Enough and Time* (1950), Warren carried his investigations into the past. Each of his first three novels had included a story within a story designed to make the thematic commentary on the main narrative through a first-person account by someone else; in *All The King's Men* the someone else was a Civil War-era forebear of Jack Burden, whose journal Jack had proposed to edit. In *World Enough and Time* Warren made such a journal the principal historical source. Drawing upon the famous "Kentucky Tragedy" of the 1820s, which had been used by such writers as Poe, Simms, Charles Fenno Hoffman, and Thomas Holley Chivers, he based the narrative of Jeremiah Beaumont upon an actual document, "The Confession of Jereboam O. Beauchamp," published in Kentucky in 1826. The novel is presented by a functioning omniscient author, who introduces the situation, comments and speculates on events, motives, and meanings while relating the story, and "quotes" from the "original" document left by Beaumont. The method is central to Warren's theme, which has to do with the difficulty of fathoming the past and the always-puzzling gap between private motives and public behavior. Beaumont's love for Rachel Jordan, his decision to murder his benefactor, Colonel Cassius Fort, to avenge Fort's earlier seduction of Rachel, his suicide pact with Rachel, their trial for murder, their escape to the west and the ultimate return eastward to death—to our modern eyes these actions and the professed motives of the participants seem melodramatic and naïve, but the narrator knows better, for the men and women who lived, schemed, loved, and died in frontier Kentucky faced the same human requirements that men have always faced.

In telling his story as he does, Warren permits himself the freedom to speculate and interpret directly to and for the reader. But he also takes on a heavy responsibility, for he approaches the situation of the lyric poet: he must sustain his own direct intervention through the appropriateness of what *he* says, as authorial personality. What happens in the narrative cannot speak for itself. Let him try to make too much of a situation, or attempt to force a significance that the events will not sustain, and the result will be disbelief on the reader's part. All will depend upon the credibility of the authorial personality. To his credit, Warren brings it off very well indeed, though he lets the story itself go on too far beyond its dramatic resolution so that the authorial personality can complete his demonstration.

Each of Warren's people, whatever their time and place, faces what Jack Burden at the close of *All The King's Men* calls "the awful responsibility of time." Each must learn how to hold onto moral integrity in greatly changed conditions, a feat that can be accomplished neither by an adamant refusal to accept change nor by the abdication of individual responsibility under the guise of conforming to changed conditions. For the former results in an abstract, subjective idealism that ceases to bear a shaping relationship to the human life it is supposed to govern, and the latter course, in its surrender of all moral judgment, removes the checks upon recalcitrant human nature that alone elevate men beyond savagery and make society possible. The choice is always difficult, for those who must make it are men and women who are subject to all the temptations of pride, ambition, appetite, avarice, avoidance of pain, and moral laziness that beset human beings. It is Warren's ability to dramatize these moral issues in individual characterizations and immediate issues that makes his fiction compelling and successful.

Nor does Warren fall into the trap of easy nostalgia for simpler times. The problems that his people face are not depicted merely as the result of rapid industrialization, or the erosion of Protestant religious orthodoxy, or of any such topical event. They have always existed. Not that some times are not better than other times, but that whatever the time and place, the human moral necessity remains. For Warren the historical past is depicted not as a golden age before the fall of public or private virtue, but as a rebuke to the present through its greater simplicity for us: "it's a better rebuke than any dream of the future," he declared at the Fugitive's reunion in 1956. "It's a better rebuke because you can see what some of the costs were, what frail virtues were achieved in the past by frail men. And it's there, and you can see it, and how they had to go at it." [19]

If one thinks of agrarianism not as a movement designed to turn the South back to subsistence farming, but as a way of asserting civilized values and humane community relationships, an effort to retard and thus to humanize the South's belated but intense rush to emulate the attitudes and institutions of modern industrial society, then the continuity with Warren's first four novels is apparent. They stem thematically from the same religious, social, and moral assumptions that produced *I'll Take My Stand*; each revolves about the problem of "the awful responsibility of Time," the necessity of translating moral imperatives into the language of changing times, and each depicts the human cost of attempts to evade that responsibility. In this sense, agrarianism was a programmatical, rhetorical response, and Warren's fiction, like Tate's fiction and poetry, an artistic response to the threat of chaos, through an assertion of what Tate called religious humanism and what Warren would later claim was the province of poetry: "It keeps alive the sense of self and the correlated sense of a community."[20] Or, as Warren put it in the final section of a sequence of poems written almost four decades after the Agrarian venture, *Audubon: A Vision* (1969): "In this century, and moment, of mania,/Tell me a story."[21]

The Freedom of Poetry

To follow the career of Robert Penn Warren into the decades beyond his close association with the Nashville Fugitives and the Agrarian venture is beyond the scope and intent of this book, which has been directed at tracing out how the major Fugitive poets arrived at their involvement in agrarianism, what the commitment meant for them, and how the concerns embodied in it carried over into their subsequent writings.

Of all the Vanderbilt group, Warren has been the most prolific, most continuously active as a writer in the decades that have followed. Not only fiction and poetry, but critical essays and books, plays, commentaries on American history and society, textbooks and revisions of textbooks, have poured from his typewriter. At no time has his interest in the South abated; in particular the problems and possibilities of genuine racial integration in the region have continued to hold his attention. The Warren who wrote *Segregation: The Inner Conflict in the South* (1956) and *Who Speaks for the Negro?* (1965) is only an older and wiser version of the man who could in 1930 write these lines in an essay ostensibly devoted to a defense of segregation: "What the white workman must learn, and his education may be as long and as laborious as the Negro's, is that he may respect himself as a white man, but, if he fails to concede the Negro equal protection [under the law], he does not properly regard himself as a man."[22] The assumptions about the need for human dignity and equality under the law have not changed; the man holding the assumptions has simply come to realize long since that only through racial desegregation could that aim ever be put in the way of ultimate attainment.

One of Warren's most attractive books is the little monograph entitled *The Legacy of the Civil War: Meditations on the Centennial* (1961), in which the interests expressed as early as the biography of John Brown are brought up to date, but viewed from a perspective less purely sectional: the war is shown as having produced for the North a "Treasury of Virtue" which enabled a smug indifference to social reform and a narcissistic complacency about American superior morality that has caused trouble in foreign relations ever since, while for the South the war provided a "Great Alibi" that enabled southerners to externalize all evil and guilt as having to do with outside interference, instead of looking inside themselves for the source of much of their troubles.

Throughout the 1950s and 1960s Warren continued to produce novels, though none has achieved the lasting success of *All The King's Men*. As might be expected of the work of a writer who has written so much, Warren's fiction is uneven in quality. He is not a fastidious writer like Tate and Ransom; his willingness to plunge ahead and not worry about getting everything in order ahead of time has made it possible for him to enjoy one of the longest, most varied, and most productive careers in American literary history, but it has also meant that he has published work that is not always formally successful. If Warren has had one persistent problem with his fiction, it seems to me, it has been that of discovering the proper form for getting his fascination with ideas and values into an integral relationship with his interest in tale-telling— plot, characterization, motives, and action. Not always has he been as fortunate as in *All The King's Men*, when the characterization of Jack Burden emerged as a way both to tell and to embody the meaning of the story he had in mind. Even in *All The King's Men* I have never quite believed that Anne Stanton would ever have become Willie Stark's mistress; the thematic design, not the inevitablity of the characterization, seems to have required it. In *Band of Angels* (1955), he let his thematic concerns shape his dramatic developments to an undue extent, while in *The Cave* (1959) it was rather the other way around: that novel contains sequences and scenes that seem to be present only because Warren wanted to see what a character would do in a given situation, not because the situation is needed to develop the theme properly. Warren is simply not the kind of writer who produces perfect work; his imagination is too bold, his mind too restless to allow him the kind of lapidary technique that would avoid all flaws and imperfections. What he wrote about Joseph Conrad is appropriate—"For him the very act of composition was a way of knowing, a way of exploration."[23] Does it not follow that for such a writer, there are always going to be false leads, imperfect knowledge, incomplete insights, and that these are going to be reflected in the technique? Or as Warren wrote of Faulkner, "the unevenness is, in a way, an index to his vitality, his willingness to take risks, to try for new effects, to make new explorations of material and method."[24] As a writer Warren is almost always interesting; his fiction is always packed with life. And there has been no falling off of his talent, it seems to me. His most recent novel at the time of this writing, *Meet Me in the Green Glen* (1971), is also one of his very best.

We have seen how Warren ceased to write lyric poetry for some years following publication of *Selected Poems, 1923–1943*. I have suggested that it came just at the point at which he had discovered a style that would enable him to move with a freedom hitherto denied him in verse. In 1953, however, he brought out an unusual volume, *Brother to Dragons: A Tale in Verse and Voices*, based on a little-known episode in early Kentucky history in which a nephew of Thomas Jefferson, Lilburn Lewis, butchered

a slave for breaking a pitcher. After Lilburn and his brother Isham were indicted, they made a suicide pact to shoot
each other, but though Lilburn was killed, Isham survived and escaped, was captured and sentenced to die for
his brother's murder, but made his way to freedom and
was later reported as having been killed at the Battle of
New Orleans.

For Warren, the most fascinating aspect of the story
was what went unrecorded: its possible impact upon Jefferson, the meaning it contained for his invincibly optimistic view of the nature of man. The story is related in
verse dialogue, and to serve the function of chorus Warren uses a character he calls R.P.W., identified as "the
writer of this poem."[25] In the course of the poem Warren
explores, through description, dialogue, and colloquy,
the moral and social implication of the developing story.
At the close, in a long soliloquy, R.P.W. relates how and
why he was drawn to the scene of a long-ago crime, in the
country of his own boyhood, and he makes a commentary on what was involved not only in the story itself, but
in his wish to tell it. It is not really a soliloquy, however: it
is a lyric poem. Written in the style of the story-telling itself, it is far more flexible, colloquial, and personal than
any of the lyric poetry he had ever written previously.
The question arises, Why didn't Warren go ahead and
write *Brother to Dragons* as a novel? There are numerous
plausible reasons, having to do with the difficulty of working an historical figure like Jefferson into it without going beyond the documentation, among other things. But
I suggest that one factor in the decision, at least, may well
have been that the form he elected to use enabled him to
use R.P.W. as chorus without having to externalize him,
turn him into a Jack Burden or the like. R.P.W. could
speak directly to the meaning of the tale and also explore
his wish to search out the meaning.

Through R.P.W. in *Brother to Dragons* he seems to have
moved right into his mature style as poet. By this time he

was living in Connecticut and teaching at Yale University. His first marriage had ended in divorce in 1951, and a year later he married Eleanor Clark, herself an accomplished writer. Soon there were two children, a son and a daughter. The obvious happiness of this union seems to me to be somehow involved in the return of Warren to his first literary love, lyric poetry. For whatever reason, he now began writing new poems, personally direct in a way that his earlier style had never permitted, in a language much less "literary" and more colloquial, though by no means prosy. The poems seemed to come in sequences, and for subject matter he drew upon his own experiences, his children, his own childhood, but always through memory and meditation, with the focus of the poem on the poet's thoughts and feelings about such things. The R.P.W. of *Brother to Dragons* was now overtly the lyric poet. Though not everyone has cared for this new verse, it seems to me to be interesting and beautiful in a way that his pre-1943 work never managed. There is none of the feeling of the meaning being forced objectively upon the subject matter through rhetoric when it really belonged to the poet's feelings about the subject matter. There is a marvelous sense of freedom, of the poet's ability to move from strength to strength.

In 1969 came what I think is his finest work of poetry, the verse sequence entitled *Audubon: A Vision*. In the image of the early American painter-naturalist, who traveled throughout the wilderness of the early nineteenth-century South, shooting his birds in order to record them faithfully and capture their likeness in art, Warren sees the essential artist:

> He put them where they are, and there we see them:
> In our imagination.
> What is love?
> One name for it is knowledge.[26]

Youngest of the Fugitives, Warren has carried his art

into forms and sequences far removed from what he and his friends were doing in Nashville in the early 1920s. Allen Tate recognized his gift very early: "You know Red is pretty close to being the greatest Fugitive poet," Tate wrote to Donald Davidson in 1927. "There are certain obstructions to this realization, of course. He is the only one of us who has *power*."[27] Greater, as poet, than John Crowe Ransom, or than Tate himself? A half-century later it is difficult to say, and surely not really important: each of the three has his own unique way with language. One would not have any one of them greatly different, as poet, than he has been. But this much is undeniable. The seventeen-year-old sophomore who, as Tate remembered it, "tall and thin," came wandering into Walter Clyde Curry's rooms in 1923 to borrow the typewriter, and who "when he walked across the room . . . made a sliding shuffle, as if his bones didn't belong to one another,"[28] did not fail to take maximum advantage of his gift. If as Tate said, Warren had *power* as a poet, he has used it.

That, however, is a story different from the one I have sought to relate, and not part of the concern of this book, which has been an attempt to show how a group of young poets grew to manhood in the early years of the twentieth-century South, began writing their poems, became interested in the history and the social and economic life of the region of their birth and residence, and embarked upon a venture designed to safeguard what they found best in it and to warn against its unwitting self-destruction. Why they did so, what they meant in so doing, how each of them went about it, and what they eventually came to think about it, has been the subject of this inquiry, which has sought to examine some of the relationships, for a group of writers, between their poetry and fiction and their regional allegiance—between, that is, a literature and a society. How and why they took their stand, and what it meant for them, is the story that I have tried to tell.

Notes

CHAPTER 1

1. Willard Thorp, *American Writing in the Twentieth Century* (Cambridge, Mass.: Harvard University Press, 1960), 241–42.

2. "To the Scholars of New England," *Selected Poems*, 3rd edition, revised and enlarged (New York: Alfred A. Knopf, 1969), 88. This edition—the third—is cited hereinafter as *Selected Poems*.

3. Ralph Waldo Emerson to Evert Duyckinck, March 3, 1849, in Eleanor Melville Metcalf, *Herman Melville: Cycle and Epicycle* (Cambridge, Mass.: Harvard University Press, 1953), 59.

4. Allen Tate, "Emily Dickinson," *Essays of Four Decades* (Chicago: Swallow Press, 1968), 285.

5. Donald Davidson, "Regionalism and Nationalism in American Literature," *Still Rebels, Still Yankees and Other Essays* (Baton Rouge: Louisiana State University Press, 1957), 275.

6. Robert Penn Warren, *John Brown: The Making of a Martyr* (New York: Payson and Clarke, 1929), 245.

7. Perry Miller, "From Edwards to Emerson," *Errand into the Wilderness* (New York: Harper and Row, 1964), 196–98.

8. *Ibid.*, 201.

9. Jonathan Edwards, "The Visible Union of God's People," in Alan Heimert and Perry Miller (eds.), *The Great Awakening: Documents Illustrating the Crisis and Its Consequences* (Indianapolis and New York: Bobbs-Merrill, 1967), 567.

10. Miller, "From Edwards to Emerson," 198.

11. Quoted in C. Vann Woodward, *Origins of the New South, 1877–1913* (Baton Rouge: Louisiana State University Press, 1951), 170, Vol. IX of *A History of the South*.

12. Howard W. Odum, *The Way of the South* (New York: Macmillan, 1947), 173.

13. Holland Thompson, *The New South: A Chronicle of Social and Industrial Evolution* (New Haven, Conn.: Yale University Press, 1921), 216.

14. Quoted in Edwin Mims, *History of Vanderbilt University* (Nashville, Tenn.: Vanderbilt University Press, 1946), 28.

15. Donald Davidson, *Southern Writers in the Modern World* (Athens: University of Georgia Press, 1958), 13–14.

16. Thomas Nelson Page, "The Old South," *The Old South: Essays Social and Political* (Chautauqua, N.Y.: Chautauqua Press, 1919), 25–26.

17. Rob Roy Purdy (ed.), *Fugitives' Reunion: Conversations at Vanderbilt, May 3–5, 1956* (Nashville: Vanderbilt University Press, 1959), 106–107.

18. Mims, *History of Vanderbilt University*, 246.

19. Thomas Daniel Young, *Gentleman in a Dustcoat: A Biography of John Crowe Ransom* (Baton Rouge: Louisiana State University Press, 1976), 62–63. Hereinafter cited as *Young*.

20. *Young*, 65.

21. Ransom, "Philomela," *Selected Poems*, 63–64.

22. *Young*, 77.

23. Davidson, *Southern Writers in the Modern World*, 13.

24. William Yandell Elliott to Alex Brock Stevenson, July 23, 1915, quoted in Louise Cowan, *The Fugitive Group: A Literary History* (Baton Rouge: Louisiana State University Press, 1959), 4.

25. Davidson, *Southern Writers in the Modern World*, 14.

26. "Introduction," *Poems About God* (New York: Henry Holt, 1919), vi–vii.

27. "Grace," *Ibid.*, 20.

28. "Geometry," *Ibid.*, 27.

29. "Morning," *Ibid.*, 63.

30. "The Cloak Model," *Ibid.*, 42.

31. "Noonday Grace," *Ibid.*, 6–10.

32. "Grace," *Ibid.*, 18–23.

33. Allen Tate, *Memoirs and Opinions: 1926–1974* (Chicago: Swallow Press, 1975), 30–31.

34. Allen Tate, "To Intellectual Detachment," *The Swimmers and Other Poems* (New York: Charles Scribner's Sons, 1970), 154.

35. "Henry Feathertop" [Tate], "Sinbad," *The Fugitive*, I (April, 1922), 16.

36. "Roger Prim" [Ransom], "Ego," *Ibid.*, 3–4. Ransom retitled this poem "Plea in Mitigation" and revised it somewhat (eliminating the stanza about "take the vomit where they do") and included it in *Chills and Fever*. It does not, however, appear in his *Selected Poems*.

37. "Philomela," *Selected Poems*, 63–64.

38. "Winter Remembered," *Ibid.*, 37.

39. "Captain Carpenter," *Ibid.*, 45.

40. "Janet Waking," *Ibid.*, 12.

41. "Vaunting Oak," *Ibid.*, 16.

42. "Miriam Tazewell," *Ibid.*, 3.

43. "Vaunting Oak," *Ibid.*, 16–17.

44. "Blue Girls," *Ibid.*, 11.

45. "Piazza Piece," *Ibid.*, 9.

46. "Necrological," *Ibid.*, 42–43.

47. "Judith of Bethulia," *Ibid.*, 30–31.

48. "Captain Carpenter," *Ibid.*, 44–46.

49. "Noonday Grace," *Poems About God*, 8–10.

50. "The Equilibrists," *Selected Poems*, 85–86.

51. "Here Lies a Lady," *Ibid.*, 140. Ransom revised this poem late in his life; the earlier version, "A" in this edition, is to my mind far preferable.

52. Frank Durham, *DuBose Heyward: The Man Who Wrote Porgy* (Columbia: University of South Carolina Press, 1954), 27–28.

53. "Armageddon," *Selected Poems*, 55–57.

54. "Old Mansion," *Ibid.*, 70–71.

55. "Antique Harvesters," *Ibid.*, 83–84.

56. "Forms and Citizens," *The World's Body* (New York: Charles Scribner's Sons, 1938), 43–44.

57. *The Fugitive*, I (April, 1922), 1.

58. Cowan, *The Fugitive Group*, 73.

59. *Young*, 67.

60. Cowan, *The Fugitive Group*, 121–22.

61. *Poems About God*, vi–vii.

62. J[ohn]. C[rowe]. R[ansom]., "The Future of Poetry," *The Fugitive*, III (February, 1924), 3.

63. "Poetry: A Note on Ontology," *The World's Body*, 130.

64. Louise Cowan, *The Southern Critics* (Irving, Tex.: University of Dallas Press, 1971), 20.

65. *Southern Writers in the Modern World*, 8.

66. Allen Tate, "For John Crowe Ransom at Seventy-Five," *Shenandoah*, XIV (Spring, 1963), 7.

67. "Why Critics Don't Go Mad," *Poems and Essays* (New York: Vintage Books, 1955), 149–50.

68. *Young*, 63.

69. Cowan, *The Southern Critics*, 33.

70. *Young*, 73.

71. *The World's Body*, x.

72. "Poetry: A Note on Ontology," 138.

73. *Ibid.*, 140.

74. *Young*, 77.

75. "The Future of Poetry," 3.

76. *God Without Thunder: An Unorthodox Defense of Orthodoxy* (New York: Harcourt, Brace, 1930), ix–x.

77. *Ibid.*, 305.

78. *Ibid.*, 327–28.

79. John L. Stewart, *The Burden of Time: The Fugitives and Agrarians* (Princeton, N.J.: Princeton University Press, 1965), 128.

80. *Ibid.*, 115.

81. *God Without Thunder*, 125.

82. *Ibid.*, 125.

83. Quoted in Stewart, *The Burden of Time*, 267.

84. *Young*, 78.

85. "The School," *Poems About God*, 72.

86. "Conrad in Twilight," *Selected Poems*, 2nd ed. (New York: A. A. Knopf, 1963), 28. Ransom revised the poem beyond recognition for the 1969 edition, and also included the original text as published in *The Fugitive*. I prefer the version of 1963.

87. *God Without Thunder*, 301.

88. "Armageddon," *Selected Poems*, 56.

89. "Crocodile," 65–67.

90. *Young*, 77.

CHAPTER 2

1. John Crowe Ransom, "In Amicitia," in *Allen Tate and His Work: Critical Evaluations*, ed. Radcliffe Squires (Minneapolis: University of Minnesota Press, 1972), 14.

2. Louise Cowan, *The Fugitive Group: A Literary History* (Baton Rouge: Louisiana State University Press, 1959), 35–36.

3. "In Amicitia," 13–16.

4. *Ibid.*

5. Radcliffe Squires, *Allen Tate: A Literary Biography* (New York: Pegasus, 1971), hereinafter cited as *Squires*.

6. *Ibid.*, 18–22.

7. "A Lost Traveller's Dream," *Memoirs and Opinions, 1926–1974* (Chicago: Swallow Press, 1975), 6–7.

8. Allen Tate, *Stonewall Jackson, the Good Soldier: A Narrative* (New York: Minton, Balch, 1928), 10.

9. *Ibid.*, 48.

10. "A Lost Traveller's Dream," 17.

11. *Squires*, 18.

12. "The Swimmers," *The Swimmers and Other Poems* (New York: Charles Scribner's Sons, 1970), 38.

13. "A Lost Traveller's Dream," 7.

14. *Ibid.*, 19.

15. "In Amicitia," 13.

16. Tate, *Memoirs and Opinions: 1926–1974* (Chicago: Swallow Press, 1975), 25.

17. "In Amicitia," 12.

18. Tate to Davidson, December 12, 1929, in *The Literary Correspondence of Donald Davidson and Allen Tate*, ed. John Tyree Fain and Thomas Daniel Young (Athens: University of Georgia Press, 1974), 243–44. Hereinafter cited as *Literary Correspondence*.

19. *"The Fugitive* 1922–1925," 30.

20. "Henry Feathertop" [Allen Tate], "Sinbad," *The Fugitive*, I, (April, 1922), 16.

21. *Squires*, 32.

22. J[ohn]. C[rowe]. R[ansom]., "Editorial," *The Fugitive*, I (October, 1922), 68.

23. "Horatian Epode to the Duchess of Malfi," *The Swimmers*, 75.

24. John Crowe Ransom, "Here Lies a Lady," *Selected Poems*, third edition, revised and enlarged, (New York: Alfred A. Knopf, 1969), 140.

25. "Horatian Epode to the Duchess of Malfi," 75.

26. *Squires*, 43.

27. "Horatian Epode to the Duchess of Malfi," 75. In its original form this poem appears in *The Fugitive*, I, (October, 1922), 76.

28. T. S. Eliot, "Whispers of Immortality," 61, and "Mrs. Eliot's Sunday Morning Service," 64, in *Collected Poems: 1909–1935* (New York: Harcourt, Brace, 1936).

29. *Squires*, 44.

30. *Religion and the Intellectuals: A Symposium, Partisan Review Series Number Three* (New York: Partisan Review, 1950), 133.

31. *Squires*, 48.

32. John Crowe Ransom, "Waste Lands," *Literary Review of the New York Evening Post*, July 14, 1923, Sec. 3, pp. 825–26.

33. "Waste Lands" (Letter to the Editor), *Literary Review of the New York Evening Post*, August 4, 1923, Sec. 3, p. 886.

34. John Crowe Ransom, "Mr. Ransom Replies" (Letter to the Editor), *Literary Review of the New York Evening Post*, August 11, 1923, Sec. 3, p. 902.

35. Allen Tate, "For John Ransom at Seventy-Five," *Shenandoah*, XIV, (Spring, 1963), 7.

36. "In Amicitia," 13–14.

37. *Ibid.*, 14.

38. Tate to Davidson, February 18, 1929, *Literary Correspondence*, 226.

39. Tate, "Mr. Pope," *The Swimmers*, 125.

40. *Squires*, 71–72.

41. M. E. Bradford, *Rumors of Mortality: An Introduction to Allen Tate* (Dallas, Tex.: Argus Academic Press, 1969), 17.

42. Ferman Bishop, *Allen Tate* (New York: Twayne, 1967), 64–65.

43. John L. Stewart, *The Burden of Time: The Fugitives and Agrarians* (Princeton, N.J.: Princeton University Press, 1965), 373.

44. "The Battle of Murfreesboro," *The Fugitive*, I (October, 1922), 84.

45. Andrew Lytle, "Allen Tate: Upon the Occasion of His Sixtieth Birthday," in Squires (ed.), *Allen Tate and His Work*, 24.

46. "Last Days of the Charming Lady," *The Nation*, CXXI (Oct. 28, 1925), p. 485.

47. "Our Cousin Mr. Poe," *Essays of Four Decades* (Chicago: Swallow Press, 1968), 387.

48. "Fragment of A Meditation," *The Swimmers*, 83.

49. "Elegy: Jefferson Davis: 1808–1889," *The Swimmers*, 82.

50. "Ode to the Confederate Dead," *The Swimmers*, 18–19.

51. Allen Tate, *The Fathers* (New York: G. P. Putnam's Sons, 1938), 305.

52. "The Man of Letters in the Modern World," *Essays of Four Decades*, 13.

53. "Crane: The Poet as Hero: An Encomium Twenty Years Later," *Essays of Four Decades*, 327.

54. "Hart Crane," *Essays of Four Decades*, 321, 323.

55. "Allen Tate Interview," by James Forsyth, Tom Speight, Dan Williams, *The Rebel Magazine*, East Carolina College, XI (1965–66), 6.

56. "Last Days of the Charming Lady," 485–86.

57. "Allen Tate Interview," *The Rebel Magazine,* 6.

58. Stewart, *The Burden of Time*, 382.

59. "Narcissus as Narcissus," *Essays of Four Decades*, 602.

60. Davidson to Tate, February 15, 1927, *Literary Correspondence*, 186–67.

61. *Squires*, 74.

62. "Narcissus as Narcissus," 604.

63. *Ibid.*

64. *Ibid.*, 607.

65. "Last Days of the Charming Lady," 486.

66. "Narcissus as Narcissus," 607.

67. Conversation with present writer.

68. Tate, "Our Cousin Mr. Poe," 398.

69. "Narcissus as Narcissus," 601.

70. *Squires*, 82.

71. "Causerie," *The Swimmers*, 79–82.

72. Stewart, *The Burden of Time*, 377–78.

73. "The Subway," *The Swimmers*, 105.

74. Bradford, *Rumors of Mortality*, 14.

75. Tate to Davidson, October 24, 1928, *Literary Correspondence*, 218.

76. Tate to Mark Van Doren, January 29, 1929, quoted in *Squires*, 85–86.

77. "A Poetry of Ideas," review of *Poems 1909–1925* by T. S. Eliot, *New Republic*, XLVIII (June 30, 1926), 172–73.

78. "T. S. Eliot's Ash Wednesday," *Essays of Four Decades*, 463–64.

79. "Introduction to American Poetry," in Lord David Cecil and Allen Tate (eds.), *Modern Verse in English, 1900–1950* (New York: Macmillan, 1958), 41.

80. Tate to Davidson, February 18, 1929, *Literary Correspondence*, 223.

81. Davidson to Tate, July 29, 1929, *Literary Correspondence*, 227.

82. "A Poetry of Ideas," 172.

83. "Last Days of the Charming Lady," 486.

84. "Allen Tate Interview," *Rebel Magazine*, 17.

85. See R. K. Meiners, *The Last Alternatives: A Study of the Works of Allen Tate* (Denver: Alan Swallow, 1963), 145–52; *Squires*, 95–97; and Robert Dupree, "The Mirrors of Analogy: Three Poems by Allen Tate," *Southern Review*, VIII, n.s. (October, 1972), 774–91, esp. 778–85.

86. "The Cross," *The Swimmers*, 115.

87. "Ode to the Confederate Dead," 19.

88. *Ibid.*

89. *Ibid.*, 20.

90. "Letter from Abroad," *The Swimmers*, 10–12.

91. Bradford, *Rumors of Mortality*, 27.

92. "Emily Dickinson," *Essays of Four Decades*, 287.

93. Bradford, *Rumors of Mortality*, 28.

CHAPTER 3

1. Davidson to Tate, October 16, 1929, *The Literary Correspondence of Donald Davidson and Allen Tate*, ed. John Tyree Fain and Thomas Daniel Young (Athens: University of Georgia Press, 1974), 235.

2. Biographical material on Donald Davidson is taken from Thomas Daniel Young and M. Thomas Inge, *Donald Davidson* (New York: Twayne, 1971), 17–26.

3. *Ibid.*, 27–32.

4. Quoted *Ibid.*, 36.

5. *Southern Writers in the Modern World* (Athens: University of Georgia Press, 1958), 11.

6. Tate to Davidson, August 10, 1929, in *Literary Correspondence*, 229–33.

7. Davidson to Tate, October 26, 1929, *ibid.*, 237.

8. Tate to Davidson, December 11, 1929, *ibid.*, 246.

9. Louise Cowan, *The Fugitive Group: A Literary History* (Baton Rouge: Louisiana State University Press, 1959), 40.

10. Harriet Monroe, "The Old South," *Poetry*, XXII (May, 1923), quoted *Ibid.*, 114.

11. [Donald Davidson,] "Merely Prose," *The Fugitive*, II (July, 1923), 66.

12. "A Demon Brother," *The Fugitive*, I (April, 1922), 6–7.

13. "Old Harp," *Poems 1922–1961* (Minneapolis: University of Minnesota Press, 1966), 112.

14. "Epilogue: Fire on Belmont Street," *Poems 1922–1961*, p. 181.

15. D[onald]. D[avidson]., "The Future of Poetry," *The Fugitive*, IV (December, 1925), 125–28.

16. "Hit or Miss," *The Fugitive*, IV (December, 1925), 100.

17. "The Wolf," *Poems 1922–1961*, p. 105.

18. Allen Tate, *Memoirs and Opinions: 1926–1974* (Chicago: Swallow Press, 1975), 26.

19. "Apple and Mole," *Poems 1922–1961*, p. 94.

20. Cowan, *The Fugitive Group*, 202.

21. *Ibid.*

22. Tate to Davidson, December 12, 1929, in *Literary Correspondence*, 245.

23. Davidson to Tate, December 29, 1929, *ibid.*, 249.

24. "Theodore Dreiser," *The Spyglass: Views and Reviews, 1924–1930*, ed. John Tyree Fain (Nashville: Vanderbilt University Press, 1963), 68–70.

25. "T. S. Stribling," *Spyglass*, 13.

26. "Regionalism and Nationalism in American Literature," *The Attack on Leviathan* (Chapel Hill: University of North Carolina Press, 1938), 239.

27. "The Artist as Southerner," *Saturday Review of Literature*, II (May 15, 1926), 782–84.

28. "First Fruits of Dayton: The Intellectual Evolution in Dixie," *The Forum*, LXXIX (June, 1928), 899–907.

29. Tate to Davidson, March 7, 1927, in *Literary Correspondence*, 194.

30. Allen Tate, "Last Days of the Charming Lady," *Nation*, CXXI (October 28, 1925), 485–86.

31. Davidson to Tate, November 29, 1925, in *Literary Correspondence*, 150.

32. *Ibid.*, 151.

33. Tate to Davidson, November 25, 1925, *ibid.*, 147–49.

34. Davidson to Tate, November 29, 1925, *ibid.*, 150.

35. *The Tall Men*, in *Poems 1922–1961*, pp. 113–81. All page citations are to this edition and are given parenthetically.

36. Tate to Davidson, March 29, 1926, in *Literary Correspondence*, 162.

37. Tate to Davidson, May 14, 1926, *ibid.*, 126–27.

38. Davidson to Tate, June 14, 1926, *ibid.*, 170.

39. Allen Tate, "Message from Abroad," *The Swimmers and Other Poems* (New York: Charles Scribner's Sons, 1970), 11.

40. Davidson to Tate, July 29, 1929, in *Literary Correspondence*, 227.

41. Tate to Davidson, December 29, 1926, *ibid.*, 181–82.

42. Davidson to Tate, January 21, 1927, *ibid.*, 185.

43. Davidson to Tate, February 15, 1927, *ibid.*, 186.

44. The correspondence between Tate and Davidson concerning "Lee in the Mountains" and a discussion of the relationship between the two men in the composition of this poem are included in Thomas Daniel Young and M. Thomas Inge, *Donald Davidson: An Essay and a Bibliography* (Nashville: Vanderbilt University Press, 1965.)

45. Davidson to Tate, January 2, 1943, in *Literary Correspondence*, 331.

46. Davidson to Tate, February 23, 1940, *ibid.*, 321–22.

47. *Southern Writers in the Modern World*, 60.

CHAPTER 4

1. Malcolm Cowley, *Exile's Return: A Literary Odyssey of the 1920's* (New York: Viking Press, 1956), 217.

2. Allen Raymond, in *New York Herald-Tribune*, June 1, 1930, quoted in George B. Tindall, *The Emergence of the New South, 1913–1945* (Baton Rouge: Louisiana State University Press, 1967), 99; Gerald W. Johnson, "Greensboro, or What You Will," *Reviewer*, IV (1923–1924), 169, quoted in Tindall, *The Emergence of the New South*, 99.

3. Edwin Mims, *The Advancing South* (New York: Doubleday, Page, 1926), 112, 198–99.

4. Quoted in Virginia Rock, "The Making and Meaning of *I'll Take My Stand*: A Study in Utopian-Conservatism, 1925–1939" (Ph.D. dissertation, University of Minnesota, 1961), published in photocopy by University Microfilms, 1961, p. 207.

5. Quoted *Ibid.*, 204.

6. "Statement of Principles," Twelve Southerners, *I'll Take My Stand: The South and the Agrarian Tradition* (New York: Harper and Bros., 1930). Citations to "Statement of Principles" and the various essays in *I'll Take My Stand* are to this edition, and will hereinafter be given parenthetically.

7. Davidson to Tate, March 4, 21, 1927, February 5, 1929, Tate to Davidson, March 13, 1927, August 10, 1929, *The Literary Correspondence of Donald Davidson and Allen Tate*, ed. John Tyree Fain and Thomas Daniel Young (Athens: University of Georgia Press, 1974), 193, 195, 229–33.

8. Donald Davidson, "*I'll Take My Stand*: A History," *Agrarianism in American Literature*, ed. M. Thomas Inge (New York: Odyssey Press, 1969), 200.

9. Italics Tate's. Tate to Davidson, August 10, 1929, in *Literary Correspondence*, 229–30.

10. Davidson, "*I'll Take My Stand*: A History," 195–96.

11. *Ibid.*, 196.

12. Tate to Davidson, September 7, 1930, in *Literary Correspondence*, 255.

13. Davidson to Tate, July 21, 1930, *Ibid.*, 251.

14. *Fugitives' Reunion: Conversations at Vanderbilt, May 3–5, 1956*, ed. Rob Roy Purdy (Nashville, Tenn.: Vanderbilt University Press, 1959), 203.

15. "The Profession of Letters in the South," *Essays of Four Decades* (Chicago: Swallow Press, 1968), 529.

16. Quoted in Rock, "The Making and Meaning," 335–38.

17. Davidson, "*I'll Take My Stand*: A History," 195.

18. *Ibid.*

19. *Ibid.*

20. Davidson, "Lee in the Mountains," *Poems 1922–1961* (Minneapolis: University of Minnesota Press, 1966), 46.

21. Stark Young (ed.), *A Southern Treasury of Life and Literature* (New York: Charles Scribner's Sons, 1937), 341.

22. Tate to Davidson, March 1, 1927, in *Literary Correspondence*, 191.

23. Tate to Davidson, November 9, 1929, *ibid.*, 241.

24. Davidson to Tate, March 31, 1937, *ibid.*, 241.

25. Donald Davidson, "The 'Mystery' of the Agrarians," *Saturday Review of Literature*, XXVI (January 23, 1943), 6–7.

26. Tate to Davidson, December 4, 1942, in *Literary Correspondence*, 328–29.

27. F. Garvin Davenport, Jr., *The Myth of Southern History: Historical Consciousness in Twentieth-Century Southern Literature* (Nashville, Tenn.: Vanderbilt University Press, 1970), 79.

28. Rock, "The Making and Meaning of *I'll Take My Stand*," 433, 450.

29. Davidson to Tate, December 29, 1929, *Literary Correspondence*, 247–48.

30. Perry Miller, "From Edwards to Emerson," *Errand into the Wilderness* (New York: Harper and Row, 1964), 202.

31. Henry David Thoreau, *Walden* (New York: Thomas Y. Crowell, 1961), 119–20.

32. James Russell Lowell, "Thoreau," in *The Shock of Recognition: The Development of Literature in the United States Recorded by the Men Who Made It*, ed. Edmund Wilson, 2 vols. (New York: Grosset and Dunlap, 1955), I, 242.

33. *Walden*, 5.

34. *Ibid.*, 440.

35. Tate, "Emily Dickinson," *Essays of Four Decades*, 284.

36. Tate to Davidson, August 10, 1929, in *Literary Correspondence*, 230.

37. *Fugitives' Reunion*, 209–10.

38. Michael Millgate, "An Interview with Allen Tate," *Shenandoah*, XII (Spring, 1961), 32.

39. *Fugitives' Reunion*, 210.

CHAPTER 5

1. For a discussion of *Who Owns America?: A New Declaration of Independence*, ed. Herbert Agar and Allen Tate (Boston: Houghton Mifflin, 1936), see Virginia Rock, "The Making and Meaning of *I'll Take My Stand*: A Study in Utopian-Conservatism, 1925–1939" (Ph.D. dissertation), published by University Microfilms, Inc., Ann Arbor, Mich., in photocopy form, 387–98. See also the correspondence between Tate and Donald Davidson in *The Literary Correspondence of Donald Davidson and Allen Tate*, ed. John Tyree Fain and Thomas Daniel Young (Athens: University of Georgia Press, 1974), 292–302.

2. "Statement of Principles," Twelve Southerners, *I'll Take My Stand: The South and the Agrarian Tradition* (New York: Harper and Bros., 1930), xx–xxi.

3. Davidson to Tate, March 31, 1937, in *Literary Correspondence*, 300–301.

4. *Ibid.*, March 2, 1938, p. 310.

5. *Ibid.*, February 23, 1940, pp. 320–24.

6. Morton Dauwen Zabel, "Two Years of Poetry," *Southern Review*, V (Winter, 1940), 582–83.

7. Tate to Davidson, July 12, 1940, in *Literary Correspondence*, 324.

8. *Ibid.*, December 12, 1929, pp. 244–45.

9. Davidson, "A Mirror for Artists," *I'll Take My Stand*, 60.

10. Davidson to Tate, February 6, 1933, in *Literary Correspondence*, p. 286.

11. Davidson to Tate, October 3, 1938, Tate to Davidson, October 6, 1938, *Ibid.*, 318–19.

12. Davidson, "The 'Mystery' of the Agrarians: Facts and Illusions About Some Southern Writers," *Saturday Review of Literature*, XXVI (January 23, 1943), 6–7; Tate to Davidson, December 4, 1942, in *Literary Correspondence*, 328–29.

13. Davidson to Tate, January 2, 1943, in *Literary Correspondence*, 329–32.

14. *Ibid.*, January 4, 1962, p. 383.

15. See Ransom, "The Most Southern Poet," and John Donald Wade, "Oasis," *Sewanee Review*, LXX (January–March, 1962), 202–207, 208–12; and Tate, "The Gaze Past, the Glance Present," *Sewanee Review*, LXX (July–September, 1962), 671–73.

16. Davidson, "Lines Written for Allen Tate on His Sixtieth Birthday," *Poems 1922–1961* (Minneapolis: University of Minnesota Press, 1966), 16.

17. Ransom, "Survey of Literature," *Selected Poems* (3rd ed., Revised and Enlarged; New York: Knopf, 1969), 68.

18. Ransom, "Antique Harvesters," *Selected Poems*, 83.

19. Ransom, "Reconstructed but Unregencrate," *I'll Take My Stand*, 12, 19–20.

20. Italics mine. "Statement of Principles," *Ibid.*, xxv.

21. Thomas Daniel Young, *Gentleman in a Dustcoat: A Biography of John Crowe Ransom* (Baton Rouge: Louisiana State University Press, 1976), 78.

22. Ransom, "A Poem Nearly Anonymous," 1–28, and "Forms and Citizens," 29–54, *The World's Body* (Baton Rouge: Louisiana State University Press, 1968), 1–28, 29–54. Page references to these two essays will hereinafter be given parenthetically.

23. For a full discussion of this episode, see Young, *Gentleman in a Dustcoat*, 270–90.

24. Vivienne Koch, "The Achievement of John Crowe Ransom," *John Crowe Ransom: Critical Essays and a Bibliography*, ed. Thomas Daniel Young (Baton Rouge: Louisiana State University Press, 1968), 138–39.

25. Ransom, "What Does the South Want?" *Who Owns America?*, 185.

26. *Ibid.*, 187.

27. Davidson to Tate, March 31, 1937, in *Literary Correspondence*, 300–301.

28. Ransom, "Art and the Human Economy," *Beating the Bushes: Selected Essays, 1941–1970* (New York: New Directions, 1972), 131–34.

29. Davidson to Tate, October 3, 1945, in *Literary Correspondence*, 344.

30. Ransom, "The Communities of Letters," *Poems and Essays* (New York: Vintage Books, 1955), 116.

31. Tate, "Reflections on the Death of John Crowe Ransom," *Memoirs and Opinions, 1926–1974* (Chicago: Swallow Press, 1975), 43.

32. Italics mine. Ransom, "The Tense of Poetry," *The World's Body*, 237.

33. Tate, "Reflections on the Death of John Crowe Ransom," 45.

34. Ransom, "Captain Carpenter," *Selected Poems*, 45.

35. Tate, "A Southern Mode of the Imagination," *Essays of Four Decades* (Chicago: Swallow Press, 1968), 581–82.

36. Tate, "The Cross," *The Swimmers and Other Poems* (New York: Charles Scribner's Sons, 1970), 115.

37. Tate, "A Lost Traveler's Dream," *Memoirs and Opinions*, 7–8.

38. Tate, *Stonewall Jackson, the Good Soldier: A Narrative* (New York: Minton, Balch, 1928), 48.

39. Tate, "Emblems," *The Swimmers*, 142.

40. Tate, "Remarks on the Southern Religion," *I'll Take My Stand*, 174.

41. Tate, "Sonnets of the Blood," *The Swimmers*, 144–48.

42. Tate, "Remarks on the Southern Religion," 175.

43. *Ibid.*

44. Davidson to Tate, October 29, 1932, Tate to Davidson, December 10, 1932, in *Literary Correspondence*, 276, 280.

45. Tate, "Mediterranean," *The Swimmers*, 3–4.

46. Tate, "Message from Abroad," *The Swimmers*, 12.

47. Tate, "Aeneas at Washington," *The Swimmers*, 5–6.

48. Tate to Davidson, December 10, 1932, in *Literary Correspondence*, 279–80.

49. R. E. Lee to G. W. Custis Lee [?], quoted in Douglas Southall Freeman, *R. E. Lee: A Biography* (4 vols; New York: Charles Scribner's Sons, 1934), I, 421.

50. Tate, "The Migration," *Yale Review*, XXIV (Autumn, 1934), 83–111.

51. Unpublished letter, Allen Tate to John Peale Bishop, October 30, 1933.

52. Tate, "The Profession of Letters in the South," *Essays of Four Decades*, 527.

53. *Ibid.*, 533.

54. *Ibid.*, 546, 534.

55. Tate, *The Fathers* (New York: G. P. Putnam's Sons, 1938.) All references hereinafter are to this edition, and page numbers will be given parenthetically.

56. Radcliffe Squires, *Allen Tate: A Literary Biography* (New York: Pegasus, 1971), 135–46. See also Arthur Mizener, "*The Fathers* and Realistic Fiction," *Accent*, VII (Winter, 1949), 101–109.

57. Warren, *John Brown: The Making of a Martyr* (New York: Payson and Clarke, 1929), 322.

58. Squires, *Allen Tate*, 139.

59. Tate, "Seasons of the Soul," *The Swimmers*, 31.

60. Tate, "A Symposium: The Agrarians Today: Five Questions," *Shenandoah*, III (Summer, 1952), 38–39.

61. Tate, "The Man of Letters in the Modern World," *Essays of Four Decades*, 16.

CHAPTER 6

1. "Autumn Twilight Piece," *Double Dealer*, VII (October, 1924), 2.

2. "August Revival: Crosby Junction," *Sewanee Review*, XXXIII (December, 1925), 439.

3. "Kentucky Mountain Farm," *Selected Poems, 1923–1943* (New York: Harcourt Brace, 1944), 82.

4. *Ibid.*, 80–81.

5. Warren to author, February 9, 1975.

6. *John Brown: The Making of a Martyr* (New York: Payson and Clarke, 1929), 217.

7. "The Briar Patch," in Twelve Southerners, *I'll Take My Stand: The South and the Agrarian Tradition* (New York: Harper and Bros., 1930), 264.

8. Rob Roy Purdy (ed.), *Fugitives' Reunion: Conversations at Vanderbilt, May 3–5, 1956* (Nashville, Tenn.: Vanderbilt University Press, 1959), 208–209.

9. Interview, Robert Penn Warren and Ralph Ellison, in *Writers at Work: The 'Paris Review' Interviews*, ed. Malcolm Cowley (New York: Viking Press, 1959), 194.

10. "Literature as a Symptom," in Herbert Agar and Allen Tate (eds.), *Who Owns America?* (Boston: Houghton Mifflin, 1936), 267.

11. John Edward Hardy, "The Achievement of Cleanth Brooks," in Louis D. Rubin, Jr., and Robert D. Jacobs (eds.), *Southern Renascence: The Literature of the Modern South* (Baltimore, Md.: Johns Hopkins University Press, 1953), 414.

12. Cleanth Brooks, "Foreword" to Robert W. Stallman (ed.), *Critiques and Essays in Criticism, 1920–1948* (New York: Ronald Press, 1949), xx.

13. "Terror," *Selected Poems, 1923–1943*, 18.

14. Allen Tate, "Ode to the Confederate Dead," *The Swimmers and Other Poems* (New York: Charles Scribner's Sons, 1970), 17.

15. "The Ballad of Billie Potts," *Selected Poems 1923–1943*, 3.

16. *Ibid.*, 12.

17. *Ibid.*, 19.

18. Charles H. Bohner, *Robert Penn Warren* (New York: Twayne, 1964), 32–33.

19. *Fugitives' Reunion*, 210.

20. Warren, *Democracy and Poetry* (Cambridge, Mass.: Harvard University Press, 1975), 92.

21. Warren, *Audubon: A Vision* (New York: Random House, 1969), 32.

22. "The Briar Patch," 260.

23. "'The Great Mirage': Conrad and *Nostromo*," *Selected Essays* (New York: Random House, 1958), 58.

24. "William Faulkner," *Selected Essays*, 59.

25. Allen Tate, *Brother to Dragons: A Tale in Verse and Voices* (New York: Random House, 1953), 2.

26. *Audubon: A Vision*, 30.

27. Tate to Davidson, January 20, 1927, in *The Literary Correspondence of Donald Davidson and Allen Tate*, ed. John Tyree Fain and Thomas Daniel Young (Athens: University of Georgia Press, 1974), 184.

28. Allen Tate, *Memoirs and Opinions, 1926–1974* (Chicago: The Swallow Press, 1975), 32.

A Note on Authorities

The starting point for all students of the Fugitive poets is Louise S. Cowan's *The Fugitive Group: A Literary History* (Baton Rouge: Louisiana State University Press, 1959). John M. Bradbury, *The Fugitives: A Critical Account* (Chapel Hill: University of North Carolina Press, 1958), though it carries the story into the post-Fugitive years, is not as informative. For agrarianism, the best study remains unpublished: Virginia J. Rock, "The Making and Meaning of *I'll Take My Stand*: A Study in Utopian Conservatism, 1925–1945," a University of Minnesota doctoral dissertation which is available on xerox or microfilm form from University Microfilm, Inc., Ann Arbor, Michigan. John L. Stewart, *The Burden of Time: The Fugitives and Agrarians* (Princeton, N.J.: Princeton University Press, 1965), though written well, suffers from a bias that causes the author to evaluate the work of the leading Fugitives in accordance with their political liberalism, or lack of it; my feeling is that Stewart got his slant on the members of the group from the late Merrill Moore. Alexander Karanikas, *Tillers of a Myth: Southern Agrarians as Social and Literary Critics* (Madison: University of Wisconsin Press, 1966) is polemical and frequently imperceptive.

The only biography of John Crowe Ransom is a distinguished one indeed: Thomas Daniel Young, *Gentleman in a Dustcoat: A*

Biography of John Crowe Ransom (Baton Rouge: Louisiana State University Press, 1976). Radcliffe Squires, *Allen Tate: A Literary Biography* (New York: Pegasus, 1971) is an excellent study of that writer. Thomas Daniel Young and M. Thomas Inge, *Donald Davidson* (New York: Twayne, 1969) and Charles H. Bohner, *Robert Penn Warren* (New York: Twayne, 1964) are the best studies of those writers, and in style and content far above the customary level of the Twayne United States Authors series.

Ransom and Warren have written no memoirs; perhaps Warren will. Donald Davidson's *Southern Writers in the Modern World* (Athens: University of Georgia Press, 1958) is an invaluable source. So are the several essays about the Fugitives in Allen Tate's *Memoirs and Opinions, 1926–1974* (Chicago: Swallow Press, 1974). An extremely informative record is the correspondence that Davidson and Tate exchanged from the early 1920s onward, as published in *The Literary Correspondence of Donald Davidson and Allen Tate*, edited by John Tyree Fain and Thomas Daniel Young (Athens: University of Georgia Press, 1974.) There are also many interesting passages in the transcripts of the reunion of the Fugitives at Vanderbilt in 1956, *Fugitives' Reunion: Conversations at Vanderbilt, May 3–5, 1956*, edited by Rob Roy Purdy (Nashville, Tennessee: Vanderbilt University Press, 1959).

Index